"Few books address a subject that will benefit laypersons, pastors, and scholars. This book is the exception. Anyone interested in the vital doctrine of the work of Christ will be blessed by this work. It is comprehensive in scope, fair and balanced in assessing various views, and biblically faithful in its conclusions. I love Christology and this book increased my love for the central doctrine of the Christian faith. I will keep this book close at hand. It is that well done."

—**Daniel L. Akin**, president and professor of preaching and theology, Southeastern Baptist Theological Seminary

"The work of Christ is central to Christian Theology and this new book by John Hammett and Charles Quarles represents the best and most robust treatment of it to date. The combination of biblical and systematic theology makes *The Work of Christ* a standout contribution both in the areas of New Testament studies and theological studies respectively. The first part of the book covers the biblical material comprehensively with exegetical clarity and engagement in scholarship. The second part of the book masterfully presents the work of Christ, with specific focus on the atonement, as a systematic theological whole. This book, quite frankly, is a gold standard for studying the text of scripture theologically beyond the silos of biblical and theological disciplines. It is well written, engaging, scholarly, thorough, and faithful—it is a must read and a model to emulate."

—**Alan S. Bandy**, professor of New Testament and Greek and director of PhD Studies, New Orleans Baptist Theological Seminary

"John Hammett and Charles Quarles offer a robust account of the work of Christ worked out through a clinical exercise of biblical and systematic theology. An exemplary volume that will help readers, young and old, understand that God was in Christ reconciling the world to himself, and how Jesus lived, died, and rose for us and our salvation. A top-notch introduction by two world class scholars."

—**Michael F. Bird**, academic dean and lecturer in New Testament, Ridley College, Melbourne, Australia

"*The Work of Christ* leverages biblical and theological insight from two seasoned scholars who both deepen and broaden engagement with this vital doctrine. Quarles draws deeply on the most salient Old and New Testament texts regarding the atonement to establish a reliable biblical-theological synthesis. Hammett's systematic formulation adds breadth by exploring Christ's work, along with Father and Spirit, as creator and sovereign before focusing at length on the work of the cross in dialogue with historical, contemporary, and global perspectives. The result of their partnership moves the heart toward worship as much as it focuses the mind on the excellencies of our savior."

—**Jason S. Hiles**, dean, College of Theology and Grand Canyon Theological Seminary, Grand Canyon University

"*The Work of Christ* is exemplary, not only in content but in method. In these pages, you have a template for how theology lives in concert with biblical studies, hermeneutics, and biblical theology. Hammett and Quarles show us how the written Word of God drives us to a proper grasp of the incarnate Word of God's dramatic action. Most importantly, though, this book does what good theology is supposed to do: it deepens our understanding of what God has done for sinners like us in Christ, which, in turn, fuels our worship for our savior. From biblical analysis to theological synthesis, Hammett and Quarles help us know and love this God who has done far more than we can ask or imagine in and through the work of his Son."

—**Ryan Lister**, director, The Residency at Regents, Regents School of Austin

"This volume demonstrates the wisdom of the series, Theology for the People of God, as Chuck Quarles, a biblical scholar, and John Hammett, a theologian, competently explore the Scriptures and Christian theology on the work of Christ. Quarles expertly surveys the biblical material from both testaments and then devotes two chapters to biblical-theological summary and synthesis. Hammett expands the traditional concept of the work of Christ to include creation. He gives attention to Christ's saving deeds and the biblical metaphors that interpret those deeds. He treats historical views of the atonement, both objective and subjective. He highlights penal substitution and unlimited atonement. I recommend this volume to anyone wanting to increase their understanding of one of Scripture's most important topics—Christ's saving accomplishment."

—**Robert A. Peterson**, theologian, associate pastor, and writer

"Hammett and Quarles team up in this excellent study of Christ's work. Their work is characterized by careful exegesis and probing of the biblical text. At the same time, the systematic implications of Christ's work are explicated in conversation with both historical and contemporary scholarship. Students, pastors, and scholars will find this to be an invaluable resource on what God has accomplished in Christ for our great salvation."

—**Thomas S. Schreiner**, James Buchanan Harrison Professor of New Testament Interpretation, The Southern Baptist Theological Seminary

THE
WORK
OF
CHRIST

THEOLOGY
for the PEOPLE of GOD

THE
WORK
OF
CHRIST

John S. Hammett & Charles L. Quarles

EDITORS

David S. Dockery | *Nathan A. Finn* | *Christopher W. Morgan*

ACADEMIC
BRENTWOOD, TENNESSEE

DEDICATION

We dedicate this book to our colleagues on the faculty of Southeastern Baptist Theological Seminary, who have provided an atmosphere of community and engaged us in conversations conducive to scholarship. We are grateful to serve with them at what is affectionately known as the "happy seminary."

"One with many friends may be harmed,
but there is a friend who stays closer than a brother."
—Proverbs 18:24

ACKNOWLEDGMENTS

We are grateful to Seth Ellington and Eli Stanley who proofread Part I. Seth also verified the Scripture references. Their attention to detail and thoughtful suggestions improved this section significantly. Yeongwhi Jo produced the bibliography of the resources that were cited in the footnotes. We highly value the contribution of these emerging scholars.

CONTENTS

SERIES PREFACE

In Ephesians 4:11-16, the Apostle Paul identifies the goals of the teaching ministry of the church: to build up the church, to lead it to maturity in faith, and to lead it to unity. The goals continue to be the focus of ecclesial theologians, those Christian thinkers who understand their calling and work is to be carried out in service to the church, the people of God. Among other things, ecclesial theology must be grounded in the Scriptures; it must be Trinitarian, Christ-centered, Spirit-enabled, and doxological; it must be informed by the thinking of God's people throughout church history; and it must be ministry- and mission-focused.

Theology at its best understands the importance of influencing and speaking to the mind, the heart, as well as the hands. Ecclesial theologians in the twenty-first century must help people develop: a theologically informed way of seeing the world (the mind); a Christian response to life (the heart); and Christian motivations for ministry (the hands). We believe that this full-orbed understanding can only be addressed when we understand that theology finds its focus in the church. This is not to say that there is no place for academic theology that seeks to address the academy or for a public theology that attempts to engage culture and society. It is to say that the purpose of this series has a particular emphasis, which is grounded in a calling to serve the church. For this reason, we have titled the series Theology for the People of God.

Like other similar series, Theology for the People of God is a multi-volume effort that addresses the classical *loci* of systematic theology. What sets this series apart is its perspective, its emphasis, and its scope. In terms of its perspective, each volume in the series is co-authored by two scholars who are deeply committed to a theological outlook that is convictionally Baptist and warmly evangelical. Careful theology is an integrative task, and to that end the volumes in Theology for the People of God emphasize integration of biblical and systematic theology in dialog with historical theology and with application to church and life. Finally, the scope of this series extends beyond the classical *loci* to include other topics that are relevant to the church: spirituality, pastoral ministry, cultural engagement, and global mission.

Our audience is not first and foremost other "professional" theologians, but rather university students, seminarians, pastors, and other church and ministry leaders. However, we also believe that any thoughtful Christian will benefit from the volumes in this series. At its root, all faithful theology is simply thinking rightly about God and his world for the sake of living rightly before God in his world. To that end, all theology is for the people of God, and every believer is called to be a theologian.

It is our prayer that this series may somehow in God's good providence serve as a source of renewal for the people of God in the days to come. We hope that this will take place as people better understand what they believe and why they believe it, for it is the responsibility of theology to expound the whole counsel of God (Acts 20:7). While no single author or volume will be able to do so, together, we trust that the series in a symphonic manner will serve the church in this way. We believe that the sound, reliable theology found in this series will serve as a source of strength and hope for God's people for decades to come.

This series has been many years in the making. We pray that each volume will serve as an instrument of grace for readers and those who will be influenced by the faithful efforts of the authors who have collaborated with us in this project. We are grateful for each author and the skills and gifts that each person brings to this work. We are grateful for our friends at B&H Academic and Lifeway who have supported the idea for this series. We ultimately thank our great God for the privilege to work together with these many colleagues and co-workers.

Finally, we truly believe that healthy theology that matures the head, heart, and hands will not only enable believers to move toward maturity but will result in the praise and exaltation of God, for it is our understanding that all good and edifying theology leads to doxology. With the Apostle Paul, we, too wish to exclaim, "Oh, the depth of the riches of the wisdom and knowledge of God! How unsearchable his judgments and his paths beyond tracing out! . . . For from him and through him and to him are all things. To him be glory forever! Amen" (Rom 11:33, 36).

Soli Deo Gloria
David S. Dockery, Nathan A. Finn, and Christopher W. Morgan, editors

ABBREVIATIONS

AB	Anchor Bible
ANF	*Ante-Nicene Fathers*
BDAG	Walter Bauer, Frederick W. Danker, William F. Arndt, and F. Wilbur Gingrich. Greek-English Lexicon of the New Testament and Other Early Christian Literature. 3rd ed. Chicago: University of Chicago Press, 2000.
BECNT	Baker Exegetical Commentary on the New Testament
BST	The Bible Speaks Today
BTNT	Biblical Theology of the New Testament
CBQ	*Catholic Biblical Quarterly*
CEV	Contemporary English Version
chap.	chapter
CSB	Christian Standard Bible
CTJ	*Calvin Theological Journal*
ed.	edition; editor; edited by
EBC	Expositor's Bible Commentary
EBTC	Evangelical Biblical Theology Commentary
EGGNT	Exegetical Guide to the Greek New Testament
EQ	*Evangelical Quarterly*
ESV	English Standard Version
FC	Fathers of the Church
GNT	Good News Translation
HALOT	*The Hebrew and Aramaic Lexicon of the Old Testament.* Ludwig Koehler, Walter Baumgartner, and Johann J. Stamm. 3rd ed. Leiden: Brill, 1994–1999.
Heb.	Hebrew

ICC	International Critical Commentary
Institutes	*Institutes of the Christian Religion.* John T. McNeill, ed.; Ford Lewis Battles, trans. Library of Christian Classics, 2 vols.
JBL	*Journal of Biblical Literature*
JETS	*Journal of the Evangelical Theological Society*
JSNTSup	Journal for the Study of the New Testament Supplement
JSOT	*Journal for the Study of the Old Testament*
JSOTSup	Journal for the Study of the Old Testament Supplement Series
K&D	Keil, Carl F. and Franz Delitzsch. *Biblical Commentary on the Old Testament.* Grand Rapids: Eerdmans, 1986.
KJV	King James Version
LEB	Lexham English Bible
LW	*Luther's Works.* Jaroslav Pelikan and H. T. Lehmann et al., eds.
LXX	Septuagint
n.	note
NAC	New American Commentary
NBC	New Bible Commentary
NET	New English Translation
NETS	New English Translation of the Septuagint
NIBCOT	New International Biblical Commentary on the Old Testament
NICNT	New International Commentary on the New Testament
NICOT	New International Commentary on the Old Testament
NIGTC	New International Greek Testament Commentary
NIV	New International Version
NPNF[1]	*Nicene and Post-Nicene Fathers*, series 1
NPNF[2]	*Nicene and Post-Nicene Fathers*, series 2
NSBT	New Studies in Biblical Theology
NT	New Testament
NTS	New Testament Studies
OT	Old Testament
PNTC	Pillar New Testament Commentary
rev. ed.	revised edition

SBJT	*The Southern Baptist Journal of Theology*
STR	*Southeastern Theological Review*
TNTC	Tyndale New Testament Commentary
TOTC	Tyndale Old Testament Commentary
TynBul	*Tyndale Bulletin*
UBS[5]	*The Greek New Testament,* United Bible Societies, 5th ed.
VT	*Vetus Testamentum*
WA	*D. Martin Luthers Werke. Kritische Gesamtausgabe.* 58 vols. Weimar: Böhlau, 1833–.
WBC	Word Biblical Commentary
WTJ	*Westminster Theological Journal*

INTRODUCTION

It is most appropriate for a series titled Theology for the People of God to devote a volume to the work of Christ. The topic of the "work of Christ" focuses especially on the question, "What has Christ done for his people?" We might propose better captions for this topic instead of the traditional but rather mundane expression "the work of Christ."[1] The traditional caption may conjure images of Jesus sweating in a carpenter shop as he planes rough wood for his next project. The work of Christ is intended to refer to something vastly more important than the products of a carpenter's craftsmanship, something of far greater eternal significance than wooden tables, chairs, cribs, and bowls. Robert Letham did not exaggerate when he described "the work of Christ" as "the heart of the Christian faith" and "the most significant realities we can ever face."[2]

The doctrine of the work of Christ has traditionally focused primarily on "the saving significance of the death" and is often equated with the doctrine of the atonement.[3] Of course, the work of Christ entails much, much more. Scripture describes Christ's works of creation (John 1:3; Acts 3:15; 1 Cor 8:6; Col 1:16; Heb 1:2; Rev 3:14), governing the cosmos (Col 1:17; Heb 1:3), revelation (John 1:18; Heb 1:3), ruling (Matt 19:28; 28:18; Rev 1:5; 11:15; 19:16), judging (Matt 3:11–12; 7:21–23; 25:31–46; Rev 19:11–16), healing (Matt 4:23), etc. Due to the inseparable operations of the Trinity,

---

[1] Robert Letham describes the phrase as "dry, ponderous" and even "limp." Letham, *The Work of Christ*, Contours of Christian Theology (Downers Grove: IVP, 1993), 17.

[2] Letham, *The Work of Christ*, 17.

[3] James Leo Garrett Jr., *Systematic Theology: Biblical, Historical, and Evangelical*, 2 vols., 4th ed. (North Richland Hills, TX: Bibal, 2011), 1:607.

Christ is involved in all aspects of divine activity. The categories of work are practically endless and thus defy full and comprehensive description. The disclaimer offered by the apostle John for the limited scope of his Gospel is applicable here: "And there are also many other things that Jesus did, which, if every one of them were written down, I suppose not even the world itself could contain the books that would be written" (John 21:25).

This book is divided into two major parts. Part 1 presents the biblical theology of the work of Christ, and Part 2 treats the systematic theology of the doctrine. The two parts are necessarily distinct in their scope and approach, though these sections are complementary and interdependent.

They are different in scope because Part 1 will focus exclusively on Christ's atoning work. This specific focus is necessary in order to allow for sufficiently detailed discussion of related biblical texts. Part 2 of this book will helpfully address many aspects of Christ's work and is more comprehensive than most treatments but will appropriately emphasize Christ's atoning work.

The methodologies that guide each part are also different. Biblical theology begins with *analysis* in which the researcher seeks to "reconstruct the individual theologies of the writings or collections of writings of the Bible."[4] After the analysis of the individual texts of the individual books and corpora, the researcher proceeds to *synthesis* which seeks "to construct one single theology for the Bible in its entirety."[5] Brian Rosner observes:

> There is a temptation in studying the Bible's theology too quickly to read one part of it in the light of another and thus to miss the individual contours of the terrain and flatten out the whole. In doing biblical theology much is lost if James is read in the light of Paul, or Mark in the light of Matthew. It is more accurate and productive first to let James be James and Mark be Mark and so on, thus appreciating their particular colours and hues, before going on to see how their perspectives look on the larger canonical canvas.[6]

---

[4] Brian S. Rosner, "Biblical Theology," in *New Dictionary of Biblical Theology*, ed. T. Desmond Alexander and Brian S. Rosner (Downers Grove: InterVarsity, 2000), 6.

[5] Rosner, 6.

[6] Rosner, 6.

Most chapters of Part 1 will necessarily focus on this analysis. Concluding chapters will present a biblical-theological synthesis of the doctrine of the work of Christ in the OT, the NT, and then Scripture as a whole.

The treatment of a biblical theology of the work of Christ is necessarily selective. Few, if any, theological works have the luxury of being truly exhaustive. An initial draft of the OT theology section treated every OT prophecy that referred to any aspect of Christ's work. However, space limitations forced adoption of another approach. The treatment of the work of Christ in Old Testament theology will focus exclusively on texts that are widely recognized as *direct messianic prophecies* and that clearly refer to the Messiah's *salvific mission* and *function*.[7] Although the New Testament shows that types of Christ appear in the OT, these will not be the focus of the OT section. Instead, various OT types of Christ which portray the significance of his death will be treated as they are mentioned in the NT as seems most consistent with the biblical theology approach.

The second part of our treatment of the work of Christ builds on the exegetical work done in Part 1 by taking a systematic theology approach. The goal is to explain what the church (both the church throughout history and the global church today) has made of this biblical teaching. What beliefs and practices have Christians derived from this biblical teaching? What theological issues have been matters for controversy and question? What are the pressing matters of discussion among Christians today?

Rather than working through the whole of the Bible, section by section, our pattern of organization will be to examine the work of Christ in terms of four main eras. First, we will look at the preincarnate work of the eternal

---

[7] This, of course, is not intended to imply that all scholars will view the selected texts as messianic. Tremper Longman III wrote: "As we will illustrate below in connection with certain selected texts, it is impossible to establish that any passage [in the Torah and the Writings] in its original literary and historical context must or even should be understood as portending a future messianic figure." Longman III, "The Messiah: Explorations in the Law and Writings," in *The Messiah in the Old and New Testaments*, ed. Stanley E. Porter (Grand Rapids: Eerdmans, 2007), 13. However, in the same volume, Craig Evans suggests that Longman's view is unduly pessimistic. Evans, "The Messiah in the Old and New Testaments: A Response," in *The Messiah in the Old and New Testaments*, 231–34. On the other hand, Walter Kaiser confidently asserts: "There are six direct messianic predictions in the Pentateuch." See Walter C. Kaiser, Jr., *The Messiah in the Old Testament* (Grand Rapids: Zondervan, 1995), 36.

Son. Then, we will consider the work of Christ in the incarnation and in his earthly life and ministry. Our third and by far longest section will focus on the principal work of Christ, the cross or the work of atonement, but we will not end there. We will discuss the work of Christ in his resurrection, ascension and exaltation, concluding with the promise of future work related to his return and the full establishment of the kingdom of God.

Within each section, we will look at theological doctrines, and consider the development of these doctrines in church history, as believers have reflected on the key texts of Scripture. For example, we will look at the doctrine of Christ as Creator, based on texts like John 1:3 and Col 1:16. We will have to ask what the church has made of the teaching that Christ "emptied himself" (Phil 2:7) in becoming incarnate, and how that shapes our understanding of his earthly life and ministry. The issues of the nature and extent of the atonement have been subjects of extensive and important discussion historically and contemporarily and will occupy multiple chapters of this part of the volume. Numerous doctrines cluster around biblical teaching on the present work of Christ as the resurrected, ascended, and exalted Lord, and his future work as coming King.

To the development of these doctrines in the understanding of the church through history, we are fortunate today to be able to begin to add the voices of church across cultures, as the global church is beginning to add its insights. We are recognizing that theology developed in Western culture may have blind spots in understanding certain aspects of Scripture. Theology developed in cultural contexts quite different than ours can help us see those blind spots and add insights we would otherwise miss,[8] and we are grateful to receive help from the global church. The harvest of these insights from the global church is just beginning and is fuller on some points of the work of Christ than others, but we want to allow their work to complement and where necessary correct the understandings of Western theologians.[9]

---

[8] See E. Randolph Richards and Brandon O'Brien, *Misreading Scripture with Western Eyes: Removing Cultural Blinders to Better Understand the Bible* (Downers Grove: IVP Books, 2012).

[9] See the helpful works of Timothy Tennent, *Theology in the Context of World Christianity* (Grand Rapids: Zondervan, 2007), which surveys all the major loci of theology and gives insights from the global church for each topic; William Dyrness and Veli-Matti Kärkkäinen, eds., *Global Dictionary of Theology* (Downers Grove: IVP

At times, our discussions of aspects of the work of Christ will be analytical and technical. They may even seem pedantic. We must delve into academic debates that might spark little interest for some readers. We pray that readers will persevere even in these sections because, in the end, they make an important contribution to our understanding of the cross of our Savior and move us to worship our Lord with even greater gratitude and devotion. The details and important nuances of the doctrine of Christ's atoning death ultimately prompt us to join Charles Wesley in exclaiming, "Amazing love! How can it be that Thou, my God, should die for me!"[10]

Academic, 2008), which includes global contributions to hundreds of topics; and Gene Green, Stephen Pardue, and K. K. Yeo, eds., *Majority World Theology: Christian Doctrine in Global Context* (Downers Grove: IVP Academic, 2020), which gives the fullest presentation of global voices currently available on six of the major doctrines of systematic theology.

[10] Charles Wesley, "And Can It Be," Hymn 147 in *The Baptist Hymnal* (Nashville: Convention Press, 1991).

PART I
BIBLICAL THEOLOGY

1

The Work of Christ in the Old Testament

Describing the mission and work of the Christ (Messiah) in the OT is a hazardous enterprise, though this should not prevent us from taking up the task. Debate still rages over the frequency of explicit references to the Messiah in the OT. On one extreme, some scholars argue for a paucity of references to the Messiah. Near the end of the twentieth century, Ron Clements correctly observed: "[V]irtually all of the major books on Old Testament theology say very little at all about such messianic hope and, even when they do, do so in a very guarded and circumscribed way."[1] J. Gordon McConville did not exaggerate when he wrote: "Modern Old Testament scholarship has been largely informed by the belief that traditional Christian messianic interpretations of Old Testament passages have been exegetically indefensible."[2]

At the other end of the spectrum stand scholars who insist that the primary theme of the OT is the messianic hope. James Hamilton wrote that

---

[1] Ron E. Clements, "The Messianic Hope in the Old Testament," *JSOT* 43 (1989): 4. One must not, however, overstate the case. See the discussion of David as "anticipatory ideal figure" in Rolf Rendtorff, *The Canonical Hebrew Bible: A Theology of the Old Testament,* Tools for Biblical Studies Series 7, trans. David Orton (Dorchester: Deo, 2011), 570–74.

[2] J. Gordon McConville, "Messianic Interpretation of the Old Testament in Modern Context," in *The Lord's Anointed: Interpretation of Old Testament Messianic Texts,* ed. Philip Satterthwaite, Richard Hess, and Gordon Wenham (Eugene, OR: Wipf and Stock, 2012), 2.

"from start to finish, the OT is a messianic document, written from a messianic perspective, to sustain a messianic hope."[3] He added that "the NT seems to regard the whole of the OT as pointing to and being fulfilled in the one it presents as the Messiah, Jesus of Nazareth."[4]

One of the most important texts for establishing the messianic purpose of the OT is Luke 24:27, a key element of the resurrected Jesus's discussion with the two men on the road to Emmaus: "Then beginning with Moses and all the Prophets, he interpreted for them the things concerning himself in all the Scriptures." Michael Rydelnik and Edwin Blum explain:

> The Lord's point was not that there is one verse in each section of the Hebrew Bible that points to the Messiah. Rather, Jesus was saying that the whole Hebrew Bible, down to the DNA level, was messianic. The Messiah was to be found in the overall message of the Hebrew Bible, not just in some selected proof-texts.[5]

Glenn Kreider has also commented: "Surely Jesus does not mean that every word in every verse in the Scripture must be interpreted as an explicit reference to the Messiah, but that every text must be understood in light of Him."[6]

For others, the claim that the purpose of the OT as a whole is to reveal the Messiah does not go far enough. Some scholars appeal to Luke 24:13–35 to argue that the entire Old Testament is so thoroughly messianic that Christ is the focus of every passage. David Murray titled his book on the Christocentric interpretation of Scripture *Jesus on Every Page*. He describes his adoption of this interpretive approach as an Emmaus Road experience in which "I discovered Jesus on every page. He wasn't just here and there—He was everywhere."[7] However, this approach deserves careful and thoughtful

---

[3] Hamilton, "The Skull Crushing Seed of the Woman: Inner-Biblical Interpretation of Genesis 3:15," *SBJT* 10.2, no. 2 (2006): 30.

[4] Hamilton, 30.

[5] Michael A. Rydelnik and Edwin A. Blum, eds., *The Moody Handbook of Messianic Prophecy: Studies and Expositions of the Messiah in the Old Testament* (Chicago: Moody, 2019), 26.

[6] Glenn Kreider, "The Deity of the Messiah in the Old Testament," in *Moody Handbook of Messianic Prophecy*, 149.

[7] David Murray, *Jesus on Every Page: 10 Simple Ways to Seek and Find Christ in the Old Testament* (Nashville: Thomas Nelson, 2013), 16. The statements of Hamilton, Rydelnik, Blum, and Kreider should not be assumed to support Murray's more

evaluation. Despite its attraction to Christian scholars, the claim is problematic on several grounds.

First, such an assumption is not supported by the grammar, structure, and context of the Greek text of Luke 24:27. Luke's intention is to show that Jesus explained to the two men the predictions and descriptions of the Messiah that were contained in all the major sections of the Old Testament writings. The first clause of verse 27 shows that Jesus began his explanation with the first major section of the OT, the Torah or five books of Moses, then proceeded to the next major section of the OT, the Prophets. He then continued this approach by explaining the things concerning himself "in all the Scriptures." Interpreted in light of the introductory clause, "all the Scriptures" probably refers to all three of the major sections of Scripture, not only the Law and the Prophets, but also the Writings. Luke 24:44 confirms that this was the intention of Jesus's words: "These are my words that I spoke to you while I was still with you—that everything written about me in the Law of Moses, the Prophets, and the Psalms must be fulfilled." Here Jesus explicitly lists all three major sections of the Old Testament. "Psalms" replaces a reference to the Writings since Psalms is the first book in the Writings in the order of the Hebrew canon and contains more promises about the Messiah than other books in that corpus.

The approach that Jesus used here is exemplified in rabbinic literature. In b. Sanhedrin 90b, Gamaliel defends the doctrine of resurrection in response to challenges from the *minim* (in this case, the Sadducees) by arguing, "It is proved from the Torah, from the Prophets, and from the Writings." Gamaliel then appealed to Deut 31:16 (Law), Isa 26:9 (Prophets), and Song of Solomon 7:9 (Writings). This was a common approach to establishing the biblical authority for a particular claim.[8] By using this approach, Jesus was not insisting that every passage is messianic, but that the sufferings of Jesus,

---

extreme position. Hamilton ("Skull Crushing Seed of the Woman," 30), for example, clarified, "I am not suggesting that we should look for 'Jesus under every rock' or in every detail of the description of the temple, a straw man which at times seems to be the only thing conceivable to certain 'OT only' interpreters when they hear the suggestion I am making."

[8] See also b. B. Bat.7b; b. Sab. 115a (in which "all Holy Scriptures" is defined as Law, Prophets, and Writings; cf. b Qidd 49a); b. Moed Qat. 18b; b. Erub 17a; b. Makk. 10b; b. Abod. Zar. 19b.

which had caused these two disciples to doubt that Jesus was the Messiah (Luke 24:21), were foretold in all three major sections of the Old Testament. Thus, the biblical argument supporting the sufferings of the Messiah could not be stronger. The sufferings of the Messiah were not merely foretold in a single OT proof-text that might be subject to a myriad of interpretations and the topic of endless debate. The three-fold witness of the major sections of Scripture firmly established that the Messiah must suffer and then enter his glory. Thus, Scripture as a whole (and not just one isolated part of it) foretold Jesus's suffering and his glory.

It is important to note that Luke does not merely say that "the things concerning himself" were *recorded* or *foretold* "in all the Scriptures." Luke 24:27 reports that Jesus *interpreted for them* the things concerning himself in all the Scriptures. Jesus *explained for them* the things concerning himself wherever they appear in the Scriptures from beginning to end. If the OT is so thoroughly messianic that the Messiah appears on every page, this interpretation would have taken an enormous amount of time. However, Luke indicates that Jesus's conversation with the disciples on the road to Emmaus occurred on a single day and during a seven-mile walk. Even at a very slow pace, such a walk would take only a few hours. Time would simply not afford an explanation of how every single passage in every single OT book foretold about Jesus, if Jesus is on *every* page. The details that Luke supplies make it practically impossible that "in all the Scriptures" was intended to refer to every page or passage of Scripture.

Second, an insistence that the Messiah is the focus of every page or passage of Scripture overlooks explicit statements about Holy Scripture which demonstrate its more comprehensive purpose.[9] For example, 2 Tim 3:16–17 shows that the God-breathed Scriptures are useful for teaching, rebuking, correcting, and training in righteousness. Paul also insists that many OT narratives were written to provide moral examples for Christians: "Now these things took place as examples for us, so that we will not desire evil things as they did" (1 Cor 10:6). Paul emphasizes this point a few verses later: "These

---

[9] Murray acknowledges that despite an early inclination to reject any use of the Old Testament narratives to serve as examples or warnings, he ultimately recognized that it was "going too far to the other side by rejecting any exemplary lessons from the Old Testament." Murray, *Jesus on Every Page*, 54–55.

things happened to them as examples, and they were written for our instruction, on whom the ends of the ages have come" (1 Cor 10:11).

Several scholars have argued that some of the rabbis recognized that the entire Old Testament was written to describe the Messiah. Some appeal to b. Ber. 34b in which Hiyya bar Abba quoted r. Yohanan as saying, "All of the prophets prophesied only concerning the days of the Messiah."[10] This initially compelling quotation is assumed to be equivalent to the statement of Jesus in Luke 24:27, 44–45 which is interpreted as implying that the entire OT is a messianic document. However, the use of Yohanan's statement in this manner fails to appreciate the meaning of the statement in its original context. In fact, the quotation misleadingly breaks off Yohanan's original words in the middle of the sentence. The statement continues by citing Isa 64:4 to argue, "but as to the world that will come [thereafter], 'Eye has not seen, God, beside you.'" Thus, Yohanan was insisting that the prophets did not see beyond the messianic era (which many viewed as only temporary) to the eternal age that would follow. He was clearly *not* arguing that every OT prophet's entire message focused on the Messiah. The statements of Yohanan that immediately precede and follow his statement about the messianic age serve to confirm this.

Daniel Block's study of the Messiah in the Old Testament led him to conclude:

> As a matter of fact, the books that make up the Old Testament are not obviously preoccupied with the messiah. Within this variegated record of divine action and revelation, the messianic hope is embedded like a diamond, precious not only because of its intrinsic value, but in the Hebraic sense also because of its rarity. Inasmuch as the Old Testament is a record of God's gracious reach to fallen humankind within history, it is indeed filled with hope, but to characterize this as an overtly and pervasively messianic hope is to overstate the case. Explicit references to the messiah in the Pentateuch can

---

[10] See James Hamilton, "The Skull Crushing Seed of the Woman," 30; and Craig Evans, "The Old Testament in the New," in *The Face of New Testament Studies*, ed. Scot McKnight and Grant R. Osborne (Grand Rapids: Baker, 2004), 136. R. Yohanan's statement is quoted twice in this regard in Rydelnik and Blum, eds., *The Moody Handbook of Messianic Prophecy*, 26, 123.

be counted on a single hand, and their relative frequency increases only slightly as we move through the Former Prophets to the Latter Prophets, and then the Writings.[11]

I generally concur with this assessment.[12] Although I share the high view of the Lord Jesus that stands behind the view that every page of the OT is to be interpreted in a Christocentric fashion, I fear that the approach has some unforeseen negative consequences. The quest to find Jesus everywhere may unwittingly diminish the importance and apologetic force of those texts that explicitly predict his coming(s), the nature of his person, and (for our purposes here) his mission and work.

In a familiar movie trope, a person is lured by an opponent into a Hall of Mirrors where he encounters hundreds of images of an armed villain which he wrongly assumes to be the opponent himself. His distraction with the multitude of images prevents him from sensing the presence of his flesh-and-blood opponent, even though he may be only inches away. In a similar way, the desire to find Jesus everywhere in the OT, in every conceivable type, as the hero in every story, as the referent of every allegorical reading, may result in an unintentional depreciation of those scores of messianic prophecies that explicitly predict the Messiah's birth, his deity and humanity, his atoning death, his bodily resurrection, and his glorious resurrection centuries before his coming. Reducing the OT to a messianic Hall of Mirrors in which the reader is surrounded by countless images of Jesus may prevent the reader from seeing the stunning implications of the prophets' explicit and literal predictions about the coming Messiah. Thus, our study of the OT discussion of Christ's atoning work will focus on explicit messianic prophecies. Our examination of New Testament theology will expand this focus to various OT types.

---

[11] Daniel Block, "My Servant David: Ancient Israel's Vision of the Messiah," in *Israel's Messiah in the Bible and the Dead Sea Scrolls*, ed. Richard Hess and M. Daniel Carroll R. (Downers Grove: Baker Academic, 2003), 21–22.

[12] I would wish to emphasize the importance of the adjective "explicit" in the final sentence of the statement and to clarify that the OT is both a record of revelatory acts and is itself divine revelation.

2

The Work of Christ in the Pentateuch

Introduction

Our study of the work of Christ in the OT naturally begins where Christ's explanation of his suffering and glory in Luke 24:27 began—with Moses, that is, the Five Books of Moses. Jesus elsewhere referred to these books as the "Law" (translating the Hebrew term "Torah"). The Greek OT describes these five books as the "Pentateuch."[1] These books contain messianic prophecies that are foundational to the messianic hope and Jesus's fulfillment of those hopes in the remainder of Scripture.

Discussion

Genesis 3:15

The first messianic promise of Scripture appears in God's curse on the serpent after his deception of Eve and Adam. God declared, "I will put hostility between you and the woman, and between your offspring and her offspring. He will strike your head, and you will strike his heel" (Gen 3:15). The identity of this seed is not specifically stated. Although the singular noun "offspring"

---

[1] The Greek term τεῦχος could refer to a roll of writing material, thus a book, scroll, or volume.

(*zera*ʿ) is often used to speak of one's progeny in general,[2] specific features of the text suggest that it here refers to a single descendant of the woman. First, the pronoun (*hûʾ*) that refers to the "offspring" is masculine singular. When the noun refers to progeny in general, plural pronouns are used in biblical Hebrew (cf. Gen 15:13; Exod 32:13).[3] When the noun refers to an individual, singular pronouns are used (cf. Gen 4:25; 21:13; 1 Sam 1:11; 2 Sam 7:12–17; 1 Chr 17:11–13; Isa 41:8). Second, when the woman later uses the noun "offspring" (Gen 4:25), the term clearly refers to a single descendant. This suggests that she understood the noun in Gen 3:15 to refer likewise to a single descendant.

The Septuagint translator seems to have interpreted the passage to refer to an individual. Although the Greek noun for "seed" (*sperma*) is neuter singular, the translator used a masculine singular pronoun to refer to the seed. When "seed" is collective, the translator of the Pentateuch consistently uses masculine plural pronouns. R. A. Martin thus argued that the Septuagint offers "the earliest Messianic interpretation of Gen 3:15."[4]

John Sailhamer has argued that Gen 3:15 is designed to prod the reader to question the identity of the seed:

> There remains in this verse a puzzling yet important ambiguity: Who is the "seed" of the woman? It seems obvious that the purpose

---

[2] Although the noun appears 229 times in the Hebrew Bible, it assumes the plural form only once (1 Sam 8:15). In this exceptional occurrence, the context suggests that the noun refers to grain fields rather than to seeds.

[3] For a more detailed argument, see C. J. Collins, "A Syntactical Note (Genesis 3:15): Is the Woman's Seed Singular or Plural?" *TynBul* 48 (1997): 139–48. When "seed" is collective, it may use singular or plural verbal inflections. Naturally, adjectives are consistently singular. However, pronouns are consistently plural. When seed refers to an individual, writers use singular verbs, adjectives, pronouns, and pronominal suffixes.

[4] R. A. Martin, "The Earliest Messianic Interpretation of Genesis 3:15," *JBL* 84 (1965): 425–27. Note also that church fathers of the second century viewed the passage as messianic. See Irenaeus, *Haer.* 4.40.3. The reference to Gen 3:15 in Justin, *Dial.* 102 is more ambiguous though it is often cited in favor of the messianic interpretation. The Targums are often cited as evidence for an early messianic interpretation of the second half of the curse of the serpent. However, the Targums see the seed as a reference to multiple descendants, even though the curse against the serpent will be finally fulfilled in the messianic era.

of verse 15 has not been to answer that question, but rather to raise it. The remainder of the book is, in fact, the author's answer.[5]

Although the grammar of Gen 3:15 offers clues that an individual descendant is in view, the identity of the seed must be determined by later references to the "seed" in the Pentateuch and later OT references.[6] Daniel Block wrote:

> Although complex, the Old Testament picture of the messiah gains in clarity and focus with time. But the messianic hope is a single line that begins in broadest terms with God's promise of victory over the serpent through "the seed of the woman" (Gen. 3:15), then is narrowed successively to the seed of Abraham (Gen. 22:18), the tribe of Judah (Gen. 49:10), the stem of Jesse (Isa. 11:1), the house/dynasty of David (2 Sam. 7), and finally the suffering and slain servant of Yahweh (Isa. 53).[7]

The promised seed will crush the head of the serpent who is the source of all evil in God's good world. Through the Messiah, good will triumph over evil.

Genesis 22:18

The promises to Abraham also contain references to a promised seed. Several of the promises regarding the seed of Abraham are clearly collective and refer to his progeny. For example, Gen 13:15–16 promises that the seed will multiply until Abraham's descendants are as numerous as the particles of dust on the earth. Genesis 17:8 uses a plural pronoun to refer to the seed. Then Gen 17:9–10 refers to multiple generations of the seed, and the mark of the seed, circumcision, is commanded for all male descendants of Abraham throughout all generations.

Similarly, Gen 22:17 describes the seed/offspring of Abraham as numerous. However, in the final sentence of the verse, both a singular verb (which

---

[5] John Sailhamer, *The Pentateuch as Narrative: A Biblical-Theological Commentary* (Grand Rapids: Zondervan, 1992), 108.

[6] For a helpful defense of the messianic interpretation, see Hamilton, "The Skull Crushing Seed of the Woman," 30–54 (see chap. 1, n. 3).

[7] Daniel Block, "My Servant David: Ancient Israel's Vision of the Messiah," 56 (see chap. 1, n. 11).

is not unusual with the collective sense) and singular pronominal suffixes (which are unprecedented for the collective sense) refer to the seed.[8] The surprising shift in grammar suggests a focus on one specific descendant of Abraham. Thus Gen 22:18 ("All nations of the earth will be blessed by your offspring") seems to refer to a single descendant.[9] This is likely the feature that signaled to the New Testament writers that Gen 22:18 is messianic. Furthermore, T. D. Alexander has noted that Ps 72:17 appears to allude to Gen 22:18 and to find its fulfillment in "a king whose reign surpasses by far that of Solomon." He adds, "Indeed, this future monarch is described as ruling the entire earth, bringing deliverance to the oppressed by defeating their enemies (cf. Ps. 72:4–14)."[10] Steinman observes: "Thus, the last two of these three promises [in Gen 22:17–18] are specifically messianic in nature and find their fulfillment in Christ."[11]

If Gen 22:17b–18 refers to the Messiah, the promise indicates that the Messiah will conquer his enemies.[12] This resonates well with the promise of the seed crushing the head of the serpent in Gen 3:15. Now the promise is expanded to describe the defeat of all the Messiah's enemies. However, the promise also assures that the Messiah will bless all nations. The preceding narrative hints at the nature of this blessing. The Messiah will provide the offering that fulfills God's demand (Gen 22:1–16).

Genesis 49:8–12

Genesis 49:8–12 shows that this seed will come from the line of Judah.[13] This passage tells "what will happen to you [the sons of Jacob] in the days

---

[8] Collins, "A Syntactical Note (Genesis 3:15): Is the Woman's Seed Singular or Plural?" 143.

[9] For a similar view, see T. Desmond Alexander, "Further Observations on the Term 'Seed' in Genesis," *TynBul* 48 (1997): 363–67.

[10] Alexander, "Further Observations on the Term 'Seed' in Genesis," 366.

[11] Andrew E. Steinmann, *Genesis: An Introduction and Commentary*, TOTC 1 (Downers Grove: InterVarsity, 2019), 222.

[12] Although the NIV, CSB, and several other versions translate Gen 22:17b "their enemies," the Heb. text refers to "his (sg.) enemies."

[13] For a similar view, see John Sailhamer, *The Meaning of the Pentateuch: Revelation, Composition and Interpretation* (Downers Grove: IVP Academic, 2009), 321–23.

to come" (Gen 49:1). The prophecy regarding Judah initially emphasizes his supremacy ("your father's sons will bow down to you"). This element of the prophecy appears to be an allusion to Gen 27:29, Isaac's blessing on Jacob: "May your mother's sons bow in homage to you." Genesis 27:29 continues with an allusion to Gen 12:3. This serves to establish a link between Gen 12:3, 27:29, and 49:8 and thus identify the king from Judah as Abraham's "seed."[14] The blessing promises victory in conflict ("your hand will be on the necks of your enemies"). This second emphasis is reminiscent of the promises of victory in Gen 3:15 and 22:17. The line of Judah will rule with scepter and staff until a specific descendant arises who bears the right to command the obedience of all the peoples. Although the interpretation of Gen 49:10 is debated, evidence shows that a messianic interpretation was very early. A Qumran text (4Q252 5:1–7) explains that the prophecy refers to "the righteous Messiah, the Branch of David." Similarly, Targum Onqelos paraphrases the debated expression of the verse "until the Messiah comes to whom the kingdom belongs and whom the nations will obey." This interpretation is also supported by some manuscripts of the Septuagint.[15] The final element of the prophecy (Gen 49:11–12) foretells that the promised descendant of Judah will make the earth amazingly bountiful. Grape vines will be so massive that a stubborn donkey tethered to the vine cannot snap them when he tugs on his halter rope.[16] Grape juice will be as abundant as water so that wine may replace it as the liquid in which garments are washed. This suggests that the Messiah's reign will reverse the curse of Gen 3:17–19 and restore the earth to the fertility it enjoyed before sin wrecked God's good creation.

Deuteronomy 18:15–19

The final prophecy about the salvific work of a coming Messiah in the Pentateuch appears in Deut 18:15–19. The prophecy describes the coming of a prophet who would resemble Moses in remarkable ways. This prophet would be an Israelite ("from among your own brothers"). Like Moses, he

---

[14] See Sailhamer, 474–75.

[15] These manuscripts translate *šilōh* as "[the one] to whom it belongs."

[16] This is viewed as a messianic prophecy by r. Hiyya bar Abba (b. Ber. 57a).

would be a mediator between God and the nation. He would represent God to the people and speak on God's behalf so they would not be destroyed by direct encounter with God's fiery glory or killed by the power of God's own voice. God would place his words in the prophet's mouth and he would speak on God's behalf. The commands given by the prophet would not be his commands, but God's. The people were obligated to fulfill these commands and God would hold them accountable if they disobeyed. The commandments delivered by Moses belonged to the old covenant (cf. Deut 4:12–14). The prophet like Moses would deliver new commandments above and beyond those already delivered by Moses. This implies that the prophet like Moses would either add to the demands of the old covenant or be the mediator of a new covenant, a covenant that would be described later by the prophets (e.g., Jer 31:31–34).

Although some interpreters believe that this prophecy was fulfilled either by Moses's immediate successor, Joshua, or by the succession of OT prophets,[17] Deuteronomy 34:10–12 clearly precludes the former view since the statement, "No prophet has arisen again in Israel like Moses," immediately follows mention of Joshua's prophetic ministry. Moses's close communion with God was unique since he was the only prophet "whom the LORD knew face to face." Furthermore, Moses was "unparalleled for all the signs and wonders" and "for all the mighty acts of power and terrifying deeds" that Moses performed. This suggests that the passage should be understood as a messianic prophecy.[18] This interpretation is affirmed in the New Testament (e.g., Acts 3:22–23). The Dead Sea Scrolls (4Q175 and 1QS 9:11) identify the prophet like Moses as an eschatological prophet who will

---

[17] This view is based on the opinion that the singular "prophet" functions as a "collective." See John Thompson, *Deuteronomy*, TOTC 5 (Downers Grove: IVP Academic, 1974), 234; and Eugene Merrill, *Deuteronomy*, NAC 4 (Nashville: Broadman and Holman, 1994), 272. Merrill suggests that "the ambiguity of the individual and collective both being expressed in the grammatical singular is a common Old Testament device employed to afford multiple meanings or applications to prophetic texts." Note, however, that the plural form of the noun appears 149 times in the Hebrew Bible including one occurrence in the Pentateuch (Num 11:29).

[18] This view was widely affirmed in early Christian history. See especially Eusebius, *Dem. ev.* 3:2; *Ps.-Clem. Rec.* 1:57; Aphraates, *Dem.* 21:10; Basil the Great, *Spir.* 33. For additional references, see Dale C. Allison Jr, *The New Moses: A Matthean Typology* (Minneapolis: Fortress, 1993), 103–6.

arise together with the Messiahs of Aaron and Israel. However, the sages in rabbinic literature reasoned from the similarities between descriptions of Moses in the Pentateuch and descriptions of the Messiah in OT prophecies that the prophet like Moses must be the Messiah.[19]

Figure 1: References to the Work of Christ in the Pentateuch[20]

Scripture	Content
Gen 3:15	The seed of the woman will crush the head of the serpent.
Gen 22:18	The seed of Abraham will bless all the nations.
Gen 49:6–12	A descendant of Judah will rule over the peoples and his kingdom will enjoy amazing prosperity.
Deut 18:15–19	A prophet like Moses will serve as mediator between God and his people and issue divine commands.

Summary

The Pentateuch offers several descriptions of the salvific work of the Messiah that will prove to be foundational in biblical theology. First, the Messiah is a conqueror who will crush the head of the serpent (Gen 3:15). Second, the Messiah is a descendant of Abraham who will bless people of all nations

---

[19] This rabbinic conviction led to the formulation of the maxim: "Like the first redeemer [Moses], so the last redeemer [Messiah]" (Pesikta Rabbati 15:10 and Ruth Rabbah 2:14). For a discussion of this theme in rabbinic literature, see Charles Quarles, "'Out of Egypt I Called My Son': Intertextuality and Metalepsis in Matthew 2:15," *STR* 8.1, no. 1 (2017): 13–15.

[20] Some scholars have argued that Gen 9:25–27 contains a messianic promise. See Charles Briggs, *Messianic Prophecy: The Prediction of the Fulfilment of Redemption through the Messiah: A Critical Study of the Messianic Passages of the Old Testament in the Order of their Development* (New York: Scribner, 1886), 79–83; Kaiser, *The Messiah in the Old Testament*, 42–46 (see introduction, n. 7). However, this view is dependent on the doubtful claim that the implied subject of the verb "dwell" is "God" rather than Japheth. This view was affirmed in Targum Onqelos (though not by Philo as Briggs claimed) which reads, "May his Shekinah dwell in the tents of Shem." Even if this is the proper sense, a messianic interpretation is not thereby supported.

on earth (Gen 22:18), not merely the people of Israel. The context of the promise seems to imply that he will bless them by offering the sacrifice that fulfills God's demands (Gen 22:1–16). Third, the Messiah will serve as a mediator between God and his people (Deut 18:15–17) who converses with God face-to-face and relays God's words to those who cannot stand in God's glorious presence themselves. He will issue new divine commands. These commands will either add to the demands of the old covenant or constitute a new covenant. The Messiah will speak with divine authority and God will hold his people accountable for obeying everything that the Messiah teaches and commands (Deut 18:18–19).

3

The Work of Christ in the Historical and Wisdom Books

The Work of Christ in the Historical Books

The "Historical Books" include Joshua, Judges, Ruth, 1–2 Samuel, 1–2 Kings, 1–2 Chronicles, Ezra, Nehemiah, and Esther. Compared to the Pentateuch, Psalms, and Prophets, the historical books have a paucity of references to the Messiah. Nevertheless, one can make a persuasive case that these books do display a messianic trajectory.[1]

The most important messianic text in this section of the OT is undoubtedly the prophecy of Nathan known as the Davidic covenant (2 Sam 7:4–16). Admittedly, this text does not explicitly refer to the Messiah's salvific work. Nevertheless, many of the later messianic prophecies that do refer to the salvation Messiah brings are in some way dependent on this important prophecy. The significance of this text for the development of messianic expectation is hard to overestimate. Ronald Clements refers to the prophecy as the "seed-bed of the messianic hope."[2] Although some scholars see all of 2 Sam 7:11–16 as directly messianic, most of the prophecy seems to

---

[1] My understanding of this trajectory has been influenced by T. D. Alexander, *The Servant King: The Bible's Portrait of the Messiah* (Vancouver: Regent College, 2003), 41–96; and Andrew T. Abernethy and Gregory Goswell, *God's Messiah in the Old Testament: Expectations of a Coming King* (Grand Rapids: Baker, 2020), 28–84.

[2] Ronald Clements, "The Messianic Hope in the Old Testament," *JSOT* 13 (1989): 12.

refer directly to Solomon.[3] Solomon is David's direct descendant who would expand the borders of David's kingdom (7:12), construct the temple (7:13), and require God's loving discipline for his sins (7:14–15). However, verses 13b ("I will establish the throne of his kingdom forever") and 16 ("Your house and kingdom will endure before me forever, and your throne will be established forever") clearly look far beyond Solomon and his personal reign. David himself recognized that the Lord was speaking about his house "in the distant future" (2 Sam 7:19).[4]

The repeated use of the expression "forever" makes the promise especially significant. The Davidic dynasty would rule over Judah for the next four centuries before that rule ended in 587 BC. The prophets foresaw the demise of the Davidic dynasty but recognized that God's covenant with David would still be fulfilled, not through an enduring succession of Davidic kings but through the eternal rule of a single Davidic descendant, the Messiah (e.g., Amos 9:11; Isa 9:6–7; 11:1–9). Recognition that only the Messiah could fulfill 2 Sam 7:13b and 16 prompted interpreters to see the Messiah as the fulfillment of other aspects of the prophecy as well (e.g., Heb 1:5). The Dead Sea Scrolls interpret the Davidic covenant as a prophecy about the Messiah. After quoting 2 Sam 7:11–14, 4Q174 explains:

> He is the Branch of David who shall arise with the Interpreter of the Law [to rule] in Zion [at the end] of time. As it is written, "I will raise up the tent of David that is fallen" (Amos 9:11). That is to say, the fallen tent of David is he who shall arise to save Israel.

Nathan's prophecy has impressive similarities to an earlier messianic prophecy (Gen 49:10: "the scepter will not depart from Judah") since both prophecies promise that Israel's rulers will come from a specific line and both stress the longevity of the royal line. The Davidic covenant offers greater

---

[3] The interpretation adopted here is supported by Carl F. Keil, and Franz Delitzsch, *Biblical Commentary on the Old Testament* (Grand Rapids: Eerdmans, 1986), 2:346; Joyce G. Baldwin, *1 and 2 Samuel*, TOTC (Downers Grove: IVP Academic, 1988), 227–28; A. A. Anderson, *2 Samuel*, WBC (Dallas: Thomas Nelson, 2000), 121–23; and Mary J. Evans, *1 and 2 Samuel*, NIBCOT (Peabody, MA: Hendrickson, 2000), 168–69.

[4] Although Targum Onqelos on 2 Samuel 7 does not explicitly mention the Messiah, it seems to imply a messianic interpretation in David's words, "You have spoken even concerning the house of Your servant concerning the world to come."

specificity to the earlier promise. Kingship belongs to the line of David within the line of Judah. Since Gen 49:10 sees the enduring reign of the tribe of Judah culminating in the reign of a single individual, attentive readers should have anticipated that 2 Sam 7:16 would also culminate in the reign of a single individual—the Messiah.

OT scholars do not exaggerate in their profuse descriptions of the importance of this text. Gordon famously described 2 Sam 7 as the "'ideological summit', not only in the 'Deuteronomistic History' but also in the Old Testament as a whole."[5] Baldwin described the chapter as "the source of the messianic hope as it developed in the message of prophets and psalmists."[6] Bergen asserted that words of the Davidic covenant "play the single most significant role of any Scripture found in the Old Testament in shaping the Christian understanding of Jesus."[7]

Figure 2: References to the Work of Christ in the Historical Books

Scripture	Content
2 Sam 7:13b, 16	A descendant of David will reign forever.

Summary

God promised that he would permanently establish David's throne. The Davidic dynasty would rule eternally. This eternal rule would not be accomplished through the reign of an unbroken succession of Davidic descendants. Instead, God's promise would be fulfilled through the reign of a single descendant of David, the Messiah, who would reign forever.

The Work of Christ in Wisdom and Poetic Literature

For our purposes, Wisdom and Poetic Literature will include Job, Psalms, Proverbs, Ecclesiastes, Song of Solomon, and Lamentations. Various

---

[5] Robert P. Gordon, *1 and 2 Samuel* (Exeter: Paternoster, 1986), 235.

[6] Baldwin, *1 and 2 Samuel*, 228.

[7] Robert D. Bergen, *1, 2 Samuel*, NAC 7 (Nashville: B&H, 1996), 337. Cf. Clements, "The Messianic Hope in the Old Testament," 12–13.

scholars have argued that each of these books contains references to the Messiah. On the other hand, Walter C. Kaiser has argued, "There is little predictive material in these books."[8] Within Wisdom and Poetic Literature, he finds direct references to the Messiah only in Psalms. This assessment is probably correct.[9]

Psalms

The richest deposit of messianic material in the Wisdom and Poetic Literature of the OT is definitely found in the Psalms.[10] Some interpreters, like the church father Augustine, have seen the Messiah in nearly every psalm.[11] Others, like Franz Delitzsch, see "only a single one," Psalm 110, as a direct and explicit messianic prophecy in which David "looks forth into the future of his seed and has the Messiah definitely before his mind."[12] Still

---

[8] Kaiser, *The Messiah in the Old Testament*, 90 (see introduction, n. 7).

[9] The first draft of this chapter contained detailed discussions of purported messianic references in each of these books. Unfortunately, these treatments had to be deleted to remain within the prescribed length for the book.

[10] Of the 1,313 pages devoted to explaining messianic prophecy in the OT, *The Moody Handbook of Messianic Prophecy* devotes 270 pages (one-fifth of the entire book) to Psalms. This compares to 226 pages devoted to Isaiah and 554 pages dedicated to the entire corpus of the Prophets.

[11] Augustine's first sentence in his exposition on the first psalm is, "This is to be understood of our Lord Jesus Christ, the Lord Man." See A. Cleveland Coxe, ed., *St. Augustine: Expositions on the Book of the Psalms*, NPNF 1.8 (New York: Christian Literature Company, 1888), 1. Coxe observed that Augustine's expositions "are part of the system which the Church had received, of which Christ was the Alpha and the Omega, and in which the foreshadowing David was nowhere." More recently, Richard Belcher Jr. has argued that every psalm somehow anticipates Jesus Christ. Belcher Jr., *The Messiah and the Psalms: Preaching Christ from All the Psalms* (Fearn, Scotland: Mentor, 2006).

[12] K&D 5:66. Note, however, that Delitzsch (K&D 5:68–70) distinguishes five classes of Psalms that are in some sense messianic: 1) directly eschatologically messianic psalms, 2) typically messianic psalms, 3) typico-prophetically messianic psalms, 4) indirectly eschatologically messianic psalms, and 5) eschatologically Jehovic psalms. Psalms belonging to this first category "are only distinguished from prophecy proper by their lyric form; for prophecy is a discourse and the psalms are spiritual songs" (68).

others see no messianic content in the Psalms at all. Sadly, the non-messianic approach dominated twentieth-century scholarship on the Psalms.

However, evidence is mounting that this skeptical approach should be abandoned. The individual psalms show numerous signs of having been carefully and thoughtfully arranged to form a unified literary composition.[13] The introduction climaxes with Psalm 2 which describes the king as God's vice-regent who rules from Zion over a kingdom that extends to the ends of the earth. This theme of Davidic royalty will permeate the Psalter as a whole. The five books that follow are joined by literary seams. The seams between the first, second, and third books (Psalms 2, 41, 72, 89) also emphasize kingship and the Davidic covenant. The composition of the Psalter as a single book is clearly post-exilic, since Ps 107:3 and 126:1 refer to the return from the Babylonian exile. This longing for God to fulfill the Davidic covenant in a composition of this date implies that the Psalter should be read as a messianic document. Brevard Childs argued convincingly, "Indeed, at the time of the final redaction, when the institution of kingship had long since been destroyed, what earthly king would have come to mind other than God's Messiah?"[14]

Promises of the Messiah appear with special frequency in the psalms ascribed to David. David, like the OT prophets, was controlled by "the Spirit of the LORD" (1 Sam 16:13). David's final words identified himself as a prophet: "The Spirit of the LORD spoke through me, his word was on my

---

[13] Gerald Wilson revolutionized studies of the Psalms by demonstrating that the Psalter consists of five books with an introduction and conclusion. Wilson, *The Editing of the Hebrew Psalter*, Society of Biblical Literature, Dissertation Series 76 (Chico, CA: Scholars Press, 1985). For a helpful summary of Wilson's findings, see Seth D. Postell, "Messianism in the Psalms," in *The Moody Handbook of Messianic Prophecy: Studies and Expositions of the Messiah in the Old Testament*, ed. Michael Rydelnik and Edwin Blum (Chicago: Moody, 2019), 460–65; Abernethy and Goswell, *God's Messiah in the Old Testament*, 182–96. Abernethy and Goswell more closely follow Wilson in their conclusions. They agree that Wilson's understanding of the order and structure of Psalms "give it a distinctly non-messianic cast" by "moving away from hopes centering on the Davidic royal house toward an exclusive reliance on YHWH as king" (193).

[14] Brevard Childs, *Introduction to the Old Testament as Scripture* (Philadelphia: Fortress, 1979), 516.

tongue" (2 Sam 23:2).[15] Thus, we should not be surprised that several of the Psalms are clearly and explicitly messianic.

Psalm 2 is an example of direct messianic prophecy. Both ancient Jewish and Christian interpreters recognized this. The messianic interpretation is confirmed by the Father's statements at Jesus's baptism (Mark 1:11) and transfiguration (Mark 9:7), both of which allude to Ps 2:7. Early Christian quotations of Ps 2 also consistently treat the psalm as messianic (Acts 4:25–26; 13:33; Heb 1:5; 5:5). In addition, the messianic interpretation is apparent in 4Q174, which interprets the "Son" of 2 Sam 7:8–14 as a reference to the eschatological Messiah and associates the Davidic covenant with Psalm 2 and Amos 9:11–12.

Several internal features of the psalm support the messianic interpretation. The psalm specifically refers to the Lord's "Anointed One" or Messiah whom the nations oppose. The psalm identifies this Messiah as the Lord's begotten Son. Furthermore, the psalm promises that this Messiah will inherit the nations and possess the "ends of the earth," promises that were not fulfilled in the reigns of any of the historic kings of the Davidic dynasty. This psalm portrays the work of the Messiah as ruling over the nations (Ps 2:8) and conquering those who rebel against his authority (Ps 2:1–5, 9).

Psalm 2 may also imply the Messiah's priestly role which will be clearly affirmed later in the Psalter. The Hebrew text of Ps 2:6 says, "I have installed my king on Zion, my holy mountain." The throne of the Anointed One is in Zion, Jerusalem, God's "home" and his "resting place forever" (Ps 132:13–14) where the "dwelling for the Mighty One of Jacob" (Ps 132:5) is located. God has set him as king on the "holy mountain." This was a reference to Moriah, the temple mount, where Abraham had offered Isaac (Gen 22:2) and where God had commanded David to set up an altar and offer burnt offerings and fellowship offerings to the Lord to end a plague on Israel decades before the construction of the temple (2 Sam 24:18–25; cf. 2 Chron 3:1). By God's own command, King David had performed the priestly role of offering sacrifices on the holy mountain before any Aaronic priest ever had. The Targum on the

---

[15] Jesus taught that David spoke in his psalms "by the Holy Spirit" (Mark 12:36; Matt 22:43). The apostles repeatedly affirm the inspiration of David's psalms, describe him as a prophet who saw what was to come, and insist that David wrote about Jesus (Acts 1:16; 2:25, 30–31; 4:25).

Psalms paraphrases Ps 2:6: "And I have anointed my king and appointed him over my sanctuary." Precisely in what sense the Messiah is "over my sanctuary" is unclear. One might argue that he is over the sanctuary as the protector of the holy city who ensures that its courts remain sacrosanct by warding off potential invaders who might desecrate the sacred space. On the other hand, the language may imply that the Messiah presides in some sense over the sanctuary and thus serves a priestly function, though he would seem to exhibit an authority greater than that of the high priest himself. The Targum on Ps 122:5 says, "For there thrones have been placed; in Jerusalem thrones are in the sanctuary for the kings of the house of David." The Targum seems to assert that the heavenly Jerusalem ("Jerusalem that is built in the firmament") is like "a city that has been joined together on earth" (Targum on Psalm 122:3). Since the temple in the earthly Jerusalem has thrones for the Davidic kings, the Messiah has a throne from which he exercises authority from within and over the temple. Because Psalm 2 forms the second half of the introduction to the Psalter, it prompts the reader to expect the messianic promise to be a prominent theme of the Psalter as a whole.

Delitzsch is correct that Psalm 110 is a "directly eschatologically mes-sianic psalm" in the sense that David is clearly speaking of a future ruler distinct from himself who is exalted to a position far beyond that assumed by any mere human king. Psalm 110 was interpreted by Jesus as a mes-sianic psalm that demonstrated the Messiah was both David's descendant and David's Lord (Matt 22:44; 26:64; Mark 12:36; 14:62; Luke 20:42–43; 22:69; cf. Acts 2:34–35; Heb 1:13). David speaks of the figure in the psalm in the second person and describes him as "my Lord." The Hebrew text and LXX, if taken literally, imply that the Messiah will live forever since the Lord says, "You are a priest forever" (Ps 110:4). The LXX also seems to affirm the preexistence of the Messiah, "From the womb, before the Morning-star, I brought you forth" (Ps 110:3).[16]

David's Lord is enthroned at the right hand of Yahweh where he reigns as God's own co-regent, conquers all his enemies by divine power, crushes kings, and judges the nations "over the entire world" (Ps 110:6). The LXX translator picks up on some of the connections to earlier messianic prophe-cies. For example, he translates Psalm 110:6 not as "he will crush leaders" but

---

[16] New English Translation of the Septuagint.

as "he will crush the heads of many upon the ground."[17] The allusion to Gen 3:15 and Num 24:17 is unmistakable.

Psalm 110:4 introduces a new role of the Messiah that has not been explicit in preceding messianic prophecies. In addition to being king, judge, and warrior, David's Lord will also be an eternal priest.[18] Like Melchizedek in Gen 14:18, he will fill the offices of both king and priest. He is a priest "forever" since his priesthood is established by an irrevocable divine oath. He can serve in his priestly role forever only if he is eternal. In this priestly role he will undoubtedly serve as a mediator between God and his people. His priesthood is patterned after that of Melchizedek who pronounced the blessing of the Abrahamic covenant on Abraham. In Gen 12:2 the Lord promised to bless Abram in the future, "I will bless you." Melchizedek then pronounces and enacts the blessing in Gen 14:19, "He [Melchizedek] blessed him [Abraham] and said: Abram is blessed by God Most High, Creator of heaven and earth."[19] Since the Messiah will be a priest according to the pattern of Melchizedek, he will also mediate a covenant between God and his people. This will evidently be a new covenant that replaces the Mosaic covenant, a "better covenant, which has been established on better promises" (Heb 8:6).

The primary function of a priest is to intercede for those he represents (Heb 7:25; cf. 7:22). His intercession entails the presentation of offerings and sacrifices. Neither Levites (Num 18:6–7) nor kings had the privilege of entering the sanctuary to present offerings and sacrifices to God. The law specified that the priests alone were responsible for the ministry of the altar (Num 18:3–5, 7). Thus, the offering of sacrifice was one of their distinctive

---

[17] The Targum on Psalms likewise renders verse 6: "he smote the heads of kings on the earth, very many." The Targum sees the psalm as a promise to David that "you are appointed leader in the age to come, because of the merit that you were a righteous king." Translations of the Targum on Psalms are by Edward Cook.

[18] The dual role of the Messiah as both ruler and priest will also be emphasized in Jer 33:14–26 and Zech 3:8; 4:1–14; 6:9–15. For a discussion of this dual role, see Martin J. Selman, "Messianic Mysteries," in *The Lord's Anointed*, 295–97 (see chap. 1, n. 2).

[19] Abraham acknowledged Melchizedek's superiority by paying a tithe of all the plunder that he had seized when he defeated the kings of Shina, Ellasar, Elam, and Goiim. Thus, David's Lord is likewise Abraham's Lord, one who is superior to both Israel's founding father and her greatest king.

and most solemn duties. The priestly role of David's Lord naturally implies that he must present a sacrifice as well (Heb 8:3).

Figure 3: References to the Work of Christ in the Wisdom and Poetic Books

Scripture	Content
Psalm 2	The Messiah, the Lord's begotten Son, will inherit the nations, possess the ends of the earth, and exercise authority over the temple mount.
Psalm 110	David's Lord will sit enthroned at Yahweh's right hand, judge the nations, conquer and rule over his enemies, and be an eternal priest according to the order of Melchizedek.

Summary

Although other indirect references to the Messiah may appear elsewhere in the Wisdom and Poetic books, the clearest direct references to the Messiah are contained in the Psalms. The Psalms describe the work of the Messiah in kingly, priestly, and prophetic terms. First, the Psalms promise that the Messiah will reign over a worldwide and eternal kingdom, judge the peoples, punish the wicked, defeat all his enemies, and bless all nations. Second, the Psalms describe the Messiah as an eternal priest who will intercede with God on behalf of his people, preside over the temple, and (implicitly at least) offer sacrifice. Third, the Psalms describe the Messiah as one who has divine grace upon his lips, seemingly indicating that like David before him, the Messiah will be a prophet.

4

The Work of Christ in the Prophetic Books

The Prophetic Books mention the Messiah and his work more frequently than any other portion of the Old Testament. All four of the Major Prophets (Isaiah, Jeremiah, Ezekiel, and Daniel) and about half of the Minor Prophets (Hosea, Joel, Amos, Micah, Haggai, Zechariah, and Malachi) refer to the Messiah, some multiple times, and describe various aspects of his mission and activity.

The Work of Christ in the Major Prophets

The Major Prophets contain a heavy concentration of references to the Messiah. Of the four Major Prophets, Isaiah undoubtedly contains the richest deposit of messianic prophecies.[1] However, Jeremiah and Ezekiel also contain important descriptions of the Messiah. Daniel is sometimes considered one of the Historical Books of the Old Testament, but here we include Daniel with the Major Prophets.

---

[1] Matthew used his famous fulfillment formula eleven times (1:22; 2:15, 17; 2:23; 4:14; 8:17; 12:17; 13:35; 21:4; 26:56; 27:9). Six times he specifically identified the OT book from which he was quoting. All six of the identified sources belong to the Major Prophets. Four times Matthew identifies Isaiah as his source, and twice he identifies Jeremiah as his source.

Isaiah

The NT quotes Isaiah far more frequently than any other prophet.[2] The frequency is due in part to the recognition that Isaiah is thoroughly messianic. Matthew explicitly identifies nineteen different OT prophecies that were fulfilled by Jesus. Nine of these, nearly half, are from the book of Isaiah.[3] The apostle John described Jesus's many miracles as well as the stunning disbelief of those who witnessed them (John 12:37) and argued that Isaiah had prophesied both. He explained that "Isaiah said these things because he saw his [Jesus's] glory and spoke about him" (John 12:41).

Isaiah 2:1–4 foretells events that will occur "in the last days" (Isa 2:2). These events include all nations streaming to the Lord's house to worship Yahweh and receive his instruction and the establishment of peace among all the nations. Although the prophecy does not explicitly mention the Messiah, descriptions of the work of the Messiah later in Isaiah will show that the Messiah is the divine instructor and the bringer of universal peace. These intratextual connections prompted rabbinic commentators to recognize that the prophecy refers to the messianic age.[4]

The first explicit reference to the Messiah appears in Isa 4:2–4. The prophet refers to the beautiful and glorious "Branch of the LORD." "Branch" or "Sprout" (ṣemaḥ) may be used of a plant that springs up (Gen 19:25; Isa 61:11; Ezek 16:7; Hos 8:7; Ps 65:10). Since the term is associated with the "fruit of the earth," one might argue that the "sprout" merely refers to plants that will sprout in the land of Israel as it is restored by the Lord. However,

---

[2] The "Index of Quotations" in the UBS[5] (859) lists fifty-five texts from Isaiah that are quoted in the NT (several of these are quoted multiple times in different NT books). Only four texts from Jeremiah, two from Ezekiel, and one from Daniel are quoted. Over the various editions, the UBS committee changed the criteria, the results, and the headings.

[3] See Charles L. Quarles, *A Theology of Matthew: Jesus Revealed as Deliverer, King, and Incarnate Creator* (Phillipsburg, NJ: P&R, 2013), 28–29.

[4] Rambam, Radak, Ibn Ezra, and Rashi interpreted this prophecy as referring to the reign of the Messiah. See Rabbi Nosson Scherman, *Isaiah: The Later Prophets with a Commentary Anthologized from the Rabbinic Writings*, Milstein Edition (New York: Mesorah, 2013), 17–19, cited in J. Randall Price, "Isaiah 2:2–4/Micah 4:1–5: The Restoration of Israel in the Messianic Age," in *The Moody Handbook of Messianic Prophecy*, 785, 800.

the OT prophets often used the term to refer to the Messiah (Jer 23:5; 33:15; Zech 3:8; 6:12). Furthermore, Isaiah later uses another term from the same semantic field to describe the Messiah as a "shoot" (*nēṣer*) that "will grow from the stump of Jesse" and "bear fruit" (Isa 11:1). These factors are likely what influenced the author of the Targum of Jonathan to use the gloss: "The Messiah of the Lord will be joyous and majestic." Three of the Greek translations of Isaiah 4:2 substitute ἀνατολή κύριος ("the Dawn, the Lord" [NETS]) for the expression "Branch of the Lord." Since they also make the same substitution in Jer 23:5–6; 33:14–18; Zech 3:7–9 and 6:11–13—texts which are obviously messianic—the Greek translators appear to regard Isaiah's text as messianic as well. Gregory R. Lanier has shown that the Greek translators' ἀνατολή probably means "arising one" in these contexts rather than "Dawn," and refers to the emergence of a deliverer figure.[5]

The reign of the Messiah will be accompanied by the spiritual cleansing and purification of the remnant in Jerusalem so that all of God's people will be called holy. The messianic age will also result in the return of the Shekinah to Mount Zion (Isa 4:3–4, 5–6). God's presence with his people will be as obvious and powerful as it was during the Exodus because God's glory will surround those assembled to worship the Lord and will provide shelter from storm and shade from the heat.

Isaiah refers to this Messiah again in Isa 7:14. Of course, scholars still debate the identity of Isaiah's Immanuel. Michael Rydelnik did not exaggerate when he referred to this text as "the most controversial of messianic prophecies."[6] Space does not permit serious engagement with this debate here. Evangelical scholars generally recognize that this text is messianic in some sense. However, most recent evangelical scholars argue that the verse refers to the birth of the Messiah via typology[7] or a progressive fulfillment

---

[5] Gregory R. Lanier, "The Curious Case of צמח and ἀνατολή: An Inquiry into Septuagint Translation Patterns," *JBL* 134 (2015): 505–27.

[6] Michael Rydelnik, *The Messianic Hope: Is the Hebrew Bible Really Messianic?* NAC Studies in Bible & Theology (Nashville: B&H, 2010), 147.

[7] Paul Wegner, "A Reexamination of Isaiah IX 1–6," *VT* 42 (1992): 127; James M. Hamilton Jr. "'The Virgin Will Conceive': Typological Fulfillment in Matthew 1:18–23," in *Built Upon the Rock: Studies in the Gospel of Matthew*, ed. Daniel M. Gurtner and John Nolland (Grand Rapids: Eerdmans, 2008), 228–47; Abernethy and Goswell, *God's Messiah in the Old Testament*, 88–89 (see chap. 3, n. 1).

that followed an initial fulfillment in Ahaz's time.[8] Neither typology nor progressive fulfillment constitutes the direct predictive prophesy set as a criterion for treatment in this section.

However, several recent scholars have offered a persuasive case for the traditional view that Isa 7:14 is a direct predictive messianic prophecy.[9] We can only briefly summarize the key arguments here:

1. The sign "as deep as Sheol or as high as heaven" offered in Isa 7:11 seems to be a miraculous sign, and the "sign" in 7:14 is expected to be as well.

2. The sign need not occur in Ahaz's lifetime since Ahaz refused the sign (Isa 7:12) at which point the prophecy is addressed to the entire "house of David" (Isa 7:13) and second person plural pronouns are then used.

3. The most detailed semantic study of the Hebrew term ʿalmâ concludes that the word describes the mother of Immanuel as a female adolescent who is a virgin, thus confirming the LXX translation παρθένος.[10]

4. The prophecy cannot be fulfilled by either a child of Ahaz (Hezekiah)[11] or a son of the prophet Isaiah (Maher-shalal-hash-baz) since the child cannot reach the age of accountability for moral decisions until *after* the sixty-five-year period described in Isa 7:8, i.e., until after the completion of the deportation of Israel by Assyria in 671 BC (cf. Ezra 4:2; 2 Kgs 17:1–33).[12]

---

[8] Kaiser, *The Messiah in the Old Testament*, 158–62 (see introduction, n. 7).

[9] Rydelnik, *The Messianic Hope*, 147–63; Paul House, *Isaiah*, 2 vols. (Fearn, Tain, Ross-Shire, Great Britain: Mentor, 2019), 1:214–35; Christophe Rico and Peter J. Gentry, *The Mother of the Infant King, Isaiah 7:14;* ʿalmâ *and* parthenos *in the World of the Bible: A Linguistic Perspective* (Eugene, OR: Wipf and Stock, 2020). Cf. Gary V. Smith, *Isaiah 1–39*, NAC 15A (Nashville: B&H, 2007), 201–19; Charles L. Quarles, *Matthew*, EBTC (Bellingham, WA: Lexham, 2023).

[10] Rico and Gentry, *The Mother of the Infant King, Isaiah 7:14*, 66–160.

[11] Note that the second-century church father, Justin Martyr, rejected this interpretation (Justin, *Dial.*, 43).

[12] See esp. House, *Isaiah*, 1:214–35; Smith, *Isaiah 1–39*, 201–11. Scholars who see an initial fulfillment in Ahaz's day avoid the chronological problem by interpreting Isa 7:16 to mean merely that "both kings harassing the house of David will be removed." Kaiser, *The Messiah in the Old Testament*, 162; cf. John D. W. Watts, *Isaiah*

5.   The messianic interpretation best suits the broader literary structure, especially the references to the coming king in Isa 9:1–7 and 11:1–9.

What then does Isa 7:14 say about the work of the Messiah? First, the Messiah will embody the presence of God so that God dwells among his people. Second, the Messiah's coming will bring the assurance that God has not abandoned his people and God will bring them deliverance through this promised Messiah. Immanuel's diet of "curds and honey" shows that the land has been devastated (Isa 7:20–25). No farmer tills the soil and no vineyards remain. Animals graze on the thorns and briers that are abundant on the terrain, and the few survivors of the devastation live on the milk products from these animals and the wild honey from the bees that have built their hives in the rocks and thornbushes. Immanuel arises in the context of this judgment, but his name signals deliverance, the end of exile, the restoration of God's people.

Isaiah also refers to the Messiah as Yahweh's "servant." This identification is not universally accepted. Some scholars insist that the Servant is either corporate Israel, a prophet (such as Isaiah or Jeremiah), a king (such as Cyrus or Hezekiah), or a priest (such as Onias or Joshua).[13] However, a strong case can be made that the Servant is none other than the prophet like Moses of Deut 18, a figure rightly equated with the Messiah. The Dead Sea Scrolls (11QMelch 18–25) identify Isaiah's Servant as the Messiah described in Dan 9:26. Rabbi Simlai of the Babylonian Talmud (b. Sotah 14a) and many later Jewish interpreters regarded Isaiah 53 as a description of Moses. Many modern scholars also recognize allusions to Moses in the Servant Songs and argue that the Servant is a second Moses figure.[14]

1–33 (Waco, TX: Word, 1985), 97. Note, however, that the verse refers not to the destiny of the kings of Syria and Israel but to the abandonment of their lands. John Oswalt states that since the 1892 commentary by Bernhard Duhm, nonconservative scholars have generally rejected the messianic interpretation of Isa 7:14 "because of a refusal on the part of most scholars to accept a view of inspiration that would allow the possibility of genuinely predictive prophecy." Oswalt, *Book of Isaiah: Chapters 1–39*, NICOT (Grand Rapids: Eerdmans, 1986), 207.

[13] For a good overview of these options, see G. P. Hugenberger, "The Servant of the Lord in the 'Servant Songs' of Isaiah: A Second Moses Figure," in *The Lord's Anointed*, 105–19 (see chap. 1, n. 2).

[14] See especially Gerhard von Rad, *Old Testament Theology*, trans. D. M. G. Stalker, 2 vols. (New York: Harper & Row, 1962), 2:261–62, 273–77; Allison Jr. *The*

We have already seen that ancient Jews, the NT writers, and early Christians recognized the prophet like Moses as the Messiah. Evidence abounds that Isaiah himself saw the Davidic Messiah described in Isaiah 7, 9, and 11 as the second Moses described in the Servant Songs. The description of David as "my servant" in Isa 37:35 (cf. Ps 18:1; 36:1) implies that the Servant is both a new Moses and new David. Both the Servant and David are described by Yahweh as "my chosen one" (Isa 42:1; Ps 89:3). Strong intratextual connections exist between the description of the Messiah in Isa 11:1–3 and the description of the Servant in Isa 42:1–4. The Spirit of the Lord rests on the Davidic king in Isa 11:2 and on the Servant in Isa 42:1. The Davidic king will "execute justice" (11:3, 4), and Isaiah's Servant "will bring justice to the nations" (42:1) and establish "justice on earth" (42:4). The exaltation of the Servant (52:13) and the silence (52:15) and prostration (49:7) of kings in his presence seem to imply the Servant's royal identity. The comparison of the Servant to a "young plant" and a "root out of dry ground" (53:2) are reminiscent of the description of the Messiah as the "root of Jesse" (11:10) and "shoot" and "branch" (11:1), even though different vocabulary is used.

The identification of the Davidic Messiah and the Servant is very important for understanding the Messiah's mission and work. The Servant Songs demonstrate that the Messiah's work entails vastly more than the ruling and reigning described in Isaiah 9 and 11. The first Servant Song (42:1–4)[15] shows that the Messiah will embody God's covenant with his people who include not merely Israelites but also the nations, the Gentiles (42:6). The Messiah will be a teacher, because "the coasts and islands"—that is, the inhabitants from earth's most distant lands—"will wait for his instruction (*tôrâ*)" (42:4). The new Moses will deliver a new torah that people will eagerly obey, resulting in the restoration of justice and righteousness in the world.

The second Servant Song (49:1–6) offers still more insights into the work of Christ. The Servant is identified as Israel. The reference is clearly

---

New Moses: A Matthean Typology, 68 (see chap. 2, n. 18); Hugenberger, "The Servant of the Lord in the 'Servant Songs' of Isaiah," 119–39.

[15] The utterances of the Father at Jesus's baptism and transfiguration (Mark 1:11; 9:7) allude to Isa 42:1 and confirm that this first Servant Song is fulfilled in Jesus.

not to the nation of Israel. Isaiah 42:18–25 explained in detail why the nation was disqualified from fulfilling the role that God had assigned to it. Israel was spiritually deaf and blind and completely ignored God's words. Isaiah 42:24b summarizes: "They were not willing to walk in his ways, and they would not listen to his instruction." Isaiah 48:1–2 charged that Israel was not true to its name and thus unworthy of its name since its profession was "not in truth or righteousness."[16] Israel's treacherous rebellion was depicted using the strongest metaphors for stubbornness imaginable, an iron neck and a bronze forehead (Isa 48:4, 8). Thus the Lord has now called a new Israel, the Servant, who will succeed in the mission that national Israel failed to fulfill. Furthermore, Isa 49:5 clearly distinguishes the Servant from national Israel since this new Israel will bring Jacob/Israel back to God.

The mission of the Messiah will be greater in both scale and scope than the mere restoration of Israel. The dignity and majesty of the Messiah is so much greater that merely restoring a small nation is beneath him. Yahweh promises: "I will also make you a light for the nations, to be my salvation to the ends of the earth" (49:6b). As the "light," the Messiah will illuminate and reveal. He will lead the people to God and guide them on the path of righteousness (Isa 2:5; 42:16; 50:10; 51:4–5). He will be God's provision for "salvation." This salvation clearly is more than liberation from oppression since this salvation is not only for exiled and imprisoned Israelites but even for the very nations that have oppressed them. This salvation is clearly spiritual salvation. The cry, "This is our God . . . and he has saved us" (Isa 25:9) shows that this salvation entails destroying death (v. 8), wiping every tear from the eyes of his people (v. 8), conquering God's enemies (vv. 10–12). This salvation involves the forgiveness of iniquity and the healing of all sickness (33:22, 24; cf. 35:4–6), the removal of shame (45:17; cf. 42:17; 44:9, 11), and the justification and glorification of God's people (45:22–25). The description of the Messiah as "my [Yahweh's] salvation" not only identifies him as Yahweh's agent, but also closely associates him with Yahweh who has

---

[16] The niphal verb translated "are called" is probably reflexive ("call themselves") and indicates that the people identify themselves as Israel (cf. Isa 44:5), but the context implies that the claim is spurious. See Chris Franke, *Isaiah 46, 47, 48: A New Literary-Critical Reading* (Winona Lake, IN: Eisenbrauns, 1994), 170; Gary Smith, *Isaiah 40–66*, NAC (Nashville: B&H, 2009), 315–16.

repeatedly insisted that he alone is the Savior (43:11; 45:21; cf. 43:3; 45:15; 49:26; 60:16; 63:8).

The third Servant Song (50:4–9) is appropriately called "the Gethsemane of the Servant."[17] The Messiah knows how "to sustain the weary with the word" (50:4). Thus, encouraging those who are exhausted so they can press on another day is one important aspect of his work. The description of his work focuses primarily on his obedient suffering. The Servant offers his back to those who beat him and his face to those who rip out his beard (50:6), and he exposes his face to the spitting of his torturers. God will vindicate the Servant and will severely punish those who wrongly condemned and abused him.

The fourth Servant Song (52:13–53:12) elaborates on the suffering of the Servant introduced in the third Servant Song and on the salvation provided by the Servant described in the second Servant Song. It clarifies that the suffering is the very means of salvation. The Servant suffers such horrible disfigurement that he no longer looks human (52:14) so that he may "sprinkle many nations" (52:15). This sprinkling is probably a reference to a priest sprinkling blood to secure atonement (Lev 4:6, 17; 5:9; 16:14, 19) or, less likely, to consecrate (Lev 8:11, 30).[18] The descriptions of the Servant's suffering and death as vicarious (Isa 53:4, 5, 6, 9, 10, 11, 12) strongly support the view that this sprinkling is related to atonement for sin. This statement is closely related to the descriptions of the Messiah as priest that occur in Psalms (Ps 110:4; cf. 2:6). This priestly role is confirmed in Isa 53:12, in

---

[17] This expression was coined by Christopher North in *The Suffering Servant in Deutero-Isaiah: An Historical and Critical Study* (London: Cumberlege, 1956), 146.

[18] The grammar of the expression in Isa 52:15 most closely matches Lev 4:6, 17 since the construction lacks a preposition and instead uses a direct object. Admittedly, difficult text-critical issues exist here. Although the MT says, "sprinkle," the LXX has "cause to marvel" and the Targum of Jonathan has "scatter." The verb in the MT best fits the context since the Servant is compared to a slaughtered lamb (Isa 53:7) and since his death is described as a "guilt offering" (Isa 53:10). For a helpful defense of the reading and sense of "sprinkle" with a sacrificial meaning, see Edward J. Young, *Studies in Isaiah* (Grand Rapids: Eerdmans, 1955), 199–206; and Peter Gentry, "The Servant Sprinkles Many as Anointed Priest," Text and Canon Institute Blog, July 18, 2022, https://textandcanon.org. Gentry follows the Great Isaiah Scroll (1QIsaᵃ) in seeing 52:14 as a reference to the Servant's anointing (to be a priest) rather than his marring or disfiguring.

which the Servant "interceded for the rebels." In the Hebrew construction used here, the verb means "to plead with someone on behalf of someone else" (cf. Gen 23:8).[19] The meaning is identical to that of Isa 59:16 in which the verb likely refers to an advocate who pleads one's case before a judge,[20] interceding on behalf of others like Abraham did in Gen 18:22–33 and Moses did in Exod 32:11–14.

The Servant is not only the priest who offers the atoning sacrifice; he is the sacrifice as well. The Servant "bore our sicknesses" and "carried our pains" (Isa 53:4). Sickness and pain were specified results of breaking the covenant with God. The curses of the covenant included "wasting disease, fever, inflammation" (Deut 28:22), "the boils of Egypt, tumors, a festering rash, and scabies, from which you cannot be cured" (v. 27), "painful and incurable boils on your knees and thighs—from the sole of your foot to the top of your head" (v. 35), "wondrous plagues . . . , severe and lasting plagues, and terrible and chronic sicknesses" (v. 59), "all the diseases of Egypt" (v. 60), and "every sickness and plague not recorded in the book of this law" (v. 61). Deuteronomy 29:22 warned covenant breakers that "future generations of your children who follow you and the foreigner who comes from a distant country will see the plagues of that land and the sicknesses the LORD has inflicted on it." Thus, the curses of the covenant are suffered by the Servant.

Many people will despise the Servant because they assume that he has personally broken the covenant and is thereby deserving of his horrible suffering (Isa 53:3). Observers regard the Servant as "stricken, struck down by God, and afflicted" (53:4). The verb "regard" (*ḥšb*) when used with the accusative and the preposition *lᵉ* or with the double accusative (the construction in Isa 53:4) ordinarily means "to presume wrongly." Just as Judah wrongly presumed that the veiled Tamar was a prostitute (Gen 38:15) and Eli wrongly presumed that Hannah was drunk (1 Sam 1:13), many will wrongly presume that the Servant is a terrible sinner deserving of God's fiercest wrath. Yet the prophet repeatedly emphasizes the Servant's complete innocence. The

---

[19] I concur with Franz Delitzsch that the Hiphil is equivalent to the Qal in this context. Delitzsch, *Biblical Commentary on the Prophecies of Isaiah*, trans. James Kennedy, Clark's Foreign Theological Library, vol. 44 (Edinburgh: T&T Clark, 1890), 2:312.

[20] The Targum of Jonathan took the verb in this sense: "there was no man who would stand and petition on behalf of them."

Servant is "righteous" (Isa 53:11). He "had done no violence and had not spoken deceitfully" (Isa 53:9).

The innocent Servant suffers the curses of the covenant because he suffers and dies in the place of others. The prophet implies this already in Isa 53:4. Smith explains:

> [T]he source of the Servant's suffering is connected to "our" suffering by claiming that he suffered because "he himself" was the one who "carried, bore" the consequences that belonged to "us." The act of "carrying, bearing" could suggest either participation with others by helping them carry their load (46:7; Exod 18:22; Num 11:17), or the verb could communicate the idea of "carrying" something for someone else by taking away the load that others were bearing (40:24; 41:16). The next two verses and 53:11–12 will make it clear that the Servant will take away the suffering that others were supposed to bear.[21]

What has already been strongly implied in Isa 53:4 is explicitly stated later in the prophecy. The Servant suffered "because of our rebellion" and "because of our iniquities" (Isa 53:5). The Lord punished the Servant "for the iniquity of us all" (Isa 53:6) and "because of my people's rebellion" (Isa 53:8). He "will justify many" because he "will carry their iniquities" (Isa 53:11). He allowed himself to be "counted among the rebels" so that he could bear "the sin of many" (Isa 53:12). Finally, the Servant is described as a "guilt offering" (ʾāšām; Isa 53:10). In Levitical law, this specific offering was given to seek atonement for various sins (Lev 5:6–6:7). Delitzsch explains:

> The trespass-offering was a restitution or compensation made to God in the person of the priest, a payment or penance which made amends for the wrong done, *a satisfactio* in a disciplinary sense. And

---

[21] Smith, *Isaiah 40–66*, 449. Smith adds, "The verbs נָשָׂא 'to bear, carry' and סָבַל 'to carry, shoulder' are synonyms that communicate the idea that "he carried" something that belonged to someone else." John Oswalt argues that "This is the language of the cult, especially from Leviticus. There the sacrificial animal carries (nāśāʾ) the sins of the offerers away, so that the offerer does not carry them anymore." Oswalt, *The Book of Isaiah: Chapters 40–66*, NICOT (Grand Rapids: Eerdmans, 1998), 386.

this is implied in the name; for just as חטאת denotes first the sin, then the punishment of the sin and the expiation of the sin, and hence the sacrifice which cancels the sin; so 'âshâm signifies first the guilt or debt, then the compensation or penance, and hence (cf., Lev 5:15) the sacrifice which discharges the debt or guilt, and sets the man free.[22]

The law declares that the sinner "is guilty and he will bear his iniquity" (Lev 5:17). However, through the presentation of the guilt offering, "the priest will make atonement on his behalf . . . and he will be forgiven" (v. 18). One can hardly imagine how Isaiah could have stated more clearly or emphatically that the Servant's death provided penal substitutionary atonement.

The prophecy stresses that the Servant will experience severe suffering and a brutal death. He is beaten so viciously that he is no longer recognizable as a human being (Isa 52:14). He is a "man of suffering" (53:3) who is "pierced" (53:5), a term normally referring to some type of fatal stabbing (cf. Isa 51:9; Job 26:13). He is "crushed" (Isa 53:5, 10) and "punished" (vv. 5–6). He suffers "wounds," probably a reference to the lacerations on his back and face from his bloody beating and the ripping out of his beard (50:6). He is "oppressed and afflicted" (53:7), "struck" (vv. 4, 8), and "cut off from the land of the living" (v. 8). He dies (vv. 8–9) only after suffering unimaginable "anguish" (v. 11).

Despite the vivid descriptions of the Servant's suffering and death, the prophet emphasizes his success and exaltation. The prophecy both begins and ends on a triumphant note. Many scholars see the reference to the Servant's success and exaltation in Isa 52:13 and the reference to God granting him "the many as a portion" and "the mighty as spoil" (53:12) as an inclusio that indicates that this is the primary theme of the prophecy.[23] The statements that God will "prolong his days" (53:10) and that even after his anguishing death, the Servant "will see light and be satisfied" (53:11) implies that the exaltation referred to in Isa 52:13 entails resurrection.[24] Thus the suffering Servant will be a powerful, victorious conqueror.

---

[22] K&D 7:333 (see chap. 3, n. 3).

[23] An inclusio is a literary device in which similar features appear at the beginning and end of a section to alert the reader to the primary theme of that section.

[24] J. Alec Motyer notes that the threefold exaltation in Isa 52:13 is "a trio which many link with the threefold exaltation of Jesus Christ in resurrection, ascension

Another description of the Messiah appears in Isa 61:1–3. Jesus clearly interpreted this text as messianic and stated that he fulfilled it. He read this passage in the synagogue in Nazareth and said, "Today as you listen, this Scripture has been fulfilled" (Luke 4:16–22). Although the Targum (and some modern scholars) identifies the figure in this passage as Isaiah, an important first-century Jewish text (11Q13; cf. 4Q521) recognizes that the passage refers to the Messiah.

Several details of the text support this messianic interpretation. First, the statement "he has anointed me" identifies the figure as an "anointed one" and hence messianic in some sense. Second, the statement "the Spirit of the Lord God is on me" is reminiscent of the descriptions of the Messiah in Isa 11:2: "the Spirit of the Lord will rest on him—a Spirit of wisdom and understanding, a Spirit of counsel and strength, a Spirit of knowledge and of the fear of the Lord" (cf. 42:1; 50:4–5). Third, his ministry to the "poor" recalls Isa 11:4 in which the Messiah "will judge the poor righteously and execute justice for the oppressed of the land." Fourth, his ministry will make God's people righteous (Isa 61:3), an effect of the ministry of the Servant in 53:11 (cf. Isa 11:5). Fifth, his ministry of releasing the prisoners echoes themes of Isa 49:8–12. Other parallels with earlier messianic prophecies in Isaiah exist that demonstrate that Jesus's interpretation of Isa 61:1–3 was sensitive to the original context and faithful to the intention of the divinely-inspired author.[25]

The prophecy details clearly the work of the Messiah. He will "bring good news to the poor" (Isa 61:1). He will proclaim the good news that those who are helpless, who have been subject to the abuses of powerful people, and who have suffered constant hardship will be rescued and their suffering brought to an end.[26] He will "heal the brokenhearted" (v. 1). The

---

and heavenly enthronement." Motyer, *The Prophecy of Isaiah* (Downers Grove: IVP, 1993), 374–75.

[25] After a thorough discussion of the parallels between this text and earlier descriptions of the Messiah, Oswalt (*The Book of Isaiah: Chapters 40–66*, 564) concludes that "to apply the passage to an unknown prophet or group is asking too much." He adds, "This is the Messiah, and he is being consciously associated with the Servant by showing that the Messiah does the Servant's work."

[26] See the descriptions of the fate of the poor in Isa 3:14–15; 10:2; 11:4; 32:7; 41:17; 58:7.

verb translated "heal" means to "bind up" or "bandage." Isaiah used this term in 1:6 to describe a "sinful nation, people weighed down with iniquity" who have "abandoned the Lord" and "despised the Holy One of Israel" (1:4) and thus been beaten with a rod of discipline until their entire body is covered with welts "not cleansed, bandaged, or soothed with oil" (1:6). In Isa 30:18–26, the Lord "bandages his people's injuries and heals the wounds he inflicted." By bandaging God's people, the Messiah will bring an end to God's judgment on them. Those who were cursed from breaking covenant with God will now be blessed through the Messiah. The Messiah will also proclaim the liberation of captives and prisoners. Isaiah often refers to those under God's judgment as prisoners (Isa 10:4; 24:22), especially God's people who are in exile (Isa 14:17; 42:22; 51:14). The Messiah will bring an end to the exile and captivity that fulfilled the covenant curses (Deut 28:30–32, 36–37, 48, 64–68). The Messiah will proclaim "the year of the Lord's favor" (Isa 61:2), a phrase associated with the "day of salvation" in Isa 49:8. This time of salvation for God's repentant people will also be the "day of our God's vengeance" for the wicked who oppressed them. Isaiah describes this day of vengeance with graphic imagery in 63:1–6, another text fulfilled by the Messiah who will "trample the winepress of the fierce anger of God" (Rev 19:15). The Messiah will "comfort all who mourn" (Isa 61:2). These mourners are grieved by the anger of God that has befallen them due to their sinfulness (57:16–19). The Messiah brings the comfort of divine forgiveness, the comfort described in Isa 40:1–2 that comes when his people's "time of hard service is over" and her "iniquity has been pardoned." God's people will trade their mourning garments for festal robes and crowns. Those who were characterized by wickedness in the past (Isa 59:1–8) will produce the fruit of righteousness that brings God glory (Isa 61:3).

Jeremiah

The prophet Jeremiah gives four direct messianic prophecies that echo themes already prominent in the prophecies of Isaiah: Jer 23:5–6; 30:8–9; 30:21–22; and 33:15–16. Jeremiah 23:5–6 promises that God will "raise up a Righteous Branch for David" in the coming days. The Targum recognizes that this Branch is the same figure described in Isaiah 4:2 (which uses the same noun as Jer 23:5) and 11:1 and thus paraphrases verse 5: "Behold, days

are coming, says the Lord, when I will establish a Messiah of righteousness for David." This branch will sprout from the apparently dead stump of
the Davidic dynasty to fulfill God's covenant with David (2 Samuel 7). The
emphasis on the Messiah's righteousness is reminiscent of Isa 9:7; 11:3, 5;
and 53:9, 11. The mission of the Messiah is to be a Ruler and a Savior. Unlike
many other kings in the line of David, the Messiah will "reign wisely as
king and administer justice and righteousness in the land," a promise which
echoes themes from early messianic prophecies (e.g., Isa 9:7; 11:3–4). "In his
days Judah will be saved" implies that the Messiah will be the divine agent
of salvation. The related prophecy that immediately follows also begins with
"Look, the days are coming" and promises Israel's return from exile, a return
that mirrors and yet exceeds their deliverance in the Exodus from Egypt
(Jer 23:7–8). The combined prophecies imply the Messiah's identity as the
prophet like Moses who will lead a new exodus by delivering God's people
from their exile, the exile that resulted from their rebellion against him.

Jeremiah 30:21–22 describes the messianic king as a leader and ruler
who will arise from among the descendants of Jacob (cf. Jer 30:20). F. B.
Huey notes that the reference to the Messiah rising from among them is
"a reference to the Mosaic promise (Deut 17:15) of a divinely chosen king
'from among your own brothers' (cf. 1 Sam 16:1–13)."[27] This king also enjoys
the privileges of a priest since he is invited to enter the Lord's presence in
the manner in which only the high priest was allowed to do (Exod 28:34–35;
Leviticus 16).[28] When Uzziah, another Davidic king, entered the sanctuary
and acted as a priest by burning incense on the incense altar, eighty-one
priests rebuked him for usurping priestly privileges, and the Lord struck him
with leprosy (2 Chron 26:16–23). The messianic Son of David, however, is
granted the privileges of the Aaronic priesthood and enters the Lord's presence without any risk of divine judgment. The promise made immediately

---

[27] F. B. Huey, Jr., *Jeremiah, Lamentations*, NAC 16 (Nashville: Broadman &
Holman, 1993), 267.

[28] J. A. Thompson noted: "To enter the divine presence unbidden was to risk
death. The ruler thus appears to be undertaking a sacral or priestly function rather
than one that is specifically political. The picture is of a ruler-priest performing
both political and priestly duties." Thompson, *The Book of Jeremiah*, NICOT (Grand
Rapids: Eerdmans, 1980), 562. For a similar view, see Block, "My Servant David," 42
(see chap. 1, n. 11).

after the reference to the Messiah, "You will be my people, and I will be your God" (Jer 30:22), is a covenant formula used frequently in the Old Testament (e.g., Gen 17:7–8; Exod 6:7; 19:6; Lev 26:12; Jer 7:23; Ezek 36:28). The formula appears only a chapter later (Jer 31:33) as part of the new covenant promise of Jer 31:31–34. The connection seems to imply that the priest-king of Jer 30:21 will be the mediator of this new covenant which promises the internal transformation of God's people (31:33), a personal relationship with God, and the complete forgiveness of sins (31:34).[29]

Ezekiel

The book of Ezekiel contains four direct messianic prophecies (Ezek 17:22–24; 21:25–27; 34:23–31; 37:15–28).

A reference to the Messiah's salvific work probably appears in Ezek 21:26–27. The phrase "until he comes" is widely recognized as a reference to the messianic promise in Gen 49:10, "until he whose right it is comes."[30] If so, the turban and crown—which Zedekiah was unworthy to wear and was commanded by God to remove—rightly belong to the coming Messiah. This confirms that the Messiah will rule as the king of God's people. The reference to the "turban" may also imply that the Messiah will serve as priest since the word "turban" normally refers to the headdress of the high priest (Exod 28:4, 37, 39; 29:6; 39:28, 31; Lev 8:9; 16:4). The Targum on Ezekiel described the turban as the one belonging to "Seraiah the high priest." However, the grammar of the Hebrew text implies that both the turban and the crown are worn by the same figure, the king, and Zedekiah does not appear to have

---

[29] Huey, *Jeremiah, Lamentations*, 267. Although Gerald Keown, Pamela Scalise, and Thomas Smothers do not explicitly make this connection, they acknowledge that this oracle "concentrates on his mediatorial function" and further note that on the occasion of the old covenant, only Moses was allowed to approach God in the manner described here (Exod 20:21; 24:2). Keown, Scalise, and Smoothers, *Jeremiah 26–52*, WBC 27 (Dallas: Word, 1995), 104. Hetty Lalleman observes that the message "sounds like a messianic promise" and that Jer 30:22 sets the stage for the promise of the new covenant in Jer 31:31–34. Lalleman, *Jeremiah and Lamentations*, TOTC 21 (Downers Grove: IVP Academic, 2013), 277.

[30] Ralph Alexander describes the expression as "a definite reference to Genesis 49:10 and the king-priest Messiah." Alexander, "Ezekiel," in *Isaiah, Jeremiah, Lamentations, Ezekiel*, EBC 6 (Grand Rapids: Zondervan, 1986), 845.

ever assumed a priestly role.[31] The prophecy contrasts Zedekiah as a "profane and wicked prince of Israel" (Ezek 21:25) with the righteous Messiah whose righteousness uniquely qualifies him to rule.

Although some scholars challenge the messianic interpretation of Ezek 21:26–27, Ezek 34:23–31 is clearly and unmistakably messianic. After a blistering indictment of Israel's shepherds (34:1–10), her wicked and abusive past kings, God promised that he would personally shepherd his people (34:11–22). He will bring the exiles from other countries back to their homeland and prevent the wealthy and privileged from taking advantage of the weak and poor. Then the prophet launches into a powerful messianic promise. God would establish over them "one shepherd" (34:23). This divinely appointed shepherd would obviously be a king who loved the sheep and expressed God's own care for them by seeking the lost, bringing back the strays, bandaging the injured, strengthening the weak, and preventing the fat sheep from abusing the weaker sheep (cf. 34:16). The appointment of "one shepherd" stands in stark contrast to the multiple shepherds mentioned in 34:2, 7–10. The reference to "one" shepherd has two important implications. The aforementioned shepherds were a line of successive kings. The reference now to a single shepherd emphasizes that God is not replacing a corrupt and wicked line with a new succession of kings. Instead, he will fulfill the Davidic covenant (2 Sam 7:16) through a single descendant of David, the Messiah.[32] As Ezek 37:25 will stress, the Messiah "will be their prince forever." Furthermore, God's people would not be divided into two kingdoms, each ruled by a different king. The divided kingdom would be reunited under the rule of the Messiah (Ezek 37:15–24). The description of the Messiah as "my servant" indicates that he will reign in service to God and as an expression of God's own regency.

The Messiah's reign will be accompanied by God's "covenant of peace" (34:25). Block appropriately titles Ezek 34:23–24 "The Human Agent of Peace."[33] The Messiah will enact this covenant of peace and bring the

---

[31] For additional evidence of a linguistic nature, see Block, *Ezekiel: 1–24*, 690n189.

[32] Lamar E. Cooper, *Ezekiel*, NAC (Nashville: Broadman and Holman, 1994), 302.

[33] Daniel Block, *The Book of Ezekiel: Chapters 25–48*, NICOT (Grand Rapids: Eerdmans, 1998), 297.

promised peace to the covenant beneficiaries. This peace is more than just the absence of war and conflict. Block persuasively argues from their numerous parallels that "the inspiration for Ezekiel's description of *šālôm* derives from the ancient covenant blessings as recorded in Lev. 26:4–13."[34] This peace is *shalom* in its fullest sense and includes liberation from captivity and slavery, elimination of dangers from predators, fertile fields, abundant rain, and protection even from fear and insult (Ezek 34:25–31). Although some scholars insist that this covenant of peace is distinct from the new covenant, the reference to this same covenant of peace in the final messianic prophecy of Ezekiel strongly implies that the two expressions refer to the same covenant.

Ezekiel 37:24–28 closely resembles the prophecy in 34:23–31. This prophecy also describes the Messiah as "my Servant David" who will be the "one Shepherd for all of them," that is, for all people in the reunited kingdom of Israel. It insists that the reign of the Davidic Messiah will be forever (Ezek 37:25). However, this prophecy clearly associates the Messiah's reign with the spiritual salvation of God's people. God promises, "I will save them from all their apostasies by which they sinned, and I will cleanse them" (37:23). This salvation includes both forgiveness and transformation. In the reign of the Messiah, "they will follow my ordinances, and keep my statutes and obey them" (v. 24). This echoes the promise of the giving of the Spirit in Ezek 36:26–27:

> "I will give you a new heart and put a new spirit within you; I will remove your heart of stone and give you a heart of flesh. I will place my Spirit within you and cause you to follow my statutes and carefully observe my ordinances."

Thus the "covenant of peace" is none other than the new covenant promised in Jer 31:31–34. Although Ezekiel does not explicitly state that the Messiah will be the agent through whom God bestows his Spirit on his people, the association of the Messiah's reign with the transformation of sinners and the covenant of peace strongly implies this. The covenant of peace also entails a new relationship with God and closeness to him. God will not be isolated or distant from his people. He will place his sanctuary among them forever and make his dwelling place with them (Ezek 37:26–27).

---

[34] Block, *Ezekiel 25–48*, 303.

Daniel

Two direct messianic prophecies appear in Daniel: the Son of Man prophecy in Dan 7:13–14[35] and the Seventy Weeks prophecy in 9:24–27.

Daniel explicitly refers to the salvific work of the Messiah in this latter text. Messiah appears again in the Seventy Weeks vision in Dan 9:24–27.[36] Gabriel's prophecy anticipates the coming of an "Anointed One, the prince" who will appear after sixty-nine sets of sevens of years have passed since the imperial decree to restore and rebuild Jerusalem.[37] This ruler appears to be the Messiah. Daniel Block noted:

> Remarkably, Dan. 9:25–26 and Isa. 61:1 represent the only instances outside Psalms in which the verb *māšaḥ* and/or its cognate noun *māšiaḥ* refer to someone whose role approximates that of the messiah as understood by the definition quoted earlier: "a figure who will play an authoritative role in the end time, usually the eschatological king."[38]

---

[35] For a more detailed discussion of the prophecy and its interpretation in early Jewish and Christian texts, see Charles L. Quarles, "Lord or Legend: Jesus as the Messianic Son of Man," *JETS* 62, no. 1 (2019): 103–24.

[36] J. N. Oswalt ("משח," *NIDOTTE* 2:1123–27) argues that Dan 9:25–26 is the only certain reference to an eschatological messiah in the OT.

[37] Scholars continue to debate whether the chronology of the prophecy is to be interpreted literally or symbolically. Early Christians like Julius Africanus and Eusebius of Caesarea argued that the prophecy showed "that the time of the Saviour's Coming from above was known to the ancient prophets, and clearly handed down in writing" (Eusebius, *Dem. ev.* 8.1 §380–81). Julius Africanus interpreted the prophecy as referring to seventy sets of seven literal years that culminated in the ministry of Jesus (Chronography 5, quoted in Eusebius *Dem. ev.* 8.2 §§ 389–91). Eusebius regarded the "Anointed One" in Dan 9:25 as a reference to the succession of high priests who ruled Israel up to the time of Jesus and the "coming ruler" in v. 26 as Herod the Great. However, he viewed the covenant in Dan 9:27 as the new covenant enacted by the Messiah and on those grounds saw Daniel's prophecy culminating in the death of Jesus. Eusebius saw the "abomination of desolation" as Pilate's act of desecrating the temple by bringing images of Caesar into the temple (Eusebius, *Dem. ev.* 8.2 §§ 402–403; Josephus, *Ant.* 18.3 and *J.W.* 2.9.2; Philo, *Embassy* 38). Many modern commentators argue that the timeframe is symbolic and refers to an indefinite period. See Michael Shepherd, *Daniel in the Context of the Hebrew Bible*, Studies in Biblical Literature 123 (New York: Peter Lang, 2009), 95–99; Paul House, *Daniel*, TOTC 23 (Downers Grove: IVP, 2018), 159.

[38] Daniel Block, "My Servant David: Ancient Israel's Vision of the Messiah," in *Israel's Messiah*, 25.

One of the Dead Sea Scrolls (11Q13) describes the Anointed One of Dan 9:26 as the messenger of Isa 52:7 who brings the good news of salvation, the fulfillment of Isa 61:2 who comforts those who mourn, and as one anointed by the Spirit (Isa 42:1; 61:1–3). The messianic interpretation was also the dominant view among early Christians and many of their Jewish contemporaries.[39]

Gabriel said that the Messiah would be "cut off" (*yikkārēt*), a verb that meant "to kill" when applied to persons or other living creatures (e.g., Gen 9:11; Exod 31:14; Jer 9:21; 11:19). This recalls language used to describe the death of the Servant in Isaiah's fourth Servant Song, who was also "cut off [*nigzar*] from the land of the living" when he was "struck because of my people's rebellion" (Isa 53:8). The Messiah's ministry will fulfill the wonderful promises of Dan 9:24 by bringing an end to rebellion, putting a stop to sin, atoning for iniquity, bringing in everlasting righteousness, sealing up vision and prophecy, and anointing the most holy place. The description of the Messiah atoning for iniquity assigns to him a priestly function only mentioned a few times in earlier messianic prophecies. J. Barton Payne understandably referred to this text as "one of the most significant passages in the Old Testament on the priestly work of the Messiah."[40] Ending rebellion, stopping sin, and bringing in everlasting righteousness involves changing the character of God's people so they at last manifest the divine image and likeness that was so severely marred by the fall. The ministry of the Messiah will entail not only forgiveness but also transformation. "Everlasting righteousness" results from the fulfillment of the new covenant in which God writes his commandments on his people's hearts, gives them a new heart, and places his Spirit within them to cause them to keep his commandments and fulfill his ordinances.[41]

---

[39] Jerome surveyed the interpretations of the Seventy Weeks prophecy by Julius Africanus, Eusebius, Hippolytus, Apollinarius of Laodicea, Clement of Alexandria, Origen, Tertullian, and contemporary Jewish interpreters and showed that all recognized the prophecy as messianic despite differences in their understanding of the chronology. See Gleason Archer, trans. *Jerome's Commentary on Daniel* (Grand Rapids: Baker, 1958), 94–110.

[40] J. Barton Payne, *The Theology of the Older Testament* (Grand Rapids: Zondervan, 1962), 276.

[41] This affirmation is not intended to imply that the covenant of Dan 9:27 is necessarily the "new covenant." For the view that "the coming ruler" in Dan 9:26 is the

Figure 4: References to the Work of Christ in the Major Prophets

Scripture	Content
Isa 4:2–6	The Messiah will wash away the filth of the remnant of Israel, and the Shekinah that provided refuge to Israel in the Exodus will overshadow Mount Zion.
Isa 7:14	Immanuel embodies the presence of God and brings deliverance and restoration to those in exile.
Isa 42:1–9	The Davidic Messiah will bring justice and offer instruction to the nations, abolish false worship, free the oppressed, and heal the blind.
Isa 49:1–6	The Messiah is an unconquerable warrior who will defeat all who oppose his people, restore national Israel, and bring salvation to the nations.
Isa 50:4–9	The Messiah will sustain the weary with his words and suffer obediently.
Isa 52:13–53:12	The Messiah will perform the sprinkling that effects atonement, intercede on behalf of the rebels, bear the guilt and punishment of sinners despite his own innocence, die as the atoning sacrifice for his people, live again, and be exalted by God.
Isa 61:1–3	The Messiah will be empowered by the Spirit to bring good news of deliverance to the poor and oppressed, make God's people righteous, and bring an end to God's judgment on his people.
Jer 30:21–22	The Messiah will be a priest-king who will mediate the new covenant.

Messiah who will enact the new covenant (9:27), see Peter Gentry, "Daniel's Seventy Weeks and the New Exodus," *SBJT* 14, no. 1 (2010): 26–44, esp. 37–40. For the view that the coming ruler is the future antichrist, see Eugene Carpenter, "Daniel," in *Ezekiel, Daniel,* Cornerstone Biblical Commentary, ed. Philip Comfort (Carol Stream, IL: Tyndale, 2010), 428–31; Stephen Miller, *Daniel,* NAC 18 (Nashville: B&H, 1994), 268–74.

Ezek 34:23–31	The Messiah will shepherd God's people, unite the divided kingdom, and enact the "covenant of peace," the new covenant.
Ezek 37:15–28	The Messiah will shepherd the united kingdom of Israel, reign eternally, grant forgiveness, and transform God's people.
Dan 9:24–27	The Messiah will die to atone for iniquity and change the character of God's people to establish eternal righteousness.

Summary

The Major Prophets contain numerous references to the ministry of the Messiah and reveal many important features of his work. The Major Prophets emphasize that the Messiah will rule, not only over the kingdom of Israel (Jer 23:5–6; 33:15–16; Ezek 34:23–31; 37:15–28) but over all nations and people of every tribe and language (Isa 11:1–9; Ezek 17:22–24; Dan 7:13–14). These Prophets also stress that the Messiah will bring salvation to the nations (Isa 49:1–6). The Messiah will die as the atoning sacrifice that effects forgiveness for the iniquities of the repentant (Isa 52:13–53:12; cf. Dan 9:24–27). He will also mediate the new covenant that promises to transform God's people so that they are characterized by a supernatural righteousness (Jer 30:21; Ezek 34:23–31; 37:15–28; Dan 9:24–26). The Major Prophets describe the coming Messiah as a teacher who will instruct God's people in the way of righteousness (Isa 42:1–9; 50:4–9; 55:3–5; 61:1–3).

The Work of Christ in the Minor Prophets

Our study of the descriptions of the work of the Messiah in the Old Testament at last brings us to the so-called Minor Prophets. The adjective "minor" merely contrasts the length of these relatively short books with the massive size of the books of the Major Prophets: Isaiah, Jeremiah, Daniel, and Ezekiel. The "Minor Prophets" are certainly not of minor importance, especially when it comes to the topic of the promised Messiah and his future ministry.

Since at least 200 BC (Sir 49:10), the "Twelve Prophets" have been viewed as a single collection.[42] Several important features demonstrate that the collection is to be read as a single book.[43] Both the Masoretic Text and the Dead Sea Scrolls place Hosea as the first book in the collection so that it serves as the introduction to the Book of the Twelve.[44] Hosea contains several references to the Messiah and his reign (Hos 1:10–11; 3:4–5), and these references prompt the reader to expect messianic references elsewhere in the Book of the Twelve. However, these texts in Hosea do not refer explicitly to his salvific work.[45] A possible messianic prophecy in Joel 2:23 may refer to the Messiah's ministry of teaching Torah and instructing his people in the way of true righteousness. A clear messianic prophecy in Amos 9:11–12 leads to a promise of the restoration of the land in the messianic era which is reminiscent of prophetic promises of a new creation (Isa 51:3; cf. Ezek 36:35).

Zechariah

Explicit references to the Messiah appear with greater frequency in the book of Zechariah. In Zech 3:8 the Lord promises that he is about to send "my servant, the Branch." Obviously, both these descriptors of the coming person are messianic titles that are prominent in earlier prophecies.[46] "My servant" was the central figure in the four Servant Songs of Isaiah (Isa 42:1–9; 49:1–6;

---

[42] See also Acts 7:42; b. B. Bat. 14b. The Masoretic text also treats the "Book of the Twelve" as a single book. See the masora at the end of Malachi. For a brief and helpful explanation of this and other evidence, see Michael Shepherd, *A Commentary on the Book of the Twelve: The Minor Prophets*, Kregel Exegetical Library (Grand Rapids: Kregel Academic, 2018), 22–23.

[43] See Paul House, *The Unity of the Twelve*, JSOTSup 97 (Sheffield: Almond, 1990); Shepherd, *The Book of the Twelve*, 23–36.

[44] See James VanderKam and Peter Flint, *The Meaning of the Dead Sea Scrolls: Their Significance for Understanding the Bible, Judaism, Jesus, and Christianity* (San Francisco: Harper, 2002), 138–39; Shepherd, *A Commentary on the Book of the Twelve*, 21–26; Abernethy and Goswell, *God's Messiah in the Old Testament*, 125.

[45] See, however, Quarles for the argument that Hosea implicitly identifies the Messiah as the new Moses who will lead the new exodus. Quarles, "'Out of Egypt I Called My Son': Intertextuality and Metalepsis in Matthew 2:15," *Southeastern Theological Review* 8, no. 1 (2017): 3–20.

[46] The Targum of Jonathan paraphrases the two titles as "my servant the Messiah."

50:4–9; 52:13–53:12). The title may well have been drawn from descriptions of Moses in the Pentateuch (e.g., Num 12:7; cf. Josh 1:2), which suggests that Isaiah's Servant is the prophet like Moses promised in Deut 18:15–19. "The Branch" (*ṣemaḥ*) is the specific title used by Isaiah and Jeremiah to refer to the Messiah (Isa 4:2; Jer 23:5–6; 33:15) and is a synonym of another term (*nēṣer*) also used by Isaiah in a messianic sense (Isa 11:1).[47] Once again, the Messiah assumes a priestly role. The stone set before Joshua is the capstone that will complete the rebuilding of the temple and enable the return of the sacrificial system. The many sacrifices offered in the temple anticipate a future sacrifice in which the Lord promises, "I will take away the iniquity of this land in a single day" (Zech 3:9). That removal of iniquity was vividly portrayed in the scene in Zech 3:3–7. The filthy rags worn by Joshua the priest depicted the iniquity of the nation. The removal of those rags and their replacement with clean festive robes dramatized the forgiveness of God's people. The expression "on that day" is used by the OT prophets as "shorthand" for the "day of the LORD" (cf. 2:11; Isa 2:11; Joel 2:1; Zeph 1:14), a period that brings the judgment of the wicked and the salvation of the repentant (Zech 12:8; 14:3).[48] Inviting neighbors to sit under a person's vine and fig tree recalls the description of Israel's Golden Age during the reigns of David and Solomon but also exceeds that description. First Kings 4:25 says, "Throughout Solomon's reign, Judah and Israel lived in safety from Dan to

---

[47] The "stone" of Zech 3:9 has also traditionally been seen as an image of the Messiah (cf. Ps 118:22–23; Isa 8:13–15; 28:16). This identification was made by Didymus the Blind who wrote, "This person can be no one but the savior, who has descended, with a nature endowed with a seven-fold capability of seeing." Robert C. Hill, *Didymus the Blind: Commentary on Zechariah*, FC 111 (Washington, DC: Catholic University of America Press, 2006), 80. However, the "seven eyes" on the stone are probably the "seven eyes of the LORD, which scan the whole earth" and rejoice when looking upon the stone in Zech 4:10. C. J. Thomson correctly observed, "It seems unlikely to be coincidental that the only two references to 'seven eyes' in the Old Testament occur in these two consecutive chapters." Thompson, "The 'Seven Eyes' of Zech 3:9 and the Meaning of the Dual Form," *VT* 62, no. 1 (2012): 124. This supports Calvin's view that the stone is the capstone of the new temple mentioned in Zech 4:7 and 10. However, since Zech 10:4 uses the image of the "cornerstone" to symbolize the Messiah, this important stone for temple construction may represent the Messiah himself.

[48] Andrew Hill, *Haggai, Zechariah, and Malachi*, TOTC 28 (Downers Grove: IVP, 2012), 153.

Beer-sheba, each person under his own vine and fig tree." However, "on that day," both owner and neighbor will sit under the vine and fig tree. The messianic reign will thus be characterized by the forgiveness of sin, removal of guilt, unprecedented peace, and amazing prosperity.[49]

Zechariah 6:12 mentions this messianic "Branch" again.[50] The Lord instructed Zechariah to make a silver and gold crown from temple offerings and place it on the head of the high priest. This crown was to be kept in the temple, apparently to be bestowed on the promised Branch. Although many interpreters view this "branch" as Zerubbabel, Abernethy and Goswell object:

> [T]he reference in Zech. 6 must be to the building of a future (and more glorious?) temple in the consummated kingdom of God (cf. Ezek. 40–42; Hag. 2:9). A royal personage is envisaged, though he is not to be identified with Zerubbabel, for, again, a *future* figure is in mind (Zech. 6:12b–13), such that this passage cannot be indicating the imminent restoration of the monarchy in the person of Zerubbabel.[51]

They later add: "The fact that the crown is put on Joshua's head, not Zerubbabel's, again shows that the latter is not to be identified with the Sprout."[52]

The messianic Branch will "build the Lord's temple" (Zech 6:12). The statement probably looks back to the Davidic covenant which promised that God would raise up one of David's descendants who "will build a house for my name, and I will establish the throne of his kingdom forever" (2 Sam 7:13).

---

[49] First Kings 4:24 says that Solomon "had peace on all his surrounding borders." Micah 4:4 reinforced an allusion to 1 Kgs 4:25 with the expression "with no one to frighten him."

[50] The Targum of Jonathan paraphrases Zech 6:12: "Behold the man—Messiah is his name—will be revealed and he shall be magnified and shall build the temple of the Lord."

[51] Abernethy and Goswell, *God's Messiah in the Old Testament*, 167. See also Anthony Peterson, "A New Form-Critical Approach to Zechariah's Crowning of the High Priest Joshua and the Identity of 'Shoot' (Zechariah 6:9–15)," in *The Book of the Twelve and the New Form Criticism*, ed. Mark J. Boda, Michael H. Floyd, and Colin M. Toffelmire, SBL Ancient Near East Monographs 10 (Atlanta: SBL, 2015), 285–304.

[52] Abernethy and Goswell, *God's Messiah in the Old Testament*, 167.

Initially, this promise seemed to be fulfilled through Solomon. However, by Zechariah's time, the Davidic dynasty no longer ruled over Israel or Judah and the temple of Solomon had been destroyed. The temple being completed by Zerubbabel was a disappointing replacement for Solomon's impressive building (Ezra 3:12). The prophets looked forward to the construction of a new, eschatological temple of even greater grandeur than the temple of Solomon (Ezek 40–48; Hag 2:6–9).

The messianic Branch will also "bear royal splendor and will sit on his throne and rule" (Zech 6:13). The Branch is closely associated with a priest. Unfortunately, the precise relationship between the king and the priest is difficult to discern. The words "there will be a priest on his throne" seem to indicate that the priest is seated on the royal throne. Only one throne is mentioned and the Hebrew text uses the same preposition ('al) to describe both the position of the king and the priest in relationship to this throne. This may indicate that the king and the priest are one person. This would explain why Zechariah was instructed to place the royal crown on the head of the high priest before the crown was deposited for safekeeping in the temple to await the arrival of the eschatological Branch. On the other hand, the LXX clearly distinguishes the king and the priest since the king is seated on his throne but the priest is "on his right hand," and this was apparently the view of the Qumran community as well (1QS 9:11; 1QSa 2:11–22). Since earlier messianic prophecies described the Messiah as filling the dual roles of king and priest (e.g., Ps 110:2, 4) and this dual role seems to be implied in Zech 3:8, the two roles are probably fulfilled by the single messianic Branch.[53]

The Messiah is mentioned again in Zech 13:7. Some commentators understandably view this shepherd against whom the sword is raised as the worthless shepherd of 11:17 since the Lord cursed him with the words, "May a sword strike his arm and his right eye!" But one must consider the differences and not merely the similarities between the two figures. The worthless shepherd "deserts the flock" (11:17). He "will not care for those who

---

[53] See Shepherd, *A Commentary on the Book of the Twelve*, 428; Hill, *Haggai, Zechariah, and Malachi*, 177–78. George Klein argues that the Branch is Zerubbabel who serves as a type of Christ: "It would seem reasonable to claim that the imagery ultimately points to the person of Christ. A typological understanding fits both the immediate and broader canonical contexts well." Klein, *Zechariah*, NAC 21B (Nashville: B&H, 2008), 195–206.

are perishing, and he will not seek the lost or heal the broken" (11:16). In contrast, the shepherd of Zech 13:7 appears to be a faithful shepherd. His sheep scatter only after the shepherd is struck down. Furthermore, the Lord describes this shepherd as "My shepherd" which implies the shepherd's faithfulness and obedience to the Lord.[54] He even calls this shepherd "the man who is my associate," one who is closely related to the Lord. Since "shepherd" is a metaphor for a leader or king, God's shepherd is probably the messianic Branch of Zechariah's earlier prophecies.[55] This was likely the basis for Jesus's application of Zech 13:7 to describe his execution and the scattering of his disciples in Matt 26:31 and Mark 14:27.[56] The struck shepherd is also probably the "pierced" one of Zech 12:10. The reference to piercing is equivalent to Isaiah's description of the suffering Servant: "He was pierced because of our rebellion, crushed because of our iniquities" (Isa 53:5).[57] The mourning in the plain of Megiddo may be an allusion to the great mourning at the death of the good king Josiah (2 Chron 35:21–25) who was slain in the valley of Megiddo (cf. 2 Kgs 23:28–30). The men and women of Israel continued to sing of Josiah in their mourning dirges long after his death (2 Chr 35:25). If this is the intended reference in Zech 12:10, the comparison suggests that the pierced one is a king. His identification as the Lord himself ("me whom they pierced") indicates that he is the Messiah (cf. Isa 9:6). John 19:37 views the crucifixion of Jesus as the fulfillment of this messianic prophecy.[58]

These two references to the death of the Messiah (Zech 12:10; 13:7) surround a promise of salvation: "On that day a fountain will be opened for

---

[54] Although the reference to the shepherd in Zech 11:17 also ends with the *hireq yod*, this is an example of the *nomen regens* with *hireq compaginis*, not the first-person singular suffix. See *HALOT*, s.v. רעה.

[55] Although the Targum of Jonathan does not identify the shepherd as the Messiah, it paraphrases the command to strike the shepherd as "kill the king."

[56] Even the rabbis of the Babylonian Talmud recognized that Jesus of Nazareth was the fulfillment of this prophecy (b. Suk. 52a). However, they distinguished Jesus (Messiah, the son of Joseph) from Messiah, the son of David.

[57] Zechariah and Isaiah used different but synonymous terms to describe this piercing. The LXX interprets this "piercing" of the LORD as a metaphor for insult, but Klein (*Zechariah*, 366) aptly objects that mere insult does not fit well with the intense mourning for the pierced one described in the second half of the verse.

[58] See M. J. J. Menken, "The Textual Form and the Meaning of the Quotation from Zechariah 12:10 in John 19:37," *CBQ* 55 (1993): 494–511.

the house of David and for the residents of Jerusalem, to wash away sin and impurity" (Zech 13:1). This resonates with the promise of Zech 3:9, "and I will take away the iniquity of this land in a single day," a promise that is associated with the arrival of the messianic Branch. Thus, Zechariah's Messiah is not only a king, but also a Savior. His piercing will be the means by which the Lord removes the iniquity of his people. He is not only a priest, but also the sacrifice offered to secure the forgiveness of the repentant.

Malachi

Malachi 3:1–4 promises that the "LORD of Armies" will send his messenger to prepare the way for his coming. The New Testament identifies this messenger as John the Baptist and shows that this identification was affirmed by both Jesus and John himself (Matt 11:10; Mark 1:2; Luke 7:27; cf. Matt 11:3; Luke 1:17, 76; 7:19; John 3:28). The sending of this messenger precedes the arrival of "the Lord you seek." In the context of Malachi, this "Lord" appears to be the "LORD of Armies" whom the people have sought vainly through their sacrifices (Mal 1:6–14), their tears (2:13), and their complaints.

Although the title "Lord" (ʾāḏân) is distinct from the divine name LORD (yhwh) and in some contexts refers to mere human authorities, the preceding uses of the term in Malachi suggest that the title refers to God. Malachi 1:6 shows that the "LORD" is the supreme Lord who is worthy of honor from his servants, the priests. Malachi 1:12 and 1:14 use the title to identify the Lord to whom sacrifices are to be offered.

The use of the definite article with this title in Mal 3:1 confirms that this is a reference to deity. Every other occurrence of this title with the definite article in the OT refers to the God of Israel, the Lord par excellence.[59] Even if the definite article here is merely anaphoric (referring to a Lord mentioned in the preceding context), this too confirms the identification of this "LORD" as Yahweh.

This "LORD" is also the One who has ownership and authority over the Jerusalem temple to the extent that it may be fittingly described as his temple (cf. Mal 3:1, 10) just as the sacrificial table was earlier described as "the

---

[59] Hill, Haggai, Zechariah, Malachi, 333.

Lord's table" (Mal 1:12).[60] Mal 4:5 identifies the messenger whom the LORD of Armies sends as "the prophet Elijah" and this new Elijah prepares for the coming of the "great and terrible day of the LORD."[61] This strongly implies that the "Lord" of Mal 3:1 is none other than the "LORD" of Mal 4:5.

Nevertheless, the LORD refers to this "Lord" in the third person much as in Ps 110:1, a messianic text. He also identifies this Lord as "the Messenger of the covenant you delight in."[62] The parallels between Malachi's words and Exod 23:20a (cf. Exod 32:34; 33:2) suggest that the prophet was intentionally alluding to that Exodus text. The messenger/angel (*mal'ak*) of Exod 23:20 was the deliverer who would guide and protect Israel throughout the exodus and lead them to the Promised Land. He was also the bearer of the Divine Name (Exod 23:21: "my name is in him"). The promise of this messenger/angel immediately preceded the ceremony that enacted the old covenant (Exod 24). These parallels suggest that the "Messenger of the covenant" (Mal 3:1) will be a figure who bears God's name, leads God's people on a new exodus, and will initiate a new covenant. The role of the messenger of the covenant is comparable in many ways to the role of Moses. Thus, Malachi's prophecy recalls the prophet-like-Moses prophecy of Deut 18:15–19. Christian interpretation has traditionally recognized that the prophecy is messianic.[63]

---

[60] For the view that this temple is the eschatological temple, see Shepherd, *A Commentary on the Book of the Twelve*, 497.

[61] Ray Clendenen noted that "almost all scholars identify him as a prophet (cf. 2 Chr 36:15–16) and see this passage as parallel to 4:5." Clendenen, "Malachi 3:1; 4:1–5: The Messiah as the Messenger of the Lord," *Moody Handbook of Messianic Prophecy*, 1330.

[62] Although some scholars see the "Lord" and the "Messenger of the covenant" as two distinct figures, the structure and parallel ("you seek"/"you delight in") imply that the Lord is the Messenger. See Clendenen, "Malachi 3:1; 4:1–5," 1331. Elsewhere Clendenen observes that "this is one of those enigmatic Old Testament passages in which God and his unique angel/messenger ("the angel of the LORD") are spoken of as if they are one and the same (Gen 16:7–14; 18:1–19:1; 22:12; Exod 3:1–6)." Clendenen, *Haggai, Malachi*, NAC 21A (Nashville: B&H, 2004), 385. The occurrence of this phenomenon in an eschatological text related to the coming Messiah legitimizes the view that the angel of the LORD is a Christophany.

[63] Although the medieval rabbinic commentator David Kimchi frequently challenged Christian interpretations of the Old Testament, he identified the "Lord" of Mal 3:1 as "King Messiah." See *Mikraoth Gedoloth: The Twelve Prophets*, trans. A. J.

The Messiah will purify his people like fire refines precious metal (cf. Ezek 22:18–22) and bleach whitens fabric (Mal 3:2). This purification will begin with the spiritual leaders of God's people, the sons of Levi. They will once again revere and stand in awe of the Lord, offer true instruction, turn many from iniquity, and lead God's people to present sacrifices that are acceptable to him (Mal 2:5–7; 3:3–4). Those who refuse to repent will experience the Messiah's judgment. Andrew Hill's exegesis of this text led him to conclude:

> The ambiguities surrounding the precise number and identity of these eschatological figures who have roles in this theophany continue to invite scholarly discussion. Beyond specific identifications, it is important to recognize that the divine messengers carry out a thorough purification of God's people. The eschaton will witness the transformation of God's people into a holy community, by a spirit of burning, washing and cleansing (3:2–3; cf. Isa. 4:3–4; Zeph. 3:11–13, 17). The desired outcome of this difficult and painful process of 'refining' is genuine worship offered to YHWH by his faithful people—now spiritually renewed.[64]

Figure 5: References to the Work of Christ in the Minor Prophets

Scripture	Content
Zech 3:8	The Messiah will serve as a priest and through his ministry the LORD will take away the iniquity of his people. His reign will be characterized by unprecedented peace and amazing prosperity.
Zech 6:12–13	The Messiah will fulfill the Davidic covenant by building the new, eschatological temple and serve as the eschatological priest.
Zech 12:10	The Messiah will be pierced.

Rosenberg (New York: Judaica, 1996), 2:413. Block states bluntly, "In any case, in the Malachi passages, the messenger/prophet announces the coming of the messiah." Block, "My Servant David," 32.

[64] Hill, *Haggai, Zechariah and Malachi*, 337.

| Zech 13:7 | The Messiah will be struck down and his death will remove the iniquity of the people (cf. 13:1). |
| Mal 3:1–4 | The Messiah will be the messenger of the new covenant, will lead God's people on a new exodus, will purify the repentant, and judge the unrepentant. |

Summary

Several of the Minor Prophets prophesy about the coming Messiah. Messianic prophecies appear in the books of Hosea, Joel, Amos, Zechariah, and Malachi. These prophecies reveal several aspects of the work of the Messiah. The Messiah will restore the kingdom of David and reign over a reunified nation of Israel. The Messiah will extend his rule to all the nations and reign as king over the entire earth. His reign will be characterized by peace and prosperity that exceeds any ever known before. This peace and prosperity will result from the messianic king's ultimate defeat of the enemies of God's people.

Another prominent theme is the Messiah's priestly work. The Messiah will serve as the eschatological priest who takes away the iniquity of the people and purifies the repentant. Shockingly, this priest will secure atonement by offering himself as a sacrifice. The Messiah will be pierced and struck down but his own death will remove the iniquity of God's people.

The Messiah will also be a prophet and teacher who will instruct his people in the way of true righteousness. As a prophet whose ministry resembles that of Moses, the Messiah will lead God's people on a new exodus that results in liberation from their exile and deliverance from the consequences of their sin.

5

The Work of Christ in the New Testament, the Synoptic Gospels, and Acts

The messianic prophecies of the OT form a crucial foundation for the discussions of the salvific work of Christ in the NT. In the mid-twentieth century, C. H. Dodd analyzed many of the OT messianic texts treated in our previous chapters. He rightly observed that this "whole body of material . . . is common to all the main portions of the New Testament" and is "the substructure of all Christian theology and contains already its chief regulative ideas."[1] The NT writers further develop the concepts that appear in incipient form in the OT and more fully describe the benefits of the Messiah's atoning death, often looking beyond explicit messianic prophecies to various OT types.

Mark

The first clear reference to Jesus's salvific work appears in John the Baptist's prophecy about the coming Messiah in Mark 1:8. John demonstrates that the Coming One is more powerful than John himself by contrasting the baptism with the Spirit that the Messiah will perform with the baptism with

---

[1] C. H. Dodd, *According to the Scriptures: The Sub-Structure of New Testament Theology* (New York: Scribner, 1953), 127.

water that John practices. This baptism of the Spirit appears to allude to the outpouring of the Spirit described in Ezek 36:26–27 (cf. Ezek 11:18–21):[2]

> "I will give you a new heart and put a new spirit within you; I will remove your heart of stone and give you a heart of flesh. I will place my Spirit within you and cause you to follow my statutes and carefully observe my ordinances."

The sinner's change of heart and the indwelling of the Holy Spirit transform the sinner's character to produce obedience to God's commands. The prophecy repeatedly promised spiritual cleansing: "I will save you from all your uncleanness" (Ezek 36:29; cf. 36:33; 37:23). The descent of the Spirit on Jesus at his baptism verifies that Jesus is the Coming One who bears the power to baptize others with the Spirit. The baptism of the Spirit is the result of Jesus's enactment of the new covenant by his death that will soon be discussed.

Jesus not only transforms sinners, but he also grants them forgiveness. Although Jesus's words to the paralytic, "Son, your sins are forgiven" (Mark 2:5), might initially sound merely as a pronouncement that the man was forgiven by God, Jesus later clarified that he personally, as the Son of Man, had authority to forgive sins (Mark 2:10). Jesus replied to the scribes' protest that only God can forgive sins by proving his own authority to forgive through the healing of the paralytic.

Still later, Jesus portrayed himself as the great spiritual doctor who came to summon those who were spiritually sick to be made well (Mark 2:17). The analogy may imply that at least several of Jesus's miracles of physical healing functioned as pictures of spiritual salvation. This is clearly true of the healing of the paralytic since Jesus himself associates the healing with forgiveness of sin. However, this appears to be true of other healing miracles as well. In Mark 7:31–37, Jesus healed a deaf man. In Mark 8:22–26, Jesus healed a blind man. In the intervening pericope, Jesus challenges his disciples with the question, "Do you have eyes and not see; do you have ears and not hear?" (Mark 8:18). The question portrays the men as spiritually blind and spiritually deaf. The two healing miracles that immediately precede and follow the pericope imply that just as Jesus gives physical hearing and sight to

---

[2] Robert Guelich, *Mark 1–8:26*, WBC 34A (Dallas: Word, 1989), 25.

the physically deaf and blind, he also grants spiritual hearing and sight to the spiritually deaf and blind.[3]

Mark 8:31 is the first of a series of Jesus's predictions of his death (cf. Mark 9:31; 10:33–34; 14:8–9). Mark's summary of the prediction uses an expression that is highly significant theologically: "it was necessary for the Son of Man to suffer . . . and be rejected . . . and be killed." The verb translated "it was necessary" (δεῖ) implies that Jesus's impending death was ordained by God.[4] Jesus's words during his final Passover celebration demonstrate that his death was described in Israel's Scriptures: "For the Son of Man will go just as it is written about him" (Mark 14:21). In Mark, Jesus does not explicitly identify the OT prophecies about his death. Jesus's predictions likely drew details from the descriptions of the suffering of the Isaianic servant (Isa 50:4–6; 52:13–53:12; cf. Ps 22).[5] The use of the title "Son of Man" in the predictions of Jesus's death (Mark 8:31; 9:31; 10:33) may imply that the predictions appealed also to Daniel and equated the Son of Man figure from Dan 7:13 with the Anointed One (Messiah) in 9:25. If so, the references to the suffering and death of the Son of Man recall the promise of the completion of God's purpose "to put a stop to sin, to atone for iniquity, to bring in everlasting righteousness" (Dan 9:24).

One of the most important statements about Jesus's saving work in Mark appears in 10:45: "the Son of Man did not come to be served, but to serve, and to give his life as a ransom for many." The statement is almost certainly an allusion to Isa 53:12. The wording of the last clause ("giving his life . . . for many") matches the sense of Isa 53:12 (LXX): "for whom [many] his life was handed over."[6] The allusion is sufficiently obvious to

---

[3] See esp. James Edwards, *Mark*, PNTC (Grand Rapids: Eerdmans, 2002), 243. The spiritual significance of the miracles may be the reason that Jesus healed the blind man gradually and in stages. Spiritual illumination occurs over time though it is a miraculous act.

[4] Robert Stein, *Mark*, BECNT (Grand Rapids: Baker, 2008), 401.

[5] For a more detailed discussion of the OT background of Jesus's prediction, see William Lane, *Mark*, NICNT (Grand Rapids: Eerdmans, 1974), 296–303. Lane, like many others, unfortunately overlooked the possible connection to the slaying of the anointed one in Daniel 9.

[6] W. J. Moulder, "The Old Testament Background and the Interpretation of Mark x.45," *NTS* 24 (1977): 120–27; R. T. France, "The Servant of the Lord in the Teaching of Jesus," *TynBul* 19 (1968): 26–52.

prompt the reader to recall Isaiah's entire description of the Servant's vicarious death. That Jesus intends his brief allusion to trigger recollection of the entire fourth Servant Song is supported by his addition of a single word (λυτρόν) translated by the English phrase "as a ransom." A ransom was the payment required to obtain the release of a prisoner in order to rescue him from impending execution (Exod 21:30). In Exod 30:11–16 the term is a synonym for "the atonement price" or "the contribution to the LORD to atone for your lives." Although the noun does not appear in Isaiah's prophecy of the Suffering Servant, this noun aptly summarizes the role of the Servant who "was pierced because of our rebellion, crushed because of our iniquities," punished "for the iniquity of us all," and "bore the sin of many" (Isa 53:5, 6, 12). It is an insightful and vivid description of the Lord's "righteous servant" who will carry sinner's iniquities so that he may "justify many" (53:11) by serving as their "guilt offering" (v. 10).

Jesus's statement clearly describes his death as vicarious. Not only does the Son of Man give his life as a ransom to free others, he gives his life as a substitute for others. Although the CSB text translates the Greek phrase ἀντὶ πολλῶν as "for many," the alternative translation provided in the margin is probably superior: "in the place of many." The Greek preposition with a genitive object ordinarily expresses substitution.[7] Admittedly, the preposition sometimes assumes the sense of the preposition ὑπέρ and merely means "on behalf of" or "for the sake of." Yet in this instance, the preposition most likely has the same sense as in Isa 53:12 (LXX) and thus expresses that Jesus will give his life as a ransom in the place of many sinners.

Jesus describes his death as a fulfillment of Zech 13:7 (Mark 14:27). The striking of the shepherd seems to be the means by which God will fulfill his promise in Zech 13:1: "On that day a fountain will be opened for the house of David and for the residents of Jerusalem, to wash away sin and impurity." The broader context of the messianic prophecy cited by Jesus shows that his death will cleanse God's people of their sins.

Jesus's words instituting the Last Supper are especially important for understanding his salvific work. Unlike the parallel accounts, Mark's version of the words of institution does not explicitly mention the sacrificial

---

[7] See Murray Harris, *Prepositions and Theology in the Greek New Testament* (Grand Rapids: Zondervan, 2012), 52.

nature of the offering of Jesus's body. Jesus simply distributes the broken bread with the words, "Take it; this is my body" (Mark 14:22). Jesus's body, represented by the bread, seems to be functioning as a substitute for the roasted flesh of the Passover lamb that was normally distributed and consumed during the Passover meal.[8] As the slaughter of a Passover lamb protected a household from the certain death of the firstborn by prompting the Destroyer to "pass over" that household, Jesus's death will cause the wrath of God to "pass over" his disciples. The words implicitly portray Jesus's death as an atoning sacrifice.

The words, "This is my blood of the covenant, which is poured out for many" (Mark 14:24), present Jesus's death as a covenant-initiating sacrifice. When the old covenant was enacted, Moses sacrificed bulls as fellowship offerings. He splattered half of the blood at the base of the altar, then read the covenant scroll aloud to the people. They committed, "We will do and obey all that the LORD has commanded" (Exod 24:7). Then Moses splattered the other half of the blood on the people and said, "This is the blood of the covenant that the LORD has made with you concerning all these words" (Exod 24:8).

Jesus's words borrow Moses's expression from the covenant ceremony to demonstrate that his death is the sacrifice that enacts the new covenant. This new covenant was promised in numerous Old Testament texts, including Jer 31:31–34; 32:36–41; 50:2–5; Ezekiel 11:18–21; 16:59–63; 18:30–32; 34:20–31 (esp. v. 25); 36:24–32 (esp. v. 26) [cf. Isa. 59:21]; 37:15–28 (esp. v. 26); Isa 54:1–10 (esp. vv. 9–10); 55:1–5; 61:8–9; Dan 9:25–27; and Deut 30:1–10.[9] No text in this group is more important than Jer 31:31–34, a text which explicitly refers to "a new covenant."

The new covenant described by Jeremiah had three prominent features. First, the covenant entailed the transformation of sinners' moral character.

---

[8] Chronological details in the Passion account suggest that Jesus celebrated this Passover meal a day before the normal celebration since he knew that his crucifixion would prevent him from celebrating Passover at the usual time. For a defense of this position, see R. T. France, *The Gospel of Matthew*, NICNT (Grand Rapids: Eerdmans, 2007), 980–85.

[9] Peter Gentry has helpfully identified major texts related to a new covenant in Peter Gentry and Stephen Wellum, *Kingdom through Covenant*, rev. ed. (Wheaton: Crossway, 2018), 448, 541–71, 650.

God promised, "I will put my teaching within them and write it on their hearts" (Jer 31:33). God's instruction would no longer be merely external, inscribed on tablets of stone. It would be internalized, inscribed on the tablets of a person's heart. This internalized standard would impart to God's people an internal compulsion to behave and speak in a manner pleasing to God.

Second, the covenant promised full reconciliation to God. Jeremiah 31:33 used a common covenant formula: "I will be their God, and they will be my people." Sinful Israel had been alienated and rejected by God for breaking covenant with him. God had declared, "I will show them my back and not my face on the day of their calamity" (Jer 18:17) because "they have turned their back to me and not their face" (Jer 2:27) by their acts of idolatry. But now God would turn his face to his people and enable them to know him fully: "they will all know me, from the least to the greatest of them" (31:34).

Third, the covenant promised complete and perpetual forgiveness of sins: "I will forgive their iniquity and never again remember their sin" (31:34). Israel could not purge herself of her iniquities by any means: "Even if you wash with lye and use a great amount of bleach, the stain of your iniquity is still in front of me" (2:22). Their sin had been recorded indelibly with an iron stylus with a diamond point (17:1). Yet God would graciously forgive and forget their sin. Sinners' transformation, reconciliation, and forgiveness were accomplished through the new covenant that Jesus enacted by his death.

A final text in Mark that illuminates Jesus's salvific work is Mark 14:36 in which Jesus asked the Father to remove "this cup." This cup is clearly a reference to Jesus's impending suffering and death. The description of this suffering as a "cup" probably alludes to the cup of divine wrath (Ps 75:8; Jer 25:15–29; Ezek 23:31–34; Isa 51:17–23; Lam 4:21).[10] Jesus clearly does not personally deserve to drink this cup of divine wrath. The Father had verbally identified Jesus as a "beloved Son" at both his baptism (Mark 1:11) and his transfiguration (Mark 9:7) and even stated that he was "well-pleased" with him (Mark 1:11). Furthermore, Jesus's Gethsemane prayer clearly shows that this cup was not forced to Jesus's lips, but that Jesus voluntarily embraced the cup in an act of submission to the Father's will. Thus, the Gospel of

---

[10] Stein, *Mark*, 662–63.

Mark has supplied all the details necessary for the reader to recognize that the suffering of Jesus is vicarious. He drinks the cup of divine wrath that was deserved by others. This Gethsemane experience prepares the reader to understand the irony of the bystanders' taunt, "He saved others, but he cannot save himself!" (Mark 15:31). Those who witnessed the Gethsemane scene know that he could have saved himself but chose to suffer in accordance with the Father's will, and that it is by refusing to save himself that he truly saves others.

Figure 6: References to the Work of Christ in Mark

Scripture Passage	Content
Mark 1:8	Jesus will perform the baptism of the Spirit (cf. Ezek 36:26–27).
Mark 2:5, 10	Jesus forgives sins.
Mark 2:17	Jesus is the great spiritual doctor who came to heal those who are spiritually sick.
Mark 8:31	Jesus's suffering and death are necessary to the divine plan.
Mark 10:45	Jesus will give his life as a ransom for many.
Mark 14:27	Jesus's death fulfills Zech 13:7 and thus will accomplish the spiritual cleansing described in Zech 13:1.
Mark 14:22, 24	Jesus's death is an atoning sacrifice and the sacrifice that enacts the new covenant.
Mark 14:36	Jesus, by his suffering and death, drinks the cup of divine wrath.

Summary

Mark describes Jesus's death as an atoning sacrifice that will spare Jesus's disciples from divine destruction much like the Passover sacrifice spared Israel's firstborn. Jesus's death is also a "ransom for many" that redeems sinners from bondage and judgment. Jesus's sacrificial death is related to his authority to forgive sins and heal those who are spiritually sick. Jesus's death is also a covenant-enacting sacrifice that inaugurates the new covenant promised by the OT prophets and results in the baptism of the Spirit which will compel Jesus's disciples to live righteous lives that are pleasing to God.

Matthew

Although Jesus's salvific work is more prominent in Mark than many scholars have assumed, Matthew places greater emphasis on Jesus's salvific work than Mark.[11] The angel clearly announced Jesus's mission in Matt 1:21: "You are to name him Jesus, because he will save his people from their sins." The name "Jesus" is the Greek version of the Hebrew name Joshua which means "Yahweh saves." The name is appropriate because Jesus is the incarnation of Yahweh (as the name Immanuel will indicate) and will be the Savior of sinners. The promise that he will save his people from their sins is likely an allusion to Ezek 36:28–29; 37:23.[12] The verses are part of the prophecy about the new covenant which is promised in Ezekiel 36 and illustrated in Ezekiel 37. In this context within the book of Ezekiel, the verb "save" refers to release from exile (Ezek 36:24), cleansing (36:25, 29, 33; 37:23), transformation (36:26–27), restoration (37:22), and reconciliation to God (37:23). It assumes the full connotations of its original sense in its new context as well. "His people" in Matt 1:21 alludes to "My [Yahweh's] people" in Ezek 36:28 and 37:23 and thus implies Jesus's identification as Yahweh. Although readers might first assume that "his people" refers to Israel, the people from whom Jesus descended (Matt 1:2–17), the remainder of the Gospel shows that "his people" refers to Jesus's disciples (cf. Matt 12:50). This implies that Jesus's disciples constitute a restored or new Israel whom Jesus will liberate from bondage, cleanse of their defilement, transform, restore, and reconcile to God.

---

[11] To save space, I will not discuss texts in Matthew and Luke paralleled by Mark and thus already discussed in the previous session. However, these parallel texts are very important for understanding the presentation of Jesus as Savior in these Gospels as well.

[12] Nicholas G. Piotrowski, "'I Will Save My People from Their Sins': The Influence of Ezekiel 36:28b–29a; 37:23b on Matthew 1:21," *TynBul* 64 (2013): 33–54.

Matthew also emphasizes Jesus's salvific work in his presentation of Jesus as the new Moses. Matthew repeatedly highlights the amazing similarities between Jesus and the great Old Testament figure. He demonstrates that Jesus is like Moses in his infancy, his prophetic teaching ministry, his fasting, his miracles, and his transfiguration.[13] These similarities demonstrate that Jesus is the promised "prophet like Moses" (Deut 18:15–19). Matthew 2 contains a heavy concentration of parallels to Moses. Herod the Great slew the male infants of Bethlehem but God providentially spared Jesus much like how Pharoah slew the male Hebrew infants but God providentially rescued Moses (cf. Matt 2:1–23; Exod 1:8–2:10). Furthermore, when the angel announced to Joseph that it was now safe to return the holy family to Israel, the angel employs the very words used by Yahweh to announce to Moses that it was safe for him to return home (cf. Matt 2:20; Exod 4:19).

Matthew signals the theological significance of these parallels in Matt 2:15 by quoting Hos 11:1: "Out of Egypt I called my son." In its original context, Hosea was referring to the exodus of Israel from Egypt. Other texts in Hosea anticipate a new exodus, a deliverance of Israel from another "Egypt," Assyria. Assyria is repeatedly associated with Egypt in Hosea's prophecies (Hos 7:11; 9:3; 11:11; cf. 7:16; 8:13; 9:6). Hosea 11:5, however, distinguishes Assyria from Egypt to indicate that Hosea is not predicting a literal return to Egypt. Instead, "Egypt" serves as a symbol, a type, of Israel's new oppressors. Assyria, like Egypt, is a land where Israel is held in bondage and oppressed. Yet Hos 2:14–15 promised that the Lord would lead Israel into the wilderness (as he did in the exodus) and that she would respond to him "as she did in the days of her youth, as in the day she came out of the land of Egypt." Hosea 3:5 shows that this time of Israel's deliverance and return will occur "in the last days" when the people "seek the LORD their God and David their king." The purpose of Matthew's citation of Hos 11:1 is to show that Jesus is "David their king," the "prophet like Moses" who will lead this new deliverance.[14]

---

[13] See Quarles, *A Theology of Matthew*, 33–45 (see chap. 4, n. 3); Dale Allison Jr., *The New Moses: A Matthean Typology* (Minneapolis: Fortress, 1993).

[14] See G. K. Beale, "The Use of Hosea 11:1 in Matthew 2:15: One More Time," *JETS* 55 (2012): 697–715; Charles L. Quarles, "'Out of Egypt I Called My Son': Intertextuality and Metalepsis in Matthew 2:15," *STR* 8, no. 1 (Spring 2017): 3–19. Note that Hosea looks back to the exodus again in Hos 12:9 and 13:4 and adds, "The

Matthew's citation of Jer 31:15 in 2:18 seems to be part of a similar strategy. In their original context, Jeremiah's words referred to the deportation of Israelites to Babylon. However, the sad description of Israel's exile was immediately followed by the promise of deliverance: "your children will return from the enemy's land" (Jer 31:16) and "there is hope for your future" (Jer 31:17). These gracious promises are accompanied by the even greater promise of the new covenant (Jer 31:31–34), which will result in the transformation and forgiveness of God's people. Thus, the citation of this pivotal text prompts the informed reader to recall the angel's promise that Jesus will "save his people from their sins" (Matt 1:21).

Matthew 8:17 describes Jesus's healing miracles as a fulfillment of Isa 53:4. The citation demonstrates that Matthew recognized Jesus as the servant of Isaiah's Servant Songs. This has enormous implications for Matthew's understanding of Jesus's salvific work. Isaiah described the servant as a priest who would sprinkle nations for their spiritual cleansing, intercede for those who rebelled against God, and offer an atoning sacrifice. Shockingly, the priest would offer himself as this sacrifice. He would suffer vicariously the curses of the covenant and bear the guilt and punishment for the sins of others. He would offer himself as a guilt offering. The Servant would be crushed, struck, wounded, and pierced in an act of penal substitutionary atonement. Through his sacrifice, he will "justify many." Jesus's fulfillment of this crucial OT messianic prophecy is later confirmed by Jesus's own allusion to Isa 53:12 in Matt 20:28 (par. Mark 10:45).[15]

Matthew's identification of Jesus as the Isaianic Servant dovetails with his presentation of Jesus as the new Moses. Isaiah himself provides clues that the

---

LORD brought Israel from Egypt by a prophet, and Israel was tended by a prophet" (Hos 12:13).

[15] R. T. France stated that "the Servant model will become central to Jesus's explanation of his death in 20:28; 26:28 as well as probably underlying the whole concept of messianic suffering which will be developed from 16:21 on." France, *Matthew*, NICNT (Grand Rapids: Eerdmans, 2007), 322. Note that only Matt 27:57 (cf. Mark 15:43; Luke 23:50) describes Joseph of Arimathea, in whose tomb Jesus was buried, as a "rich man." Matthew probably highlights this detail because he recognizes it as another fulfillment of the fourth Servant Song. Isaiah 53:9 foretold that the Servant would be "assigned a grave with the wicked, but he was with a rich man at his death, because he had done no violence and had not spoken deceitfully."

servant is the prophet like Moses of Deut 18:15–19.[16] The very title "servant" is reminiscent of descriptions of Moses. Moses was described as Yahweh's "servant" frequently in the five books of Moses (e.g., Exod 4:10; 14:31; Num 11:11; 12:7–8; Deut 3:24; 34:5) as well as in later Old Testament books (Josh 1:1, 2, 7, 13, 15; 8:31, 33; 9:24; 11:12, 15; 12:6; 13:8; 14:7; 18:7; 22:2, 4, 5; 1 Kgs 8:53, 56; 2 Kgs 18:12; 21:8; 1 Chr 6:49; 2 Chr 1:3; 24:6, 9; Neh 1:7, 8; 9:14; 10:29; Ps 105:26; Dan 9:11; Mal 4:4) and the New Testament (Heb 3:5; Rev 15:3). The character, intercessory activity, healing ministry, sprinkling, and endowment with the Spirit are among the many similarities between Moses and the Servant.[17] Ancient interpreters recognized these similarities and associated Moses with Isaiah's Servant of the Lord.[18] Peter's sermon in Acts 3 presents Jesus as both the fulfillment of the prophet-like-Moses prophecy and the fulfillment of Isaiah's Servant of the Lord prophecies (Acts 3:17–26). He saw both sets of prophecies as messianic and likely saw Isaiah's prophecy as a further description of the prophet-like-Moses figure. In the same vein, Matthew probably recognized a close relationship between the prophet like Moses and the Servant of Isaiah's Servant Songs.

Matthew applies yet another of Isaiah's Servant Songs (Isa 42:1–4) to Jesus in Matt 12:16–21. This is the longest quotation of the OT in Matthew's entire Gospel. The climax of the quotation (and Matthew skipped the first clause in Isa 42:4 to leap to this climax) focuses on the hope of the nations or Gentiles in the name of the Servant. This Servant Song confirms that the many for whom the servant dies in Isaiah 53 include Gentiles as well as Jews. Jesus extends hope even to those previously excluded from God's chosen people. This constitutes a major theme of Matthew's Gospel that builds to the Great Commission order to "make disciples of all nations" (Matt 28:19–20).

We saw in our discussion of Mark's description of the work of Christ that Jesus described his death as the sacrifice that would enact the new covenant. In Matthew's Gospel, a specific effect of the new covenant is emphasized. The cup symbolizes "my blood of the covenant, which is poured out for many" (Matt 26:28), essentially in parallel with Mark. However, Matthew's

---

[16] Gerhard von Rad, *The Message of the Prophets*, trans. D. G. M. Stalker (New York: Harper & Row, 1965), 227–28.

[17] Quarles, *A Theology of Matthew*, 60–66 (see chap. 4, n. 3).

[18] B. Sotah 14a.

version stresses that the sacrifice is made "for the forgiveness of sins." The emphasis points to the promise of forgiveness in the new covenant that appears in Jer 31:34; Ezek 36:25, 33; 37:23.

Matthew 26:53–54 highlights the voluntary nature of Jesus's sacrificial death. During Jesus's arrest in Gethsemane, one of Jesus's disciples attempted to enable Jesus's escape by drawing a sword and striking the high priest's servant. Jesus rebuked the disciple and explained that his action was completely unnecessary. If Jesus had wished to escape, he could simply call on his Father, and he would provide him with "more than twelve legions of angels." Jesus did not need twelve human protectors when he easily could have summoned more than twelve legions of angelic warriors (approximately 72,000 angels). Jesus's point was that he chose to die in obedience to the Father's will (Matt 26:39). Since the Father would not have been willing to intervene in this manner if Jesus deserved suffering and death, Jesus's statement also implies his innocence and righteousness. The Father's willingness to rescue Jesus if he requested confirms that his death was undeserved and implies that Jesus died for the sake of others, just as the quotations and allusions to the fourth Servant Song insist.

Matthew then demonstrates that Jesus did indeed enact the new covenant by his death (as promised at the Last Supper) in a breathtaking description of the events that immediately followed Jesus's death (Matt 27:50–54). Matthew's account of the phenomena that occurred at the conclusion of the crucifixion reverberates with allusions to the Valley of Dry Bones vision in Ezekiel 37.[19] The earthquake, the opening of the tombs, and the resurrection of the dead are strongly reminiscent of the events of Ezekiel 37 as they are described in the LXX. The final clause of Matt 27:50 (CSB: "gave up his spirit") is more accurately translated: "he released the Spirit."[20] With his dying breath, Jesus releases the Spirit who resurrects the dead saints in Jerusalem in a manner that recalls the activity of the Spirit/breath of God resurrecting the dead in Ezek 37:5, 6, 9–14, an event that illustrates the fulfillment of the new covenant promise: "I will put my Spirit in you, and you

---

[19] Charles L. Quarles, "Matthew 27:52–53: Meaning, Genre, Intertextuality, Theology, and Reception History," *JETS* 59 (2016): 278–82.

[20] For evidence that the scribe who copied Codex Vaticanus (or its exemplar) interpreted Matt 27:50 in this manner, see Charles L. Quarles, *Matthew*, EBTC (Bellingham, WA: Lexham, 2022), 734n1076.

will live" (Ezek 37:14; cf. Ezek 36:27). The phenomena that accompany the crucifixion combine to make a profound theological point about the significance of Jesus's death. Jesus's death enacts the new covenant through which sins are forgiven and the Spirit is imparted to give new life with a new moral character to God's people.

Figure 7: References to the Work of Christ in Matthew

Scripture Passage	Content
Matt 1:21	Jesus will save his people from their sins.
Matt 2:15, 18	Jesus is the new and greater Moses who will lead a new and greater exodus.
Matt 8:17	Jesus is Isaiah's Suffering Servant whose suffering and death will atone for the sins of many.
Matt 12:16–21	Jesus is Isaiah's Suffering Servant who will bring hope to the nations.
Matt 26:28	Jesus's death is a sacrifice that provides forgiveness for many sinners.
Matt 26:53–54	Jesus's sacrificial death is voluntary, and he could have escaped this death if he chose to do so.
Matt 27:50–54	Jesus's death enacts the new covenant and imparts the Spirit to deceased saints, initiating the resurrection of the dead.

Summary

Matthew's Gospel, like Mark's, shows that Jesus's death is an atoning sacrifice and a covenant-enacting sacrifice. Matthew more explicitly identifies Jesus as Isaiah's Suffering Servant and thereby emphasizes that Jesus's death is a voluntary and vicarious death that will atone for sins, provide forgiveness, and bring hope to the nations. Matthew also emphasizes Jesus's identity as the new and greater Moses who will enact the new covenant and lead a new exodus that rescues Jesus's disciples from their slavery to sin.

Luke-Acts

In addition to the descriptions of Jesus's saving work which Luke shares in common with Mark, Luke contains important unique material that is also significant for understanding the Messiah's mission to save sinners. In Luke 2:10–12, the angel proclaims the gospel message.[21] The angel summarizes the essential truths of the gospel under three names or titles of Jesus which express his identity as Savior, messianic king, and God.[22] The title emphasized in the sentence structure is "Savior." In the preceding context, related words refer to salvation in a broad sense. The Song of Mary (Luke 1:46–55) described the Lord as "God my Savior" and describes him scattering the proud and toppling the mighty. Similarly, the prophecy of Zechariah (Luke 1:68–79) refers to "salvation from our enemies and from the hand of those who hate us" (1:71). However, Zechariah also foretold that John the Baptist would "go before the Lord to prepare his ways, to give his people knowledge of salvation through the forgiveness of their sins" (v. 77), which shows that "salvation" includes forgiveness.[23] Later references in Luke's Gospel will confirm that Jesus is the Savior who provides forgiveness of sin by his death. Simeon stressed that Jesus is Savior by taking the infant Christ in his arms and exclaiming, "Now, Master, you can dismiss your servant in peace, as you promised. For my eyes have seen your salvation" (2:29–30). Anna similarly proclaimed that Jesus would accomplish "the redemption of Jerusalem" (2:38).

Although all four Gospels quote some portion of Isa 40:3–4 in connection with John the Baptist's preparation for the ministry of Jesus, only Luke (3:3–6) extends the quotation to Isa 40:5 (LXX) to include the promise: "and

---

[21] Note that the verb translated, "I proclaim to you good news" is εὐαγγελίζομαι.

[22] Each of the eighteen preceding occurrences of κύριος in Luke referring to someone other than Jesus use the term as a substitute for the Hebrew divine name (1:6, 9, 11, 15, 16, 17, 25, 28, 32, 38, 45, 46, 58, 66, 68, 76; 2:9 [2x]). In Luke 1:43, Elizabeth refers to Mary as "the mother of my Lord." Her statement to Mary contains two uses of κύριος, and the other (1:45) is clearly a reference to the God of Israel. Thus, the preceding context has thoroughly prepared the reader to understand the description of Jesus as "Lord" as a reference to his deity.

[23] Robert Stein recognizes that the use of this expression "reveals that Luke understood the Benedictus to refer to a spiritual rather than a political salvation." Stein, *Luke*, NAC (Nashville: B&H, 1992), 101.

everyone will see the salvation of God."[24] In this context, "salvation" probably refers specifically to the forgiveness of sins. The LXX says that all flesh will see the salvation of God "because the Lord has spoken." This appears to refer to God's statement in Isa 40:1–2 offering comfort to Jerusalem "because her sin has been forgiven." Perhaps this was the OT text that influenced the reference to the "redemption of Jerusalem" in Luke 2:38. Furthermore, Luke 3:3 demonstrated that John's ministry involved "proclaiming a baptism of repentance for the forgiveness of sins." The flow of the narrative implies that the "salvation of God" which Jesus will provide involves this forgiveness of sins.

Perhaps the most important text in Luke that confirms that the salvation Jesus brings involves forgiveness of sins is Luke 7:36–50. Although all three of the Synoptic Gospels record Jesus's pronouncement of forgiveness to the paralytic (Matt 9:2; Mark 2:5; Luke 5:20), only Luke records this pronouncement of forgiveness. Jesus explained to Simon the Pharisee that the sinful woman who washed Jesus's feet with her tears, wiped his feet with her hair, and anointed them with expensive perfume did so as an expression of her deep gratitude for the forgiveness he had granted her. Jesus pronounced, "Your sins are forgiven" (Luke 7:48), and equated this forgiveness with salvation: "Your faith has saved you" (Luke 7:50).

In Luke 22:35–38, a pericope that is unique to Luke's Gospel, Jesus explained how he would provide forgiveness to sinners. He quoted Isa 53:12, "He was counted among the lawless," explained that the prophecy was "written about me [him]," and that he must fulfill it (Luke 22:37). Jesus did not intend to isolate this one small portion of the fourth Servant Song and imply that he would fulfill only that portion. Instead, he is claiming to be the fulfillment of the entire Song of the Suffering Servant (Isa 52:13–53:12). This statement provides the key to understanding Jesus's repeated insistence that his suffering and death were both necessary and fulfilled Scripture (9:21–22; 17:25; 18:31–34; 24:6–8, 25–27, 46–47). Although others apply direct quotations of this OT prophecy to Jesus in the NT, this is the clearest example of Jesus's application of the text to himself.[25] This demonstrates that the

---

[24] For a brief discussion of the unique form of Luke's quotation, see Darrell Bock, *Luke 1:1–9:50*, BECNT (Grand Rapids: Baker, 1994), 295–98.

[25] John Nolland suggests that Luke, rather than Jesus, is the source of this quotation. Nolland, *Luke 18:35–24:53*, WBC 35C (Dallas: Word, 1993), 1077. Bock

application of Isaiah's prophecy to Jesus by the NT writers is following the precedent of Jesus's own OT interpretation.

Luke's Gospel is also the most explicit in the description of Jesus's death as the sacrifice that enacts the new covenant. Although both Matthew and Mark record Jesus's statement: "This is my blood of the covenant" (Matt 26:28; Mark 14:24), Luke specifies the covenant to which Jesus was referring: "This cup is the new covenant in my blood" (Luke 22:20). His paraphrase of Jesus's words clarifies that Jesus was referring to the "new covenant" identified in Jer 31:31, the covenant that results in the transformation of sinners and in the forgiveness of their sins.

Jesus's authority to save is clearly expressed in his conversation with the repentant criminal who was crucified at his side. Only Luke records that the man pled, "Jesus, remember me when you come into your kingdom" (Luke 23:42). And only Luke records Jesus's reply: "Truly I tell you, today you will be with me in paradise" (v. 43).

Finally, the climax of the Gospel stresses that the OT described the suffering and resurrection of the Messiah and foretold that "repentance for forgiveness of sins will be proclaimed in his name to all the nations, beginning at Jerusalem" (24:46–47). The close association of Jesus's suffering and resurrection with the forgiveness of sins implies that his suffering and resurrection were the means by which forgiveness of sins was accomplished. The statement recalls Jesus's earlier claim to be the fulfillment of the fourth Servant Song in which an innocent servant of the Lord bears the iniquities of others and suffers for their justification.

References to Jesus's atoning death in the book of Acts, the second volume of Luke's two-volume work, build on the descriptions of that death in Luke's Gospel. Acts confirms Jesus's identity as the Savior who will provide the forgiveness of sins through his death.[26] Acts 2:23 states that Jesus's crucifixion was "according to God's determined plan and foreknowledge." Acts 3:17–21 presents the Messiah's sufferings as the basis for sins being wiped out. This text also implies that the Messiah will accomplish the "restoration

---

shows that the Greek quotation reflects the MT rather than the LXX which "suggests the use of tradition and argues for the age and authenticity of Luke 22:37." Bock, *Luke 9:51–24:53*, BECNT (Grand Rapids: Baker, 1996), 1748.

[26] Acts 2:38; 5:31; 10:43; 13:38; 26:18.

of all things" at the time of his return. Acts 4:12 shows that salvation is possible only through Jesus: "There is salvation in no one else, for there is no other name under heaven given to people by which we must be saved." In Acts 5:31, Peter calls Jesus the "Savior" and explains that God exalted Jesus "to give repentance to Israel and the forgiveness of sins." Similarly, Acts 10:43 insists that anyone who believes in Jesus receives forgiveness of sins and that forgiveness through Jesus's name is an important part of the testimony of the Old Testament prophets (cf. Acts 17:2–3).

The most important text in Acts regarding the means by which Jesus accomplished salvation for repentant believers is probably Acts 8:26–40. The Ethiopian eunuch was reading Isaiah 53, the song of the Suffering Servant, aloud in his chariot and asked Philip, "Who is the prophet saying this about—himself or someone else?" (Acts 8:34). Philip used Isaiah 53 to explain "the good news about Jesus" (Acts 8:35). Just as Jesus applied Isaiah 53 to himself in Luke 22:37, Philip also identifies Jesus as the Suffering Servant who died to atone for the iniquities of others. This explanation of Isaiah 53 confirms that Luke regarded Jesus's death as an act of penal substitutionary atonement.

In Acts 13:38–39, Paul adds his testimony about the salvation accomplished by Jesus to the earlier testimonies of Peter and Philip. Paul argues that Jesus provided "forgiveness of sins" to believers. He explained this forgiveness in terms of justification: "Everyone who believes is justified through him from everything that you could not be justified from through the law of Moses." Paul would later explain this doctrine of justification in greater detail in his letters to the Romans and Galatians.[27] The verb "justify" ($\delta\iota\varkappa\alpha\iota\acute{o}\omega$) means "to declare righteous." It is a legal term referring to the final verdict of a defendant by a judge in which the defendant is pronounced "not guilty." Paul insists that the law of Moses condemns sinners and does not provide viable means for their acquittal by the eschatological judge. Only through Jesus can the sinner be pronounced righteous in the sight of the holy God and acquitted of the indictments that the law imposes.[28]

---

[27] See Gal 2:16; 3:11, 24; Rom 2:13; 3:20, 24, 28; 4:2, 5; 5:1, 9; 8:30, 33; 1 Cor 6:11. For a detailed summary of the doctrine of justification in Paul's letters, see Douglas Moo, *A Theology of Paul and His Letters* (Grand Rapids: Zondervan, 2021), 469–91.

[28] The verb $\delta\iota\varkappa\alpha\iota\acute{o}\omega$ may mean "set free" in some contexts, and the ESV, NASB, and increasing numbers of commentators suggest that nuance here. However, the

Paul's address to the Ephesian elders at Miletus in Acts 20:17–38
includes another important statement explaining the means by which Jesus
provided salvation to sinners. Paul urged the elders to "shepherd the church
of God, which he purchased with his own blood" (Acts 20:28). The statement couples a very high Christology together with an affirmation of the
redemption that Jesus accomplished by his sacrificial death. The antecedent
of the pronoun "he" (implied in the third person singular verb form) and the
referent of the adjective "his own" in this statement is God. Thus, Paul identifies the one who bled on the cross as the incarnation of deity.[29] Furthermore,
Paul explains that Jesus's death, signified by the blood he shed in his crucifixion, was an act by which God purchased the church. The expression which
Paul employed here does not emphasize the situation from which the person
was rescued in the manner that "ransom" and "redemption" do. The emphasis
of the verb περιποιέω is on the acquisition of property or possessions. The
notion is that sinners who did not previously belong to God do belong to him
now. They are his and his exclusively.[30] F. F. Bruce notes that the LXX used

---

immediately preceding statement focused on "forgiveness of sins," and Luke does
not elsewhere use δικαιόω to refer to liberation. That sense is also very rare in Paul's
writings. Romans 6:7 may be the only example of this usage in the Pauline corpus
out of twenty-seven total occurrences. Some scholars have argued that the use of the
preposition ἀπό is inconsistent with the sense "justify" (e.g., C. K. Barrett, *Acts*, ICC
[Edinburgh: T&T Clark, 1994], 650). For a persuasive response to this objection, see
Scott Kellum, *Acts*, EGGNT (Nashville: B&H Academic, 2020), 162–63.

[29] This interpretation is based on the conclusion that the τοῦ ἰδίου is functioning as an attributive adjective in the secondary attributive position as in Acts 1:25.
This is the interpretation affirmed by the CSB, NIV, ESV and most other English
translations. The alternative translation, "the blood of his own Son," that appears in
the NRSV, NET, CEV, LEB, GNT, and a few other translations regards the adjective
as substantival. Although Luke occasionally uses the plural masculine substantive to
refer to one's associates or relatives (Acts 4:23; 24:23), in the only other instance in
Luke-Acts in which he used the adjective to refer to a single relative, he chose to use
a noun with the attributive adjective (Acts 24:24) to remove any possible ambiguity.
Thus, one would have expected him to supply the noun υἱοῦ in this context if he had
intended to refer to "his own Son." Ancient scribes attempted to remove the ambiguity of the original construction and clearly specify the meaning "his own blood"
by placing the adjective in the primary attributive position (e.g., L 323 614 1241
Athanasius Chrysostom Didymus).

[30] A few Greek manuscripts (p41 D 2344) stress this nuance of the verb by adding the pronoun εαυτω (for himself).

this same verb and the related noun to refer to God's acquisition of Israel. He adds that although Paul prefers the verbs "buy" (ἀγοράζω) and the concept of redemption (ἀπολύτρωσις) to refer to God's acquisition of his people, the construction that Paul uses here is paralleled in Eph 1:14 (cf. 1 Pet 2:9).[31]

David Peterson observed that Paul clearly presents Jesus's blood as the price paid for divine redemption, a claim that Paul explains in greater detail in Rom 3:24–25; 5:9. He correctly argues that Paul is employing "specifically covenantal language" that is reminiscent of Jesus's claim at the Last Supper to enact the new covenant through his own sacrificial death.[32] An essential element of the new covenant was God's unique possession of his people that resulted in him alone being their God: "I will be their God and they will be my people" (Jer 31:33; cf. Ezek 36:28; 37:23, 27).

Figure 8: The Work of Christ in Luke

Scripture Passage	Content
Luke 2:11	Jesus is the Savior who will provide forgiveness of sins (cf. Luke 1:77).
Luke 2:30	Jesus brings salvation.
Luke 2:38	Jesus brings redemption.
Luke 3:6	Because of the coming of Jesus, "everyone will see the salvation of God" (Isa 40:5 LXX).
Luke 7:48, 50	Jesus forgives and saves a sinful woman.
Luke 22:35–38	Jesus identifies himself as Isaiah's Suffering Servant who will be punished for the iniquities of others.
Luke 23:43	Jesus grants entrance into paradise.
Luke 24:46–47	Jesus's suffering and resurrection fulfill OT prophecies and are associated with forgiveness of sins.

---

[31] F. F. Bruce, *The Book of Acts*, NICNT (Grand Rapids: Eerdmans, 1988), 393n66.

[32] David Peterson, *The Acts of the Apostles*, PNTC (Grand Rapids: Eerdmans, 2009), 570.

Figure 9: The Work of Christ in Acts

Scripture Passage	Content
Acts 2:23	God planned and orchestrated Jesus's death.
Acts 3:17–21	Through Jesus's sufferings, God wipes out the sins of those who repent.
Acts 4:12	Salvation is possible only through Jesus.
Acts 5:31	God exalted Jesus as Savior to provide forgiveness of sins.
Acts 8:34–35	Jesus is Isaiah's Suffering Servant who died to atone for the iniquities of others.
Acts 10:43	Faith in Jesus is necessary to receive forgiveness of sins.
Acts 13:38–39	Through Jesus, sinners are forgiven and justified.
Acts 20:28	Jesus's sacrificial blood is the ransom that purchases God's people.

Summary

Luke, like Matthew, explicitly identifies Jesus as Isaiah's Suffering Servant who died a substitutionary death to provide atonement and justification to sinners. This identification appears in both volumes of Luke's two-volume work. Furthermore, in Luke 22:35–38, the Evangelist shows that Jesus's identity as the Suffering Servant was claimed by Jesus himself and not merely those who came after him. Because of Jesus's sacrificial death, he provides forgiveness of sin, salvation, redemption, justification, and grants entrance into paradise.

6

The Work of Christ in John's Gospel, Epistles, and Revelation

The apostle John is the author of five NT books: his Gospel, three letters, and the book of Revelation. Naturally, the descriptions of the salvific work of Christ in these five books are very similar and complementary. Consequently, they are best treated together. Rather than proceeding through each book separately and in order, as has been our normal approach, this discussion will seek to integrate them to form a coherent picture of John's theology of the work of Christ.

John's writings especially emphasize Christ's work of providing forgiveness of sins through his sacrificial death. The Prologue to John's Gospel hints that Jesus will forgive sinners by applying a phrase from Exod 34:5–7 to Jesus in John 1:14. John explains that Jesus is the incarnation of Deity, the tabernacle of the glory of God. He further describes Jesus as "full of grace and truth." This phrase is quoted from the supreme revelation of Yahweh in the Old Testament: "The LORD—the LORD is a compassionate and gracious God, slow to anger and abounding in faithful love and truth." John's expression, "full of grace and truth," is an obvious translation of the Hebrew expression translated as "abounding in faithful love and truth" in the CSB. God's compassion, grace, and faithful love compel him to maintain "faithful love to a thousand generations, forgiving iniquity, rebellion, and sin." This revelation of the character of God was renowned and the essence of it is repeated in Num 14:18; Neh 9:17; Pss 86:15; 103:8; and Joel 2:13. John's application of this phrase to the incarnate Word demonstrates that Jesus possesses God's character, which prompts him to forgive and prepares the reader for the later descriptions of Christ's provision of atonement.[1]

The Prologue certifies the witness of John the Baptist concerning the true Light (John 1:6–9). John's testimony includes the exclamation that Jesus is "the Lamb of God, who takes away the sin of the world" (John 1:29; cf. 1:36). Scholars still debate the primary background of this lamb reference. Various scholars have proposed that the lamb is to be understood as a reference to an apocalyptic warrior-lamb who brings judgment like the one that appears in 1 Enoch; the ram of Gen 22:8, 13, and 14; the Passover lamb; or the lamb to which the Suffering Servant is compared in Isa 53:7.[2]

The primary background is almost certainly the Passover lamb. The chronology of Jesus's Passion in John indicates that Jesus died as the Passover lambs were being sacrificed (John 18:28; 19:14). John also argues that Jesus's legs were not broken by the Roman soldiers and that this fulfilled the Scripture which said, "Not one of his bones will be broken" (John 19:36). The Scripture to which John referred was probably the instructions related to the consumption of the Passover lamb in Exod 12:46 and Num 9:12.[3] The reference to the use of the "hyssop branch" in John 19:29 may also be significant since Exod 12:22 specified that a cluster of hyssop should be used to smear the blood of the Passover lamb on the lintel and doorposts.[4] The description of Jesus as the Lamb of God likely anticipates these later references and thus identifies Jesus as the fulfillment of all that the Passover lamb prefigured. The blood of the Passover lamb served as a "distinguishing mark" of the Israelites during the final plague of the Exodus. When the Lord passed through Egypt striking down the firstborn males of both people

---

[1] Colin Kruse, *John*, TNTC 4, 2nd ed. (Downers Grove: IVP, 2017), 64.

[2] For a brief presentation of these options, see Andreas Köstenberger, *A Theology of John's Gospel and Letters*, Biblical Theology of the New Testament (Grand Rapids: Zondervan, 2009), 414–16.

[3] Some scholars suggest that John was instead referring to Ps 34:20. However, the form of John's quotation more closely matches the texts from the Pentateuch. See Craig Keener, *The Gospel of John*, 2 vols. (Peabody, MA: Hendrickson, 2003), 2:1155–56. John probably recognized a connection between the Passover instructions and the psalm and intentionally borrowed features from both sources.

[4] Raymond Brown, *The Gospel According to John*, AB 29, 2 vols. (Garden City, NY: Doubleday, 1966), 1:62.

and animals, he promised to "pass over" the homes marked by the blood of the lamb. The Passover lamb ensured the Israelites' protection from destruction and was associated with their redemption from slavery in Egypt. By his death, Jesus would save his people from destruction and accomplish their spiritual exodus—deliverance from their slavery to sin (John 8:34).[5]

The description "who takes away the sin of the world" clearly portrays the lamb as an atoning sacrifice. Some scholars object that this description is inconsistent with the association of the lamb with Passover since the Passover lamb was not considered an offering that sought forgiveness. However, this description is not incompatible with portrayal of Jesus as the Passover lamb since Paul described the Passover lamb as a sacrifice in the middle of the first century (1 Cor 5:7) and Josephus, another first-century Jew, described the Passover lamb as a "sacrifice" that "purified their houses with the blood."[6]

John probably associated the Passover lamb with the lamb of Isa 53:7.[7] Isaiah used the image of "a lamb led to the slaughter" to portray the silent suffering of the messianic servant who "bore the sin of many" (Isa 53:12) and whom the Lord punished "for the iniquity of us all" (Isa 53:6). John 12:37–38 explicitly claims that Jesus fulfilled the Song of the Suffering Servant. Although John cites only the first verse of Isaiah 53, his intention is to apply the entire Servant Song to Jesus. Other echoes of Isa 53 in this Gospel confirm this conclusion. Jesus lays down his life voluntarily (John 10:11, 15, 17–18; 15:13) just as the Servant "willingly submitted to death" (Isa 53:12). The high priest's unwitting prophecy that Jesus was going to die for the people (John 11:50–52; 18:14) is reminiscent of the description of the Servant's substitutionary death in Isa 53:5, 6, 8, and 11. John's description of Jesus's sacrificial death as an act of divine glorification (John 3:14; 12:32) probably appeals to Isa 52:13 in which the Suffering Servant is "raised and lifted up and greatly exalted."

---

[5] Philo saw Passover as symbolizing a spiritual exodus in which a person abandoned the sinful passions that previously dominated him. See Philo, Alleg. 3:84, 154, 165.

[6] Jos. Ant. 2.14.6 §312.

[7] Cf. Brown, *Gospel According to John*, 1:63; Rudolph Schnackenburg, *The Gospel According to St. John*, 3 vols., trans. Kevin Smyth, ed. J. Massingberd Ford and Kevin Smyth (New York: Herder and Herder, 1968–1980), 1:300. Keener views the combination as "feasible" (*John*, 1:454).

The letters of John very clearly describe Jesus's death as an atoning sacrifice (1 John 2:2; 4:10) and insist that "the blood of Jesus his [God's] Son cleanses us from all sin" (1 John 1:7; cf. 3:5). The term that John uses to describe this sacrifice (ἱλασμός) was employed in extrabiblical Greek literature to refer to an offering that placated the wrath of a god whom the offeror had offended. Some scholars have objected that this cannot be the sense of the term in the NT. They argue that Scripture affirms expiation (removal of sin which prohibits a relationship with God) rather than propitiation (placating the wrath of God). But the noun and related terms imply that Jesus's death was an act of sacrifice that satisfied the justice of God and placated the wrath of God.[8] In the LXX, these terms are used to refer to the "Day of Atonement" (Lev 25:9), the atonement ram "by which the priest will make atonement for the guilty person" (Num 5:8), the forgiveness by which the Lord refrains from keeping an account of iniquities (Ps 130:4), and the sin offering necessary for the purification of a priest who was defiled by coming into contact with a corpse (Ezek 44:27). This OT usage implies that the atoning sacrifice was a propitiation, an act of appeasement.[9] Although some modern thinkers have been repulsed by such assertions, even going so far as to describe propitiation as "morally repugnant" or "cosmic child abuse,"[10] John presents this sacrifice as the supreme expression of the Father's love (1 John 4:10). The echo of John 3:16 here is unmistakable.

The expressions "takes away the sin of the world" and "cleanses us from all sin" are essentially equivalent. Both expressions refer to a removal of guilt

---

[8] Colin Kruse argues that the "atoning sacrifice" of 1 John 2:2 is a propitiation rather than merely an expiation since this sacrifice is juxtaposed with Jesus's advocacy for sinners: "Jesus is the one who speaks to the Father in our defense when we sin. This suggests that he is, as it were, pleading for mercy for sinners, and this in turn suggests that his role as the atoning sacrifice is to secure that mercy; that is, he is, in this context, the propitiation for our sins." Kruse, *Letters of John*, PNTC, 2nd ed. (Grand Rapids: Eerdmans, 2020), 79.

[9] Although the issue is still debated, I. H. Marshall boldly asserts, "There can be no real doubt that this [propitiation] is the meaning." *The Epistles of John*, NICNT (Grand Rapids: Eerdmans, 1978), 118. Commentators who argue that the atoning sacrifice involves both expiation and propitiation include Smalley, Witherington, and Robert Yarbrough, *1–3 John*, BECNT (Grand Rapids: Baker, 2008), 78.

[10] Simon Gathercole helpfully assembles several such quotations in his *Defending Substitution: An Essay on Atonement in Paul* (Grand Rapids: Baker, 2015), 24–25.

in which "our sin is removed and forgiven; its defiled effects no longer condemn us in the sight of God."[11] This cleansing from sin is a reference to forgiveness of sins since 1 John 1:9 associates forgiveness with cleansing (cf. Jer 33:8).[12] Furthermore, if this cleansing were moral transformation, cleansing from all sin would imply a moral perfection which John immediately insists that the believer does not presently possess (1 John 1:8).

Jesus refers to this cleansing again in John 13:8–10. When Peter objects to Jesus's intention to wash Peter's feet, Jesus replies, "If I don't wash you, you have no part with me." Peter then urges Jesus to wash him completely, including his feet, his hands, and his head. Jesus replied, "One who has bathed doesn't need to wash anything except his feet, but he is completely clean." Although the shifts from physical washing to spiritual cleansing can be confusing, Jesus unmistakably describes his true disciples (excluding Judas) as those who have been washed so that they are "completely clean." Peter's denial of Jesus shortly thereafter shows that he has not experienced complete moral transformation. He is "completely clean" because he is totally forgiven.[13] The guilt of his sin has been entirely removed. These references to cleansing are closely related to the references to washing in the book of Revelation (Rev 7:14; 22:14). However, Revelation refers to the washing of one's robes rather than the cleansing of the body, perhaps to emphasize that the righteousness that results from this cleansing is imputed rather than imparted, an alien righteousness rather than one's own.

The references to Jesus as the Lamb of God in John's Gospel and the atoning sacrifice in John's letters are closely related to the frequent portrayal of Jesus as the Lamb in Revelation. Revelation refers to Jesus as the Lamb twenty-eight times, making it the most frequently used title of Jesus in the entire book.[14] By contrast, Revelation refers to Jesus as the "Messiah" or

---

[11] I. H. Marshall, *The Epistles of John*, 112.

[12] Colin G. Kruse, *The Letters of John*, 70.

[13] George Beasley-Murray explains that this cleansing is the one accomplished "through his redemptive death" and entails "remission of guilt" and "a part with him in the eternal kingdom." Beasley-Murray, *John*, WBC 26, 2nd ed. (Dallas: Word, 1999), 234.

[14] Rev 5:6, 8, 12, 13; 6:1, 16; 7:9, 10, 14, 17; 12:11; 13:8; 14:1, 4 (2x), 10; 15:3; 17:14 (2x); 19:7, 9; 21:9, 14, 22, 23, 27; 22:1, 3. In the one additional use of the word "lamb" in Revelation, the portrayal of the beast as "like a lamb" probably indicates

"Christ" seven times (1:1, 2, 5; 11:15; 12:10; 20:4, 6), "Lord" seven times (11:8; 14:13; 17:14; 19:16; 22:6, 20, 21), the "Son of Man" twice (1:13; 14:14), "the faithful [and true] witness" twice (1:5; 3:14), the "Word of God" once (19:13), and the "Son of God" once (2:18). Although the Lamb is described as an enthroned ruler (5:13; 7:17; 22:1, 3) and a conquering warrior (17:14), he is just as frequently described as one "slain" or "slaughtered" (5:6, 12; 13:8) and who has shed his blood (7:14; 12:11). The slaughtered Lamb has the authority to grant salvation (7:10). He inscribes the names of those to be saved in his "book of life" (13:8). His shed blood cleanses sinners of their guilt since they "washed their robes and made them white in the blood of the Lamb" (7:14). The Lamb "redeems" humans as firstfruits for God and for himself (14:4).

In addition to his lamb imagery, John uses other images to portray Jesus as the one who died a substitutionary death to save sinners. Jesus explains his saving work by describing himself as the "good shepherd" who "lays down his life for the sheep" (John 10:11; cf. 10:15). The expression "lays down his life" refers to a voluntary act of self-sacrifice. Jesus explicitly states that "no one takes it [my life] from me, but I lay it down on my own" (John 10:18) even though Jesus's sacrifice had been commanded by the Father. The phrase "for the sheep" uses the preposition ὑπέρ with the genitive object which may mean either "for the sake of the sheep" or "instead of the sheep." In this instance, the context shows that the two nuances overlap. The analogy that Jesus used to portray his death is that of a shepherd who dies defending his sheep against a ravenous wolf. The shepherd's death is for the benefit of the sheep, but it is also in place of the sheep. If the shepherd had not intervened and battled the wolf to the death, the wolf would have inevitably snatched some and scattered the rest, leaving them defenseless against other predators as well. Carson is undoubtedly correct when he writes:

---

that he imitates Jesus in some way. Grant Osborne notes that the beast "parodies the description of Christ as the Lamb with seven horns in 5:6." Grant, *Revelation*, BECNT (Grand Rapids: Baker, 2002), 511. The seventh-century commentary on Revelation by Oecumenius, our earliest Greek commentary on the book, noted that "the wretch pretends to be Christ (though he is not)." See John N. Suggit, trans., *Oecumenius: Commentary on the Apocalypse*, FC 112 (Washington, DC: Catholic University of America Press, 2006), 123.

The words "for (*hyper*) the sheep" suggest sacrifice. The preposition, itself ambiguous, in John always occurs in a sacrificial context, whether referring to the death of Jesus (6:51; 10:11, 15; 11:50ff.; 17:19; 18:14), of Peter (13:37–38), or of a man prepared to die for his friend (15:13). In no case does this suggest a death with merely exemplary significance; in each case the death envisaged is on behalf of someone else.[15]

Borchert agrees but goes further: "The expression *hyper tōn probatōn*, 'for the sheep' (better 'on behalf of the sheep,' 10:11, 15) implies a self-sacrificing perspective. Indeed, the use of *hyper* in relation to the death of Jesus (cf. 6:51) seems in this Gospel to carry a substitutionary meaning."[16]

The concepts of sacrifice and substitution are combined again in John 11:47–53. Caiaphas calls for the arrest and execution of Jesus and explains, "it is to your advantage that one man should die for the people rather than the whole nation perish" (John 11:50). Again, John uses the preposition ὑπέρ with the genitive object and one can make a good argument that the preposition expresses benefit, "for the sake of." However, the next clause states the alternative to the death of one man for the people—the destruction of the whole nation. This refers to the destruction of the temple and the slaughter of the people that the chief priests and Pharisees feared as a result of Jesus's popularity with the people (John 11:48). Since the option is that either Jesus die or that the nation be destroyed, Jesus's death is both for the benefit of the nation and as a substitute for the nation (and for God's children scattered throughout the world).[17] Caiaphas's unwitting prophecy is very important to John and he reminds his readers of this important statement in his description of the proceedings that led to Jesus's execution (John 18:14).

---

[15] D. A. Carson, *The Gospel According to John*, PNTC (Grand Rapids: Eerdmans, 1991), 386.

[16] Gerald Borchert, *John 1–11*, NAC 25A (Nashville: B&H, 1996), 334.

[17] Leon Morris observes: "We should not overlook that this way of putting it means a definitely substitutionary death. Either the nation dies or Jesus dies. But if he dies the nation lives; it is his life instead of theirs." Morris, *The Gospel According to John*, NICNT, rev. ed. (Grand Rapids: Eerdmans, 1995), 504. Grant Osborne likewise notes that the construction used here refers "to a substitutionary or atoning sacrifice in which he died in their place." Osborne, *The Gospel of John*, Cornerstone Biblical Commentary 13, (Carol Stream, IL: Tyndale House, 2007), 174.

The substitutionary element in these earlier uses of the preposition ὑπέρ prepares the reader to recognize the same nuance in 15:13: "No one has greater love than this: to lay down his life for his friends." When Jesus continues by identifying his disciples as his friends, it becomes clear that he will lay down his life for them. Jesus is the good shepherd and his disciples are the sheep.

The substitutionary nature of Jesus's death is confirmed by John's quotation of Isa 53:1 in John 12:38. The citation is probably an example of metalepsis in which reference to a small portion of a text is intended to prompt recollection of the entire section. John's point is that the disbelief of those who witnessed Jesus's miracles fulfills Isa 53:1 because Jesus is the Suffering Servant who will die for the iniquities of others. The Song of the Suffering Servant is probably the source that prompts Jesus to equate his passion with his exaltation. Jesus describes his crucifixion/exaltation as being "lifted up" (John 3:14; 12:32, 34) because Isaiah described the Servant as "raised and lifted up and greatly exalted" (Isa 52:13).

The theme of Jesus's substitutionary death resurfaces in John 18:11. When Peter resorts to violence in a futile effort to prevent Jesus's arrest, Jesus replies, "Am I not to drink the cup the Father has given me?" The question appears to be a reference to Jesus's prayer in Gethsemane, even though John does not record that struggle (Mark 14:36; Matthew 26:39, 42).[18] The "cup" likely has the same associations here as in Mark and Matthew where it appears to refer to the cup of suffering and the wrath of God (Ps 75:8; Isa 51:17, 22; Jer 25:15; Ezek 23:31–33; Rev 14:10; 16:19). Morris confidently commented, "We cannot doubt but that in this solemn moment these are the thoughts that the term arouses."[19]

One of the most striking features of John's descriptions of Jesus's atoning sacrifice is his repeated insistence that this sacrifice was offered for the world. Jesus is the Lamb of God who "takes away the sin of the world" (John 1:29). God demonstrated his love for "the world" by giving his one and only Son (3:16) and God sent his Son "to save the world through him" (3:17).

---

[18] Colin Kruse and George Beasley-Murray both recognize an allusion to the Synoptic account of Jesus's Gethsemane prayer. Kruse and Beasley-Murray, *John*, WBC 36, 2nd ed. (Dallas: Word, 1999), 323, 408.

[19] Leon Morris, *The Gospel According to John*, 661.

The Samaritan woman describes Jesus as "the Savior of the world" (4:42). Jesus "gives life to the world" (6:33) and gives his flesh "for the life of the world" (6:51). Jesus came "to save the world" (12:47). This prominent theme of John's Gospel appears in his letters as well. There John not only asserts that the Father sent the Son to be "the world's Savior" (1 John 4:14); he even insists that "he himself is the atoning sacrifice for our sins, and not only for ours, but also for those of the whole world" (1 John 2:2).

Most interpreters acknowledge that John's statements indicate that God loves and Jesus died for the entire human race.[20] John's use of the word "world" in his writings precludes equating "world" with the elect or believers only. John frequently describes the world as standing in hostile rebellion against God. The world hates Jesus (John 7:7; 15:18–19; cf. 17:14). The world is ruled by Satan and is under divine judgment (John 12:31; cf. 14:30; 16:11). The world is not able to receive the Spirit (John 14:17). In most cases in which the word "world" has a restricted sense, the term does not refer to Jesus's disciples, the church, or the elect but describes humanity distinct from and opposed to Jesus's disciples.[21] For example, in his intercessory prayer for his disciples, Jesus explicitly contrasted those whom the Father had given to him with "the world" (John 17:6, 9).

Furthermore, the argument that "world" refers merely to the elect cannot satisfactorily explain 1 John 2:2. In this text, the world is distinguished from the apostle John and his fellow believers, not in the sense that it excludes this group but in the sense that includes far more than this group. Additionally, John stresses the inclusive sense of the term by use of the adjective "whole," a modifier that obviates the notion that John was singling out only a portion of the world and strongly implies that John intends to include every individual in the human race as an intended beneficiary of Jesus's atoning sacrifice.

---

[20] John Calvin, *The Gospel According to John, Part 1:1–10,* Calvin's New Testament Commentaries, vol. 4, trans. T. H. L. Parker, Commentary on John (Grand Rapids: Eerdmans, 1961), 74–75.

[21] Carson sees John 1:29 as a clear exception. He argues that in this text "world" refers to "all human beings without distinction" (i.e., "not restricted in its purpose or effectiveness to the Jewish race") instead of "all without exception" since John 1:11–12 restricts salvation to those who believe in the name of the Son of God. Carson, *John,* 151.

Augustine and Calvin argued that "the whole world" in 1 John 2:2 referred to the whole church that was scattered throughout every region of the world.[22] This explanation suits some of the references to the salvation of the world in John's writings quite well. This interpretation is supported by Rev 5:9 in which the four living creatures and the twenty-four elders sing that the Lamb "purchased people for God by your blood from every tribe and language and people and nation" (cf. Rev 7:9; 14:6; 15:3–4; 22:2). Furthermore, John seems to use the word "world" in an inclusive and not necessarily exhaustive sense repeatedly in his Gospel. A prime example is John 4:42: "This really is the Savior of the world." That confession was uttered by the Samaritans in a pericope in which the Samaritan woman expressed shock that Jesus would share the water ladle with her since, as John explains parenthetically, "Jews do not associate with Samaritans" (John 4:9). It also follows Jesus's earlier statement that "salvation is from the Jews" (v. 22). At the Samaritan villagers' request, Jesus has stayed with them two days, evidently as a guest in a Samaritan home (John 4:40). Thus, recognition that Jesus is the Savior "of the world" in this context means that Jesus is far more than the Savior of Jews but is also Savior of people from other groups such as Samaritans and even Gentiles.[23]

Another example is John 11:49–52. Caiaphas called for the apprehension and execution of Jesus on the grounds that "it is to your advantage that one man should die for the people rather than the whole nation perish" (v. 50).

---

[22] See Augustine, Hom. 1 John 1.8; John Calvin, *The Gospel According to St. John, Part 2:11–21, and the First Epistle of John*, Calvin's New Testament Commentaries, vol. 5, trans. T. H. L. Parker (Grand Rapids: Eerdmans, 1959), 244. Although he acknowledged that the "solution" that "has commonly prevailed in the schools" said "Christ suffered sufficiently for the whole world, but efficiently only for the elect" and although he admitted the truthfulness of the theological axiom, Calvin denied that the solution fit the context of this specific passage. Calvin, however, soon changed his view from the opinion on 1 John 2:2 in his commentary on the General Epistles (dedicated to Edward VI on January 24, 1551) to the opinion on John 3:16 in his commentary on the Gospels (dedicated on January 1, 1553). Origen's position differed from Augustine's. He interpreted "the whole world" in 1 John 2:2 to refer to "sinners in all parts of the world."

[23] Grant Osborne noted that the confession of Jesus as the Savior of the world "would be especially true for the Samaritans who recognized that their *taheb* was also the Jewish Messiah and, therefore, the only Messiah for the whole world." Osborne, *The Gospel of John*.

John explains that Caiaphas's words were an unwitting prophecy since Jesus "was going to die for the nation, and not for the nation only, but also to unite the scattered children of God" (vv. 51–52). These "scattered children" are distinct from the nation of Israel, thus Gentiles. Consequently, Jesus has the authority over "all people" so that he can give eternal life to everyone that God has given to him (John 17:2; cf. 10:16).

In John 12:20, some Greeks, evidently Gentile God-fearers, asked to see Jesus. This episode is closely related both to what immediately precedes and follows it in the context of John's Gospel. Immediately before the appearance of the Greeks, the Pharisees complain, "Look, the world has gone after him!" (12:19). The spiritual quest of these Greeks confirms the Pharisees' statement and shows that "the world" includes Gentiles. Immediately after the appearance of these Greeks, Jesus says, "The hour has come for the Son of Man to be glorified" (v. 23). In the same conversation, Jesus equates his glorification with his "lifting up" and exclaims, "If I am lifted up from the earth I will draw all people to myself" (v. 32). In context, "all people" seems to refer not to every individual, but to people of all ethnicities including the Greeks that have just approached Jesus.

Jesus's statement, "I am the light of the world" (John 8:12) is probably an appeal to messianic prophecy. Isaiah described the Servant of the Lord, the Messiah, as "a light to the nations" (Isa 42:6). After explaining that restoring Israel alone was too small a task for the Servant, God promised: "I will also make you a light for the nations, to be my salvation to the ends of the earth" (Isa 49:6). If the statement "I am the light of the world" is an allusion to these two messianic prophecies, "world" serves as a reference to all the nations from one end of the earth to the other.

Thus, John's writings have several notable examples in which "world" has an inclusive rather than truly universal sense. One can make a good case that the context suggests this inclusive sense in John 3:16 as well. Jesus has just compared the lifting up of the Son of Man to Moses lifting up the bronze snake in the wilderness. The OT miracle was performed for the benefit of Israelites during their conquest of Gentile peoples in the land of Canaan (Num 21:4–9), a time when the Lord "handed the Canaanites over to them, and Israel completely destroyed them and their cities" (Num 21:3). Thus, the analogy that Jesus used could have easily led John's readers to assume that Jesus was lifted up for the benefit of Israelites exclusively. The insistence that

God loved the world and demonstrated that love through the sending of his Son was a powerful deterrent to this misunderstanding of Jesus's mission.

Although the inclusive interpretation makes sense in several texts in John's Gospel, this interpretation faces serious difficulties in 1 John. First John offers no hint of concern regarding Gentile exclusion or tensions between Jewish Christians and believers from other ethnic backgrounds. John does not mention any of the points of contention that sometimes disrupted the fellowship of Jewish and Gentile believers, issues such as circumcision, Sabbath, and dietary laws. No evidence suggests that his opponents were Judaizers. The debate with the secessionists did not focus on whether Jesus was the Savior *of all*, but whether he was Savior *at all*. The secessionists claimed that they had not sinned (1 John 1:6–2:2) which made Jesus's sacrifice unnecessary in their view. They apparently denied that Jesus had come "in the flesh" (1 John 4:2) and consequently denied his atoning death, his blood sacrifice (1 John 5:6–8).[24] In the face of these challenges, the claims that Jesus's atoning sacrifice was for the sins of the whole world and that Jesus is the Savior of the world stress that Jesus is not merely a savior but the all-sufficient Savior. His sacrifice is sufficient to cleanse us "from all unrighteousness" (1 John 1:9) and his forgiveness is available to "anyone" who sins (1 John 2:1). Daniel L. Akin rightly concludes:

> Although it is possible to say that 'the whole world' is John's way of saying all the nations (but not intending every single person), and that "the propitiation for the sins of the whole world" is meant to stress the exclusivity of Jesus' work (i.e., Jesus is the only propitiation for all alike), such a view does not provide a satisfactory answer to John's "not only for ours but also for. . . ."[25]

The inclusive sense of "world" (meaning both Jew and Gentile) often fits the context of the usages in the Gospel of John. Nevertheless, the universal sense of "world" (meaning the entire human race) best fits the references in 1 John.

These texts do not suggest universalism. John emphasizes the necessity of faith for salvation. He explicitly states that "everyone who believes in him will not perish but have eternal life" (John 3:16). He clarifies that "anyone who does

---

[24] See the excellent discussion in Kruse, *The Letters of John*, 177.

[25] Daniel L. Akin, *1, 2, 3 John*, NAC (Nashville: B&H, 2001), 85.

not believe is already condemned" (John 3:18). Andreas Köstenberger observes that these texts are "John's way of holding in tension the fact that Jesus renders universal atonement while saving effectually only those who respond to him in faith and accept his substitutionary sacrifice on their behalf."[26] These texts do show, however, that Jesus's death made salvation possible for every individual. Through Jesus's death, salvation was afforded for all, though it is applied only to believers. Through Jesus's atoning sacrifice, forgiveness was procured for all, though it is secured only for those who repent and believe.[27]

John's writings show that the work of Christ includes the new covenant ministry of imparting the Holy Spirit to believers. The Prologue to the Gospel of John describes the Word who came into the world as the one who gives "the right to be children of God" (1:12) to those who believe on his name. They become children of God not through mere legal adoption but through spiritual birth. Although Jesus will describe the Spirit as the one who is the direct agent performing this birth in his conversation with Nicodemus (John 3:5, 8), the Prologue specifies that the Word is the authority who grants this privilege to believers. Jesus will later explain that the Father gives the Spirit at the Son's request (14:16). Those whom Christ authorizes to become God's children are "born, not of natural descent, or of the will of the flesh, or of the will of man, but of God" (1:13). In this spiritual birth, sinners enter a new relationship with God. Those who were formerly children of Satan (John 8:44; 1 John 3:8) and thus enemies of God become enemies of Satan and children of God (1 John 3:1, 2, 10; 4:4). Through this spiritual birth, sinners are also characterized by a new resemblance to God. The child inherits characteristics from the parent. Thus, "whatever is born of the flesh is flesh, and whatever is born of the Spirit is spirit" (John 3:6).[28] As John later explains in his first letter (1 John 3:9), God's children are

---

[26] Köstenberger, *A Theology of John's Gospel and Letters*, 226. Köstenberger also recognizes that John's Gospel is combatting the notion that the Messiah merely came to save Israel. Jesus is the Savior of Gentiles as well, the "scattered children of God" (John 11:52; cf. 10:16). See pp. 415, 463.

[27] This formula distinguishing sufficiency and efficiency appears in Peter Lombard, *IV Libri Sententiarum* 3.5.3; Thomas Aquinas, *Summa Theologicae* 3a.2.5; and is affirmed in the Second Heading of the Canons of the Synod of Dordt.

[28] Carson rightly emphasizes that Jesus's point is that "it is God's Holy Spirit who produces a new nature." Carson, *The Gospel According to John*, 196–97.

spiritually conceived by God's "seed." The impartation of that seed ensures that the believer will exhibit characteristics of the heavenly Father just as surely as the seed by which a child is physically conceived guarantees that the child will exhibit characteristics of the biological father. This spiritual conception and birth results in a radical transformation of the sinner's moral character. John explained, "Everyone who has been born of God does not sin, because his seed remains in him; he is not able to sin, because he has been born of God" (1 John 3:9). He added that a person's character and behavior clearly reveal whether a person is the progeny of God or a child of the devil. God's children will be characterized by righteousness and love (2:29; 3:9; 4:7–8). The devil's children will be characterized by unrighteousness and the absence of love (3:8, 10). John stresses that the new birth will produce obedience to God's commands (3:1–3; 5:2–4, 18). It will especially result in obedience to the command to love fellow believers (3:11, 14) since love is one of the Father's primary characteristics (4:7–8) and is necessarily transmitted to those whom he spiritually conceives. This love results not only from the new character given to the believer, but also from the new relationship established with fellow believers through the new birth. When God becomes our Father through spiritual conception, believers necessarily become spiritual siblings. Consequently, "everyone who loves the Father also loves the one born of him" (1 John 5:1). Since love is the essence of God's moral law, love produces a lifestyle of holiness and righteousness (1 John 5:2; 2 John 5–6). This divine love will express itself both in word and in action (1 John 3:16–20).

The Prologue identifies Jesus as the one who grants new birth and thus authority to become children of God since Jesus is the one who performs the baptism of the Spirit (John 1:33). This baptism of the Spirit refers to the outpouring of the Spirit that fulfills the new covenant (Ezek 36:26–27). The Synoptic Gospels demonstrate that Jesus's death served as the sacrifice that initiated this new covenant. John confirms that Jesus's death is essential to the impartation of the Spirit. The Gospel repeatedly explains that Jesus's glorification at the time of his departure (death) was necessary if the Spirit was to come (John 7:39; 16:7).[29] Jesus imparted the Spirit to the ten

---

[29] Gerald Borchert correctly recognizes that the departure of John 16:7 is not the ascension, but "the atoning death of Jesus" since the "Spirit era" begins in John

disciples assembled together on the evening of Resurrection Sunday (John 20:19–23). He reenacted the creation of humanity in Gen 2:7 by breathing on the disciples and saying, "Receive the Holy Spirit" (John 20:22). Jesus's gesture portrays the impartation of the Spirit as an act of new creation, a portrayal that is closely associated with the concept of spiritual conception and birth.[30]

John repeatedly emphasizes that salvation is possible only through Jesus. In John's account of Jesus's teaching, the Savior uses several different images to show that sinners can have a relationship with God through Jesus exclusively. After comparing Nathaniel to Israel after Jacob repented of the deceitful character expressed by his name (John 1:47), Jesus said, "You will see heaven opened and the angels of God ascending and descending on the Son of Man" (John 1:51). Jesus was describing himself as the stairway that Jacob saw in his dream at Bethel (Gen 28:12), a stairway that extended from the ground to heaven itself, the point of access to heaven and thus to God.[31]

Similarly, Jesus described himself as "the gate for the sheep" (John 10:7; cf. 10:9), the entryway into the flock of the divine shepherd. He is the exclusive entry point. Those who attempt to enter another way are guilty of criminal trespassing. These intruders are like thieves and robbers who have broken into a place where they have no right to be (John 10:1).

Jesus makes this same point yet again when he proclaims, "I am the way" (John 14:6). The way or road (ὁδός) leads to the most important destination. By this road a sinner comes to the Father. Once more Jesus insists that no other means of access to the Father exists: "No one comes to the Father except through me."

20:22 before the ascension. Borchert, *John 12–21*, NAC 25b (Nashville: B&H, 2002), 165.

[30] The relationship of this event to the outpouring of the Spirit at Pentecost has long been a topic of debate. For an explanation of the issue, see Charles L. Quarles, "New Creation: Spirituality according to Jesus," in *Biblical Spirituality: God's Holiness and Our Spirituality*, ed. Christopher W. Morgan, Theology in Community (Wheaton: Crossway, 2019): 79–106.

[31] Beasley-Murray notes that the analogy portrays Jesus as "the point of contact between heaven and earth, the focus of the 'traffic' that brings heaven's blessings to mankind." Beasley-Murray, *John*, 28. Carson argues that Jesus is comparing himself to Jacob rather than the ladder or staircase. Carson, *The Gospel According to John*, 163–64.

Jesus also uses several different expressions to show that he is the source of eternal life. Two of the most urgent necessities of life are food and drink. Jesus describes himself as both. He is the one who gives someone the "living water" that "will become a well of water springing up in him for eternal life" (John 4:14). Jesus later explains that "the Son gives life to whom he wants" (5:21) and "the dead will hear the voice of the Son of God, and those who hear will live" (5:25).

Jesus is also "the bread of life" (John 6:35) who satisfies all spiritual hunger and thirst. Those who receive this bread "will live forever" (6:51, 58) because "everyone who sees the Son and believes in him will have eternal life and I will raise him up on the last day" (6:40; cf. 11:25–26).

Jesus is not only the source of resurrection life, but also the source of new life here and now. Jesus promises that the one who believes in him will have "streams of living water flow from deep within him" (John 7:38). Jesus taught that this promise had already been made in "the Scripture." John explains that the living water symbolized the Holy Spirit whom Jesus would give after he was glorified (7:39).

The transformation wrought by Christ in his enactment of the new covenant is accompanied by spiritual liberation, redemption from slavery to sin. Although this doctrine is most commonly associated with the teaching of the apostle Paul (Gal 4:3–5; 5:1; Rom 6:15–23), it appears in the Gospel of John as well. Jesus explained that sinners are enslaved to sin (John 8:34). Consequently, they seek to fulfill the desires of their spiritual father, the devil (8:44). However, Jesus's disciples "will know the truth, and the truth will set you [them] free" (8:32). Jesus added, "If the Son sets you free, you really will be free" (v. 36). A fellow slave did not have the authority to emancipate a slave. The master's son, however, did have such authority. Since Jesus is the one and only Son of the heavenly Father, he has the full right and authority to set sinners free from their slavery to sin. It is important to insist that this liberation does not consist of freedom *to* sin but freedom *from* sin. Although spiritual liberation in the Gospel of John has several important aspects such as "freedom from condemnation (5:24), darkness (8:12), the power of the evil one (17:15; cf. 1 John 5:18) and death (5:24; 8:51),"[32] the primary focus in this text is deliverance from sin's domination so that the believer is free to live

---

[32] Kruse, *John*, 238.

righteously. The hallmark of the slave to sin is a lifestyle dominated and characterized by sin (John 8:34). John emphasizes that the disciple of Jesus abandons a sinful lifestyle (John 5:14; 1 John 2:1; 3:4, 6, 8–9; 5:18). This emphasis is closely related to John's claim that the believer has a different "walk" (John 8:12; 11:9–10; 12:35; 1 John 1:6–7; 2:6, 11; 2 John 4, 6; 3 John 3–4; Rev 3:4). Both Greek and Hebrew speakers used terms for "walk" to refer to a person's moral and ethical lifestyle. John clearly does so as well.

Jesus's death also results in the vanquishing of Satan. As Jesus anticipated his impending death, he declared, "Now is the judgment of this world. Now the ruler of this world will be cast out" (John 12:31; cf. 16:11; Rev 12:9). This occurs when Jesus is "lifted up from the earth" (John 12:32), a reference to Jesus's exaltation in his crucifixion (v. 33).[33] The ruler of this world is Satan (cf. John 14:30; 16:11; 1 John 5:19). Therefore, the casting out of Satan seems to be equivalent to his judgment mentioned in John 16:11.

The use of the title "ruler of this world" suggests that the casting out involves expulsion from the throne, a violent removal from his position of authority.[34] Because of Satan's deposition, disciples of Jesus may now be guarded and protected from the evil one (John 17:15). He is no longer an internal, dominating force but a mere external threat.[35] Believers are no longer children of the devil performing the bidding of their evil father (John 8:44; 1 John 3:10). The devil's goal is to inspire sin (John 13:2), but Christ came to "destroy the devil's works" (1 John 3:8). By Jesus's death, Satan's tyranny is brought to an end.

However, when viewed in the context of John's writings as a whole, the casting out of Satan seems to have even farther-reaching implications. This casting out likely refers to Satan's expulsion and banishment from heaven. Revelation 12:7–9 seems to offer a vivid description of this expulsion.[36]

---

[33] Carson, *The Gospel According to John*, 444.

[34] Borchert refers to this as "the unseating of the world's prince." Borchert, *John 12–21*, 57.

[35] Augustine entertains the question, "Since the devil is thus cast out of the hearts of believers, does he now tempt none of the faithful?" He replies, "Nay, verily, he does not cease to tempt. But it is one thing to reign within, another to assail from without" (*Tract. Ev. Jo.* 52.9).

[36] Carson describes the casting out of the prince of the world as "analogous to the apocalyptic scene in Revelation" and cites Rev 12:11 in support. Carson, *The*

Satan's role in heaven was to prosecute believers before the heavenly Judge. He was "the accuser of our brothers and sisters, who accuses them before our God day and night" (Rev 12:10). Because he was "cast out" of heaven, he is no longer able to accuse believers "before our God." His accusations are not permitted in heaven's courtroom. Since "the blood of the Lamb" has atoned for believers' sins, Satan's accusations were ruled out of order by the Judge. The Judge held him in contempt of court and ordered that he be disbarred. He will never be permitted to argue his case before the court again. The irony of John 16:11 is that the accuser—the prosecutor—has himself been judged, convicted, and condemned.[37]

The casting out is clearly not his expulsion from the world. Satan still roams the earth freely and wages war against the saints (Rev 12:13–17). Though Satan may persecute believers, he cannot prosecute believers. Even in martyrdom, the saints conquer the accuser "by the blood of the Lamb and by the word of their testimony" (Rev 12:11).

Figure 10: The Work of Christ in John's Writings

Scripture Passage	Content
John 1:12–13	Jesus imparts the new birth and makes sinners children of God who are marked by the Father's own character.
John 1:14	Jesus is the God full of grace and truth who forgives iniquity, rebellion, and sin (cf. Exod 34:5–7).
John 1:29 (cf. 1:36)	Jesus is the Lamb of God who takes away the sin of the world.

Gospel According to John, 444. Cf. Kruse, *John*, 314; Ian Paul, *Revelation*, TNTC (Downers Grove: IVP Academic, 2018), 221.

[37] Grant Osborne notes, "The main point is that in 12:7–10 victory in war becomes also victory in God's legal courtroom. . . . Satan can no longer prosecute the people of God, for he has lost his place in heaven." Osborne, *Revelation*, BECNT (Grand Rapids: Baker, 2002), 475.

John 1:33	Jesus performs the baptism of the Spirit in fulfillment of the new covenant.
John 1:51; 10:7; 14:6	Jesus is the stairway, gate, and road that leads to God.
John 3:14; 12:32	Jesus will be exalted in his death like Isaiah's Suffering Servant (Isa 52:13).
John 3:17	God sent Jesus to save the world.
John 4:14; 5:21, 25; 6:35, 40	Jesus is the source of spiritual and resurrection life.
John 7:38	Jesus grants the Spirit to believers to cleanse them spiritually.
John 8:36	Jesus sets believers free from their slavery to sin.
John 11:50–52; 18:14	Jesus dies for the sins of the people.
John 12:31	Jesus dethrones Satan, the ruler of this world.
John 12:37–38	Jesus is Isaiah's Suffering Servant who dies for the sins of God's people.
John 13:8, 10	Jesus cleanses sinners completely.
John 18:28; 19:14	Jesus is the Passover Lamb who causes God's wrath to pass over his people and initiates their spiritual exodus, deliverance from their slavery to sin (John 8:34–36).
John 20:22	Jesus performs the miracle of new creation by imparting the Holy Spirit to his disciples.
1 John 1:7; 3:5	Jesus's blood cleanses believers of their sins.
1 John 2:2; 4:10	Jesus's death is a sacrifice that provides atonement.
Rev 5:6, 12; 7:10, 14, 17; 12:11; 13:8; 14:4	Jesus is the Lamb who was slain to purify and redeem God's people.

Summary

John's writings present Jesus as the human sacrificial lamb whose death provides atonement to sinners and initiates their spiritual exodus that liberates them from bondage to sin. Jesus also purifies and cleanses his followers. He imparts the Holy Spirit, resulting in the spiritual birth and new creation of believers. Jesus also vanquishes Satan so that he cannot rule over Jesus's followers as he did in the past.

7

The Work of Christ in Paul's Letters

The apostle Paul's theology was Christocentric and his soteriology was cruciform. Thus, it is not surprising that some of the most powerful and poignant discussions of Jesus's saving death appear in Paul's letters. This section will discuss Paul's explanations of Jesus's saving work by working through these letters in a roughly chronological order from the early letters to the chief letters to the prison letters and finally to the personal letters.

Early Letters

Galatians

Paul is so eager to affirm the truths essential to salvation to the churches of Galatia that he does not wait until the body of the letter to introduce these truths. Galatians 1:1 not only identifies the author of the letter but also shows that Paul's gospel was by divine revelation, that Jesus is far more than a mere man, and that the Father raised him from the dead. Galatians 1:3–4 not only expresses a greeting but also describes the Lord Jesus Christ as the one "who gave himself for our sins." The use of the active participle and reflexive pronoun (τοῦ δόντος ἑαυτόν) clearly portray Jesus's death as an act of self-giving, a voluntary death. The preposition ὑπέρ with the genitive of thing (our sins) assumes the force of a purpose clause. BDAG forcefully states that the construction used here "must be variously translated . . . *in order to atone for (the) sins* or *to remove them*"[1] and lists Gal 1:4 among several examples.

Paul states that one purpose of Jesus's atoning death is "to rescue us from this present evil age." Paul's opponents might argue that the view that forgiveness is based on Christ's substitutionary atonement alone and that believers are not obligated to keep the Torah fosters reckless and immoral behavior. Paul anticipated the objection even before it was raised and insisted that Jesus's sacrificial death was not only intended to grant the believer forgiveness but also to rescue him from the corrupting influences of a depraved age.[2] This and nothing less fulfilled God's will for the believer. The believer is rescued from the present evil age when he recognizes that he belongs to the coming age and begins to live in light of this awareness (Rom 12:2; Col. 3:1–17).[3] The coming age is the resurrection age, the era of new creation in which the believer will be fully delivered from his corruption, and is the age in which Christ will bring all things into subjection. Galatians 6:15 shows that this new creation has already begun as Christ transforms believers, and the new creation that they have experienced is now their standard for living (Gal 6:16).

Galatians 2:20 will clarify that Jesus's atoning death is substitutionary. Jesus gave himself for our sins (Gal 1:4), but he also "loved me and gave himself for me" (2:20). Galatians 3:10–14 will confirm the substitutionary nature of Jesus's sacrifice. However, Gal 2:20 shows that Jesus's death is also participatory: "I have been crucified with Christ." Jesus not only dies *for* and *instead of* the believer; he involves the believer in his death so that when Jesus dies, the believer also dies together with him. Jesus's crucifixion was a co-crucifixion due to the believer's union with Christ. The "I" who

---

[1] "ὑπέρ," BDAG, 1030. Douglas Moo detects the influence of Isaiah 53 here. Moo, *Galatians*, BECNT (Grand Rapids: Baker Academic, 2012), 72.

[2] Paul is also anticipating another element of his argument against the Judaizers: the Torah belongs to this age rather than to the age in which believers belong. See Richard Longenecker, *Galatians*, WBC (Dallas: Word, 1990), 9; David DeSilva, *Galatians*, NICNT (Grand Rapids: Eerdmans, 2018), 120.

[3] Moo rightly states: "In keeping with the typical NT perspective of inaugurated eschatology, Paul claims that, though this present evil age continues in force, believers are rescued from this present age of evil, sin, and death and find their true identity in the new age that has broken into history through Christ's epochal death and resurrection." Moo, *Galatians*, 72.

experienced this crucifixion refers to the believer's previous identity when he was enslaved to sin (3:22), the law (2:16; 3:23; 4:24–25), and false gods (4:8; cf. 4:3). With the death of the old "I," a new "me" came into existence. This "me" is indwelled by Christ (2:20) who influences the way that Paul lives every aspect of his life. Longenecker is probably correct that the "righteousness" that results from Jesus's death in Gal 2:21 is both forensic (thus appealing to the discussion in verses 15–16) and ethical (referring to the discussion in verses 17–20).[4] Jesus's death results in the believer's new standing before God and a new identity and character that produces righteous living.

Paul revisits the theme of his participation in Jesus's death at the conclusion of this letter (Gal 6:14). By his involvement in Jesus's crucifixion, Paul was "crucified . . . to the world." The "world" is roughly equivalent to "this present evil age" and refers to the dangerous influence of a corrupt society over which sin reigns. Crucifixion to the world and of the world initiates the "new creation" (6:15) which is the basis for the believer's new character and behavior.[5]

Paul's most detailed explanation of Jesus's atoning death in this letter appears in Gal 3:10–14. Through his death, Christ "redeemed us from the curse of the law" (v. 13). The "curse of the law" refers to the curse described in Gal 3:10, the curse incurred by those who relied on the works of the law to secure salvation but failed to keep the law perfectly. Paul argued that no one is justified before God by the law since justification through the law required keeping all of the law all of the time. Paul adds the word "everything" to his quotation of Deut 27:26 to emphasize the necessity of perfect obedience to the law.[6] This addition, however, is no distortion of the text that he cites since the immediate context of the verse repeatedly stressed keeping "all his commands" (cf. Deut 27:1; 28:1, 15). Paul also stresses that a person who relies on the law must "remain" or "continue" in it. The force of the Greek construction (ἐμμένει . . . τοῦ ποιῆσαι) is not fully captured by the reduction of the two verbs to "do" (CSB). Many

---

[4] Longenecker, *Galatians*, 95.

[5] Moo, *A Theology of Paul and His Letters*, 84–86 (see chap. 5, n. 27).

[6] Paul is not following the LXX, but his wording is similar to the sense of the LXX which used the expression, "in all the words of this law."

translations use expressions such as "continue," "keep on," or even add the adverb "always" (NIV, NET, and NCV respectively) to demonstrate that the verb prohibits even a single departure from God's commands. As the citation of Deut 27:26 implies, the "curse" is detailed in Deut 27:9–26 and 28:15–68. To be redeemed from this curse is to be rescued from the consequences of breaking God's commandments, to escape the punishment for breaking God's covenant.[7] Jesus accomplished this redemption by "becoming a curse for us" (Gal 3:13). Paul argues that the very form of Roman execution which Jesus suffered demonstrates that he suffered the curse of the covenant. Roman crucifixion, in which a person was hung by nails to a piece of wood, was so similar to the treatment of the corpse of someone who had committed a capital offense in Deut 21:23 that few Jewish readers would have had any doubt that Jesus died under a divine curse.[8] This is probably what Paul refers to as the "offense of the cross" (Gal 5:11) and why he refers to "Christ crucified" as a "stumbling block to the Jews" (1 Cor 1:23). If Jesus were truly the Messiah, how could he have died under God's curse? Galatians 3:13 supplies the answer. Christ did not merely become a curse. He became a curse "for us." Longenecker follows Klaus Berger in referring to the curse that Jesus suffered as an "exchange curse" (*ein Tauschgeschäft*).[9] Jesus suffered the curse deserved by those who had broken the covenant so they could escape the curse of the covenant. One can hardly imagine a clearer reference to Jesus's penal substitutionary atonement.[10]

Paul continues by describing the granting of the Spirit as a purpose of Jesus's sacrificial death (Gal 3:14). Although Paul does not explain how Jesus's death resulted in believers receiving the Spirit in this context, he likely assumes here what he will later explicitly state—Jesus's death is the sacrifice that enacts the new covenant (1 Cor 11:25) in which the Spirit is given to God's people (Joel 2:28–32; Ezek 36:22–32; Isa 44:3). The Spirit

---

[7] Moo, *A Theology of Paul and His Letters*, 71–72.

[8] This seems implied by the many references to Jesus hanging "on a tree" (Acts 5:30; 10:39; 13:29; 1 Pet 2:24). See Timothy George, *Galatians*, NAC (Nashville: B&H, 1994), 238–39.

[9] Longenecker, *Galatians*, 121.

[10] George suggests that this text is "the genesis of the Christian doctrine of penal substitutionary atonement." George, *Galatians*, 240.

will transform believers so that their lives are characterized by the qualities listed in Gal 5:22–23, qualities leading to a lifestyle consistent with the law's moral demands. Thus, Jesus's death not only results in redemption from the curse deserved because of sin but even redemption from the character that promoted sin.

1–2 Thessalonians

Paul's letters to the Thessalonians make few references to Jesus's salvific work. First Thessalonians mentions Jesus's death on two occasions (1 Thess 2:15; 4:14). Paul also identifies Jesus as the one "who rescues us from the coming wrath" (1:10). This "wrath" will be poured out in the "sudden destruction" that accompanies the great Day of the Lord, a destruction which sinners cannot possibly escape on their own (5:2–3). Initially, Paul does not directly link Jesus's death with this rescue from wrath. We may presume that Paul feels no need to do so because he had explained how Jesus's death was the basis for divine forgiveness and salvation from sin clearly and recently in his preaching in Thessalonica.[11] However, Paul explicitly connects Jesus's death and the sinner's forgiveness in 1 Thess 5:9–10: "For God did not appoint us to wrath, but to obtain salvation through our Lord Jesus Christ, who died for us, so that whether we are awake or asleep, we may live together with him." Gordon Fee correctly observes that this clause "presents us with all the essential data for Paul's understanding of 'salvation in Christ.' In Paul's own order—the *goal*: 'the obtaining of salvation'; the *agent*: 'through our Lord Jesus Christ'; and the *means*: 'who died on our behalf.'"

The statement that Jesus "died for us" once again implies more than that Jesus's death was for our benefit. The association with rescue from wrath and obtaining salvation suggests that Jesus bore the wrath of God in the sinner's place in order to rescue the sinner from the coming wrath and grant them salvation.[12] Jeffrey Weima wrote:

---

[11] Gene L. Green, *The Letters to the Thessalonians*, PNTC (Grand Rapids: Eerdmans, 2002), 243; Jeffrey Weima, *1–2 Thessalonians*, BECNT (Grand Rapids: Baker, 2014), 368.

[12] Cf. G. K. Beale, *1–2 Thessalonians*, IVP New Testament Commentary (Downers Grove: IVP, 2003), 154.

As brief as the prepositional phrase "for us" may be, it clearly has in view the substitutionary character of Christ's death for believer's sins. This can be deduced from a number of instances in Paul's Letters where he uses either exactly the same language ("to die for": Rom. 5:6; 14:15; 1 Cor. 15:3; 2 Cor. 5:15) or similar wording ("to give oneself for": Gal. 1:3–4; 2:20; Rom. 8:32; Eph. 5:25; 1 Tim. 2:6; Titus 2:14) and then follows up these phrases with explicit statements about the atoning consequence of Christ's death.[13]

Jesus's death enables the repentant sinner to "live together with him," the blessed state promised earlier in 1 Thess 4:17.

Figure 11: The Work of Christ in Paul's Early Letters

Scripture Passage	Content
Gal 1:4	Christ died a voluntary death to atone for sin and rescue believers from corruption.
Gal 2:20	Christ's death was a substitutionary act and an act in which the believer participates and shares in Jesus's experience.
Gal 3:10–14	Christ redeemed believers from the curses of the Mosaic covenant by suffering those curses in their place. Jesus's death enacts the new covenant and imparts the Spirit to believers.
Gal 6:14	The believer died to the world by participation in Jesus's crucifixion.
1 Thess 1:10	Christ rescues believers from the coming wrath.
1 Thess 5:9–10	Christ grants salvation to believers by dying for them. Because of Jesus's death, believers will live together with him.

---

[13] Weima, *1–2 Thessalonians*, 368.

Chief Letters

1 Corinthians

First Corinthians stresses the importance of Jesus's atoning death. Paul rebukes those who say, "I belong to Paul," by asking, "Was Paul crucified for you?" (1 Cor 1:12–13). His point is that the Corinthians only truly belong to the one who was crucified for them and that person is Christ. The expression "for you" clearly expresses the sacrificial and even substitutionary nature of Jesus's crucifixion.

Paul's major concern over the Corinthians' desire to have the gospel preached with "eloquent wisdom" was that the cross of Christ would be "emptied of its effect" (1 Cor 1:17). Paul spends most of several chapters arguing the message about the cross is so powerful on its own that no preacher needs to add his own human wisdom to it.[14] Paul clearly sees the simple message of the cross as sufficient for the salvation of any sinner. He refers to his gospel as "the word of the cross" (v. 18), the message of "Christ crucified" (v. 23), and exclaims, "I decided to know nothing among you except Jesus Christ and him crucified" (1 Cor 2:2).[15] Paul's gospel was intentionally centered on Jesus's atoning death.

The emphasis on the importance of Jesus's crucifixion at the beginning of this letter is matched by a similar emphasis at the end of the letter. In 1 Cor 15:3, Paul identified the truths that he passed on to the Corinthians in his personal ministry in Corinth. The first truth is that "Christ died for our sins according to the Scriptures." As seen in previous discussions, the prepositional phrase "for our sins" portrays Jesus's death as sacrificial and substitutionary. Jesus died to pay the penalty for the sins of others. The Scriptures to which Paul referred as describing this sacrificial death include

---

[14] Brian Rosner and Roy Ciampa noted that, "as 1 Corinthians 1:10–4:17 itself demonstrates, for Paul even the most practical ills, such as divisions and problems of leadership in the church, are remedied by focusing on the cross. For Paul, Christ crucified is more than just the means of forgiveness and salvation; rather, it informs his total vision of the Christian life and ministry." Rosner and Ciampa, *1 Corinthians*, PNTC (Grand Rapids: Eerdmans, 2010), 114.

[15] This was not a new strategy that Paul was adopting but a resolution to continue his normal practice (Gal 3:1). See Gordon Fee, *The First Epistle to the Corinthians*, NICNT (Grand Rapids: Eerdmans, 2014), 94.

Isa 52:13–53:12,[16] but likely also include several of the Psalms as well as texts in Jeremiah and the Minor Prophets.[17] Due to the emphasis on Jesus's death in his preaching in Corinth, Paul feels little need in the Corinthian letters to go into the in-depth explanations of Jesus's death and its significance that he detailed in Romans. Nevertheless, several statements explain why Jesus's crucifixion is so important.

Paul confirms the sacrificial nature of Jesus's death in 1 Cor 5:7. He urges the Corinthians to purge the leaven of malice and evil from among them like the Jews purged leaven from their households during the Feast of Unleavened Bread held in conjunction with Passover. This was appropriate since "Christ our Passover lamb has been sacrificed." Paul recognizes that it was no accident that Jesus was crucified at Passover. The timing of the crucifixion demonstrated that Jesus was the true Passover lamb. Just as the Passover lamb was slain to ensure that destruction would "pass over" the households which applied the lamb's blood to their door frames, Christ was slain so that the wrath of God would pass over believers. Paul explains that because of Jesus's Passover sacrifice, "indeed you are [a new unleavened batch]." Leaven, dough which had fermented, served as an appropriate symbol for the sinner's corruption—his moral rot. In 1 Cor 5:8, Paul associates leaven with "malice and evil." Just as Passover required Israelites to locate and remove any leaven from their houses (Exod 12:14–20) and their entire territory (Exod 13:6–7), Jesus's Passover sacrifice resulted in a metaphorical purging of the leaven in which the Corinthian believers were cleansed of evil.

Paul uses two powerful adjectives to describe the spiritual state of believers that resulted from Jesus's sacrifice. They are "new" (νέος), a term Paul uses in Col 3:10 to describe the believer's new identity, character, and practices that result from being renewed according to the image of the Creator. This "newness" is the result of the believer's spiritual circumcision and his participation in Jesus's death, burial, and resurrection (Col 2:11–13). They are

---

[16] Thomas Schreiner, *1 Corinthians*, TNTC (Downers Grove: IVP Academic, 2018), 303.

[17] C. H. Dodd, *According to the Scriptures*, 126–27, demonstrates that large sections of these OT Scriptures were interpreted in light of their whole contexts and based "upon intelligible and consistent principles," and this material "in particular . . . provided the starting point for the theological constructions of Paul, the author to the Hebrews, and the Fourth Evangelist."

also "unleavened," purged of the evil that previously permeated every aspect of their lives. The two terms combine to portray the dramatic change that Christ wrought in the believer in which former sexually immoral people, idolaters, those engaged in sexual perversions, thieves, greedy people, drunkards, verbally abusive people and swindlers were "washed," "sanctified," and "justified" (1 Cor 6:9–11). Believers should seek to live daily in light of this transformation (1 Cor 5:8). Thus, Jesus's Passover sacrifice not only ensures that the believer will be protected from divine wrath, but it also ensures that they will live a new life of purity, sincerity, and truth.[18]

These two benefits of Jesus's sacrifice also surface in 1 Cor 11:23–26. Paul recognizes the significance of Jesus's words at the Last Supper: "This cup is the new covenant in my blood" (v. 25). Jesus's death on the cross is both an atoning sacrifice and the sacrifice that enacts the new covenant. The new covenant promises forgiveness (Jer 31:34) and transformation since God's teaching is etched on the believer's heart (Jer 31:33) so that he is compelled from within to obey God's instructions, and God places his Spirit in the believer to "cause you [him] to follow my statutes and carefully observe my ordinances" (Ezek 36:27). The new covenant causes the believer to "serve in the newness of the Spirit" (Rom 7:6), to fulfill "the law's requirement" (Rom 8:4; cf. 8:1), and results in life and righteousness (2 Cor 3:1–18).

2 Corinthians

Paul's first description of Christ's atoning work in 2 Corinthians is difficult to understand since the statement is elliptical. Most recent commentators interpret 2 Cor 5:14 to mean, "If one [Christ] died for all, then all died [in or with Christ]."[19] This death in Christ is variously interpreted as death to

---

[18] David Garland commented: "What is important to Paul in this context is that Christ's death is supposed to effect a change in their moral behavior." Garland, *1 Corinthians*, BECNT (Grand Rapids: Baker, 2003), 180.

[19] For examples of this view, see George Guthrie, *2 Corinthians*, BECNT (Grand Rapids: Baker, 2015), 305; Ralph Martin, *2 Corinthians*, WBC 40, 2nd ed. (Grand Rapids: Zondervan, 2014), 289–90; Mark Seifrid, *The Second Letter to the Corinthians*, PNTC (Grand Rapids: Eerdmans, 2014), 244; Linda Belleville, *2 Corinthians*, IVP New Testament Commentary (Downers Grove: IVP, 1996), 150–51; David Garland,

self,[20] dying to death as the penalty for sin,[21] or experience of the condemnation sin deserved through Christ's substitution.[22] However, many commentators are clearly troubled by their own conclusions and consequently argue either that all only potentially died with or in Christ[23] or that all (which referred to humanity universally in the first clause) must refer only to "his people" or "those who accept Jesus" in the second clause.[24]

Although one is naturally hesitant to reject this modern consensus, Chrysostom's position seems to make better sense. Chrysostom argued, "That if one died for all, then all died" means that Jesus died "because all were lost" and explained, "For except all were dead, He had not died for all."[25] Chrysostom's view takes the particle ἄρα as expressing an inference rather than a result. In other words, the idea is not that all died as a consequence of Christ's death on their behalf. Instead, Christ's death for all established the fact that all were previously under the sentence of death and thus needed substitutionary atonement. R. V. G. Tasker dismissed Chrysostom's view "because it construes the aorist *apethanon* as if it was an imperfect."[26] But it does no such thing. In Chrysostom's view, the aorist ἀπέθανον matches the aorist ἀπέθανον in Rom 5:15. The statements "all died" in 2 Cor 5:14 and "many died" in Rom 5:15 are equivalent since Rom 5:12 identifies the many who died as "all people." Chrysostom appears to have remembered that Paul, in his earlier correspondence with the Corinthians (1 Cor 15:22) had described the death of all as a result of participation in Adam, *not* Christ.

---

2 Corinthians, NAC (Nashville: B&H, 1999), 279–80; Paul Barnett, *The Second Epistle to the Corinthians*, NICNT (Grand Rapids: Eerdmans, 1997), 290.

[20] Martin, *2 Corinthians*, 289.

[21] Barnett, *Second Epistle to the Corinthians*, 290.

[22] Guthrie, *2 Corinthians*, 305; Seifrid, *Second Letter to the Corinthians*, 244; Garland, *2 Corinthians*, 280.

[23] Barnett, *Second Epistle to the Corinthians*, 290; Seifrid refers to an "interruption between Christ's accomplishment of salvation and its distribution by the Gospel, an interruption that remains unexplored and unexplained by the apostle" and which "cannot be bridged by any rational formula." Seifrid, *Second Letter to the Corinthians*, 244.

[24] Martin, *2 Corinthians*, 289; Belleville, *2 Corinthians*, 150–51.

[25] Chrysostom, *Hom. 2 Cor.* 11.3 (*NPNF*[1] 12, 331–32).

[26] R. V. G. Tasker, *The Second Epistle of Paul to the Corinthians*, TNTC (Grand Rapids: Eerdmans, 1958), 86.

Union with Adam results in death; union with Christ results in life. Paul maintains this same distinction in his most detailed comparison of Adam and Christ (Rom 5:14–15, 17, 18). Thus, Paul's line of thought here is from solution to plight. Christ's death for all establishes the fact that all died in Adam. Many commentators have rightly seen that the categories "in Adam" and "in Christ" are key to understanding 2 Cor 5:14. Unfortunately, they appear to overlook the distinctions between the two categories that Paul carefully and consistently delineated.

This understanding prevents the puzzling inconsistency of identifying the "all" in the first clause as all humanity and in the very next clause as all believers. "All" in both clauses of 2 Cor 5:14 is roughly equivalent to "the world" in verse 19. If the understanding of the logical relationship between the two clauses in 5:14 explained above is correct, the "all" for whom Christ died includes all who died in Adam. Thus, Guthrie is correct that Paul's statement is inconsistent with a view of limited atonement that denies the sufficiency of Jesus's atoning work to accomplish the salvation of the world.[27]

Jesus's death for all imposes on all the responsibility and obligation of living, not "for themselves," but "for the one who died for them and was raised" (2 Cor 5:15). The thought here is similar to the portrayal of Jesus's death as an act that purchased those that it ransomed and redeemed in 1 Cor 6:19–20 and 7:23. Those so purchased are obligated to live as Jesus's obedient servants.

Second Corinthians 5:19 shows that God was reconciling to himself people who had been alienated from him because of sin. God accomplished this work of reconciliation in and through Christ. The great barrier to the restoration of God's relationship with humanity was sin. Thus, reconciliation required forgiveness, "not counting their trespasses against them." The preceding context has already explained how God's righteousness and justice are maintained in this process. "Their trespasses" were counted against Jesus when "one died for all." The following context (2 Cor 5:21) will offer a still more detailed explanation.

Second Corinthians 5:21 raises difficult questions, however, regarding the extent of the atonement. The "world" in 5:19 is the entire human world, all those who were in Adam. Thus, the verse may seem to imply that

---

[27] Guthrie, *2 Corinthians*, 305.

all humanity has been both forgiven and reconciled to God in Christ. The grammar and structure of this verse is rather complicated. Important decisions made in the syntactical analysis of the verse will significantly impact the theological implications of the verse. If one follows those translations that take the verbal construction as an imperfect periphrastic (CSB, NET, NIV),[28] the imperfect may be inceptive: "God was beginning to reconcile," in which case the completion of the reconciliation may require the sinner's repentance and faith.[29] On the other hand, Harris supports the translation, "God was in Christ, reconciling the world to himself" (cf. NASB, NLT, CEV) and suggests that the participle is "less verbal than adjectival in import" and could almost be translated "as a reconciler."[30] Neither sense would affirm that God actually reconciled the entire world to himself or forgave the sins of the entire world, but only that he made this reconciliation and forgiveness possible. This would explain why Paul must still urge sinners, "Be reconciled to God" (2 Cor 5:20), a plea which indicates that reconciliation and forgiveness of the entire world was not an accomplished fact but, in some sense, depended on the sinner's decision to be reconciled and forgiven. It also explains the shift from the reference to the "world" in 2 Cor 5:19 to the much more exclusive "us" and "we" in 5:21.

Second Corinthians 5:21 explains how God maintains his own righteousness when "not counting their trespasses against them" (5:19). God made the sinless One to be sin for us. The description of the Savior as the "one who did not know sin" means that Jesus had no familiarity or personal experience with sin because he never sinned in any way (John 7:18; 8:46; 14:30; 1 John 3:5, 7; Heb 4:15; 7:26–28; 9:14; 1 Pet 1:19; 2:22; 3:18). This sinlessness qualified Jesus to become the substitute for sinners

---

[28] The imperfect periphrastic is rare in Paul (Gal 1:22–23; Phil 2:26). Furthermore, the structure here is different from Paul's other uses of the construction. See Murray Harris, *The Second Epistle to the Corinthians*, NIGTC (Grand Rapids: Eerdmans, 2005), 441–42.

[29] Martin argues that "the periphrastic tense (participle + verb ἦν, "was") denotes an element of contingency, in that although the reconciliation is complete from God's side, there is the possibility that some people may not accept it. . . ." Martin, *2 Corinthians*, 314. Similarly, Garland notes, "The imperfect tenses convey the idea of incomplete action, but it is incomplete only in the sense that God's act of reconciliation requires a human response." Garland, *2 Corinthians*, 293.

[30] Harris, *The Second Epistle to the Corinthians*, 439–40.

and is reminiscent of the "unblemished" state of sacrificial animals that were fit for the altar (e.g., Exod 12:5, 29:1; Lev 1:3, 10; 4:3). God caused him "to be sin." Some translations (CJB, NLT) assume that the word "sin" (ἁμαρτία) refers to a sin offering, a sense that the word carries in several OT texts (Exod 29:14; Lev 4:24; Num 18:9).[31] However, neither Paul nor other NT writers use the term elsewhere in this way. The statement means that God treated Jesus as sin—the very embodiment and personification of sin—during his suffering on the cross. Jesus bore the guilt of the sins of others and suffered the divine wrath that those sins deserved.[32] Harris expresses the idea well: "In a sense beyond human comprehension, God treated Christ as 'sin,' aligning him so totally with sin and its dire consequences that from God's viewpoint he became indistinguishable from sin itself."[33] He did so "for us" (ὑπὲρ ἡμῶν), a phrase which consistently expresses both benefit and substitution.

The result of the imputation of our sin to Christ is "so that in him we might become the righteousness of God." While the verb "might" implies contingency in English, no element of contingency exists in the Greek text, and although the aorist verb is in the subjunctive mood, this is required by the use of ἵνα which expresses result. As a result of the imputation of our sin to the sinless one, we become the righteousness of God. Just as "was made sin" refers to status and standing, (Jesus being treated as a sinner rather than transformed into one so that he personally sinned), "become the righteousness of God" refers to status and standing, rather than transformation. Paul certainly affirms that a transformation takes place (2 Cor 5:17), but that is not his point here. In 2 Cor 3:9, "righteousness" was the opposite of "condemnation." Here also, "righteousness" is forensic. God does not count our trespasses *against* us (2 Cor 5:19) because he counts Christ's righteousness *for* us.

---

[31] This view has a rich heritage reaching back to Ambrosiaster and Augustine. See S. Lyonnet and L. Sabourin, *Sin, Redemption, and Sacrifice: A Biblical and Patristic Study,* AB 48 (Rome: Biblical Institute, 1971), 185–296.

[32] See esp. Harris, *2 Corinthians*, 453–54. Chrysostom, *Hom.* 2 Cor. 11.5, rightly interpreted the expression, "[Jesus] suffered as a sinner to be condemned, as one cursed to die" and bore "not only punishment, but also disgrace." He interprets the "righteousness of God" as "when we are justified not by works . . . but by grace."

[33] Harris, *2 Corinthians*, 454.

Romans

Since the primary theme of Romans is "the gospel of God" (Rom 1:1), we might expect this letter to contain repeated references to Jesus's saving work. Romans more than fulfills that expectation. Even the introduction to the letter, which focuses more on Christ's identity than his work, refers to Jesus as the "powerful" Son of God (1:4). The Son's power is primarily a reference to his power to save sinners, the same power specified in Rom 1:16.

Romans 3:21–26, one of the key soteriological passages in the letter, explains that Jesus saves sinners through his sacrificial death. Rather than using the noun ἱλασμός, meaning "atoning sacrifice" (1 John 2:2; 4:10), Paul uses the cognate term ἱλαστήριον. In early Jewish and Christian literature, the term often refers to a "place" of atonement. The term was used in the LXX (Exod 25:17, 18, 19, 20 [2x], 21, 22; 31:7; 35:12; 38:5, 7 [2x], 8; Lev 16:2 [2x], 13, 14 [2x], 15 [2x]; Num 7:89), the Pseudepigrapha, Philo, and Hebrews (Heb 9:5) to refer to the "mercy seat" which was sprinkled with blood from the slaughtered sin offering on the Day of Atonement.[34] Early Greek church fathers such as Origen (3rd c.) and Theodoret of Cyrrhus (5th c.) as well as the Latin fathers affirmed that Paul's use of the term was based on the Old Testament sacrificial system and referred to the atonement cover of the ark of the covenant. This understanding was affirmed by the Protestant reformers as well. Although this view has been vigorously challenged by scholars such as Adolf Deissmann and C. H. Dodd, many modern commentators still affirm it.[35] The New English Translation follows this interpretation of Rom 3:25: "God publicly displayed him at his death as the mercy seat accessible through faith." The most recent update of the CSB similarly translates the clause, "God presented him as the mercy seat by his blood, through faith."

---

[34] Amos 9:1 and Ezek 43:14 (3x), 17, 20, use the term to refer to the "propitiatory," the area of the temple in which the sacrificial altar was located.

[35] See esp. the discussion in Douglas Moo, *The Letter to the Romans*, NICNT, 2nd ed. (Grand Rapids: Eerdmans, 2018), 252–58; Thomas Schreiner, *Romans*, BECNT, 2nd ed. (Grand Rapids: Baker, 2018), 202–3. For a detailed defense of this view, see N. S. L. Fryer, "The Meaning and Translation of ἱλαστήριον in Romans 3:25," *EQ* 59 (1987): 99–116; Daniel P. Bailey, "Jesus as the Mercy Seat: The Semantics and Theology of Paul's Use of *Hilasterion* in Romans 3:25" (PhD diss., University of Cambridge, 1999).

The interpretation of this relatively brief clause is affected by several exegetical decisions. For example, does the verb προτίθημι mean "offer" (cf. ESV) or "display publicly" (NASB, NET)? Does the noun ἱλαστήριον refer to an atoning sacrifice (NIV, ESV)[36] or to the mercy seat (CSB, NET)? And does the prepositional phrase "through his blood" modify the verb (CSB, NET, NASB1995) or the noun "faith" (KJV, LEB)? Although a detailed defense of the position is not possible here and some of these questions are difficult, the preponderance of evidence supports the view that God publicly displayed Jesus as the mercy seat where atonement is made. The blood that covered Jesus due to his brutal scourging and crucifixion served to identify him as the new mercy seat.[37] This blood that was splattered on Jesus's body provides atonement to those who believe.

The most extensive defense of a reference to the "mercy seat" in Romans 3:25 is by Daniel Bailey, who argued:

> By contrast [to the meaning "propitiatory gift" which does not fit the context of Rom 3:25], a more specialized allusion to the biblical "mercy seat" . . . does fit Paul's context, with plenty of support from lexicography (cf. LXX Pentateuch). Paul focuses on "the law and the prophets" and then more particularly on the Song of Moses in Exodus 15. The combination of God's righteousness and redemption in Exodus 15:13 (ὡδήγησας τῇ δικαιοσύνῃ σου τὸν λαόν σου τοῦτον, ὃν ἐλυτρώσω) closely parallels Romans 3:24 (δικαιόω and ἀπολύτρωσις). Furthermore, Exodus 15:17 promises that the exodus would lead to a new, ideal sanctuary established by God himself. God's open setting

---

[36] Although the NIV translates the noun as "sacrifice of atonement," it acknowledges in a footnote that the Greek noun "refers to the atonement cover on the ark of the covenant (see Lev. 16:15, 16)."

[37] Bailey, "Jesus as the Mercy Seat," 221, describes Rom 3:25 as referring to the "installation" of Jesus as the mercy seat and compares it to the reconsecration of the OT mercy seat by the sprinkling of blood in Lev 16:16: "As the old mercy seat and the shrine of which it was a part had to be reconsecrated and atoned for by the Yom Kippur blood rites once a year 'because of the impurities of the people of Israel and because of their iniquities, even concerning all their sins' (Lev 16:16 LXX), so now the death of Jesus is the ritual for his initial consecration or investiture (cf. ὁρίζω, Rom 1:4) as the mercy seat following not just a year and an entire age since which passed under God's forbearance (cf. ἐν τῇ ἀνοχῇ τοῦ θεοῦ)."

out of Jesus as the new ἱλαστήριον—the centre of the sanctuary and focus of both the revelation of God (Ex. 25:22; Lv. 16:2; Nu. 7:89) and atonement for sin (Leviticus 16)—fulfils this tradition.[38]

Bailey is mistaken, however, when he suggests that "the idea of atonement for sin is presupposed rather than emphasized"[39] by Paul. If Leviticus 16 provides the background to Rom 3:25 as Bailey recognizes, atonement is the primary focus.

By sprinkling the mercy seat with blood, the priest "will make atonement for the most holy place in this way for all their sins because of the Israelites' impurities and rebellious acts" (Lev 16:16). Although the sprinkling of the blood served to purify the objects in the Tent of Meeting,[40] this sprinkling at the same time secured atonement for the people. Mark Rooker insightfully states that although the scapegoat on the Day of Atonement "pictures the *effect* of atonement, the removal of guilt," the male goat whose blood was sprinkled on the mercy seat "pictures the *means* for atonement, the shedding of blood in the sacrificial death."[41] This view is confirmed by the description of the slaughtered goat as "the people's sin offering" (Lev 16:15; cf. 16:9). Paul's statement presents Jesus as both the place of atonement—the new mercy seat—and his death as the sacrifice that secures atonement—the new Day of Atonement sacrifice. A footnote in the NET objects that this view "creates a violent mixed metaphor" since "[w]ithin a few words Paul would switch from referring to Jesus as the place where atonement was made to referring to Jesus as the atoning sacrifice itself."[42] However, Thomas Schreiner persuasively argues that the mixed metaphors are part of Paul's intention of presenting Jesus as the comprehensive solution to the sin problem:

---

[38] Daniel P. Bailey, "Jesus as the Mercy Seat: The Semantics and Theology of Paul's Use of *Hilasterion* in Romans 3:25," *TynBul* 51 (2000): 155–58.

[39] Bailey, 211.

[40] Mark Rooker, *Leviticus*, NAC (Nashville: B&H, 2000), 218–19.

[41] Rooker, 221. Emphasis added.

[42] Oddly, the interpretation suggested in the NET does not seem to avoid this supposed problem. The NET follows Bailey's view that the mercy seat blood ritual was an initiation ritual (see especially Bailey, "Jesus as the Mercy Seat," 209–11) and the blood thus served to install Jesus as the new mercy seat of the eschatological temple. But even in this view, the blood is that shed by Jesus and his blood functions like that of the OT sacrifice.

That Jesus functioned as the priest, victim, and the place where the blood is sprinkled should not trouble us. Paul is trying to communicate that Jesus fulfills the sacrificial cultus, and the fulfillment transcends the cult. . . . What Jesus accomplished on the cross transcended previous categories and constituted their fulfillment.[43]

Paul associates Jesus's role as the mercy seat with several aspects of salvation. First, Paul associates Jesus's atoning work with justification (Rom 3:24), an act in which the divine judge pronounces the ungodly (Rom 4:5) righteous or, in the modern legal parlance, "not guilty."[44] Jesus's death was necessary if God was to maintain his own righteousness while declaring believers righteous (Rom 3:26). For God to judge the ungodly to be righteous apart from Jesus's atoning work would have compromised his own justice. The opposite of "justification" is "condemnation." Paul emphasizes later that Jesus's death prevented the believer's condemnation (Rom 8:34) which naturally led to the believer's justification. Romans 8:3 shows that Jesus suffered the condemnation that the sinner deserved in the sinner's place. Although Paul does not explicitly use the term for the OT "sin offering" in Rom 8:3, his phrase περὶ ἁμαρτίας is most frequently used in the LXX to refer to sacrifice[45] and the sacrificial connotations are obvious here. Christ became a fitting representative for sinful humanity by taking on flesh in his incarnation. His flesh was like that of fallen humanity and thus subject to physical exhaustion, sickness, and death. However, Paul's insistence that Jesus came in the "likeness" of sinful flesh preserves a distinction between Jesus and other humans. Jesus felt the full force of temptation but he never succumbed to temptation like all others do. However, God "condemned sin in the flesh," that is, in the flesh of Christ

---

[43] Schreiner, *Romans*, 202–3. See the similar argument in Fryer, "The Meaning and Translation of Hilasterion in Romans 3:25," 110. Fryer adds that Heb 9:11–22 portrays Jesus as both the high priest and the sacrificial victim which demonstrates "that in a typological interpretation of Christ's work we may expect to find an interplay of motifs which does not necessarily satisfy the precise definition demanded by modern logic."

[44] For an explanation of the most important features of Paul's doctrine of justification, see Andreas Köstenberger, Scott Kellum, and Charles Quarles, *The Cradle, the Cross, and the Crown: An Introduction to the New Testament*, 2nd ed. (Nashville: B&H Academic, 2016), 623–32.

[45] See Moo, *Romans*, 502n919.

Jesus. Jesus's physical body suffered the condemnation sinners deserved as their substitute. Because Christ suffered the believer's condemnation for him, "there is now no condemnation for those in Christ Jesus" (Rom 8:1).

Second, he links Jesus's atoning death with redemption (Rom 3:24). Redemption refers to the act of making the payment necessary to liberate a slave from bondage. In Eph 1:7 and Col 1:14, Paul defines redemption as the forgiveness of sins. In Titus 2:14, Christ offers himself as a sacrifice "to redeem us from all lawlessness and to cleanse for himself a people for his own possession, eager to do good works." Thus redemption includes not only forgiveness, but deliverance from slavery to sin and bringing people into Christ's possession to serve him as their Master (Rom 6:6–7, 17–18).

Romans 5:6 and 8 reaffirm the sacrificial nature of Jesus's death: "Christ died for the ungodly" and "while we were still sinners, Christ died for us." The allusions to those rare instances in which a person might be willing to die for someone who is just and good suggest that the preposition "for" (ὑπέρ) entails substitution and not just benefit.[46] When a person dies to save the life of another, he is dying for their sake; but he is also dying in their place. Paul adds that "we have now been justified by his blood" (Rom 5:9). Thus, present justification is the result of blood atonement, an allusion to the Day of Atonement ritual which provided the background for Paul's earlier discussion in Rom 3:25.

Paul extends his explanation of Jesus's atoning death in Rom 5:10. He clarifies that Jesus's death not only accomplishes atonement, justification, and redemption, it also results in reconciliation. Sinners were God's enemies. They declared open rebellion against God, defied his divine authority, shook a recalcitrant fist in his face, and ignored his holy commands. Although Paul often stresses the human dimension of this enmity (Rom 1:30; 8:7; Col 1:21), Kruse correctly observes: "But in the previous verse (5:9) Paul has just said that believers have been saved from 'God's wrath' through Christ, and this indicates that there was also hostility on God's side towards sinners."[47] God's wrath against sinners is no mere parenthetical thought. Paul has repeatedly warned that unrepentant sinners are under divine wrath (Rom 1:18; 2:5), and

---

[46] Cf. Grant Osborne, *Romans*, IVP New Testament Commentary (Downers Grove: IVP, 2004), 133.

[47] Kruse, *Romans*, 237.

this is a primary theme of the first major section of the letter (1:18–3:20). While sinners were in this state of enmity and thus alienated and estranged from God, God reconciled sinners to himself "through the death of his Son" (5:10). Through this reconciliation, the very sinners who had rebelled against God and were under his wrath now have peace with him (5:1). Those who were formerly God's enemies become God's friends. The full extent of this reconciliation will not become clear until Rom 8:12–17, which explains that believers are adopted by God so that they become his children and his heirs.

Romans 6:1–10 emphasizes that Jesus's death involved the participation of the believer and not merely substitution for the believer. Baptism, the moment of publicly confessing faith in and devotion to Christ, signified the believer's incorporation into Christ. Through union with Christ, the believer participated in Jesus's death, burial, and resurrection. The believer was "united with him in the likeness of his death" (6:5). Verse 6 results in three amazing benefits to the believer: 1) the "old self was crucified with him," 2) the "body ruled by sin" was stripped of its power, and 3) the believer was liberated from sin's mastery that he "may no longer be enslaved to sin." Paul will spell out the practical implications of this further in Rom 6:15–23. Through participation in Jesus's death (and resurrection), the believer is emancipated from slavery to sin and enslaved to God and righteousness.

Romans 14:9 illuminates another dimension of Paul's theology of Jesus's death. Paul has argued in the preceding context that the believer belongs entirely to the Lord Jesus so that every aspect of his existence—including observance of days, eating, living and dying—is for the Lord's glory and pleasure. Paul grounds this claim on the assertion that "Christ died and returned to life for this: that he might be Lord over both the dead and the living." Although "Lord" often serves in Romans as a substitute for the divine name, in Rom 14:4 it referred to the master of a household servant. That nuance likely continues in 14:6, 8–9 (though this does not prohibit the term from implying Jesus's deity even in this context). Christ's death establishes his lordship over believers. Paul will explain precisely why this is true in 1 Cor 6:19–20: "You are not your own, for you were bought at a price." He reaffirms this principle in 1 Cor 7:22–23: "He who is called as a free man is Christ's slave. You were bought at a price." Christ's death was a ransom price which emancipated believers from their slavery to sin but also made them Christ's property and established him as their new master (cf. Eph 6:9; Col 4:1).

Romans 15:3 appeals to Jesus's sacrificial death in an ethical exhortation. Believers should live sacrificially and curtail even some of their own liberties for the sake of those whose consciences are weak. They should not live to please themselves (Rom 15:1). Christ is the supreme example of this selfless, sacrificial lifestyle: "For even Christ did not please himself" (Rom 15:3). The ascensive καί ("even") implies that if anyone ever deserved to pursue his own pleasure and live for himself, Christ certainly did. Yet he relinquished that right for the benefit of others (cf. Phil 2:6–8). Paul cites Ps 69:9 in support because he sees clear parallels between the psalmist's experience and the experience of Christ who suffered great insults while he hung on the cross. Although the emphasis in Paul's explanation of Jesus's death in Romans clearly lands primarily on penal substitutionary atonement and secondarily on the believer's participation in that death, Paul also sees the sacrificial nature of Jesus's death as setting an example of other-centeredness that is vital to true Christian living.

Figure 12: The Work of Christ in Paul's Chief Letters

Scripture Passage	Content
1 Cor 1:18, 23; 2:2	Christ's death on the cross is the heart of the gospel message.
1 Cor 5:7	Christ's death was like that of the Passover lamb. His death caused God's wrath to pass over the believer and resulted in the purging of their corruption so that they enjoy a new identity and character.
1 Cor 6:19–20	Christ's death purchased believers so they belong to him and should be devoted to his service.
1 Cor 11:23–26	Christ's death atones for sin and enacts the new covenant.
1 Cor 15:3	Christ's death was sacrificial and substitutionary. His atoning death fulfilled the Scriptures and is of the greatest importance.

2 Cor 5:14	Christ died for all people since all were under the sentence of death.
2 Cor 5:15	Christ's death purchased sinners so they belong to him and should live for him.
2 Cor 5:19	Through Christ, God forgave and reconciled sinners to himself.
2 Cor 5:21	Christ bore the guilt of the sins of others and suffered the divine wrath that they deserved so that they may be declared righteous in God's sight.
Rom 1:4	Jesus is the Son of God with the power to save (cf. 1:16).
Rom 3:24–25	Christ's bloody death marked him as the "mercy seat" where God provides atonement. Jesus's death accomplishes the believer's justification and redemption.
Rom 5:6, 8	Christ died as the substitute for ungodly sinners.
Rom 5:10	Christ's death reconciles sinners to God.
Rom 6:1–10	The believer participated in Jesus's death so that he is liberated from slavery to sin and his character is transformed.
Rom 8:3	Jesus suffered the condemnation that sinners deserve in their place.
Rom 14:9	Christ purchased believers by his death so that he has become their master and they his servants.
Rom 15:3	Christ's death serves as a profound example to believers of selflessness and sacrifice for the benefit of others.

The Prison Letters

Philippians

In Phil 2:5–8, Paul presents the incarnation, condescension, and crucifixion of Jesus as the greatest examples of humility, treating others as more important than oneself, and prioritizing the interests of others above one's own (Phil 2:3–4). Jesus's crucifixion is an act of supreme obedience to the Father's will. He obeyed God to the point of laying down his life in the most humiliating and scandalous fashion—by being nailed to a cross. The Father responded to Jesus's humble obedience by conferring on him the name that is above every other name, the divine name, Lord. Paul then applies to Jesus an OT text (Isa 45:23) describing the worship of Yahweh. The conferral of the divine name and the worship and confession of Jesus as God show that the depth of Jesus's humiliation was matched by the height of his exaltation. Jesus's experience in humbling himself and then being exalted by God illustrates and confirms Jesus's teaching that "whoever humbles himself will be exalted" (Matt 23:12; cf. Matt 18:4).

In Phil 3:10, Paul's attention shifts from Jesus's death as an example to his death as an event in which believers participate by virtue of their union with Christ. To know and experience "the fellowship of his sufferings, being conformed to his death" means to recognize that the believer suffered and died together with Christ (Gal 2:19; Rom 6:6) and to live in light of that participation in Jesus's death by considering himself dead to sin and alive to God (Rom 6:11).[48] In light of the description of Jesus's crucifixion in 2:8, conformity to Jesus's death produces selfless obedience to God that places the needs of others above one's own.

Paul later refers to those who are enslaved to their sensual appetites[49] as enemies of the cross of Christ (Phil 3:18–19). They neither exhibit the moral transformation that results from death with Christ nor follow the example

---

[48] See Richard Melick, *Philippians, Colossians, Philemon*, NAC (Nashville: B&H, 1991), 136; Gerald Hawthorne and Ralph Martin, *Philippians*, WBC 43, rev. ed. (Nashville: Thomas Nelson, 2004), 199.

[49] The context supports the identification of those for whom Paul wept as the immoral and self-indulgent rather than Jewish legalists. See Chrysostom, Hom. Phil. 13; Walter Hansen, *Philippians*, PNTC (Grand Rapids: Eerdmans, 2009), 265–66.

of Jesus's selfless obedience. Perhaps they claim to be "friends" of the cross because they affirm that forgiveness was provided through Jesus's death, but they are, in fact, enemies of the cross because they deny the transformation of the believer effected through Jesus's death.

Ephesians

Paul opens Ephesians with praise to God for all the spiritual blessings that he has bestowed on the believer through Christ. Throughout this doxology, Paul repeatedly uses the expression ἐν Χριστῷ which is ordinarily translated "in Christ," implying that the believer's incorporation into Christ and union with him is essential to experiencing "every spiritual blessing" (Eph 1:3). However, the preposition ἐν is capable of expressing a wide variety of nuances. The Greek preposition is clearly not a simple equivalent of the similar sounding English preposition. The preposition sometimes serves as a marker of personal agency.[50] The use of the less ambiguous διά with the genitive to express intermediate agency in Eph 1:5 suggests that ἐν Χριστῷ has a similar sense here.[51]

Ephesians 1:7 identifies Jesus as the personal agent through whom the Father provided redemption. Redemption involves offering payment to deliver someone from bondage or punishment. The redemption price was "his blood," a reference to Jesus's atoning death. However, the term "blood" raises important associations with the blood sacrifices of the OT that a simple reference to death would not (cf. Exod 12:7; 23:18; 24:8; etc.). An appositional construction defines "redemption" as consisting primarily (though not exclusively) of "the forgiveness of our trespasses." This suggests that the

---

[50] "ἐν," BDAG, 329.

[51] Andrew Lincoln suggests that the construction in Paul most frequently means "through Christ's agency." However, he sees an additional nuance of incorporation in this doxology. Lincoln, *Ephesians*, WBC 42 (Dallas: Word, 1980), 21. John A. Allan argued that "the most characteristic use" of the phrase in Ephesians is the instrumental sense and that the uses of parallel phrases in Ephesians in which the preposition marks both the personal instrument and an impersonal instrument "point unmistakably to this instrumental sense." He adds, "It is no doubt possible to read into any or all of these the deeper Pauline meaning, but in every case it is possible to give a very satisfactory interpretation of the verse on the basis of a simply instrumental use of the formula." Allan, "The 'In Christ' Formula in Ephesians," *NTS* 5 (1958): 54–62.

notion of redemption in this context is rescue from punishment more than release from bondage.

In Eph 2:13–16, Jesus's atoning death is the basis on which Gentiles who were "far away" from God "have been brought near." Again, Paul refers to Jesus's death as "the blood of Christ," recalling the blood rituals of the OT. In reconciling both Jews and Gentiles to God, he also reconciled the two groups to each other. He replaced hostility with peace and created from the two groups "one new man," a new humanity in which old distinctions no longer matter. Since Jesus's death effected the new covenant which replaces the old covenant, he nullified the law with its many ordinances intended to separate Jew from Gentile. Thus it was through the cross that the old hostility between Jew and Gentile was put to death at last (Eph 2:16).

Sacrificial imagery surfaces again in 5:2. Christ's love for sinners compelled him to "give himself for us." The use of the reflexive pronoun and the insistence that Christ's love motivated him to give himself combine to emphasize the voluntary nature of Jesus's sacrificial death. "For us" indicates that Jesus's sacrifice was for our benefit and in our place, as seen often before. Paul further describes Jesus's death as "a sacrificial and fragrant offering." The Greek text literally refers to Christ as "an offering and sacrifice to God for the purpose of a fragrant aroma." The combination of the terms "offering" and "sacrifice" identifies Jesus's death as the fulfillment of all of the various offerings and sacrifices of the OT.[52] The only OT text to use both of these terms is Ps 40:6 (LXX 39:7): "You do not delight in sacrifice and offering." Hebrews interprets this as a statement of the coming Messiah and appeals to it to confirm that the OT sacrifices cannot possibly "take away sins" (Heb 10:4–7). By contrast, God does delight in the sacrifice of Jesus. The "fragrant aroma" produced by Jesus's sacrifice indicates that the sacrifice was acceptable and pleasing to God (e.g., Gen 8:21; Exod 29:18; Lev 4:31; Ezek 20:41; cf. Lev 26:31). Jesus's sacrificial love serves as an example that believers are to follow.

Paul urges husbands to express this selfless love of Christ toward their wives. Christ expressed his love to the church when he "gave himself for her"

---

[52] Harold Hoehner, *Ephesians: An Exegetical Commentary* (Grand Rapids: Baker Academic, 2002), 649. The CSB follows Lincoln's (*Ephesians*, 312) suggestion that the construction is a hendiadys for the entire sacrificial system.

(Eph 5:25). Jesus's sacrifice atones, but it also purifies and cleanses. It makes the church "holy" (an adjective used repeatedly [5:26, 27]) and blameless. Jesus's sacrifice will enable him ultimately to present (an eschatological term) the church to himself "in splendor, without spot or wrinkle or anything like that." The unblemished beauty of Christ's bride, a metaphorical depiction of her moral and spiritual perfection, results from Jesus's sacrifice.[53]

Colossians

As Paul introduces the Christological hymn of Col 1:15–20, he explains that through "the Son he loves," the Father has provided "redemption, the forgiveness of sins" (1:13–14).[54] At the climax of the hymn, Paul asserts that God acted through Christ "to reconcile everything to himself" (1:20). "Everything" refers to all creation. Paul uses the neuter form of the adjective, not with the intention of excluding persons, but with the intention of showing that reconciliation includes them but extends beyond them. Verses 21–22 clearly demonstrate that sinners who were alienated from God and hostile to God were among those Christ reconciled to God. The reference to "everything . . . whether things on earth or things in heaven" shows that "all" is truly exhaustive. However, Paul is not affirming universal salvation. Colossians 2:15 shows that Christ conquers "the rulers and authorities" that oppose him, rather than befriending them. As Doug Moo comments, "The spiritual beings to which Paul refers explicitly in [chapter 1] v. 20 are not saved by Christ but vanquished by him."[55] Although Jesus is "making peace" through his blood shed on the cross, this "peace" is not the result of atonement which satisfies the justice of God and appeases the wrath of God. This "peace" is the forced surrender, the permanent armistice, that ends creation's hostility against the Creator and brings it into submission to him.

Christ's work of reconciliation will result in sinners being presented in eschatological judgment as "holy, faultless, and blameless before him." This aspect of reconciliation is contingent upon one's steadfast faith in the hope

---

[53] Hoehner, *Ephesians*, 528.
[54] See the discussion of Eph 1:7.
[55] Douglas Moo, *The Letter to the Colossians*, PNTC (Grand Rapids: Eerdmans, 2008), 135.

of the gospel (Col 1:22–23). But for those who reject this faith, the cross will not be an instrument of atonement; it will be a weapon of war. It will disarm, disgrace, and defeat the unrepentant sinner (3:6) just as surely as it will disarm, disgrace, and triumph over the rulers and authorities with whom they are unwitting allies in their rebellion against the Almighty (Col 2:15).

Colossians 2:11 contains an unparalleled explanation of the benefits of Jesus's sacrificial death. Jesus's death is the means of spiritual circumcision. The "circumcision of Christ" is probably a circumcision that Jesus experienced, rather than one that he performs. Circumcision was a removal of the male foreskin, a piece of flesh, and this removal of flesh was paralleled by Jesus's physical death in which he put off the body of flesh. Jesus's death was thus a circumcision of sorts.[56] Because of the believer's union with Christ, he has participated in that circumcision. The believer has experienced a "circumcision not done with hands," a circumcision that is spiritual rather than physical and performed by God rather than a human being.

The doctrine of spiritual circumcision has a rich OT background. Deuteronomy 10:16 commanded the Israelites: "Therefore, circumcise your hearts and don't be stiff-necked any longer." The condition of being "stiff-necked" refers to an animal being driven by its master that locks up the muscles of its neck and refuses to yield to the pull of the reins. A stiff-necked beast insists on going its own way and thus rebels against the master's will. Circumcision of the heart, however, corrects this tendency. Circumcision of the heart results in eager compliance with the master's instructions, joyful obedience to God's commands. Although Deut 10:16 commanded the people to circumcise their own hearts, in Deut 30:6 God promised to circumcise the hearts of his people. This spiritual circumcision performed by God would have two life-changing results: 1) "you will love him with all your heart and all your soul" and 2) "you will again obey him and follow all his commands I am commanding you today." Spiritual circumcision produces wholehearted devotion to God and eager, joyful obedience to the commands of God. The believer experiences this spiritual circumcision through his union with Jesus in his death. This circumcision marks the believer, as a

---

[56] Peter O'Brien, "Colossians," NBC, 4th ed. (Downers Grove: IVP, 1994), 1271; Scot McKnight, *The Letter to the Colossians*, NICNT (Grand Rapids: Eerdmans, 2018), 238–39.

member of the covenant people, one transformed inwardly by the Spirit and ensures that he will be praised by God in final judgment (Rom 2:25–29).

Jesus's sacrificial death is also the means by which God "forgave us all our trespasses" (Col 2:13). Rabbinic discussions of eschatological judgment portrayed God as a heavenly accountant who kept an enormous ledger on which he recorded all our sins on the debit pages of our individual account.[57] Paul employs this imagery when he refers to the spiritual "certificate of debt," a list of all our trespasses which serves to indict us in final judgment. Jesus canceled this certificate of debt so that it no longer requires us to pay for our sins by bearing divine punishment (v. 14). He did so in an unusual way. Ordinarily, a debt was canceled by writing the Greek letter *chi* (which resembles a capital X) through the certificate. X-ing out the debt meant that it was now null and void.[58] However, although the debt was now eliminated, the record of the debt was still clearly visible. This ordinary manner of cancelation was not sufficient to illustrate how complete and powerful divine forgiveness is. Thus, Paul insists that our debt was not merely X-ed out. It was completely erased. Parchment and papyrus could be erased very effectively in Paul's day by washing away the ink with a damp sponge or by scraping the ink off the page with a long, sharp, straight blade. By these means, the page could be so completely erased that the original text written on it was no longer visible. To the ordinary eye, the page was as clean as new, as if it had never been written on before.[59] This served as a vivid illustration of God's complete forgiveness of the sinner.

God erased the spiritual certificate of debt by taking it away and by "nailing it to the cross" (v. 14). In Roman crucifixion, the crimes for which the accused would be tortured and killed were written on a wooden placard that was nailed to the top of the cross above the head of the condemned.[60] The Gospels record the content of the placard on Jesus's cross: "Jesus of Nazareth, the king of the Jews" (John 19:19; cf. Matt 27:37; Mark 15:26; Luke 23:38). As far as the Roman government was concerned, Jesus was crucified for the crime of insurrection—for claiming to be the king of God's people. But Paul

---

[57] M. Avot 3:15–16.

[58] "χιάζω," LSJ 1991.

[59] Chrysostom (Hom. Col. 6) wrote: "He even wiped them out; he did not scratch them out merely; so that they could not be seen."

[60] See John Granger Cook, *Crucifixion in the Ancient Mediterranean World*, WUNT 327 (Tübingen: Mohr Siebeck, 2014), 427, esp. notes 57 and 58.

asserts that the heavenly Judge saw a very different list of charges recorded on that placard.[61] He saw our spiritual certificate of debt, the list of our sins that demand punishment from a holy God. The point could not be made any more clearly. Jesus died for our sins in our place. Thus, this passage rivals Gal 3:13 as the clearest expression of penal substitutionary atonement in the letters of Paul and, perhaps, in the entire NT.[62]

In Col 2:20, Paul explains that the believer's participation in Jesus's death has still another benefit—the believer died "to the elements of this world." Moo did not exaggerate when he quipped that the meaning of the expression "the elements of this world" is "one of the more intractable problems in New Testament interpretation."[63] Until recently, most modern scholars viewed these elements as spiritual beings and this interpretation is assumed in over a dozen contemporary English translations (TNIV; RSV; NRSV; ESV; NET; REB; TEV; CJB; GNT; LEB; NCV; NLT; Mounce). However, no evidence for this meaning of the phrase is found elsewhere before the third century. Thus, an increasing number of evangelical commentators are abandoning this popular interpretation in favor of the view that the expression refers to the material elements of the universe with the understanding that pagan gods or spirits were closely associated with those elements. In the first half of the first century, Philo observed that people of other nations "have made divinities of the four elements, earth and water, and air and fire" (On the Decalogue 53). By their obsession over material objects, including the food one consumed, the beverages one drank, and the things one touched (2:16, 21), the Jewish legalists that Paul was combatting were acting as if they worshipped these objects as deities.[64] If this is correct, the point is that

---

[61] Melick, *Philippians, Colossians, Philemon*, 264.

[62] Although Scot McKnight stated that he was "unconvinced that propitiatory soteriology forms the heart of Pauline theology and missiology or that such a soteriology is present in this hymn [Col 1:15–20] or letter," he commented on Col 2:14: "The certificate is in fact nailed to the cross, which means that the indebtedness is forgiven and the charge is canceled by the death of Christ, depicted thus as a substitutionary death." McKnight, *The Letter to the Colossians*, NICNT (Grand Rapids: Eerdmans, 2018), 164, 250.

[63] Moo, *Colossians*, 187.

[64] The view is affirmed by Moo, *Colossians*, 189–91; G. K. Beale, *Colossians and Philemon*, BECNT (Grand Rapids: Baker, 2019), 240–44; and McKnight, *The Letter to the Colossians*, 226–28.

Christ has delivered his people from obsession with earthly things as if they contributed to or prevented a relationship with him.

Figure 13: The Work of Christ in Paul's Prison Letters

Scripture Passage	Content
Phil 2:5–8	Christ's death is the supreme example of humble obedience to God and placing others above oneself.
Phil 3:10	Believers are conformed to Jesus's death, producing selfless obedience to God.
Phil 3:18	Since Jesus's death transforms the believer, those who live immorally are enemies of the cross.
Eph 1:7	Christ accomplishes the redemption and forgiveness of believers through his sacrificial death.
Eph 2:13–16	Christ's atoning death is the means by which God reconciled sinners to himself and Jews and Gentiles to one another.
Eph 5:2	Christ's sacrificial death was voluntary, substitutionary, and pleasing to God.
Eph 5:25–27	Christ's sacrificial death sanctifies and cleanses the church and serves as a model for marital love.
Col 1:14	Christ provides redemption, the forgiveness of sins.
Col 1:20	Through his sacrifice, Christ reconciled everything to God.
Col 1:22	Through his death, Christ reconciles sinners to God and presents them to the eschatological Judge as holy, faultless, and blameless.
Col 2:11	Christ's death results in the believer's spiritual circumcision, which produces their loving obedience to God.

Col 2:13	Christ paid the penalty for the sins of believers so that they are forgiven and their sins are erased from the record of the divine Judge.
Col 2:15	Christ's death vanquishes the rulers and authorities.
Col 2:20	Through his death, Christ has delivered believers from an obsession with earthly things.

Pastoral Letters

1 Timothy

Since the Pastoral Letters were written to church leaders whom Paul had mentored and who knew the gospel well, the sparsity of references to Jesus's atoning death is not surprising. The purpose of the first two letters (1 Timothy and Titus) was to equip these church leaders to guide the churches well in Paul's absence. These are highly occasional documents addressing specific needs of the churches in Ephesus and Crete.

Nevertheless, the few references to Jesus's atoning death in these letters are very important and significantly enrich our understanding of Paul's theology of Jesus's saving work. The first statement regarding Jesus's death is emphasized as a saying that is "trustworthy and deserving of full acceptance" (1 Tim 1:15). This completely reliable confession focuses on two aspects of Jesus's life and ministry: his incarnation and his atoning death. The reference to Jesus coming into the world implies that he existed in heaven before being born on the earth.[65] Jesus speaks of his coming in a similar fashion in both Luke (5:32; 19:10) and especially John (6:38, 41, 51, 58; 7:28; 8:14, 42; 9:39; 13:3; 16:27; 17:8; 18:37). The primary purpose for his incarnation was "to save sinners." The verb "save" implies that sinners were in a situation of grave peril from which they were unable to deliver themselves. First Timothy 2:5 implies that the sinner faced

---

[65] Philip Towner, *Letters to Timothy and Titus*, NICNT (Grand Rapids: Eerdmans, 2006), 146.

alienation from God, since the sinner needed a mediator who would bring God and humanity into peaceful relations and enable the sinner to have access to God. By referring to Christ as the sole mediator between God and humanity, Paul is likely implying Jesus's role as the one who brings the new covenant. Paul's only other use of the term "mediator" (μεσίτης) describes Moses as the mediator of the law, the old covenant (Gal 3:19–20). Hebrews thrice describes Jesus as the mediator of the new covenant (8:6; 9:15; 12:24). Christ is able to fulfill his role of bringing God and sinners together because he "gave himself as a ransom for all" (1 Tim 2:6). The active voice of the verb "gave" and the reflexive pronoun "himself" once again stress the voluntary nature of Jesus's self-giving. The term translated "ransom" (ἀντίλυτρον) occurs only here in the New Testament. Josephus used this term to describe a bar of gold that was paid to the Roman general Crassus by Eleazar, the guardian of the sacred treasures of the temple, to prevent him from ransacking the rest of the temple treasures.[66] The term refers to the price paid to save something or someone. The noun λύτρον, even without the prefixed preposition, means "ransom" (Matt 20:28; Mark 10:45). However, the preposition ἀντί ("instead of") reinforces the notion of substitution. Since the preposition ὑπέρ assumes the same meaning in the Koine period, the entire phrase "could be emphasizing almost exclusively the idea of substitution."[67]

Jesus, by his death, paid this ransom "for all." One may more easily state what this expression does not mean than explain precisely what it does mean. Paul is clearly not affirming universalism. In Titus 2:14, Paul uses a very similar expression: "who gave himself for us to redeem us." The verb translated "redeem" (λυτρόω) is a cognate of the noun "ransom" ([ἀντί]λυτρον). The expressions have an identical meaning except for the substitution of "us" for "all," a rather odd substitution if Paul intends to affirm universalism. Furthermore, many texts in Paul's writings require faith in Christ as a condition for receiving the gift of salvation. It is possible that "all" here means "all kinds of people." If the reference is retrospective, this would include even

---

[66] Jos. Ant. 14.7.1 §107.

[67] William Mounce, *Pastoral Epistles*, WBC 46 (Nashville: Thomas Nelson, 2000), 90.

the pagan authorities who rule over believers in Ephesus (1 Tim 2:2). If the reference is prospective, this would include not only Jews but also Gentiles (1 Tim 2:7). Probably, one should not sharply distinguish these two categories since the "kings and all those who are in authority" were invariably also Gentiles, especially in Ephesus and the other major cities of Asia Minor. The category "all people" should definitely include these political officials since it was mention of these leaders that prompted Paul to say that "God our Savior . . . wants everyone to be saved and to come to the knowledge of the truth" (1 Tim 2:3–4).[68] Since "everyone" whom God desires to be saved and "all" include pagan rulers, efforts to somehow identify the "everyone" and "all" as believers or the elect seem strained.

If 1 Tim 2:3–4 is taken as affirming universalism, then one must assume that all people "come to the knowledge of the truth." If God's desire for all does not result in all coming to the knowledge of the truth, to argue that his desire for all results in universal salvation is logically inconsistent. In the Greek text, the position of the prepositional phrase, "to the knowledge of the truth," is forwarded, probably to emphasize it. This emphasis is likely part of an effort to prevent any suggestion that any may be saved apart from knowledge of (and belief in) the gospel. The "truth" which one must know is none other than the gospel that Paul taught among the Gentiles as a herald and apostle (1 Tim 2:7). The "truth" is "the sound teaching that conforms to the gospel concerning the glory of the blessed God, which was entrusted to [Paul]" (1 Tim 1:10–11).

Consequently, the most natural understanding of Paul's statements is that God desires the salvation of every human being (though not all will be saved) and that Jesus's death was a ransom sufficient for the salvation of every single sinner, provided they come to knowledge of the truth (though many will, in fact, reject this knowledge).

---

[68] See also Titus 2:11 where "bringing salvation to all people" probably refers in context to the various categories of people just mentioned in 2:2–10: older men, older women, young women, young men, and slaves. Cf. Mounce, *Pastoral Epistles*, 422; George Knight III, *The Pastoral Epistles*, NIGTC (Grand Rapids: Eerdmans, 1992), 319. Chrysostom (*Hom. Tit.* 5) sees the statement as addressed specifically to slaves, a view later affirmed by Calvin, Locke, and many others. Philip Towner objects that this widely accepted view "seems foreign to the text." Towner, *The Letters to Timothy and Titus*, 746n11.

Titus

After a powerful assertion of the deity of Christ ("our great God and Savior, Jesus Christ"), Titus 2:14 repeats the main thought of 1 Tim 2:6 but specifies precisely what Christ ransomed us from and the implications of this redemption: "He gave himself for us to redeem us from all lawlessness and to cleanse for himself a people for his own possession, eager to do good works." Once again, "redeem" refers to the act of purchasing someone's liberation from bondage or rescue from punishment. In this case, the context suggests the nuance of liberation from bondage. "Lawlessness" refers to the most heinous form of sin, deliberate defiance to God's law. The anarthrous singular use of πᾶς emphasizes individual acts: "every single act of lawlessness." Paul draws expressions from Ps 130:8 and Ezek 37:23 to explain that, by his voluntary act of sacrifice, Christ redeemed us from all lawlessness. Lawless deeds are portrayed as wicked taskmasters that once compelled sinners to do their will. Christ set believers free from their tyranny by the ransom that he paid.[69] Sinners were not emancipated from their old masters to become autonomous individuals. They were cleansed to become Christ's possession. This element of the statement probably alludes to Ezek 37:23 ("I will cleanse them. They will be my people"), a text which belongs to the promise of the new covenant.[70] In the OT context, the cleansing is definitely one that results in moral and spiritual transformation. Those who are cleansed no longer defile themselves by their idolatry or transgressions. Similarly, the redemption and cleansing in Titus 2:14 produces eagerness to do good works. Those that formerly found great pleasure in rebellion against God now find their greatest pleasure in righteous deeds. This cleansing results from the "washing of regeneration and renewal by the Holy Spirit" (Titus 3:4–6), which are granted through Jesus's enactment of the new covenant by his sacrificial death.

2 Timothy

Second Timothy 1:10 describes "our Savior Christ Jesus" as the one "who has abolished death and has brought life and immortality to light through

---

[69] Knight, *The Pastoral Epistles*, 328.
[70] Towner, *The Letters to Timothy and Titus*, 762.

the gospel." The reference to abolishing death is reminiscent of 1 Cor 15:26 where Paul refers to Christ abolishing death. There Paul explains that after Jesus's second coming, he will put all his enemies under his feet and "the last enemy to be abolished is death." Here Paul describes the abolishment of death as a past, completed event. The verb "abolish" (καταργέω) is capable of expressing two related but distinct ideas. It may refer to causing something to lose its power or ending its very existence.[71] Paul intends the latter sense in 1 Cor 15:26 but the former sense in 2 Tim 1:10. Paul does not intend to imply that death no longer exists at all since he clearly anticipates his own impending physical death in this very letter (2 Tim 4:6–8). Thus, death still exists. However, death has been stripped of its power. As a consequence of Adam's transgression, "death reigned" (Rom 5:14, 17). However, death was vanquished so that it no longer rules since "Christ, having been raised from the dead, will not die again. Death no longer rules over him" (Rom 6:9).

Second Timothy 2:11 uses a "trustworthy" saying to remind Timothy that believers died together with Christ because of their union with him. Thus, death no longer rules over the believer either. Though the believer may experience physical death, that will be followed by "life and immortality" (2 Tim 1:10). According to the pattern established by Jesus's own experience, the believer will live again never to die again. Paul describes this physical resurrection and immortality as being "brought . . . to light" through the gospel since the gospel enlightens the believer so that they understand and eagerly anticipate these coming events, even though they have not yet experienced them.

Figure 14: The Work of Christ in Paul's Pastoral Letters

Scripture Passage	Content
1 Tim 1:15	Christ came into the world to save sinners, including the worst of them.
1 Tim 2:5	Christ serves as the mediator between God and sinners.

---

[71] "καταργέω," BDAG, 525; Mounce, *Pastoral Epistles*, 485.

1 Tim 2:6	Christ voluntarily died in the place of sinners to pay the ransom that would save them.
Titus 2:14	Through his sacrificial death, Christ paid the price that redeemed believers from their slavery to sin and purified them morally so they are characterized by good works.
2 Tim 1:10	Christ abolished death.
2 Tim 2:11	Believers participated in Christ's death.

Summary

Paul's letters make a major contribution to an understanding of the work of Christ. Like the Synoptics, Acts, and John's writings, he describes Jesus's death as an atoning sacrifice that grants forgiveness to believers. On several occasions (Gal 3:13; 2 Cor 5:21; Col 2:14), he unambiguously describes Jesus's death as an act of penal substitutionary atonement. Jesus became sin for us, bore the curse of the old covenant for us, and died with our sin list nailed to the top of his cross.

Like these other NT documents, Paul also describes Jesus's death as the sacrifice that enacts the new covenant. He adds that Jesus's death is the means of the believer's spiritual circumcision which results in our eager and joyful obedience to God.

Paul stresses that since Jesus's death served as our ransom, our lives now belong to him and must be dedicated to his service. The ransom that he paid liberated us from our old spiritual bondage and rescued us from the punishment that our sins deserved. Jesus's death reconciles us to God and to each other, breaking down old barriers so that Christians can gather as a true spiritual family. Jesus's death also redeems us from our old way of life.

Paul's writings, more clearly than any other NT documents, stress that believers participated in Jesus's death. This participation transforms believers' identity and character, rescues them from bondage to sin, Satan, and the corrupting influences of the world, and nullifies the authority of the old covenant which had exacerbated sin and sentenced them to death.

Paul repeatedly presents Jesus's sacrificial death as the supreme example of selfless obedience to God and sacrificial service to others. He urges believers to imitate Jesus's example by prioritizing the needs of others above our own and by devoting ourselves to service to others.

Paul also describes the death of Jesus as the moment of Satan's defeat. Through Jesus's death on the cross, God reconciled all things to himself and broke their rebellion. He disarmed, disgraced, and triumphed over the demonic rulers and authorities. It is no exaggeration to say that Paul's understanding of Jesus's atoning death is so robust as to include the views theologians now classify as penal substitution, moral example, and Christus Victor. However, even these theories do not fully exhaust Paul's rich and complex view of Christ's salvific work.

8

The Work of Christ in the General Epistles

Hebrews

Hebrews contains one of the richest deposits of references to the atoning death of Christ in the entire NT. The panoramic description of Christ's nature and work in the introduction to the book (Heb 1:1–4) mentions that "after making purification for sins, he sat down at the right hand of the Majesty on high." The statement has a close parallel in Heb 10:12: "After offering one sacrifice for sins forever, [he] sat down at the right hand of God." The parallel demonstrates that the purification was made through sacrifice, a reference to Jesus's atoning death. Sin defiles the sinner and this defilement precludes access to the holy God. The blood atonement that Jesus provided removes this defilement so that "we have boldness to enter the sanctuary through the blood of Jesus" (10:19). The purification not only cleanses the believer externally but, more importantly, purifies him internally by sprinkling the heart so that it becomes clean and the "evil conscience" is removed (v. 22). The bad conscience is a conscience plagued by guilt and characterized by "consciousness of sin" (v. 2). Christ's atoning work removes this sense of shame and perfects the worshipper's conscience (9:9) in a way that the OT sacrifices never could. The blood of Christ will "cleanse our consciences from dead works so that we can serve the living God" (9:14) and opens for us a new and living way through the curtain that separated the sinner from God (9:8; 10:20).[1]

By God's grace, Jesus tasted death for everyone (2:9). Again, the grammar implies that Jesus not only died for the benefit of others but that he also died as their substitute. In terms reminiscent of Isaiah 53, Heb 9:28 says that Christ was "offered once to bear the sins of many" (cf. Isa 53:12). He bore their sins in the sense that he took the guilt of their sin upon himself and suffered the punishment that their sins deserved. Christ accomplished "the removal of sin by the sacrifice of himself" (Heb 9:26). His death granted full forgiveness, once and for all, to believers (10:18; cf. 9:22).[2] This forgiveness is the result of Jesus dying as an atoning sacrifice ("sacrifice for sins"; Heb 10:12).

One of the great contributions of Hebrews is the comparison of Jesus's death to the Day of Atonement ritual. Barnabas Lindars wrote that, in an "astute move," Hebrews describes Jesus's death in connection with the Day of Atonement ritual "which is not explicitly used in connection with the sacrificial death of Jesus elsewhere in the New Testament."[3] Paul Landgraf even suggests that the structure of Hebrews is determined by various features of the Day of Atonement.[4] The purpose of this comparison is to "prove that everything that is essential for atonement has been done in the sacrifice of Christ."[5]

Jesus's death also serves as a covenant-enacting sacrifice. The blood that Jesus shed is "the blood of the covenant" (10:29), that is, the blood that certifies the new covenant and by which Jesus guarantees the new covenant

---

[1] For a discussion of the cleansing of the conscience through Jesus's atoning death, see Douglas Kennard, *A Biblical Theology of Hebrews* (Eugene, OR: Wipf and Stock, 2018), 103–5.

[2] Barnabas Lindars describes the argument for the permanent efficacy of Christ's sacrificial death as "a major contribution to the theology of the New Testament" since "Hebrews alone tackles the subject comprehensively and systematically. . . ." Lindars, *The Theology of Hebrews* (Cambridge: Cambridge University Press, 1991), 125.

[3] Lindars, *The Theology of Hebrews*, 84, cf. 1.

[4] Paul Landgraf, "The Structure of Hebrews: A Word of Exhortation in Light of the Day of Atonement," in *A Cloud of Witnesses: The Theology of Hebrews in Its Ancient Contexts*, LBS 387, ed. Richard Bauckham et al. (London: T&T Clark, 2008): 19–27.

[5] Lindars, *The Theology of Hebrews*, 84.

(7:22).[6] This sacrificial blood establishes a covenant that, unlike the old covenant, is everlasting (13:20). Hebrews 10:15–17 quotes the new covenant promise of Jer 31:31–34 and concludes that the new covenant offers full forgiveness (Heb 10:18) per God's promise, "I will never again remember their sins and their lawless acts" (10:17). Hebrews 12:24 associates Jesus's enactment of the new covenant with "sprinkled blood," a reference to the ceremony that inaugurated the Mosaic covenant (Exodus 24). The text emphasizes the forgiveness that was a major aspect of the new covenant by explaining that Jesus's "sprinkled blood . . . says better things than the blood of Abel." Although the blood of Abel cried out to God for judgment on Cain because of his murder of his brother (Gen 4:10–12), the blood of Jesus calls out to God to show mercy and forgive sinners[7] in the manner promised in the prophecy regarding the new covenant in Jer 31:34.

Hebrews 2:14–15 describes yet another dimension of the work of Christ—Jesus's death as victory over Satan. Jesus took on full humanity ("flesh and blood") "so that through his death he might destroy the one holding the power of death—that is, the devil." Scripture claims that God is sovereign over life and death (Deut 32:39). However, Satan can be said to hold power over death since his deceitful enticement of Eve and Adam to defy God's command (Gen 3:1–7) resulted in death entering God's good creation in the first place (Gen 2:16–17; 3:19). The one who has been a "murderer from the beginning" (John 8:44) continues to keep sinners under the sentence of death by his deceptions. The author of Hebrews may have known and would have agreed with the view expressed in Wisdom 1:13 and 2:24: "God did not make death nor does he delight in the destruction of the living" and "Through the envy of the devil death entered the world, and those who belong to his party experience it."[8] John Owen also interpreted this text

---

[6] Lindars identifies "three principal strands" of the argument of Hebrews on the sacrifice of Christ. One of these is Christ's inauguration of the new covenant which "gives to Christ's sacrifice its permanent efficacy, because it opens the era of salvation in which fresh sacrifices for sin are no longer required." Lindars, *The Theology of Hebrews*, 71–72.

[7] B. F. Westcott, *The Epistle to the Hebrews: The Greek Text with Notes and Essays*, 3rd ed. (London: Macmillan, 1903), 419; Gareth Cockerill, *The Epistle to the Hebrews*, NICNT (Grand Rapids: Eerdmans, 2012), 658–59.

[8] NETS.

in Hebrews along these lines citing Rom 5:12 in support: "[Satan] was the means of bringing death into the world. He was able to introduce sin and so he had power to bring in death also."[9]

Jesus's own death is the means by which God strips the devil of his power. The verb translated as "destroy" in the CSB is the same verb used to describe making death powerless in 2 Tim 1:10. It likely has that sense here as well. Christ's death did not destroy the devil in the sense that it wiped him out of existence. Instead, it stripped him of his authority to keep sinners enslaved. This statement is a close parallel to Paul's assertion that by his death Jesus "disarmed the rulers and authorities and disgraced them publicly; he triumphed over them" (Col 2:15). Jesus's death served to "free those who were held in slavery all their lives by the fear of death" (Heb 2:15). People understandably fear death because it is the prelude to eschatological judgment (9:27). Apart from Jesus's sacrifice, the thought of death is horrifying because the thought of eschatological judgment is "a terrifying expectation" (10:27) since "it is a terrifying thing to fall into the hands of the living God" (v. 31). Since Jesus's sacrificial death provides full atonement, believers no longer have tormented consciences wracked by guilt that inspires fear of divine judgment and thus fear of death. Satan's power over them is broken by the confidence that God "will never again remember their sins and their lawless acts" (v. 17).

Schreiner's observations about the theological implications of this statement are worth repeating in full:

> [T]here is clearly a Christus Victor theme here. The devil exercised power over human beings, and those who belong to Jesus Christ are freed through Jesus's death. It seems here that Christus Victor and substitutionary themes come together, for only through Jesus's death is the devil's reign over death cancelled. If the devil's rule over death ends only through Jesus' death, it seems that Jesus' death functions as the means by which death's reign is destroyed. The penalty for sin is death, and Jesus paid that penalty.[10]

---

[9] John Owen, *Hebrews*, Crossway Classic Commentaries (Wheaton: Crossway, 1998), 44.

[10] Thomas Schreiner, *Hebrews*, EBTC (Bellingham, WA: Lexham, 2020), 105.

1 Peter

Peter first mentions the redemptive work of Christ in 1 Pet 1:2 in the expanded address for his letter when he describes his readers as those "sprinkled with the blood of Jesus Christ." This appears to be an allusion to Exodus 24.[11] When God enacted the Mosaic covenant, he commanded Moses to sacrifice bulls as a fellowship offering and then sprinkle half of the blood on the altar and half of the blood on the people (Exod 24:3–8). As Moses splattered the blood on the Israelites, he exclaimed, "This is the blood of the covenant that the LORD has made with you concerning all these words" (Exod 24:8). The sprinkled blood of Christ enacts the new covenant, a theme introduced in Jesus's own institution of the Lord's Supper and reinforced by Paul, the author of Hebrews, and now the apostle Peter. The closest NT parallel is Heb 12:24 which connects Jesus's role as mediator of the new covenant with "the sprinkled blood, which says better things than the blood of Abel."

First Peter 1:10–12 takes up the topic of the sufferings of Christ again. Although Peter does not detail how these sufferings accomplished our salvation, he associates Christ's sufferings with salvation. Most importantly, he states that Christ's sufferings were foretold by the OT prophets. As we will soon see, those prophets clearly include Isaiah whose prophecies about the suffering of the Messiah will be the focus of 1 Pet 2:21–25.

Peter emphasizes the amazing privilege of witnessing this fulfillment of the prophecies about the Messiah's sufferings and glory (through the gospel preached to them) by adding, "Angels long to catch a glimpse of these things" (1 Pet 1:12). The verb translated "catch a glimpse" in the CSB means "to bend over for the purpose of looking."[12] In *1 Enoch* 9:1, this verb describes angels looking down from heaven to view events on earth. Thus, Peter may refer to the angels longing to view Jesus's provision of atonement from heaven above. Another possibility is that Peter's statement appeals to the OT ritual for the Day of Atonement. Exodus 25:17–22 offers a detailed description of the OT mercy seat, or atonement cover, that formed the top of the ark of the covenant. Two cherubim, or angels, made of gold were

---

[11] Peter Davids, *A Theology of James, Peter, and Jude: Living in the Light of the Coming King*, BTNT 6 (Grand Rapids: Zondervan, 2014), 165.

[12] Παρακύπτω, BDAG, 767.

positioned at each end of the atonement cover. They were to face each other but look down toward the atonement cover. During the Day of Atonement, blood would be sprinkled on this atonement cover (Lev 16:11–17) to atone for the sins of Israel. The cherubim were thus positioned to gaze down upon this sacrificial blood. Peter's reference may imply that the cherubim were not satisfied with the blood of animals and longed to see blood of the only true and worthy sacrifice, Jesus Christ. This would closely parallel Paul's description of Jesus as the mercy seat in Rom 3:25. It also suits Peter's emphasis on the significance of Jesus's blood (1 Pet 1:2, 19) and his focus on Jesus's atoning death.[13]

Peter offers a more detailed explanation of Jesus's atoning death in 1:18–19. Christ's "precious blood" was the price paid to redeem sinners. Redemption from bondage is certainly in view here since this redemption delivered believers "from [their] empty way of life inherited from [their] ancestors." This way of life inherited from their earthly fathers stands in sharp contrast to the character inherited from their spiritual Father due to the new birth (1 Pet 1:3). Those who experience the new birth become "obedient children" (1:14) because they have now inherited the Father's own character, prompting Peter to write: "As the one who called you is holy, you also are to be holy in all your conduct; for it is written, **Be holy, because I am holy**" (vv. 15–16).

Peter contrasts Jesus's "precious blood" with "perishable things like silver or gold." His obvious point is that Jesus's atoning death is far more valuable and precious than earth's greatest treasures. However, he is likely implying more. In 1:23, Peter contrasts the "perishable" with the "imperishable," that which endures forever. He reasons that birth that results from a perishable seed is likewise perishable, while life produced through an imperishable seed endures forever. He probably anticipates that argument already in the contrast between a "perishable" redemption price versus a "precious" redemption

---

[13] Although this view is not supported in recent NT commentaries, Walter Kaiser cites 1 Pet 1:12 in reference to Exod 25:20. Kaiser, "Exodus," in *Genesis–Numbers*, EBC (Grand Rapids: Zondervan, 1990), 455. John Gill also mentions the possibility that 1 Pet 1:12 is an allusion "to the cherubim on the mercy seat, a type of Christ, which looked to one another, and to the mercy seat (Exodus 25:20)." Gill, *An Exposition of the New Testament from Galatians 2:1 to Revelation 21:21*, vol. 3 of Expositions of the New Testament (London: Matthews and Leigh, 1809).

price. Jesus's blood is a far more valuable redemption price than perishable silver and gold because a perishable redemption price effects a temporary redemption, but an imperishable redemption price effects an eternal redemption. It is this reasoning that prompts Peter's claim that Jesus "suffered for sins once for all" (3:18).

Peter compares Jesus's blood shed on the cross to that of an "unblemished and spotless lamb" (1:19). Peter is obviously portraying Jesus as the atoning sacrifice that fulfills all that the sacrificial rituals of the OT anticipated.[14] John Elliott is likely correct that Peter interprets Jesus's statement in Mark 10:45 and 14:24 in light of Isa 52:13–53:12.[15] Peter recognizes that the physical perfection of the sacrifice ("unblemished and spotless") was intended to picture the moral perfection of Jesus that qualified him to serve as our atoning sacrifice. Isaiah had stressed that the Suffering Servant was "righteous" (Isa 53:11; cf. 53:9) and was punished for the iniquities of others, not his own (Isa 53:5, 6, 8, 11, 12). Peter explicitly quotes Isa 53:9 in 1 Pet 2:22 to confirm that Jesus "did not commit sin." Similarly, Peter writes that "Christ also suffered for sins once for all, the righteous for the unrighteous, that he might bring you to God" (3:18).

First Peter 2:21–25 presents Christ as an example of one who does what is good and yet suffers (2:20). The primary purpose of the passage is to hold Jesus up as "an example, that you should follow in his steps" (v. 21). Yet Peter seems unable to refer to Jesus's suffering without declaring the greater significance of his Passion. In this declaration, Isaiah 53 is prominent.[16] The paragraph contains no less than three direct quotations of the prophecy. Verse 22 quotes Isa 53:9. Verse 24 quotes Isa 53:5. Verse 25 quotes Isa 53:6. The triad of quotations shows that Peter regards Jesus as the fulfillment of the entire song of the Suffering Servant. Jesus "bore our sins" (2:24) because

---

[14] Davids suggests that the background is "one of the Torah's sacrificial pictures (e.g., the tamid of Exod 29:38; cf. Num 28:3; the purification offering of Lev 14:10; the Pentecost lambs of Lev 23:18; Nazirite offering of Num 6:14; the Sabbath offering of Num 28:9)" since these texts refer to an unblemished lamb. Davids, *Theology of James, Peter, and Jude*, 165.

[15] John Elliott, *1 Peter*, AB 37B (New York: Doubleday, 2000), 369, 373–74.

[16] Elliott states that "the clear use of material from Isa 52:13–53:12 here in v 22 as well as in vv 24a, 24d, and v 25a makes it likely that this Isaian passage has influenced much of the content of this section." Elliot, *1 Peter*, 529.

the Servant was punished "for the iniquity of us all" (Isa 53:6). He died as a "guilt offering" (Isa 53:10) to "justify many" (53:11). Peter probably refers to the cross on which Jesus was crucified as a "tree" to allude to Deut 21:22–23. Though not as explicitly as Paul in Gal 3:13, Peter hints that Jesus died under God's curse for sin because he bore the curse for us. In yet another apparent parallel with Paul, Peter insists that believers died to sins so that they might live for righteousness. Although the verb translated as "died to" does not necessarily refer to death, the contrast with the reference to life strongly indicates that it has this nuance here. The association of death to sinful acts with Jesus's own death implies that same participation in Christ's death that is fundamental to Pauline soteriology. In this manner, Peter demonstrates why those who once were like straying sheep have now returned to the Shepherd.

2 Peter

Second Peter contains only one reference to Jesus's atoning death in the phrase "the Master who bought them" (2 Pet 2:1). This "Master" is almost certainly Jesus Christ. Second Peter is probably dependent on Jude, and this statement parallels Jude's reference to "Jesus Christ, our only Master and Lord" (Jude 4). In 1 Pet 2:18, "master" (δεσπότης) refers to the master of a slave, a meaning also intended in 1 Tim 6:1 and Titus 2:9. Although the term refers in other contexts to a ruler, the slave imagery seems required here by the verb "bought." Rulers do not buy their subjects; masters do buy their slaves. The imagery of the slave market seems unmistakable. Those who were enslaved to another have now been purchased by Christ so that they belong to him and are to serve him with their lives (cf. 1 Cor 6:19–20; 7:22–23; Rom 6:15–23; Rev 5:9). The reference assumes the common NT doctrine of redemption. Christ, by his sacrificial death, paid the ransom to liberate sinners from their slavery to sin, the flesh, and the devil. In this process, believers became Christ's own possession.

Some of those bought by the Master eventually deny him (2 Pet 2:1). This has become an important text in the debate over eternal security and the extent of the atonement. Three basic interpretations of this clause have emerged. First, "bought" may mean "truly save" and "denying the Master" may mean "committing apostasy" so that authentic Christians lose their salvation.[17] This view may be rejected since 2 Pet 1:3–11 describes a powerful divine call that ensures believers partake of the divine nature and enjoy entry into the eternal kingdom of our Lord and Savior. Second, "bought" may mean "truly save" and "denying the Master" may refer to something less than full apostasy.[18] This view may be rejected since the denial brings swift destruction, a destruction that is vividly described over the next two chapters and is associated with the Day of the Lord (2 Pet 3:7). Third, "bought" may mean something less than "truly save," and "denying the Master" may refer to actual apostasy. This third view takes two different forms, both of which qualify "bought" in some fashion. One view interprets "bought" to mean that Jesus paid the penalty for the sins of all, even those who never believe or are apostate. This provision makes salvation possible for all, even though it accomplishes salvation only for those who repent and believe. However, "bought" does not ordinarily mean merely to "pay a price" or offer the ransom for those who were enslaved to another. Instead, the Master "bought" them by both paying the ransom and bringing them into his own possession so that he became their owner and authority, their Master. Thus, the most satisfactory explanation of the passage is that offered by Schreiner:

> I would suggest that Peter used phenomenological language. In other words, he described the false teachers as believers because they made a profession of faith and gave every appearance initially of being genuine believers. . . . Their denial of Jesus Christ reveals that they did not truly belong to God, even though they professed faith.

---

[17] Davids argues, "Our author does not believe in eternal security—in fact, he knows of some folk who have 'lost their salvation' and for whom it would have been better never to have been 'saved'." Davids, *Theology of James, Peter, and Jude*, 240. Cf. Richard Bauckham who states that "2 Peter does not deny that the false teachers are Christians, but sees them as apostate Christians who have disowned their Master." Bauckham, *Jude, 2 Peter*, WBC 50 (Dallas: Word, 1983), 240.

[18] Jerome Neyrey suggests an alternative view. Rather than qualifying "bought," he prefers to qualify "deny" and suggests that this is "probably not a total denial of allegiance to Christ" but a denial of divine judgment. Neyrey, *2 Peter, Jude*, AB 37C (New York: Doubleday, 1993), 188–89.

Peter said that they were bought by Jesus Christ, in the sense that
they gave every indication initially of genuine faith.[19]

Several other pieces of evidence lend additional support to the use of phenomenological language in this text. First, the immediately preceding context emphasizes the falsity of these persons. They are false teachers and are
compared to false prophets (2 Pet 2:1). They attempt to exploit the church
with their "made-up stories" (2 Pet 2:3), their false, fabricated discourses.
This context strongly implies that their confession of faith and professed
devotion to Christ were equally suspect. Second, this letter contains several other descriptions of persons that seem to be phenomenological. In
2 Pet 1:9, the person who lacks goodness, knowledge, self-control, endur-
ance, godliness, brotherly affection, and love is described as one who "has
forgotten the cleansing from his past sins." Since these characteristics are
necessary to the "divine nature" imparted to true believers through the new
birth (2 Pet 1:3–4; 1 Pet 1:3–2:3), these persons apparently never experienced conversion, true forgiveness, or the accompanying moral transformation. "Cleansing from his past sins" may refer to removal of the defilement
that creates a barrier between the sinner and God (i.e., forgiveness) or to
a purification of the sinner's moral character so that he leads a new life.
Since this context stresses the importance of godly character in the believer,
the latter interpretation is most compelling. Furthermore, the "cleansing"
or "purification" (καθαρισμός) seems equivalent to escaping the "world's
impurity" in 2 Pet 2:20, a reference to the "corruption" that enslaves (2:19)
which is depicted by the vomit of a dog and the mud of a hog wallow in
2:22. In either view, the statement that such a person "has forgotten the
cleansing from his past sins" likely does not assert that they were actually purified and cleansed, but merely that they gave that initial appearance
through making a verbal confession and receiving water baptism. The reference to "having escaped the world's impurity through the knowledge of the
Lord and Savior Jesus Christ" in 2:20 also appears to be phenomenological.
The "world's impurity" is the "corruption that is in the world because of
evil desire" (2 Pet 1:4). Since the false teachers have just been described as

---

[19] Thomas R. Schreiner, *1, 2 Peter, Jude*, NAC 37 (Nashville: Broadman &
Holman, 2003), 331.

"slaves of corruption" (2:19) who are defeated by sin, it is hard to imagine how they could possibly have escaped worldly impurity. The descriptions of their horrible spiritual state in 2:21–22 show that there never was a genuine escape. Peter implies this through the use of the adverb ὀλίγως ("barely") to describe their escape in 2:18. The adverb is rare but its cognates show that it means "just a little" or "in a small way."[20] The adverb implies that the escape was initiated but just begun and far from complete.[21] Consequently, this text does not provide compelling evidence that Jesus's death provided redemption for every individual.

Figure 15: The Work of Christ in the General Epistles

Scripture Passage	Content
Heb 1:3	Christ made purification for sins.
Heb 2:9	Christ died as the believer's substitute.
Heb 2:14	Christ's death destroys the devil who holds the power of death.
Heb 7:22; 10:29; 12:24	Christ's death effects the new covenant and he serves as the mediator of the new covenant.
Heb 9:14	Christ's death cleanses the believer's conscience.
Heb 9:26	Christ's sacrifice effected the removal of sin.
Heb 9:28	Christ bore the sins of many.
Heb 10:12	Christ offered one sacrifice for sins forever.
Heb 10:19–20	Christ's sacrifice enables believers to enter God's presence boldly.

---

[20] An increasing number of commentators argue that the adverb means "just recently."

[21] See Grant Osborne for a discussion of the text-critical issues and proper translation. Osborne, "2 Peter," in *James–Revelation*, Cornerstone Biblical Commentary 18 (Carol Stream, IL: Tyndale House, 2011), 236, 238.

1 Pet 1:2	Christ's death enacts the new covenant by sprinkling the people of God with his blood.
1 Pet 1:10–12	Christ's sacrificial death was foretold by the OT prophets and pictured by the atoning rituals of the old covenant.
1 Pet 1:18–19	Christ's death permanently redeemed sinners from their old empty way of life and fulfills Isa 52:13–53:12.
1 Pet 2:24	Christ died on the tree bearing the curse of sin and fulfilling Isa 52:13–53:12.
1 Pet 2:21–25	Christ's death serves as an example to believers who should also suffer righteously.
1 Pet 3:18	Christ, though righteous, suffered for sins of the unrighteous once for all in order to reconcile them to God.
2 Pet 2:1	Christ's death purchased sinners so that he is now their Master and they are his servants.

Summary

The General Epistles highlight many of the aspects of Christ's salvific work already seen in other NT documents. Both Hebrews and 1 Peter describe Jesus's death as an atoning sacrifice that fulfills prophecies and types in the OT. Hebrews presents Jesus's death as an act of penal substitution in which Jesus bore the sins of many (Heb 9:28; cf. 2:9) and the righteous suffered for and in the place of the unrighteous (1 Pet 3:18). 1 Peter also implies this by describing Jesus's death as the fulfillment of Isa 52:13–53:12 (1 Pet 2:21–24). The General Epistles see Jesus's sacrifice as the fulfillment anticipated by various rituals in the OT sacrificial system (Heb 9:22). In Hebrews, Jesus's sacrifice is an offering effecting purification (Heb 1:3) and the removal of sin (Heb 9:26), the fulfillment of both annual (Heb 10:3) and daily sacrifices (Heb 10:11), and a sacrifice like that which the priest offered as a prerequisite for entering the Holy of Holies (Heb 10:19–20). Both Hebrews and 1 Peter portray Jesus's death as the sacrifice that enacts the new covenant (Heb 7:22; 10:29; 12:24; 1 Pet 1:2).

Even when one of these two books mentions aspects of Jesus's saving work that are absent in the other, other NT parallels exist. Peter's description of Jesus's sacrifice as a ransom that redeems from slavery to sin (1 Pet 1:18–19) parallels a prominent theme of Pauline soteriology (e.g., Rom 6:15–23). His affirmation that Jesus's death purchases believers as Christ's own servants (2 Pet 2:1) is similar to the theme of 1 Cor 6:19–20; 7:23; 2 Cor 5:15; Rom 14:9; Titus 2:14. The statement that Jesus's death destroys death and the devil (Heb 2:14) is reminiscent of texts such as John 12:31; 16:11; Rom 6:8–11; Col 2:15; 2 Tim 1:10. The use of Jesus's exemplary death to inspire believers to righteous living evokes remembrance of Paul's appeal to Jesus's death as a challenging example of humble obedience to God and selfless service to others (e.g., Phil 2:5–11).

9

The Old Testament and New Testament's Contribution to a Biblical Theology of the Work of Christ

The Old Testament

The direct messianic prophecies of the Old Testament provide powerful and explicit descriptions of the work and mission of the coming Messiah. The Old Testament description of the work of the Messiah is far more robust and detailed than this brief summary can express. Nevertheless, some of the most important features of the Messiah's salvific work may be categorized under the following headings: Prophet, Priest, and Savior.

Prophet

The Pentateuch promised a coming Messiah who would be a prophet like Moses and thus serve as a mediator between God and his people and deliver God's own commandments to his people. The Major Prophets show that the Messiah will mediate the new covenant that promises the transformation of the moral character of God's people and produces a righteousness in them that the Mosaic law never produced. The Major Prophets also repeatedly portray the Messiah as a teacher who, like a prophet, will instruct God's people in the way of righteousness. This element of the Messiah's work is confirmed by the Minor Prophets as well.

Priest

The Psalms insist that the Messiah will be an eternal priest according to the order of Melchizedek. As a priest, the Messiah would intercede with God on behalf of his people, preside over the temple, and offer sacrifice. The Minor Prophets portray the Messiah as a priest who will remove the iniquity of the people by offering his own life as an atoning sacrifice. He will suffer for the sins of his people to provide forgiveness, justification, and spiritual cleansing.

Savior

The Pentateuch promised the coming of a descendant of the first couple who would crush the head of the serpent. These books foretold of a descendant of the patriarchs of Israel through whom all nations on earth would be blessed. They also announced the coming of a prophet like Moses, the leader of the Exodus and mediator of the old covenant.

The Prophets later promise a new covenant that will grant complete forgiveness to God's repentant people. This new covenant will result in their moral transformation by inscribing God's righteous demands on their hearts and placing God's Spirit within them to compel them from within to do what is right and pleasing to the Lord. The new Moses is presumably to be the mediator of this new covenant.

The Messiah will bring salvation to the nations by dying as the atoning sacrifice that grants forgiveness to repentant sinners. The Minor Prophets confirm that the Messiah will be pierced and struck down, yet his death will atone for the sin of the people.

The New Testament

The OT provided a solid foundation for NT teaching regarding the salvific work of the Messiah. The Lord Jesus and the NT authors expound the clear teaching of the OT regarding the mission and work of the Messiah.

They also demonstrate that the OT has far more to say about the saving work of the Messiah than examination of direct messianic prophecies explicitly reveals. The entire sacrificial system of the Mosaic law anticipates the Messiah's atoning death and provides types and images that illuminate the significance of Jesus's Passion.

The Synoptic Gospels and Acts

Mark 10:45 and Matt 20:28 preserve Jesus's statement that the Son of Man came "to give his life as a ransom for many." Jesus's words are almost certainly an allusion to Isa 53:12 (LXX) which describes Isaiah's Suffering Servant giving his life and bearing the sins of many. The term "ransom" is not taken from Isaiah's prophecy. It may be used here in a sacrificial (Exod 30:11–16) rather than judicial (Exod 21:30) sense to serve as a synonym for "the atonement price." If so, Jesus is interpreting the death of the Servant as the fulfillment of the atoning rituals of the Pentateuch.

Matthew apparently recognized the allusion to Isaiah 53 in Jesus's words since he explicitly presents Jesus as the fulfillment of this important prophecy (Matt 8:17) and portrays Jesus as the fulfillment of another of Isaiah's Servant Songs (Matt 12:16–21). Luke identifies Jesus as the Suffering Servant in each of his two volumes (Luke 22:37; Acts 8:34–35) and, in the first reference, Jesus himself describes the prophecy as "what is written about me."

In all three of the Synoptics, Jesus claims authority to forgive sinners and confirms that he possesses that authority through a miraculous healing (Mark 2:5, 10; Matt 9:2, 6; Luke 5:20, 24). All three also show that Jesus's suffering and death are no accident of history. Jesus's Passion is necessary to God's plan (e.g., Mark 8:31; Matt 16:21; Luke 9:22). All three Synoptics and Acts claim that Jesus's death is a fulfillment of OT prophecy.

Through their accounts of the Last Supper, the Synoptics all associate Jesus's death with the sacrifice of the Passover lamb. This suggests that Jesus's death will cause the wrath of God to "pass over" Jesus's disciples. They also portray Jesus's death as the sacrifice that enacts the new covenant, much like how the sacrifices of Exod 24 enacted the old covenant. Jesus's inauguration of the new covenant forms important background to the promise that Jesus will perform the baptism of the Spirit.

All three of these Gospels describe Jesus's agony in Gethsemane and demonstrate Jesus's death was voluntary. The expression "give his life" (Mark 10:45; Matt 20:28) also implied this. Matthew especially emphasizes that Jesus could have escaped this death if he chose (Matt 26:53–54).

The Writings of John

Although the Synoptic Gospels show that John the Baptist announced that Jesus, the coming Messiah, would perform the baptism of the Spirit, the Gospel of John shows that the prophet's message contained still another gracious promise—Jesus is "the Lamb of God who takes away the sin of the world" (John 1:29; cf. 1:36). John's lamb Christology ultimately becomes a major motif of his writings. In fact, John's book of Revelation refers to Jesus as the "Lamb" more frequently than by any other Christological title.

The portrayal of Jesus as the "Lamb" clearly alludes to the Passover lamb since John emphasizes that Jesus was crucified at the time the Passover lambs were being slaughtered (John 18:28; 19:14) and shows how the treatment of Jesus's corpse was similar to the treatment of the carcass of the Passover lamb (John 19:36; cf. Exod 12:46; Num 9:12). However, the clause "who takes away the sin of the world" indicates that John also recognized Jesus's death was an atoning sacrifice like the many sacrifices in the OT rituals that sought forgiveness, purification, and reconciliation to God. John also explicitly stated that Jesus fulfilled Isaiah 53 (John 12:37–38). A good argument can be made that various features of Isaiah's Song of the Suffering Servant permeate the Gospel. John likely recognized that this text was key to understanding how Jesus, the Lamb, takes away sin. John's letters refer to Jesus's death as a "propitiation" or "atoning sacrifice" (1 John 2:2; 4:10) and describe his blood cleansing believers of all sin (1 John 1:7; cf. 3:5). This cleansing is probably the very cleansing that Jesus referred to in John 13:8, 10, a cleansing that makes Jesus's disciples "completely clean."

A certain tension exists in John's descriptions of those for whom Christ died. On one hand, some descriptions refer to specific groups. Jesus lays down his life "for his sheep" (John 10:11), "for his friends" (John 15:13), and "for us" (1 John 3:16). Yet at other times, John seems to go beyond Isaiah's prophecy and the Synoptic Gospels by insisting that Jesus did not merely die "for many" (Isa 53:12 [cf. 53:11]; Mark 10:45; Matt 20:28) but for the "world" (John 1:29; 6:51; 1 John 2:2; cf. John 3:16–17; 4:42; 6:33; 12:47). Although "world" may refer to the "many nations" whom the Messiah sprinkles and cleanses (Isa 52:15) in several of these texts, at least 1 John 2:2 (and probably John 3:16–17) seems to imply that Jesus's death somehow benefits every person.

John's writings strongly emphasize the substitutionary and voluntary nature of Jesus's death. Jesus "lays down his life" (John 10:11; cf. 15:13). Although John does not record Jesus's prayer in Gethsemane and his surrender to the Father's will to suffer and die, he confirms the Synoptic Gospel's assertion that Jesus could have escaped this suffering if he chose (John 10:18; 18:11). He also lays down his life "for" others, and the preposition indicates that Jesus died for their benefit and in their place.

John shows that the work of Christ includes the impartation of the Spirit to believers (e.g., John 1:33; 20:22). He also indicates that Jesus's death was a prerequisite to the gift of the Spirit (John 7:39; 16:7). This suggests that John, like the authors of the Synoptics, recognized that Jesus's death enacted the new covenant, even though John does not record Jesus's words to that effect at the institution of the Lord's Supper.

Finally, John sees Jesus's death as the supreme example of self-denying love for others. Thus believers should lay down their lives for their spiritual brothers and sisters as Jesus "laid down his life for us" (1 John 3:16). This does not mean that Christians can die an atoning death on others' behalf. It does mean that they should share their resources with fellow believers when they are in need (1 John 3:17) and express sacrificial love in their words and actions (1 John 3:18).

The Epistles of Paul

Paul's letters are especially rich in references to the salvific work of Christ. Like the Gospels, Acts, and John's writings, Paul appeals to the sacrifices of the OT to explain the significance of Jesus's suffering and death. Clearly familiar with Jesus's words that instituted the Lord's Supper, Paul portrays Jesus's death as the sacrifice of the Passover lamb (1 Cor 5:7) and as the sacrifice that enacts the new covenant (1 Cor 11:25). However, Paul points to another specific sacrifice as well. Alluding to the ritual performed on the Day of Atonement, Paul describes Jesus as the "mercy seat," on which sacrificial blood was poured by the high priest, to explain that Jesus's sacrificial blood accomplished our justification and redemption (Rom 3:24–26). In Eph 5:2, he compares Jesus's death to the sacrifice of a burnt offering. Paul recognizes that Jesus's death fulfilled the Holy Scriptures (1 Cor 15:3; cf. Rom 1:2; 3:21). His discussions of Jesus's death suggest that he not only saw that death as the fulfillment of direct messianic prophecies (e.g., Isa 52:13–53:12; cf. Rom 15:21; Rom 10:16) but of numerous types in Israel's sacrificial system as well.

Like Mark and Matthew, Paul also describes Jesus's death as a "ransom" (1 Tim 2:6). Since a cognate term described the OT "atonement price" (Exod 30:11–16), this description may cohere with portrayals of Jesus's death as an atoning sacrifice. However, Paul's metaphor probably looks beyond the sacrificial system of the OT to the secular world to illustrate one aspect of the significance of Jesus's death. Jesus's death is like the price paid to liberate a person from slavery. This meaning coheres with Paul's view that Christ is the believer's master (cf. Eph 6:9; Col 4:1) and the believer is "Christ's slave" who was "bought with a price" (1 Cor 7:22–23; cf. 6:19–20). Paul likely found that the imagery drawn from the slave market communicated more clearly to Gentiles who had not attended synagogue than the sacrificial imagery did.

Paul also uses secular imagery that would be especially apropos for Gentile readers to explain how Jesus's death provided forgiveness in Col 2:14. The believer's spiritual "certificate of debt," a record of every sin committed which was listed in the accounting ledger of the divine Judge, was nailed to the top of Jesus's cross. This certificate served as the placard listing the offenses for which the crucified one had been condemned. Because Jesus paid the penalty for the sins of believers by his own death, he presents them to the eschatological Judge as "holy, faultless, and blameless" (Col 1:22). The image offers one of the clearest and most poignant descriptions of Jesus's death as an act of penal substitution in all of Scripture. Paul also affirms penal substitution using imagery especially appropriate for a Jewish audience by insisting that the method by which Jesus was executed shows that he died under the divine curse that the Israelites deserved for their failure to fulfill the demands of the old covenant (Gal 3:10–14).

Perhaps Paul's most important contribution to an understanding of Jesus's salvific work is his doctrine of the believer's union with Christ in his death. This union results in a co-crucifixion—the believer is crucified together with Christ (e.g., Gal 2:19–20; Rom 6:6; Col 2:20; 3:3; 2 Tim 2:11). Through participation in Christ's death, believers died to the tyranny of sin (Rom 6:10–11), to the authority of the old covenant (Rom 7:4–6), to the domination of their flesh (Gal 5:24), and to the enticements of a sinful world (Gal 6:14). This participation is equivalent to putting off the old self (Col 3:9) and enables the believer to "put to death what belongs to your earthly nature" (Col 3:5). Christ's death resulted in the believer's spiritual circumcision (Col 2:11) which produces eager and loving obedience to God. Thus, Jesus's death is not only the means by which sinners are forgiven, but it is also the means by which their lives are transformed. Since the cross results in both forgiveness and moral transformation, those who see the cross as an excuse to continue living immorally are "enemies of the cross" (Phil 3:18).

Like John, Paul sees Jesus's death as dealing the deathblow to Satan. Through Jesus's death, God "disarmed" demonic spirits, the "rulers and authorities," "disgraced them publicly," and "triumphed over them" (Col 2:15). "Through his blood, shed on the cross" (Col 1:20), Christ crushed the authority of Satan and his demons. The decisive victory over our spiritual foes was won at the cross. Christ's victory is the basis for the fulfillment of the old promise of Gen 3:15 that "the God of peace will soon crush Satan under your feet" (Rom 16:20).

Like John, Paul presents Jesus's death as an example for believers to follow (Rom 15:3; Phil 2:5–11). In light of this example, believers should not live to please themselves. They should seek to serve others with humility and prioritize the needs of others above their own.

The General Epistles

Descriptions of Jesus's death in the General Epistles mirror descriptions in other NT documents, especially the letters of Paul. Both Hebrews and 1 Peter interpret Jesus's death against the background of the OT sacrificial system. Jesus's death is a sacrifice that atones for sin (Heb 9:26, 28; 10:12), bears the curse of sin (1 Pet 2:24), purifies and cleanses the sinner (Heb 1:3; 9:14), enacts the new covenant (Heb 7:22; 10:29; 12:24; 1 Pet 1:2), and removes all barriers to fellowship with God (Heb 10:19–20). Like Paul, Peter appears to describe Jesus as the fulfillment of the Day of Atonement ritual since his sufferings are compared to the blood poured on the top of the atonement cover and gazed on by the cherubim (1 Pet 1:10–12). Hebrews, in particular, seems to present Jesus as the fulfillment of many different categories of sacrifices from the OT cultus.

The death of Jesus has a transforming effect since it redeems sinners from their old, empty way of life (1 Pet 1:18–19). This resonates with the Pauline theme of Jesus's death as a redemption price or ransom. It is probably evidence of Peter's memory of Jesus's statement that he came to be "a ransom for many" (Mark 10:45).

Jesus's death also serves as an example to believers. Jesus was a righteous sufferer who was unjustly condemned. Similarly, believers should make sure that any suffering they experience is undeserved (1 Pet 2:21–25). Christ's sufferings are a model that believers should seek to emulate, a path that they should seek to follow.

The General Epistles also affirm a penal substitutionary view of the atonement. Peter regards Jesus's death as a fulfillment of Isa 52:13–53:12 in which the Messiah bears the iniquities of others (1 Pet 2:24). Hebrews describes Jesus's death in a manner that likely alludes to this text as well (Heb 9:28).

10

A Biblical-Theological Synthesis of the Work of Christ in Scripture

From beginning to end, from Genesis to Revelation, Scripture extols the salvific work of Christ. Although the direct messianic prophecies of the OT most emphasize the Messiah's role as ruler and king, even the earliest of these prophecies introduce the Messiah as the one who will crush the head of the serpent and bring God's blessing to the nations. The prophets reveal that the Messiah will accomplish his mission through his sacrificial death. The sovereign Messiah will also be a suffering Messiah. Although explicit references to the Messiah's atoning death are modest in terms of volume in the messianic prophecies, their relative rarity makes them all the more breathtaking. Even the few direct prophecies are stunningly sweeping in scope. The Messiah will present himself as a guilt offering, sprinkle many nations with purifying blood, wash away sin and impurity, bear the sin of many, bring rebellion to an end, put a stop to sin, atone for iniquity, and bring in everlasting righteousness (e.g., Isa 52:13–53:12; Dan 9:24; Zech 13:1). The Messiah will be both the interceding priest (Ps 110:4) and the bloody sacrifice (Isa 53:10) that provides full atonement for sin.

Jesus of Nazareth, the supremely authoritative interpreter of the Hebrew Scriptures, shows his disciples that there is more to the OT story of the Messiah's salvific work than initially meets the eye. The OT has numerous types and pictures of the Messiah's work of redemption, images ranging from guilt offerings to a bronze serpent. Jesus's disciples and those instructed by them point to many of these Old Testament images in the New Testament documents. Together the two Testaments reveal that Jesus's death was more than a tragic miscarriage of justice by Jewish leaders and Roman officials, more than the execution of a righteous martyr, more than a death that affected only a weeping mother and grieving followers viewing the heartbreaking sufferings of son, teacher, and friend atop the Place of the Skull. This death, this brutal, excruciating, horrifying death, was the fulfillment of God's eternal plan to bring salvation—a spectacularly gracious and glorious salvation—to all who repent and believe.

Christ's Death Fulfills Isaiah 52:13–53:12

Details of Isaiah's description of the Servant in his four Servant Songs indicate that this Servant is the Messiah. Like Ps 110:4 and possibly 2:6, Isaiah's fourth Servant Song describes the Servant-Messiah as a priest. He will perform the priestly function of sprinkling many nations (Isa 52:15) in order to atone for their sins. He will also "intercede for the rebels" (53:12) like a priest intercedes for his people. But the Servant is both priest and sacrifice. He will suffer and die as a "guilt offering" (53:10). The Servant's death is a vicarious, substitutionary death in which the Lord punishes him "for the iniquity of us all" (v. 6). By his death, the Servant "will justify many" (v. 11).

This prophecy clearly influences the explanations of the work of Christ given by Jesus and the NT writers. Christ applied this prophecy to himself in Luke 22:35–38 and probably in Mark 10:45 and Matt 20:28 as well. Matthew (Matt 8:17), Luke (Acts 8:32–33), John (John 12:38), Paul (Rom 10:16; cf. Rom 15:21), and Peter (1 Pet 2:22) explicitly describe Jesus as the fulfillment of this prophecy. It is difficult to imagine any single text more important for a biblical theology of the atoning work of Christ. Isaiah's prophecy is the clearest OT description of the significance of the Messiah's death and is foundational to descriptions of the work of Christ in the NT documents.

Christ's Death Fulfills the OT Sacrificial System

Isaiah describes the Messiah's death as a "guilt offering" (Isa 53:10), a sacrifice that removes the guilt of a sinner's iniquity, makes atonement on his behalf, and grants him forgiveness (Lev 5:6–6:7). Jesus and the NT authors taught that other OT sacrifices also depicted the significance of his death. They compare Jesus's death to the Passover sacrifice, the sacrifice that enacted the Mosaic covenant, the Day of Atonement sacrifice, and sacrifices for purification of the unclean. In fact, Jesus's death is compared to so many of the OT sacrifices that one seems justified in concluding that the entire OT sacrificial system foreshadows Jesus's death and its effects in some way.

Although the OT sacrificial system provides rich background for explaining the significance of Jesus's death, the NT points to other OT images of Jesus's suffering and death as well. For example, Jesus himself taught that his crucifixion was like the lifting up of the bronze serpent that rescued the Israelites from divine punishment (John 3:14; Num 21:4–9). He also quoted the psalms of lament (e.g., Ps 22:1) to describe the agonies of his crucifixion (Matt 27:46; Mark 15:34; cf. John 19:24; Heb 2:12). This quotation was especially appropriate since the psalmist writes, "They pierced my hands and my feet" (Ps 22:16), and describes other details which remarkably fit Jesus's crucifixion.

Christ's Death Causes God's Wrath to Pass Over the Believer

Jesus's words at the Last Supper appear to compare his body to the flesh of the Passover lamb that was consumed at the Passover feast (e.g., Mark 14:22). This comparison is also recorded by Matthew (Matt 26:26), Luke (Luke 22:19), and Paul (1 Cor 11:24). John highlights similarities between Jesus and the Passover lamb. He shows that Jesus's crucifixion occurred at the time that the lambs were being sacrificed (John 19:14). He also argues that the treatment of Jesus's corpse by the Roman soldiers matched the instructions for the treatment of the carcass of the Passover lamb (John 19:33, 36; Exod 12:46). Paul likewise writes that "Christ our Passover lamb has been sacrificed" (1 Cor 5:7).

Like the Passover sacrifice, Jesus's death protects his people from wrath and destruction (Heb 11:28). Like the Passover sacrifice, it also initiates an exodus. This new exodus is liberation from slavery to sin and to Satan. The OT exodus was remembered as a time of deliverance and redemption. Thus, the description of Jesus as the Passover sacrifice parallels and sometimes overlaps with descriptions of his death as a ransom or redemption price.

Christ's Death Atones for Sin

Jesus's death is also reminiscent of the sacrifices offered on the Day of Atonement. Paul refers to Jesus as the "mercy seat" on which blood was poured in the annual atoning ritual and Jesus's own blood shed in his crucifixion as the sacrifice blood poured on that mercy seat (Rom 3:25). Peter appears to describe Jesus's blood as the blood poured on the mercy seat where two cherubim looked down (1 Pet 1:11–12; Exod 25:17–22). Comparisons to the Day of Atonement sacrifices demonstrate that Christ made atonement for all the sins, impurities, and rebellious acts of his people (cf. Lev 16:16).

Jesus's death was the means by which he, as a "merciful and faithful high priest" was able to "make atonement for the sins of the people" (Heb 2:17; cf. Heb 9:6–14). Thus, the Apostle John declares, "He himself is the atoning sacrifice for our sins, and not only for ours, but also for those of the whole world" (1 John 2:2; cf. 4:10). Because of Jesus's sacrifice, "we have now been justified by his blood" (Rom 5:9) and through that blood have received "the forgiveness of our trespasses" (Eph 1:7).

Christ's Death Purifies Believers

Paul, John, and the author of Hebrews compare Jesus's death to the OT sacrifices that purified the sinner or consecrated objects after they had experienced defilement (Eph 5:25–26; Heb 1:3; 9:22; 1 John 1:7; cf. John 13:10). Jesus's death cleanses the believer's conscience (Heb 9:14) and qualifies the believer to enter God's presence boldly (Heb 10:19–20). Thus, Jesus is able to both "forgive us our sins and to cleanse us from all unrighteousness" (1 John 1:9).

Christ's Death Enacts the New Covenant

Jesus's words at the Last Supper compare his death to the sacrifice that enacted the Mosaic covenant (Mark 14:24). This comparison is also recorded by Matthew (Matt 26:28), Luke (Luke 22:20), and Paul (1 Cor 11:25). Like the sacrifices of Exod 24:5–8, Jesus's death enacts a covenant (e.g., 1 Pet 1:2; Heb 12:24). This covenant is the new covenant promised by the OT prophets. In this covenant, God promises that he "will forgive their iniquity and never again remember their sin" (Jer 31:34). He will put his teaching within them and "write it on their hearts" (Jer 31:33) so that God's instructions are no longer merely external standards for living, but internal compulsions. God's people will love his instruction and long to live according to it. Furthermore, God promises, "I will place my Spirit within you and cause you to follow my statutes and carefully observe my ordinances" (Ezek 36:27). The indwelling Spirit radically changes the believer's character and behavior. The Spirit produces the "fruit" of a Christian lifestyle that is consistent with the Law's moral demands (Gal 5:22–23).

Christ's Death Ransoms Believers

The NT uses imagery related to the slave market to portray the effects of Jesus's death. Jesus's death is like the "ransom" (Matt 20:28; Mark 10:45; 1 Tim 2:6) that a person pays to emancipate a slave or to transfer the slave from the possession of the former master to his own possession. This "ransom" is sometimes referred to by Paul simply as "the price" (τιμή). Twice Paul tells the Corinthians, "You were bought at a price" (1 Cor 6:20; 7:23). That price is a reference to Jesus's death, sometimes signified by his "blood" (e.g., 1 Pet 1:18–19), by which Christ redeemed sinners.

Believers were redeemed from "your [their] empty way of life inherited from your [their] ancestors" (1 Pet 1:18), the kind of life that characterized "slaves to impurity" (Rom 6:19) and "slaves of sin" devoid of true righteousness (Rom 6:20). They were redeemed for humble and obedient service to Christ. Due to the ransom that Christ paid, the totality of the believer, including his body (1 Cor 6:20) and his service (1 Cor 7:23), belongs to Christ. Christ is now the believers' "Master" (Eph 6:9; Col 4:1), their owner and authority.

Christ's Death Involves Believers

The words of the resurrected Christ to Paul on the Damascus Road introduced the doctrine of the believer's union with Christ. Jesus's indicting question equated Paul's persecution of the church with persecuting "me" (Acts 9:4). The clear implication is that Christ experienced what his disciples experienced. This principle would become foundational to Paul's ethic (e.g., 1 Cor 6:15–17). Christ's statement would also deeply influence Paul's soteriology. Paul recognized that if Christ was united with his disciples in such a way that he participated in their experiences, they also necessarily participated in his. Consequently, the believer participated in Jesus's death.

The believer was "crucified with Christ" (Gal 2:20). This meant that the old person who existed before the believer's conversion was dead and gone. He could exclaim, "I no longer live" (Gal 2:20). The believer thus "put off the old self with its practices" (Col 3:9). By union with Christ in his death, the believer died to sin's domination so that he is no longer "enslaved to sin" (Rom 6:6). He was "crucified . . . to the world" (Gal 6:14), the "present evil age" that presses a person to adopt its perverted standards and depraved lifestyle (Gal 1:4; cf. 5:19–21). Participation in Jesus's death also transferred the believer from the authority of the old covenant to the authority of the new covenant. The law, like a marital covenant, has authority over a person only as long as the person lives (Rom 7:1–3). Therefore, the believer has died to the old covenant, that covenant that exacerbated sin and condemned the sinner (Rom 7:5–6). Set free from "the law of sin and death" (Rom 8:2), the believer came under the new covenant that provides forgiveness of sin and the indwelling of the Spirit so that "we [he] may serve in the newness of the Spirit and not in the old letter of the law" (Rom 7:6).

Christ's Death Sets an Example for Believers

Jesus's call to discipleship commanded sinners, "Follow me" (Mark 1:17). This entailed following Jesus's example, emulating his character and conduct. But the NT writers show that believers are to follow Jesus's example, not only in life but also in death. Jesus's death serves as a model of selfless love for others. The apostle John urges believers to lay down their lives for their fellow believers by sharing their resources with those who are in need. The incentive for this sacrificial lifestyle is that Jesus "laid down his life for us" (1 John 3:16). Paul presents Jesus's death as an example of abandoning the pursuit of self-pleasure (Rom 15:3) and serving others with humility that prioritizes them above oneself (Phil 2:5–11). Peter too appeals to Jesus's death as an example. Believers must be sure that if they suffer at the hands of government authorities, they suffer like Christ as those falsely accused and wrongly condemned (1 Pet 2:21–25), not like the thieves at Jesus's side who were receiving exactly what they deserved. Thus, although the moral example theory of Jesus's death clearly must not be posited as an alternative to penal substitution, it should be affirmed alongside and as a complement to penal substitution.

Christ's Death Vanquishes Satan and His Demons

As Jesus anticipated his impending death, he declared, "Now is the judgment of this world. Now the ruler of this world will be cast out" (John 12:31; cf. 16:11; Rev 12:9). At the very least, this casting out refers to Satan's dethronement in which he is stripped of his tyranny over those who were once his children but are now children of God. However, since Rev 12:7–12 seems to serve as John's commentary on Jesus's statement, it appears that this casting out also ends Satan's ability to accuse believers before God. Jesus's sacrifice atoned for believers' sins, so Satan has no grounds to bring accusations against them. Satan is expelled from heaven's courtroom because he has been conquered "by the blood of the Lamb" (Rev 12:11).

Paul and the author of Hebrews also describe Jesus's death as his decisive victory over Satan. Paul explains that "through his blood, shed on the cross," God forced the submission of all those on earth and in heaven who had rebelled against him (Col 1:20). He clarifies that through Jesus's cross, God "disarmed the rulers and authorities and disgraced them publicly" (Col 2:15). The author of Hebrews insists that "through his death," Jesus acted to "destroy the one holding the power of death—that is, the devil" (Heb 2:14). Thus, while the penal substitutionary view of Jesus's death is most prevalent in the Scriptures, aspects of the Christus Victor view (like the moral example view) must be recognized as thoroughly biblical as well.

Christ's Death Is for Believers and the Entire World

Descriptions of the extent of the atonement are often limited to a group within humanity. In the Fourth Servant Song, the Messiah is pierced because of "our" rebellion, dies for the iniquity of "us," and through his death will justify and bear the sin of "many" (Isa 53:5, 6, 11, 12). Similar delimitations are common in the NT. Jesus refers to laying down his life for his "friends," and he explains, "You are my friends if you do what I command you" (John 15:13–14). He exclaims that he came to give his life as a ransom for "many" (Mark 10:45; Matt 20:28). John explains that Jesus came to be the atoning sacrifice "for our sins" (1 John 4:10). Paul writes that Christ died for "us" (1 Thess 5:10; Rom 5:8) and for "our" sins (1 Cor 15:3).

Yet other texts are far more inclusive and describe the scope of Jesus's sacrificial death in the most sweeping terms. In John's writings, Jesus is the "Lamb of God who takes away the sin of the world" (John 1:29) and died as an expression of God's love for the "world" (John 3:16) and as "the Savior of the world" (John 4:42). John even exclaims that Jesus Christ "is the atoning sacrifice for our sins, and not only for ours, but also for those of the whole world" (1 John 2:2). Paul also writes that not only did Christ die "for the ungodly" (Rom 5:6), he died "for all" (2 Cor 5:14–15). He insists that Christ "gave himself as a ransom for all" and that God brings "salvation for all people" (1 Tim 2:5–6; Titus 2:11).

In some of these contexts, the intention seems to be to include people of all nations, especially both Jews and Gentiles, as objects of divine grace. However, in other contexts, especially 1 Tim 2:5–6 (in which "all" seems to refer to all humanity; cf. 4:10) and 1 John 2:2 (in which the sins of "the whole world" are contrasted with "our sins" as the focus of Jesus's atoning sacrifice), the writer seems to refer to all human beings without any distinction. Since the very same writers who make these statements also very clearly assert the necessity of faith in Christ for salvation, it appears that they recognized two different intentions in the atonement. On one hand, Jesus's death promises, grants, and secures actual atonement to those who repent and believe. On the other hand, Jesus's death provides and offers atonement to all (contingent upon their repentance and faith). Jesus's own words offer the most satisfying resolution to the apparent tension. He clearly described God's giving of the Son in death as an expression of God's love for "the world" yet also insisted that only those who believe in him "will not perish but have eternal life" (John 3:16). Through the Savior's suffering, redemption is genuinely offered to all, though it is imparted only to Jesus's disciples. As Article 3 of the Second Main Point of Doctrine of the Canons of the Synod of Dordt states: "This death of God's Son is the only and entirely complete sacrifice and satisfaction for sins; it is of infinite value and worth, more than sufficient to atone for the sins of the whole world."[1]

---

[1] Article 4 proceeds to demonstrate that this complete sufficiency of Jesus's atoning death is a necessary consequence of a high Christology: "This death is of such great value and worth for the reason that the person who suffered it is—as was necessary to be our Savior—not only a true and perfectly holy human, but also the only begotten Son of God, of the same eternal and infinite essence with the Father and the Holy Spirit." Note that section 6 of the "Rejection of Errors" objects to "the distinction between obtaining and applying" only when it is accompanied by a denial of God's efficacious grace.

PART II:
SYSTEMATIC THEOLOGY

11

The Work of Christ Prior to the Incarnation

Introduction

This chapter begins our approach to the work of Christ from a systematic theology perspective. Some excellent books on the work of Christ from this perspective begin with the incarnation. Robert Letham gives his understanding of the work of Christ as "all that Christ did when he came to this earth 'for us and our salvation,' all that he continues to do now that he is risen from the dead and at God's right hand, and all that he will do when he returns in glory at the end of the age."[1] Robert Peterson follows the same pattern, with the incarnation as the first of Jesus's "saving events."[2]

While the incarnation is the obvious beginning of the work of the Incarnate One, the One who assumed flesh in the incarnation was the eternal Son, and there is important biblical teaching about his work before the incarnation. There is definite teaching on the work of Christ in creation, and intriguing hints of his possible involvement in events occurring between creation and incarnation, and that will be the focus of this chapter. In subsequent chapters, we will trace the work of Christ in a somewhat chronological

---

[1] Robert Letham, *The Work of Christ*, Contours of Christian Theology (Downers Grove: InterVarsity, 1993), 18–19.

[2] Robert Peterson, *Salvation Accomplished by the Son: The Work of Christ* (Wheaton: Crossway, 2012), 9.

fashion, looking at his work in the incarnation, followed by several chapters on the traditional systematic theology topics of the nature and extent of Christ's atoning work on the cross, and concluding with the work of Christ following the cross, from his resurrection to his return.

Christ as Creator

There are four main passages that affirm Christ as the agent of creation, or the one through whom God the Father created. In all four texts, the Greek preposition *dia* ("through") is used to express the relationship of Christ to creation. In John 1:3, the Word is identified as the one through whom "all things" are created; verse 10 specifies "the world" as being created "through him." In 1 Cor 8:6, Paul contrasts the role of the Father ("All things are from him, and we exist for him") and the role of the Son ("All things are through him and we exist through him"). Colossians 1:16 has the most expansive statement, attributing to Christ the creation of all things, "in heaven and on earth, the visible and the invisible, whether thrones or dominions or rulers or authorities." This passage also expands the relevant prepositions: all things are created "by him (*en*) . . . through him (*dia*) . . . and for him (*eis*)." Hebrews 1:2 is more succinct: God "made the universe through him."

The teaching is clear: the early church saw the Son of God as Creator of the universe, something that obviously happened before the incarnation. A fascinating question that has occasioned some discussion is "the theological framework within which such an extraordinary assertion could be made."[3] There had to be the assumption that the Son was coeternal with the Father, an assumption inherent in the orthodox understanding of the Trinity and implicit in verses reflecting the preexistence of the Son (John 1:1–2; 8:58; Phil 2:6). There may be some influence from the possible identification of Christ with the Wisdom present with God at creation in Proverbs 8:22–31. Furthermore, in calling Jesus the *Logos* (John 1:1), John used a term that called to mind the Genesis account of God creating all things by his word. But Sean McDonough argues strongly that the most important factor in the construction of the theological framework for the assertion of Christ as

---

[3] Sean McDonough, *Christ as Creator: Origins of a New Testament Doctrine* (Oxford: Oxford University Press, 2009), 2.

Creator was the early church's memories of Jesus's earthly life and ministry.[4] Throughout the Gospels Jesus acted as Lord over creation, stilling storms, walking on water, and multiplying loaves and fish. It was evidence like this that led the early church to the confession of Jesus as Messiah, and it is as Messiah that the idea of Christ creating the world makes sense. The Messiah is the Lord's anointed; as such, he acts on behalf of the Father in the act of creation. McDonough says that all of the texts on Christ as Creator "focus on the theme of messianic lordship."[5] Thus, the things Christ did in his earthly life point to his status as Lord over creation and as the one through whom God created all things, assuming his eternal existence before the incarnation.

One ongoing work of Christ is linked to his work as Creator, his work of providentially holding all things together (Col 1:17) or "sustaining all things" (Heb 1:3). This work began with creation itself and continued before, during, and after his incarnation, extending until the day of the Lord when this creation will give way to the new heavens and new earth (see 2 Pet 3:10–13).

Christophanies

The second possibility for some preincarnate work of Christ comes from Christophanies, the idea that Christ made appearances on earth before his incarnation on a variety of occasions for a variety of purposes. The most prominent figure here is "the angel of the Lord," who appears in numerous places in the Old Testament: Genesis 16 and 22, Exodus 3, Numbers 22, Judges 2, 6 and 13, 2 Kings 1 and 9, 1 Chronicles 21, Psalm 34 and 35, and Zechariah 1 and 3. There are three features that seem to give some support to the possibility that the appearances of this "angel of the Lord" are, in fact, appearances of the preincarnate Christ.

First, the angel seems at places to be clearly identified with God (Gen 16:11–13; 48:15–16; Exod 3:2–4, Judg 6:11, 14, 21, 23), and often "speaks with immediate divine authority."[6] As Charles Scobie notes, "In a number of passages it is not easy to distinguish the angel of the Lord from the Lord

---

[4] McDonough, 13.

[5] McDonough, 65.

[6] Michael Bird, *Evangelical Theology: A Biblical and Systematic Introduction* (Grand Rapids: Zondervan, 2013), 360.

himself."[7] Second, the types of things the angel of the Lord does seem fitting for Christ. Peter Schemm notes, "Both the Angel and Jesus Christ ministered through revelation, deliverance, protection, intercession, confirmation of God's covenant, and judgment."[8] There is some continuity in the work of the two. Third, Walter Kaiser points to lexical evidence in that this angel, by his very name, is, like Christ, a "sent one."[9] He says, "It is that word *sent* that ties together the angel, messenger or sent one into an Old Testament theology of christophanies, appearances of God in human form."[10] Thus the things that the angel of the Lord is sent to do on these occasions in the Old Testament could be seen as aspects of the work of Christ.

There is significant historical support for this view. This was the interpretation championed in the early church. David Bercot states, "The early church taught that in all of the Old Testament theophanies, it was the pre-incarnate Son of God who appeared."[11] But most contemporary scholarship is much more hesitant to make such claims today. Gerald Bray traces this hesitance to a change in how commentators relate the Old Testament to the New. He says,

> It was standard practice in ancient times to look for typological and prophetic foreshadowings of the coming of Christ in the Old Testament, and so we find that the Fathers saw nothing wrong in regarding epiphanies of angels, for example, as preincarnational appearances of the Son of God.[12]

---

[7] C. H. Scobie, *The Ways of Our God: An Approach to Biblical Theology* (Grand Rapids: Eerdmans, 2003), 113.

[8] Peter Schemm Jr., "The Agents of God: Angels," in *A Theology for the Church*, ed. Daniel Akin, rev. ed. (Nashville: B&H Academic, 2014), 256–57.

[9] Walter Kaiser Jr., et al., "Genesis 32:23–32: With Whom Did God Wrestle?" in *Hard Sayings of the Bible*, The Essential IVP Reference Collection (Leicester, UK: InterVarsity, 2001), CD-ROM Version. See also Scobie, *The Ways of Our God*, 113. He says of the Hebrew word for angel: "The Hebrew *mal'ākh*, from the root *l'k* = 'send,' means one who is sent, a messenger."

[10] Kaiser Jr., et al., "Genesis 32:23–32: With Whom Did God Wrestle?" 192.

[11] David Bercot, ed., *A Dictionary of Early Christian Beliefs* (Peabody, MA: Hendrickson, 2002), 643.

[12] Gerald Bray, "The Church Fathers and Their Use of Scripture," in *The Trustworthiness of God: Perspectives on the Nature of Scripture*, ed. Paul Helm and Carl Trueman (Grand Rapids: Eerdmans, 2002), 164.

It could be argued that this ancient practice fits well with the claim of the resurrected Jesus that all of the Old Testament speaks of him (Luke 24:27, 44). But Bray acknowledges that most commentators today do not see such preincarnational appearances of Christ in the Old Testament. He says of the ancient practice, "This would not meet with general acceptance today."[13] For example, Graham Cole thinks the case for seeing the angel as a representative of God is stronger than the case for seeing the angel as either a theophany or a Christophany, based on the careful way the Old Testament distinguishes between the angel of the Lord and the Lord himself [14] and the fact that the New Testament nowhere identifies Jesus with the angel of the Lord of the Old Testament.[15]

In the opinion of this author, it is a close call. On the side of seeing the angel as a preincarnate appearance of Christ, we have the arguments of Michael Bird, Charles Scobie, Peter Schemm, and Walter Kaiser, the support of many in the early church (Justin Martyr in particular), and some in contemporary evangelical life (Wayne Grudem and Billy Graham).[16] Those seeing difficulties in the preincarnate Christ position are Graham Cole, Réne Lopéz, Ronald Youngblood, Scot McKnight and "much of OT evangelical scholarship."[17] This

---

[13] Bray, 164.

[14] But as noted above, Charles Scobie thinks the Old Testament is not careful at all to distinguish between the angel of the Lord and the Lord himself; rather they are closely related. Scobie, *The Ways of Our God*, 113.

[15] See Graham Cole, *Against the Darkness: The Doctrine of Angels, Satan, and Demons* (Wheaton: Crossway, 2019), 62–65. It is interesting that in an earlier work, Cole expressed a more open assessment of the evidence: "The suggestion that the anthropomorphic theophanies were actually appearances of the preincarnate Son of God is plausible and the idea is defensible. However, it must be observed that even though this proposition is consistent with the biblical testimony it is not demanded by it." Cole, *The God Who Became Human: A Biblical Theology of the Incarnation*, New Studies in Biblical Theology, no. 30 (Downers Grove: InterVarsity, 2013), 120.

[16] See Wayne Grudem, *Systematic Theology: An Introduction to Biblical Doctrine* (Grand Rapids: Zondervan, 1994), 401. But Grudem's support is qualified, as he says the angel of the Lord may "perhaps" be the preincarnate Christ. The support of Billy Graham for this position is claimed by James Leo Garrett, Jr., *Systematic Theology: Biblical, Historical & Evangelical*, vol. 1 (Grand Rapids: Eerdmans, 1990), 360.

[17] For the arguments of Lopéz, Youngblood, and McKnight, see Cole, *Against the Darkness*, 64–65. For the position of "much of OT evangelical scholarship," see

author sees some strength in the arguments for seeing the appearances of "the angel of the Lord" as preincarnate appearances of Christ and thinks that view must be regarded as at least a strong possibility. What the angel did in the Old Testament may then be seen as quite possibly part of the work of Christ.

Less likely but also worth mentioning are two other possible appearances of Christ before his incarnation. One is the appearance of a fourth figure in the fiery furnace of Daniel 3, walking with Shadrach, Meshach, and Abednego. Some have seen this as a preincarnate appearance of the Second Person of the Trinity because that figure is described as one looking "like a son of the gods" (Dan 3:25).[18] While one writer thinks it is "naturally a Christian instinct to think of this also as a vision of the presence of the pre-incarnate Christ alongside those who are suffering for the sake of the kingdom of God,"[19] this possibility, while supported by many in the early church and some today, is again a minority position among commentators today.[20] In this writer's opinion, the biblical data here is too limited to be very definite.

Finally, there is the curious comment of Paul in 1 Cor 10:4, that the rock that followed the children of Israel in their wilderness wanderings "was Christ." The exact relationship between the rock that provided water for the Israelites and the person of Christ has been the subject of considerable scholarly discussion. Anthony Thiselton notes five possible interpretive

---

Thomas McComiskey, "Angel of the Lord," in *Evangelical Dictionary of Theology*, ed. Daniel Treier and Walter Elwell, 3rd ed. (Grand Rapids: Baker Academic, 2017), 54.

[18] Bird, *Evangelical Theology*, 360–61; Stephen Miller, *Daniel*, NAC, vol. 18 (Nashville: B & H, 1994), 123–24, and Andrew Steinman, *Daniel*, Concordia Commentary (St. Louis: Concordia, 2008), 193. Tremper Longman III, *Daniel*, NIV Application Commentary (Grand Rapids: Zondervan, 1999), 142, says of this figure in the fire, "the Christian cannot help but see a prefigurement of Jesus Christ," but he stops short of calling it a preincarnate appearance.

[19] Ronald Wallace, *The Lord Is King: The Message of Daniel*, BST (Downers Grove: InterVarsity, 1979), 68. This natural Christian instinct is reflected in a popular 2019 song from Hillsong United, "Another in the Fire," which sees the incident in Daniel 3 as a Christophany and as a promise that Christ will be with us in our fiery trials.

[20] Ernest Lucas, *Daniel*, Apollos Old Testament Commentary, vol. 20 (Downers Grove: IVP Academic, 2002), 92: "Many earlier Christian commentators . . . held that the figure here is the pre-incarnate Christ. Few would defend that view today."

options,[21] but two main camps seem to attract the most support. Some take the reference to Christ to be in some sense figurative. Some use the language of analogy, or typology, or "structural correspondence,"[22] but surprisingly, many take a more realistic view, identifying the rock as actually the pre-existent Christ. Gordon Fee says that Paul used the word "'was' to indicate the reality of Christ's presence in the OT events"; Thiselton endorses the similar view of Ben Witherington ("'Was' indicates that the divine Christ was really a part of Israel's history, providing them with life-giving water") and A. Bandstra: "Christ himself, the pre-existent Christ, was present with the Israelites in their wilderness journey."[23] But perhaps David Garland gets closest to Paul's intent in these words: "We need not be detained by views about whether he thinks of some manifestation of the pre-existent Christ (cf. Phil 2:6; Col 1:15–18), as some interpreters argue. . . . He simply assumes, without going into any elaborate theological detail, that Christ is the source of all divine gifts and succor." He is the one who is behind "both the old and new saving events."[24]

Garland's comments serve as a fitting conclusion to this examination of the work of Christ before his incarnation. These examples remind us that the Second Person of the Trinity existed in the triune Godhead from eternity past and was not idle before his incarnation. He was at work on behalf of his people even then. But that work comes to much fuller expression in the incarnation.

---

[21] Anthony Thiselton, *The First Epistle to the Corinthians*, NIGTC (Grand Rapids: Eerdmans, 2000), 727.

[22] Thiselton, *First Epistle to the Corinthians*, 727, says many commentators regard Paul's statement "as a typological comment"; Roy Ciampi and Brian Rosner, *The First Letter to the Corinthians*, PNTC (Grand Rapids: Eerdmans, 2010), 451, use the language of "analogy" as an option; Timothy Brookins and Bruce Longenecker, *I Corinthians 10–16: A Handbook on the Greek Text*, Baylor Handbook on the Greek New Testament (Waco, TX: Baylor University Press, 2016), 5, advocate seeing Christ and the rock in terms of "structural correspondence," not identity.

[23] Gordon Fee, *The First Epistle to the Corinthians*, NICNT (Grand Rapids: Eerdmans, 1987), 449; Thiselton, *First Epistle to the Corinthians*, 729, citing Ben Witherington III, *Conflict and Community in Corinth: A Socio-Rhetorical Commentary on 1 and 2 Corinthians* (Grand Rapids: Eerdmans: Paternoster, 1995), 218; and Andrew Bandstra, "Interpretation in 1 Cor. 10:1–11," *CTJ* 6, no. 1 (April 1971), 14.

[24] David Garland, *1 Corinthians*, BECNT (Grand Rapids: Baker Academic, 2003), 457–58.

12

The Work of Christ in the Incarnation and Earthly Life and Ministry

W e treat the work of Christ in his incarnation and in his earthly life and ministry together for two reasons. First, the incarnation is the necessary prerequisite for his earthly life and ministry. Second, while the work of Christ is much more evident and detailed in his earthly life and ministry than in his incarnation, there is one aspect of his work that is emphatically seen in both, the work of identification.

The Work of Christ in the Incarnation

We must first ask if the incarnation itself is an aspect of the work of Christ at all. It is certainly a prerequisite of all that Jesus did in his earthly life, but was Christ, the second person of the Godhead, active in the event of incarnation itself? The New Testament and Jesus himself repeatedly speak of the Father sending the Son (John 3:17; 5:36; Gal 4:4) and the Holy Spirit is the member of the Trinity whose activity is associated with the miraculous conception of Jesus in the virgin Mary (Matt 1:20; Luke 1:35). Is the Second Person of the Trinity totally passive in the process? John 1:14 and Phil 2:7 both speak of the Son acting in the incarnation, becoming flesh[1] and emptying himself, and so the answer would seem to be that it is proper to speak of the incarnation as one aspect of the work of Christ.

Incarnation and Theosis

The incarnation plays a significant role in the recapitulation model of the atonement held especially by the early church father Irenaeus. But in that model, the incarnation is only a part of the larger work of atonement, and so we will consider the relation of the incarnation to the atonement more fully in the next chapter's discussion of the nature of the atonement. The incarnation is much more central to what is known today as *theosis*, or deification. It reflects the biblical language of 2 Pet 1:4, which says believers "may share in the divine nature." While exactly how that happens is not clear, for Irenaeus, the incarnation is essential. In his work *Against Heresies*, Irenaeus writes, "The Word of God, our Lord Jesus Christ . . . did, through His transcendent love, become what we are, that he might bring us to be even what He is Himself."[2] Oliver Crisp gives the following in his summary of Irenaeus's doctrine: "The Word of God unites himself to human nature in order to heal humanity and enable them to participate in the divine life."[3] The Word himself is seen as acting in the incarnation.

The theme of *theosis* via incarnation is even clearer in the work of Athanasius. Though his full thought on the work of Christ includes

---

[1] The Nicene Creed sees the Son as active in the incarnation: he "came down from heaven." The Athanasian Creed says the Son becomes incarnate by the "taking of the Manhood into God" (art. 35). Other fathers speak of Christ "assuming" a human nature, most famously Gregory Nazianzus in refuting the heresy of Apollinaris: "what is not assumed is not healed." Gregory of Nazianzus, "To Cledonius the Priest against Apollinarius," in *Christology of the Later Fathers*, ed. Edward Hardy (Philadelphia: Westminster, 1954), 218.

[2] Irenaeus, *Against Heresies, ANF* (Edinburgh: T&T Clark, 1885) 1:526 (Book 5, Preface).

[3] Oliver Crisp, *Approaching the Atonement: The Reconciling Work of Christ* (Downers Grove: IVP Academic, 2020), 40.

important and multifaceted consideration of the cross, it is significant that his most important work is entitled *On the Incarnation of the Word*. In it, he says pointedly, "He was made man that we might be made God."[4] He is not denying monotheism (we do not become gods); nor do we replace God. Rather, Athanasius is saying that "Christ's work is fundamentally about enabling human beings to participate in the divine life."[5] As Christ is both God and man, if we are united to Christ, we participate in the life of God. Thus, if union with Christ is central to salvation, as it is for many,[6] salvation may be seen as deification and strongly linked to the incarnation.

This understanding of union with Christ as participation in the life of God was stronger in Eastern Orthodox theology historically than in the West, though there have been reflections of it in some Western theologians, from Thomas Aquinas to Jonathan Edwards, and it has enjoyed increased evangelical appropriation in recent years.[7] But in addition to its importance for participation in the life of God, the incarnation is also important for another aspect of the work of Christ, his identification with humans.

Identification and Kenosis

There is one important New Testament text that suggests that another work on the part of Christ was involved in the incarnation: Phil 2:7. This verse describes the work of Christ in the incarnation as a self-emptying, or a *kenosis*, from the Greek verb for to empty, *kenoō*. Verse 7 and the surrounding

---

[4] Athanasius, "On the Incarnation of the Word," *NPNF²* (Edinburgh: T&T Clark, 1891), 4:65 (para. 54).

[5] Crisp, *Approaching the Atonement*, 43.

[6] See Kenneth Keathley, "The Doctrine of Salvation," in *A Theology for the Church*, ed. Daniel Akin, rev. ed. (Nashville: B&H, 2014), 544.

[7] This is reflected in many of the contributions to Michael Christensen and Jeffery Wittung, ed., *Partakers of the Divine Nature: The History and Development of Deification in the Christian Traditions* (Grand Rapids: Baker Academic, 2007), and in the work of evangelical theologian Daniel Clendenin, "Partakers of Divinity: The Orthodox Doctrine of *Theosis*," *JETS* 37, no. 3 (September 1994): 365–79.

verses (Phil 2:5–11) have been the subject of extensive discussion among exegetes;[8] here we will only state the conclusions of our exegetical study as they relate to our topic, the work of Christ in the incarnation.

The work of Christ in the incarnation is described here as something he did not do (v. 6) and something he did do (v. 7). He did not "consider equality with God as *harpagmon.*" While there has been controversy over this word, we find the translations "something to be exploited," or "something to be used to his own advantage" to be superior to other options. As F. F. Bruce observes,

> There is no question of Christ's trying to snatch or seize equality with God: that was already his because he always had the nature of God. Neither is there any question of his trying to retain it by force. The point is rather that he did not treat equality with God as an excuse for self-assertion or self-aggrandizement; on the contrary, he treated it as an occasion for renouncing every advantage or privilege that might have accrued to him thereby, as an opportunity for self-impoverishment and unreserved self-sacrifice.[9]

Donald Macleod expresses how this decision is reflected in Christ's earthly life: "Never once does he in his own interest or in his own self-defense break beyond the parameters of humanity. . . . The power which carried the world, stilled the tempest and raised the dead was never used to make his own conditions of service easier."[10]

Positively, the work of Christ in the incarnation is described as an emptying of himself. In the late nineteenth and early twentieth century, there were a number of theologians who saw this *kenosis* as indicating that the Son of God ceased to possess certain attributes of deity in order for him to

---

[8] See any of the numerous commentaries on Philippians, along with an entire book devoted to this passage, Ralph P. Martin, *Carmen Christi: Philippians 2:5–11 in Recent Interpretation and in the Setting of Early Christian Worship* (Cambridge: Cambridge University Press, 1967).

[9] F. F. Bruce, *Philippians* (San Francisco: Harper & Row, 1983), 45.

[10] Donald Macleod, *The Person of Christ*, Contours of Christian Theology (Downers Grove: InterVarsity, 1998), 220.

become truly human.[11] But this is contrary to classical understandings of the nature of God as immutable, and contrary to classical understandings of the nature of Christ as fully God and fully man. These theologians seriously diminished the deity of the Son and are widely regarded as unorthodox.[12]

Beyond these theologians of the nineteenth and twentieth century, theologian Stephen Wellum also raises questions about some kenotic influences in contemporary evangelical Christology.[13] He distinguishes two kenotic schools, calling them ontological kenotic Christology (OKC) and functional kenotic Christology (FKC). Those within these schools perceive themselves to be within the bounds of classical Christian orthodoxy but think that some of the points of nineteenth century kenoticism make better sense of Jesus's humanity than the classical view.[14] At the same time, they think they preserve the deity of Jesus.

Those in OKC come close to making the same claims as the nineteenth-century kenoticists, "that in the incarnation the divine Son 'gave up' or 'laid aside' certain divine attributes or properties normally belonging to deity." This allowed him to live a fully human life without completely losing his deity.[15] They think they can preserve the deity of Christ by having him surrender only accidental attributes of deity, not essential attributes.[16] But such a division of divine attributes finds no support in Scripture. Wellum says

---

[11] One notable example is Charles Gore, *The Incarnation of the Son of God,* Bampton Lectures (London: John Murray, 1898).

[12] See the discussion of this so-called kenotic Christology in Stephen Wellum, *God the Son Incarnate: The Doctrine of Christ* (Wheaton: Crossway, 2016), 356–72.

[13] See Wellum, 355–93.

[14] Wellum, 374, cites C. Stephen Evans and Stephen T. Davis as among the "small number of evangelical philosophers and theologians" developing OKC. For sources by Evans and Davis, see Wellum, 374, n. 3. For FKC, Wellum, 380, lists Gerald Hawthorne, Klaus Issler, Garrett DeWeese, William Lane Craig, J. P. Moreland and Millard Erickson as "representative examples." For sources by these scholars, see Wellum, 380, n. 3, in which he slightly differentiates Erickson from the others on some points but finds even so that "the functional kenotic emphasis is strong."

[15] C. Stephen Evans, "Kenotic Christology and the Nature of God," in *Exploring Kenotic Christology: The Self-Emptying of God,* ed. C. Stephen Evans (New York: Oxford University Press, 2006), 196; Stephen T. Davis, "Is Kenosis Orthodox?" in *Exploring Kenotic Christology,* 113.

[16] Wellum, *God the Son Incarnate,* 376.

rightly that OKC's conception of Christ's deity is one that lacks "biblical and ecclesiastical warrant" and makes the classic claim that the Son is *homoousious* with the Father "problematic."[17] OKC is not a sound understanding of the *kenosis* of Phil 2:7.

Wellum sees FKC as much better than OKC in many respects. Most crucially, they do not follow OKC in seeing Christ as giving up any divine attributes in the incarnation. According to FKC, Jesus still possesses all the divine attributes but "willed to renounce the exercise of his divine powers, attributes, prerogatives, so that he might live fully within those limitations which inhere in being truly human."[18] In explaining how Jesus has supernatural knowledge and performs supernatural miracles, "FKC insists that Jesus does so, *not* by the use of his divine attributes, but by the power of the Spirit."[19]

That Jesus would choose to experience some of the limitations of human life to more fully identify with humans is an idea that we find attractive, but the way that FKC affirms it is problematic. Wellum sees FKC as departing from classical Christology at several significant points. Most important for the work of Christ is "its minimizing of Christ's *continuing exercise* of his divine attributes on earth" and "its difficulty in affirming or rejecting the *extra*."[20] These two problems are especially important for the ongoing providential work of Christ in holding all things together (Col 1:17) or "sustaining all things" (Heb 1:3). The Son must continually exercise his divine powers to accomplish this work. This is the classical understanding of the *extra-Calvinisticum*, that while walking on the earth as a human, the Son is not limited to a human nature. He still possesses something beyond his human nature, something extra. That is his divine nature, which he still possesses in full, and it is his divine powers he exercises in upholding all things.

In his earthly life, does he still exercise his divine powers? Wellum affirms this is the only way we can makes sense of the texts that identify

---

[17] Wellum, 399.

[18] Gerald Hawthorne, *The Presence and the Power: The Significance of the Holy Spirit in the Life and Ministry of Jesus* (Eugene, OR: Wipf & Stock, 2003), 208.

[19] Wellum, *God the Son Incarnate*, 383. Emphasis in original.

[20] Wellum, 382. Emphasis in original. The meaning of the *extra* will be given in the remainder of this section.

Jesus with Yahweh: "His identity is thoroughly divine, and in everything he says and does he demonstrates that he is God the Son incarnate."[21] What then are we to make of the things Jesus says and does that seem contrary to deity? Here we return to Phil 2:7.

We agree that Christ did not cease to be God, or cease to possess all the attributes of deity, but what are we to make of the two descriptive phrases following "he emptied himself," namely, "by assuming the form of a servant" and "taking on the likeness of humanity"? Christ emptied himself not by subtraction, but by addition, by taking on a full human nature, and not just any human nature, but that of a servant. As already implied by verse 6, taking on the nature of a servant means "that Jesus made an intentional and informed decision on his part not to take advantage of his position and status."[22] While Christ did not surrender his deity or any of the attributes of deity, in taking the nature of a servant and being in human likeness, he did surrender the glory he had experienced with the Father before the incarnation (John 17:5).[23]

But is there more involved in taking on a fully human nature than just the surrender of the glory of heaven? Humans are not omnipotent; they grow tired and hungry, and Jesus experienced both tiredness and hunger (John 4:6; Matt 21:18). Humans by nature are not omniscient; they lack knowledge and have to learn, and Jesus confessed lacking knowledge of at least one thing (Matt 24:36) and asked questions that seem to be more than merely rhetorical (Matt 15:34). He is specifically described as increasing in wisdom (Luke 2:52). How are these experiences compatible with the full possession of all the attributes of deity?

It seems that the decision Christ made to empty himself involved his voluntary choice to not use his divine powers *independently*. At some times in his earthly life, Jesus knew things and did things that are not in keeping with human limitations. But the divine power and knowledge evident in Jesus's life are exercised under his submission to the will of the Father. As

---

[21] Wellum, 406.

[22] Wellum, 176n83.

[23] See Daniel Akin, "The Person of Christ," in *A Theology for the Church*, 405. Akin says Jesus laid aside: "(1) the praises of heaven, (2) the position of heaven, and (3) the prerogatives of heaven."

J. I. Packer puts it, "His knowing, like the rest of his activity, was bounded by his Father's will."[24] Stephen Wellum says, "the Son, even as the incarnate Son, never acts on his own; the Son always acts in filial relation to his Father and through the Spirit," and that filial relation is one of "obedience and dependence."[25]

This explains, for example, why he did not use his power to turn a stone into a loaf of bread but did multiply loaves to feed five thousand. The Father did not will that Christ do the one but did will that he do the other. The decision Christ made in the incarnation was to live within the limitations of human nature, indeed within the limitations of the human nature of a servant. He would trust the Father to authorize when he would use his divine power and knowledge and when he would not. This seems best to explain the times when Jesus experienced human limitations and those when he exceeded them.

One final question remains. Why would Christ make such a choice? It certainly did not make his life on earth easier or more pleasant. The answer would seem to be his choice to fully identify with us in our humanness, including the painful limitations we experience. It would seem evident that in some sense God would know what it is like to be human by virtue of his omniscience. But we may doubt that God really knows and understands, thinking that knowing something by omniscience is very different than knowing by personal experience. Jesus lived a fully human life so we can know he truly knows, truly sympathizes (Heb 4:15), truly is Immanuel, God with us.

Robert Peterson asks, "So then, does Christ's incarnation save?" His answer is no in that no one is saved simply because Christ came to earth as a man, but yes in that the incarnation is "the essential precondition for the saving deeds that follow. . . . In that important sense, Christ's incarnation saves."[26] But we want to say that the incarnation is more than just an essential precondition to the saving work of Christ. The incarnation itself required work on the part of Christ: he had to decide to empty himself, with

---

[24] J. I. Packer, *Knowing God*, 20th Anniversary ed. (Downers Grove: InterVarsity, 1993), 62.

[25] Wellum, *God the Son Incarnate*, 411.

[26] Peterson, *Salvation Accomplished by the Son*, 39 (see chap. 11, n. 2).

all the implications that would mean for his earthly life. In a word, the work of Christ in the incarnation was the choice to identify with sinful humans, as a servant. And that work of identifying with humans is seen in many aspects of his human life (accepting baptism, experiencing temptation, bearing the sins of the world).

The Work of Christ in His Earthly Life

Though Jesus's earthly life was relatively short,[27] it was very full. John 21:25 says that if someone were to try to write down all that Jesus did, "not even the world could contain the books that would be written." Yet the amazing life of Jesus is often neglected in our theology. Michael Bird observes, "The sad fact is, though, that for many Christians, Jesus' life is really just the warm-up act to Paul's atonement theology."[28] We want to give due attention to those things that Jesus did in his earthly life that contribute to our understanding of the work of Jesus.

We will use the traditional rubrics of Christ's work as Prophet, Priest, and King to structure our discussion, recognizing that some acts of Christ may reflect more than one of these traditional offices. Of Christ as Prophet, Priest, and King, Bird states, "From Justin Martyr to John Calvin the *munus triplex Christi* ('threefold office of Christ') has been used to show that Jesus consummates the promises of salvation in Israel's Scriptures."[29] G. C. Berkouwer thinks it is important to emphasize that we speak of "one indivisible office" consisting of "three parts." It is one office because "[i]n fulfilling this office he accomplishes the one work of salvation."[30] At this point, we will strictly limit ourselves to events in the earthly life of Christ; his death will call for more detailed treatment later.

---

[27] Robert Stein, *Jesus the Messiah: A Survey of the Life of Christ* (Downers Grove: IVP Academic, 1996), 60, gives the dates of 7–5 BC for Jesus's birth and AD 30 or 33 as the date of his death, with an earthly life of forty years or less and an earthly ministry of from one and a half to three and a half years.

[28] Bird, *Evangelical Theology*, 357 (see chap. 11, n. 6).

[29] Bird, 364. Bird notes that the major figures in the Old Testament are prophets, priests, and kings.

[30] G. C. Berkouwer, *The Work of Christ*, trans. Cornelius Lambregtse (Grand Rapids: Eerdmans, 1965), 62.

The Work of Christ as Prophet

During his earthly ministry, Jesus was often regarded as a prophet;[31] he compared himself to a prophet on several occasions (Luke 4:24–27; Mark 6:4; Luke 13:33); and Peter and John saw Jesus as the fulfillment of the prophecy in Deut 18:15 that God would raise up for the people a prophet like Moses (Acts 3:22). Certainly, he was more than just a prophet, but "[a]ll the elements in the office of prophet are present" in his life.[32] We see his prophetic work primarily in his teaching.

Teaching is identified as one of the primary elements of Jesus's earthly ministry in the two summaries in the Gospel of Matthew. Perhaps the single most characteristic activity of Jesus was "teaching in their synagogues" (Matt 4:23; 9:35). Robert Stein points out that "within the four Gospels one of the titles most frequently used to describe Jesus is 'Teacher.'"[33] The vocational box that Jesus most clearly fit in his earthly ministry was that of itinerant teacher.[34] And it was his teaching that ultimately led his enemies to seek his death (Luke 23:5). Yet there is surprisingly little on Jesus as Teacher in most works on Christology,[35] even in books specifically on the work of

---

[31] The disciples knew that some people regarded Jesus as a prophet (Matt 16:14). The woman at the well initially thought Jesus was a prophet (John 4:19) as did the man born blind whom Jesus healed (John 9:17). When he raised the dead son of a widow back to life, the people called him "a great prophet" (Luke 7:16). At the triumphal entry, the crowds saw him as a prophet (Matt 21:11). Even the two on the road to Emmaus after Jesus's death thought he was a prophet (Luke 24:19).

[32] Letham, The Work of Christ, 94 (see chap. 11, n. 1). Of Christ as Prophet, Letham notes that Christ "never specifically claimed the office for himself" (91) and never used common prophetic formulae like "the word of the Lord came to me" or "thus says the Lord" (91, 94). Letham qualifies the notion of Jesus as prophet, pointing out how Christ's divine identity and the authority of his teaching place him in a category all to himself (94). But in the end, he does affirm a prophetic office for Christ.

[33] Robert Stein, The Method and Message of Jesus' Teachings (Philadelphia: Westminster, 1978), 1. Jesus is called "Teacher" 45 times and "Rabbi" 14 times.

[34] This provides an obvious but often overlooked explanation for why similar sayings of Jesus appear in different contexts in different Gospels. As an itinerant teacher, he probably said similar things many times in many different contexts.

[35] For example, see Wellum, God the Son Incarnate, 152–53. Wellum devotes less than two pages to Jesus as Teacher in a book of 467 pages.

Christ.[36] However, Robert Stein helpfully addresses this topic in *The Method and Message of Jesus' Teachings*.

The Forms of Jesus's Teachings. Jesus is widely recognized as a Master Teacher. In his earthly ministry, he drew large crowds, not just because he was performing miracles and healing people. Luke 5:1 records people "pressing in on Jesus to hear God's word." No doubt the content of his teaching accounts for much of the interest, but the methods of Jesus are worth noting as well. Stein notes various forms of Jesus's teaching: overstatement, hyperbole, pun, simile, and especially parables, and cautions us that these forms are not those of a scientific culture concerned with precision but those of "impressionistic language," and must be understood as such.[37]

The Content of Jesus' Teachings. In terms of the content of Jesus's teaching, a strong consensus has developed that the center of his teaching was the proclamation of the kingdom of God.[38] Part of the work of Jesus as Teacher was to announce that "The time is fulfilled," and that "the kingdom of God has come near" (Mark 1:15). Elsewhere he was more definite that the kingdom was already present: "If I drive out demons by the Spirit of God, then the kingdom of God has come upon you" (Matt 12:28). Yet in the same gospel we are commanded to pray, "Your kingdom come" (Matt 6:10), and warned elsewhere that the coming of the kingdom may not be immediate (Luke 19:11). While some choose to emphasize only the present aspect of the kingdom, and others only the future aspect, Scripture includes both, and so must we. In an important and influential book, G. E. Ladd argues that the kingdom of God is "the redemptive reign of God," and that it "will appear as an apocalyptic act at the end of this age" but "has already come into human

---

[36] Peterson, *Salvation Accomplished by the Son*, has no chapter on Jesus as Teacher, and there is no entry on Jesus as Teacher in the index to his book. He refers to the prophetic work of Jesus twice, but only as it is seen in the predictions of his death and resurrection, and in predictions of his session and second coming (68, 204). Letham, *The Work of Christ*, has a short chapter on Christ as Prophet (91–102) but only four pages focus on the teaching ministry of Christ in his earthly life; most of the chapter describes the continuing prophetic role of Jesus through the apostles and in Scripture.

[37] Stein, *The Method and Message of Jesus' Teaching*, 32.

[38] Stein, 60: "The expressions 'kingdom of God' and 'kingdom of heaven' are found in sixty-one separate sayings of Jesus in the Synoptic Gospels, and if we include the parallels, these two expressions occur eighty-five times."

history in the person and mission of Jesus."[39] It is both present and future. In Jesus, the kingdom has been inaugurated, but the consummation of the kingdom awaits his second coming. Because we live between Christ's first and second comings, we experience what is called "the tension between the already and the not yet."[40]

While the announcement of the kingdom is central to Jesus's teaching, it is not the only important element in the content of his teaching. Like no one before him, Jesus taught on and lived out a relationship to God as Father. It was not a totally unknown idea. In the Old Testament, "Father" is used with some relationship to God fifteen times. God is called or described as the Father of Israel nine times; he is described as or compared to a Father in general six times.[41] But Jesus calls God "Father" seventeen times in the Sermon on the Mount alone and teaches his followers to address God as Father in prayer. This teaching on God as Father is so much more direct and so much more emphasized in the New Testament than the Old that J. I. Packer sees it as the key difference between Christianity and Judaism:

> If you want to judge how well a person understands Christianity, find out how much he makes of the thought of being God's child and having God as his Father. If this is not the thought that prompts and controls his worship and prayers and his whole outlook on life, it means that he does not understand Christianity very well at all. For everything that Christ taught, everything that makes the New Testament new, and better than the Old, everything that is distinctively Christian as opposed to merely Jewish, is summed up in the knowledge of the Fatherhood of God. "Father" is the Christian name for God.[42]

---

[39] G. E. Ladd, *The Presence of the Future* (Grand Rapids: Eerdmans, 1974), 218.

[40] See the discussion of this important New Testament theme in Anthony Hoekema, *The Bible and the Future* (Grand Rapids: Eerdmans, 1979), 68–75.

[41] As Father of Israel, see Deut 32:6; Isa 63:16 (twice); 64:8; Jer 3:4, 19; 31:9; Mal 1:6; 2:10. As Father in general, see 2 Sam 7:14; 1 Chr 17:13; 22:10; 28:6; Pss 68:5; 89:26.

[42] Packer, *Knowing God*, 201.

This importance is seen in the fact that God is referred to as Father 258 times in the New Testament, and that his Fatherhood makes possible the blessing of adoption. Packer argues that the blessing of adoption is the highest blessing of the gospel, that it is the basis of Christian conduct, Christian prayer, and the life or faith, and that adoption shows the greatness of God's love (1 John 3:1–2).[43] This teaching on God as Father and the adoptive relationship made possible for believers, is a crucially important element in the teaching of Jesus.

A third important element in the content of Jesus's teaching is his teaching on the ethics of the kingdom. We touched on this earlier in showing the importance of seeing Jesus's ethics as kingdom ethics, applicable to us because the kingdom is inaugurated, but difficult to follow perfectly because the kingdom has not been consummated. But we want to touch now on the nature of Jesus's ethical teaching. In his teaching on loving one's enemies, on radical forgiveness, on purity and self-denial, we think it accurate to summarize Jesus's ethical teaching as calling his disciples to a deeper righteousness (Matt 5:20). It is true that not all that Jesus says is new; his great commandment is straight from the Old Testament, and there are parallels to the Golden Rule (Matt 7:12) in other bodies of ethical teaching. What was distinctive in Jesus's ethical teaching?

While Jesus took what he called the greatest commandment, and the second one like it, directly from the Old Testament, he emphasized them, and the centrality of love, more than the Old Testament does. Out of all the commandments, he chose the one calling us to love God as greatest, and put love of neighbor beside it. That is distinctive. Also distinctive in Jesus's ethical teaching is his perfect example. 'What would Jesus do?' is more than a cliché. Jesus is the perfect embodiment of his own teaching and if we do as he did, we will likely be walking in the will of God.[44] If we have any doubt as to how to interpret and flesh out his teachings, we have the perfect application of them in him.

A final key element in Jesus's teaching is his teaching on his identity. Part of his work as prophet is to reveal God. To do so fully requires that he be God incarnate. In the Gospel of John, Jesus gives his identity in seven

---

[43] Packer, 206–14.
[44] Stein, *The Method and Message of Jesus' Teachings*, 111.

"I am" statements, implying he is more than a mere man,[45] and John records seven signs for the purpose of showing Jesus to be Messiah and Son of God. It is true that there were some who doubted the true humanity of Jesus in the early church (see the warning in 1 John 4:2–3), but doubts about his true deity have been much more prominent down through church history. Jesus taught about his divine identity in numerous ways.[46] First, there are some direct claims, in the mouth of Jesus (John 8:58) and others (John 1:1–2; 20:28). Second, there are many instances in which Jesus acts in ways that show a consciousness of being divine. He taught and acted with unique authority (Matt 7:28–29), even authority over Satan (Luke 11:21–22), and eventually claimed "all authority" (Matt 28:18). Third, he assumed divine prerogatives,[47] such as claiming to be able to forgive sins (Mark 2:5–7) and accepting worship (Matt 28:17). Fourth, the titles used for Jesus constitute a claim for deity.[48] Most interesting is the title only Jesus used to refer to himself, Son of Man. Taken in isolation, it could simply mean a person. But Jesus associated Dan 7:13–14 with his claim to be the Son of Man (Mark 14:62), and the Son of Man in Dan 7:13–14 is one who is clearly divine. The historic Christian claim of the creeds that Jesus is true God and true man finds strong support in the teaching and actions of Jesus.

The Continuation of Jesus's Teaching. Does the prophetic work of Jesus continue after his death? Acts 1:1 may be seen as implying a continuation, as Luke refers to his "first narrative" (the Gospel of Luke) as recording "all that Jesus began to do and teach." Does this second narrative record all that Jesus continued to do and teach? Robert Letham thinks so. He writes of "Christ's continuing prophetic role through the apostles." He notes the authority inherent in Jesus's appointment of twelve to be his apostles. He

---

[45] John 6:35, the bread of life; 8:12, the light of the world; 10:7, the gate for the sheep; 10:11, the good shepherd; 11:25, the resurrection and the life; 14:6, the way, the truth, and the life; 15:1, the true vine.

[46] See the fuller discussion of these various ways in Wellum, *God the Son Incarnate*, 189–208.

[47] Stein, *The Method and Message of Jesus' Teachings*, 114.

[48] See Stein, 120–48, and Wellum, *God the Son Incarnate*, 199–208, for a thorough discussion of the implications in the titles Messiah, Lord, Son or Son of God, and Son of Man.

says, "Henceforth, their teaching was to be Christ's own teaching, no less."[49] Thus, Letham thinks it is "appropriate to regard Scripture itself as an aspect of the prophetic ministry of Christ," and thus he affirms "Christ's continuing prophetic role in Scripture."[50] While the doctrine of inseparable operations[51] would affirm some role for Christ in the inspiration and illumination of Scripture as a member of the triune Godhead, the doctrine of specific appropriations sees the Spirit as far more directly involved in the inspiration and illumination of Scripture. But in any case, the production of Scripture takes us far beyond the limits of this chapter, the work of Christ in his earthly life.

The Significance of the Prophetic Work of Christ. Most discussions of the work of Christ focus on his priestly work, especially the work of atonement on the cross. But early preaching about Jesus gave attention to his earthly life and ministry,[52] a life and ministry especially characterized by the prophetic role of teaching. What is the significance of this prophetic work of Christ?

It is part of how Christ fulfills the law and the prophets (Matt 5:17). He fulfills specific prophecies, such as that in Deut 18:15, in being the prophet God raised up. But he is the fulfillment of the whole prophetic office. The word of the Lord came to the prophets in the Old Testament; in Jesus, the Word itself came into the world (John 1:9). He is the prophetic word made flesh, the fulfillment of all the prophets.[53] That is why Jesus can say that all the Scriptures, specifically including the Prophets, speak of him (Luke 24:27). He is the prophet par excellence.[54]

---

[49] Letham, *The Work of Christ*, 96–97.

[50] Letham, 100.

[51] For more on the doctrine of inseparable operations, see Adonis Vidu, *The Same God Who Works All Things: An Exposition and Defense of the Doctrine of Inseparable Operations* (Grand Rapids: Eerdmans, 2020).

[52] See, for example, Acts 2:22; 10:37–38.

[53] Bird, *Evangelical Theology*, 364: "The offices of prophet, priest, and king are climactically fulfilled in the ministry of the one who would reveal, redeem, and reign on God's behalf."

[54] The early church historian Eusebius says all the prophets have reference to Christ, who is "of the prophets the Father's sole supreme Prophet." Eusebius, *Hist. Eccl.* 1.3.8–9.

Another major aspect of the prophetic work of Christ was to reveal the nature of God to the world (John 1:18).[55] Jesus did so primarily through his life on earth. He taught on the nature of God through his life and example. Who else would dare to say, "The one who has seen me has seen the Father" (John 14:9)? By his words, he taught explicitly of the goodness of God (Matt 5:45; 7:11), of his faithfulness to hear prayer and care for his children (Luke 18:6–7), of his power to do all things (Mark 10:27). By his compassion for the sick and hurting, by his love for his disciples, by his uncompromising call to holiness, he was teaching them of the nature of God.

A third significance of the prophetic ministry of Jesus was its part in fulfilling the purpose for the coming of Jesus given in 1 John 3:8: "to destroy the devil's works." Satan works to blind minds to a right understanding of God's Word. Jesus exercised the ministry of teaching to correct some of the erroneous interpretations of the law, such as in Matt 5:21–48. He contrasts what they had heard with what he says, and in so doing, speaks with authority, further verifying his nature as God incarnate.

In addition to correcting error, he had new teaching to impart, teaching on the new covenant, which would change how they saw animal sacrifices, the Sabbath, even the food laws (Mark 7:19). He gave his disciples a new command (John 13:34). They had been taught by the Old Testament to love their neighbor as themselves; the newness of Jesus's command is in the standard. They are to love as he had loved them, and that type of love was new indeed. He gave new teaching on the nature of the Holy Spirit as the comforter sent in Jesus's name, to be with the disciples forever (John 14:16–17). He had even more to teach them, but he recognized and accepted their limitations and left it to the Spirit to guide them into all truth (John 16:12–13). Even so, the teaching of Jesus himself was prized by the early church even over the teaching of the rest of the New Testament. Michael Bird notes that there are more manuscript copies of the Gospels than the other New Testament books and that the apostolic fathers and early apologists quoted more from the Gospels than any other New Testament writings.[56]

---

[55] The verb translated "revealed" in John 1:18 is *exēgēsato*, from which we get our word "exegesis." As exegesis is the process of expounding the Scriptures in a sermon, the life of Jesus is the greatest sermon ever preached on the nature of God.

[56] Bird, *Evangelical Theology*, 358.

In what follows, we will focus much attention on the priestly work of Christ, particularly the work on the cross. Such attention is justified, as the cross is the focus of much of the New Testament and has dominated discussions of the work of Christ down through history. But it should not lead us to miss the also justly important work of Christ as prophet.

The Work of Christ as Priest

The work of priests is not completely distinct from that of prophets. Robert Letham says, "Put crudely, if the prophet is God's representative before humanity, the priest is humanity's representative before God."[57] But there is certainly overlap between the two. For example, Mal 2:7 explicitly says people should seek instruction from priests, and priests are seen as having teaching responsibilities in Lev 10:11 and Deut 24:8 and especially Neh 8:1–9. Yet teaching is usually seen as a prophetic function. Still, when Heb 5:1 describes the function of the high priest (which is what Christ is called or compared to thirteen times in the book of Hebrews), he is the one "appointed in matters pertaining to God for the people, to offer both gifts and sacrifices for sins." And it is this function, offering up a sacrifice for sins, that is the focal point of discussions of Christ's priestly work, for at the cross he is both the priest offering up the sacrifice and the sacrifice itself.

This is such a massive topic, in both Scripture and church history, that we will need to devote multiple chapters to it. But our concern in this chapter is the work of Christ in his earthly life, as opposed to in his death, and there are aspects of Christ's priestly work that do take place during his earthly life.

We should notice that though Jesus himself never used the title "priest" to refer to himself, there are good reasons to affirm that he saw himself as one. He saw his body as the new temple, the place where priests minister (John 2:19–21); he offered intercession, a priestly function (Luke 22:31–32; John 17:9–26); and it is difficult to believe that the book of Hebrews would have such a strong emphasis on Jesus as priest and even high priest had the idea been totally absent from or contrary to the ministry of Jesus. It is true that Jesus was not of the tribe of Levi, the priestly tribe, but the writer of Hebrews resolves that difficulty with an appeal to

---

[57] Letham, *The Work of Christ*, 105.

the priesthood of Melchizedek. Jesus serves in that order, indeed as a high priest of the order of Melchizedek, seen as the fulfillment of the prophecy of Ps 110:4.

As priest and high priest, the first aspect of priestly work we see in the life of Jesus is the work of identification. As Stephen Wellum succinctly puts it, "representation [the priest's work] requires identification."[58] Hebrews 2:17 gives the prerequisite for representing the people before God in atonement; it is the high priestly work of identification through incarnation: "he had to be like his brothers and sisters in every way, so that he could become a merciful and faithful high priest in matters pertaining to God, to make atonement for the people." That identification began with the self-emptying at the incarnation, as discussed in the previous chapter, but continued throughout his earthly life, and is clearly seen in numerous key events.

For example, it is seen in his experiencing temptation. James 1:13 tells us that God cannot be tempted. Yet we are told that Jesus, as God incarnate, was tempted "in every way as we are," but unlike us, he overcame temptation and was "without sin" (Heb 4:15). These two affirmations—that Jesus was genuinely tempted as we are and that he did not sin—seem clear in Scripture. What has not seemed as clear to some is the answer to the question, Could Jesus have sinned? Some have said that if Jesus was truly tempted, there must have been the possibility that he could sin. But the majority view down through church history has been that, while he was truly tempted, he could not have sinned. The reason is that while Jesus possessed two natures, human and divine, he was one person. Sin is the act of a person, not a nature.[59] And the person of the God-man could not sin.[60]

---

[58] Wellum, *God the Son Incarnate*, 223.

[59] Thomas Torrance may disagree with this. According to Oliver Crisp's analysis, "in an earlier phase of his thought Torrance believed that sin was a property of persons, he later came to believe that sin is a property of natures." See the discussion in Crisp, "T. F. Torrance on *Theosis* and Universal Salvation," *Scottish Journal of Theology* 74 (2021): 14.

[60] This position that Christ could not sin is called impeccability (*non posse peccare*); the position that he could have but did not is called peccability (*posse peccare*). For a brief discussion of this issue, see Macleod, *The Person of Christ*, 229–30, or Wellum, *God the Son Incarnate*, 459–65. For a full book length treatment, see John E. McKinley, *Tempted for Us: Theological Models and the Practical Relevance of Christ's Impeccability and Temptation* (Eugene, OR: Wipf & Stock, 2009).

Yet the fact that he could not sin does not detract from the reality of his temptations, for temptation can happen within a nature. Jesus could not sin or even be tempted in his divine nature. Thus, when Scripture tells us that Jesus was tempted, we have to understand this as happening to him in his human nature. It was in his humanity, as one of us, that Jesus experienced temptation, and it was in his humanity, using no resources unavailable to us, that Jesus overcame temptation. As Bruce Ware says, in fighting temptation, Jesus made use "solely of those resources that were provided him in his humanity."[61] Indeed, Matt 4:1 says Jesus was led by the Spirit into the wilderness "to be tempted by the devil." Experiencing temptation was something that was within the Father's will for Jesus, and something that, presumably, Jesus told his disciples about.[62] And it is the experience of being tempted, and suffering when tempted, that qualifies Jesus for the high priestly work of helping those who are tempted (Heb 2:18; 4:15).

This may also relate to why Jesus received baptism (Matt 3:13–17). Why was it right for someone without sin to undergo a baptism of repentance? It was right for Jesus, because he had come to be the high priest of sinful people; it was right for him identify with sinful people. His baptism served as something of a commissioning to his priestly work.

Of course, the cross is the ultimate point of identification. Jesus so identified with sinful people that he could take their very sins upon himself, and be both the sacrifice for sins and the priest taking the sacrifice into the true Holy of Holies (Heb 9:11–12). But it doesn't end even there. As the resurrected and glorified Son, Jesus still sees persecution of his church as persecution of himself, as he asks, "Saul, Saul, why are you persecuting me?" (Acts 9:4). Jesus doesn't just remember what it is like to be human; he still is human and still identifies with his people as their high priest.

Another aspect of the work of priests is that of intercession. Intercession is especially associated with the ascension and session of the resurrected Jesus, but it began during his earthly ministry. The prayer of Jesus for his disciples in John 17 is commonly called his high priestly prayer, as he intercedes for

---

[61] Bruce Ware, *The Man Christ Jesus: Theological Reflections on the Humanity of Christ* (Wheaton: Crossway, 2013), 85.

[62] Matthew 4:1–11 and Luke 4:1–13 are not explicit, but neither mention anyone as being with Jesus when he was tempted.

his disciples then and for those who would become his disciples in the future (John 17:20). Thus present-day believers were included in the priestly work of intercession done by Jesus during his time on earth. And while we have no specific records, it is hard to believe that the intercession for Peter in Luke 22:31–32 was the only such intercession for an individual disciple or that such intercession was only one time. How deeply encouraging it must have been for Peter to have known that his High Priest was interceding for him! How deeply encouraging it should be for disciples today to know that we were included in his intercessory prayer in John 17 and that he is still interceding for us today!

But the third and most far-reaching aspect of the priestly work of Christ in his earthly life was his perfect obedience. The priests in the Old Testament went through elaborate rituals to be consecrated as priests (Exodus 29 and Leviticus 8). They had to be washed with water, clothed with proper garments, and anointed with oil. Sacrifices for atonement had to be offered, and blood from the sacrifices had to be applied to them. Only then were they qualified to serve as priests. For Christ, he is clothed in his own obedience. There is no atoning blood sacrifice made for or applied to him; he himself will be the perfect sacrifice. To represent the people before God as High Priest, Christ not only identified with them in his incarnation, baptism, and temptations; not only did he intercede for them; most of all he "lived a life of willing and sinless obedience, not only for himself but also on behalf of the entire race he represented."[63] Humans owe to God perfect obedience and praise. As our representative, Christ did this for us. Robert Letham rightly says, "It is *his* faith, *his* obedience, *his* faithfulness, *his* prayer which avails for us. As our great high priest, he offers up worship and praise acceptable to a holy God, the fruit of a life of perfect faithfulness, flawless and pure."[64] In later chapters, we will consider more fully the priestly work of Christ in his death, and rightly so, for the atoning death of Christ is the only hope humans have for forgiveness of sins. But the priestly work of Christ on earth of obedience is what qualifies him to be the high priest who can bear an atoning sacrifice for others into the presence of a holy God.

It may be appropriate at this point to note a global voice that applies the idea of Christ as priest in a distinctive way. In African culture, ancestors

---

[63] Letham, *The Work of Christ*, 116.
[64] Letham, 118. Emphasis in original.

are often seen as the mediators between humans and gods, blessing those who keep the tribal customs and traditions and punishing evildoers. Thus, Ancestor Christologies have developed as an indigenous African Christology, in which Jesus is seen as the one "whose mediatorial role between God and humanity fulfills or satisfies the mediatorial roles that are ascribed to ancestors in African indigenous religions."[65] Making such an analogy between the priestly role of Jesus and something very familiar in African culture, on the positive side, has the potential of showing that "Jesus Christ and Christianity can successfully satisfy the aspirations, hopes, and theological questions of Africans, which the indigenous religions do not satisfy."[66] Negatively, however, some believe that "Africa's ancestor cult promotes necromancy, which they judge to be an anti-Christian act or ritual" and even more seriously, that Jesus, as one charged with violating Jewish customs, would not meet "the requirements for ancestorship if he were an African."[67] Clearly, some of the priestly roles served by ancestors in some cultures may not fit the priestly work of Jesus and some of the priestly work of Jesus may not fit what Africans expect of their ancestors, but this is an example of the type of conversation that needs to happen in the global church, where differing cultures can help each other discern the positive and negative features of new developments.

The Work of Christ as King

Seeing the work of Christ as King during his earthly life and ministry is problematic. Jesus never explicitly called himself a king; his disciples never called him king; and "king" is not among the titles listed in books on Christ that discuss his titles.[68] References to Jesus as King cluster around the birth

---

[65] Victor Ezigbo, "Jesus as God's Communicative and Hermeneutical Act: African Christians on the Person and Significance of Jesus Christ," in *Majority World Theology: Christian Doctrine in Global Context*, ed. Gene Green, Stephen Pardue, and K. K. Yeo (Downers Grove: IVP Academic, 2020), 141.

[66] Ezigbo.

[67] Ezigbo, 142.

[68] Wellum, *God the Son Incarnate*, 199–208, discusses Lord, *Theos*, and God the Son as "divine titles of Christ," but does not include King. David Wells, *The Person of Christ: A Biblical and Historical Analysis of the Incarnation* (Wheaton: Crossway, 1984), 67–81, gives Word, Son of God, Suffering Servant, Lord, and Son of Man, but he also omits "King" from the list of titles for Jesus.

narrative in the Gospel of Matthew, where the magi come seeking the one
born king of the Jews and identify Jesus as that one, giving him gifts fit for a
king (Matt 2:2, 11), and at the end of all four Gospels, when Jesus is charged
before Pilate for claiming "to be Messiah, a king" (Luke 23:2), or more commonly, for claiming to be "king of the Jews" (John 18:33). Yet even in these
passion narratives, Jesus never claims to be king of the Jews. The most he
will say when asked if he is the king of the Jews is "You say so" (Matt. 27:11;
Mark 15:2; Luke 23:3) though he does add once, "My kingdom is not of this
world" (John 18:36).

So if Jesus never claimed to be king, why was he charged as such? And
why was there no clear and explicit denial of Jesus that he was king? The
answer would seem to be that Jesus had acted in ways that constituted a
claim to kingship, but it was a different type of kingship than what the people of that day saw as kingship. Moreover, the theme of the kingdom of God,
so prominent in Jesus's teaching, would imply some correlation between
Jesus and the kingdom, especially when he claims that his acts show that the
kingdom "has come" (Matt 12:28).

Yet, as we noted earlier, Jesus taught that while the kingdom had in one
sense, already come, in another sense, it was yet to come. As is commonly
said, the kingdom was inaugurated but not yet consummated. Thus, the work
of Christ as King shares some of this same tension. It is inaugurated during
his earthly life but will emerge more clearly after his resurrection and will
be consummated at the second coming.[69] In this chapter we will limit our
consideration to the work of Christ as King during his life on earth. The
ongoing present work and future eschatological work will be discussed in
later chapters.

People could easily have understood Christ to be a King because of the
unmistakable authority with which he acted in numerous spheres in his
earthly life and ministry. He acted with authority over nature. When on
the Sea of Galilee and caught in a storm, he had the authority to command
the wind and waves to be still. The disciples realized that Jesus was more

---

[69] Letham, *The Work of Christ*, 197–209, begins his discussion of the work of
Christ as king, not with his earthly life and ministry, but with "the mediatorial kingship of Christ" which began with Christ's resurrection. He gives little attention to
the work of Christ as king in his earthly life and ministry.

than a mere man. They said, "Who is this? Even the wind and the sea obey him?" (Mark 4:41). Given enough time, barley and fish can multiply and produce hundreds of loaves of barley and fishes, but Jesus could exercise authority over the processes of nature and turn five barley loaves and two fish into enough to feed five thousand men, presumably with their wives and children (John 6:6–13). The people who witnessed this miracle called Jesus "the Prophet who is to come into the world," but wanted to make him king (John 6:14–15), recognizing something kingly in Jesus's act. He acted with authority over nature.

One of the most characteristic aspects of Jesus's earthly life and ministry was healing those sick and afflicted with diseases and demons.[70] Even raising the dead happened frequently. We know that when the kingdom has fully come, there will be in it no disease or death (Rev 21:4); we know that Jesus said that his casting out of demons by the Spirit of God was evidence the kingdom was already present to some degree. It would seem that the work of Christ in healing, casting out demons, and even raising the dead is kingly work, showing the powers of the kingdom to come at work in the world today in and through the King. Even a pagan centurion recognized the authority of Jesus over disease (Matt 8:8–9), an authority that exceeds that of earthly kings but could be fitting for one who is King over all kings.

His authority is seen in sending out others. Who but a king would have the authority to send out emissaries to announce the nearness of the kingdom, not just once but twice (Matt 10:1–7; Luke 10:1–9)? The scope of his authority would be extended and the commissioning of kingdom representatives extended to all his followers after the resurrection (Matt 28:16–20), but that would take us beyond the bounds of this chapter.

One final area of kingly authority exercised by Jesus is the authority to define the nature of true kingship. The distinctive nature of Christ's kingship had been foretold in the Old Testament. Zechariah 9:9 says the king of Israel would come "righteous and victorious," but also "humble and riding on a donkey." Perhaps the clearest claim Jesus made to being a king is in fulfilling this prophecy in what is called the triumphal entry (Matt 21:1–6), including accepting the acclaim of the people, "Blessed is the King who comes in the

---

[70] See the summary statements of Jesus's ministry in Matt 4:23–24 and 9:35.

name of the Lord" (Luke 19:38). But the distinctive nature of his kingship consists in coming in humility, on a donkey, rather than a gold chariot.

He had already instructed his disciples on the true nature of authority in his kingdom. The mother of the sons of Zebedee seems to have recognized Jesus as a king, asking him to give high positions to her sons in his kingdom (Matt 20:20–21). When the others became indignant at the possibility of favoritism being shown to James and John, Jesus clarified the definition of authority in his kingdom: "whoever wants to be first among you must be your slave" (Matt 20:27). He added that he himself was giving them the example: "just as the Son of Man did not come to be served, but to serve and to give his life as a ransom for many" (v. 28). These words point us to the most central aspect of Christ's work, the work of the cross, and serve as a fitting point with which to conclude our consideration of the work of Christ in his incarnation and earthly life and ministry and transition to the awesome work of atonement.

13

The Nature of the Atonement: Historical Approaches

The Work of Christ on the Cross: Introduction

We come now to what is by common consent the great centerpiece of the work of Christ, his work on the cross. This work is usually referred to as the atonement, the means by which those separated from God are put at one with him.[1] And while some theories of the atonement include the incarnation and life of Christ as important for the atonement[2]—and most if not all theories of the atonement assume the resurrection as the validation or confirmation of the work of the cross[3]—it is the work done on the cross itself that is usually central to atonement.

The first major issue that confronts theologians is the nature of the atonement. The ravages of sin have left humans with a multiplicity of needs.

---

[1] David Allen, *The Atonement: A Biblical, Theological, and Historical Study of the Cross of Christ* (Nashville: B&H Academic, 2019), 15, traces the English word "atonement" to William Tyndale's use of it in translating the Greek term *katallagē* (usually translated "reconciliation") in Rom 5:11, expressing the concept of "at-one-ment."

[2] Irenaeus, "Against Heresies," *ANF* 1:446, 448 (Book 3, ch.18, 1, 7); Athanasius, "On the Incarnation of the Word," *NPNF²*, 4:40–41 (8–10); Thomas Torrance, *Atonement: The Person and Work of Christ*, ed. R. T. Walker (Downers Grove: IVP Academic, 2009).

[3] Fleming Rutledge, *The Crucifixion: Understanding the Death of Jesus Christ* (Grand Rapids: Eerdmans, 2015), 31. She aptly says, "*if Jesus had not been raised from the dead, we would never have heard of him*" (emphasis in original). Cf. 1 Cor 15:17.

Thus it is not surprising that most theologians today see a multiplicity of ways the Scriptures describe the work of atonement. These different ways of understanding the atonement are variously called models, theories, pictures, and even modes. While there may be some value in carefully distinguishing between terms like "motifs," "metaphors," "models," and "theories,"[4] most authors use them interchangeably, and we will follow that pattern here. The 1931 work of Gustaf Aulén was important in positing three major approaches to the atonement,[5] and many today still use three major categories.[6] Others argue for from five to thirteen models,[7] however, and there are other new models being generated.[8]

While we believe a number of these models may be interesting and intriguing,[9] in the interests of space, we must limit our study to the most important models that have emerged in the history of theology. We believe

---

[4] This is the concern of Oliver Crisp, "Methodological Issues in Approaching the Atonement," in *T&T Clark Companion to Atonement*, ed. Adam Johnson (London: T&T Clark, 2017), 315–33.

[5] Gustaf Aulén, *Christus Victor: An Historical Study of the Three Main Types of the Idea of Atonement*, trans. A. G. Hebert (London: SPCK, 1931).

[6] See James Beilby and Paul Eddy, eds., *The Nature of the Atonement: Four Views* (Downers Grove: IVP Academic, 2006). Though the title of the book says "Four Views," the fourth view, called here "the kaleidoscopic view," is not really a view but argues that there are a number of images for the atonement in the NT and that no one image or theory should be given priority (21).

[7] Henri Blocher, "Biblical Metaphors and the Doctrine of the Atonement," *JETS* 47, no. 4 (December 2004), 629–45, sees five metaphors; Christopher Morgan, *Christian Theology* (Nashville: B&H Academic, 2020), 317, and Peterson, *Salvation Accomplished by the Son*, 9–10 (see chap. 11, n. 2) both argue for six "pictures," but differ in what those pictures are; Peter Schmiechen, *Saving Power: Theories of Atonement and Forms of the Church* (Grand Rapids: Eerdmans, 2005), offers ten "theories"; and John McIntyre, *The Shape of Soteriology* (Edinburgh: T&T Clark, 1992), 44–48, has the largest list, with thirteen models of the atonement.

[8] See the contributions to "Part Four: So Great a Salvation, Soteriology in the Majority World," in *Majority World Theology: Christian Doctrine in Global Context*, 353–472.

[9] In addition to models from the Majority World (see previous footnote), the models from Denny Weaver, *The Nonviolent Atonement* (Grand Rapids: Eerdmans, 2001); Michael Gorman, *The Death of the Messiah and the Birth of the New Covenant: A (Not So) New Model of the Atonement* (Eugene, OR: Cascade, 2014); and Scot McKnight, *A Community Called Atonement* (Nashville: Abingdon, 2007) are among those worthy of further exploration.

the framework of Michael Bird, with three main approaches and a total of eight models within those three approaches,[10] includes all the major views, and will use that as the framework in the next three chapters. Bird calls his three main categories historical, subjective, and objective, and while some subdivide these categories and use different terminology, this threefold approach enjoys wide use and approval.[11]

Recapitulation, Ransom, and Victory

Recapitulation, ransom, and victory are the three terms Michael Bird groups under what he calls the historical models of the atonement.[12] Calling them "historical" seems justified for at least two reasons. They do appear early on in church history, with recapitulation especially associated with Irenaeus and ransom with Gregory of Nyssa, and in a very influential book, Gustaf Aulén has argued that the idea of Christ as Victor was the position of the early church.[13] Second, the ideas of recapitulation and victory draw on the whole

---

[10] Bird, *Evangelical Theology*, 410 (see chap. 11, n. 6).

[11] The four views in Beilby and Eddy, eds., *The Nature of the Atonement*, are essentially these three, plus a composite view, though with different names given to the three main views. Hans Boersma, *Violence, Hospitality, and the Cross: Reappropriating the Atonement Tradition* (Grand Rapids: Baker Academic, 2004), 122, references the same three main approaches, though he calls them Christus Victor, moral influence, and representative punishment. Joshua McNall, *The Mosaic of Atonement: An Integrated Approach to Christ's Work* (Grand Rapids: Zondervan Academic, 2019), subdivides what Bird calls the historical model into recapitulation and Christus Victor, and has other terms for what Bird calls subjective and objective but with much the same ideas. John Stott, *The Cross of Christ* (Downers Grove: InterVarsity, 1986), has the same three categories but with different titles for each; Millard Erickson, *Christian Theology*, 3rd ed. (Grand Rapids: Baker Academic, 2013), subdivides two of the three categories of Bird and uses different terminology throughout, but the main outlines are quite similar.

[12] Bird, *Evangelical Theology*, 410.

[13] Aulén, *Christus Victor*, 174–75. Aulén links the ideas of ransom and victory and calls this "the classic idea of the Atonement," though he also sees it as relatively undefined and ambiguous, an idea more than a theory or doctrine of atonement. For a differing position, see William Lane Craig, *Atonement and the Death of Christ: An Exegetical, Historical, and Philosophical Exploration* (Waco, TX: Baylor University Press, 2020), 110: "The notion that the Fathers were singularly committed to a *Christus Victor* theory of the atonement is a popular misimpression generated by the

story of Jesus for the atonement, not just his death on the cross. The whole history of his life, including his resurrection from the dead, plays a key role in these ideas of the atonement. Thus describing them as "historical" has some merit.

In this and subsequent chapters, we will look first at the biblical basis for these models, then note their development in church history. We will give a theological evaluation of the importance of each model and conclude with practical applications of these models for Christian life and ministry.

Biblical Basis

One of the very early ideas of the atonement is that of recapitulation: "the Savior passes through each stage of the human journey, perfectly fulfilling the broken covenant; this way, he reorders the human situation—Adam's story of fall, Israel's story of exile—by reenacting it, restoring not only the human creation but creation itself to God."[14] One verse often cited in support of this way of thinking of the atonement is Eph 1:10, where Paul speaks of God's plan "to bring everything together in Christ." One of the meanings given for the term *anakephalaiosasthai* in the standard Greek lexicon is to "sum up, recapitulate," and so some see Eph 1:10 as clear biblical support for this theme.[15] However, Markus Barth, while noting recapitulation as one possible meaning, thinks the context of Eph 1:10 points toward "to make [Christ] the head," as a better way to understand this "ambiguous Greek verb."[16] Joshua McNall, recognizing that the Greek word for head (*kephalē*) is in this verb, suggests that "one might refer to recapitulation as the process

---

secondary literature." He argues that there was no unified theory of the atonement in the writers of the patristic era. Rather, all the major NT motifs for the atonement: "sacrifice, substitutionary punishment, ransom, satisfaction, and so on—may be found in their pages" (92).

[14] Ivor J. Davidson, "Atonement and Incarnation," in *T&T Clark Companion to Atonement*, 49. Davidson adds that while this theme "is famously developed in the later second century by Irenaeus . . . it also predates him," which justifies regarding it as very early.

[15] McNall, *The Mosaic of Atonement*, 18n7: "English translations of the passage do not normally use the word *recapitulation* here, but the Greek term (*anakephalaiosasthai*) may be rendered as such."

[16] Markus Barth, *Ephesians*, AB (Garden City, NY: Doubleday, 1979), 34:91.

of 'reheadshipping.'"[17] But neither the term nor the idea of recapitulation is very prominent in Scripture.

Ransom and victory both enjoy much more explicit biblical support. In one of the few statements from the lips of Jesus concerning the meaning of his death, he said it would be "a ransom for many" (Mark 10:45), and Paul says Christ gave himself "a ransom for all" (1 Tim 2:6). Moreover, the Greek word for ransom (*lutron*) is found within the Greek word for redemption (*apolutrōsis*), and the meaning of redemption is liberation by the payment of a ransom, so the nine verses featuring the noun redemption also support the idea of Christ's death as a ransom. Redemption is clearly an important term for the atonement, indeed, seen by some as an equivalent term for atonement and salvation.[18]

Fleming Rutledge sees the New Testament teaching on redemption as drawing on and carrying forward "two major Old Testament themes." To be specific, redemption involves "liberation by a mighty power," and redemption is accomplished by "a price paid." Thus, the meaning is *"deliverance by purchase at cost."*[19] Leon Morris adds that the state from which we are liberated "is likened to slavery, a captivity which man cannot himself break," such that redemption requires outside intervention, and that the price paid for liberation "indicates an equivalence, a substitution."[20] This is seen in the preposition used in Mark 10:45, where Jesus says he would be "a ransom for [*anti*] many." The standard Greek lexicon says *anti* is used "in order to indicate that one person or thing is, or is to be, replaced by another," or "in order to indicate that one thing is equiv. to another."[21] As to the idea of a price paid, the costliness of our redemption seems to be an emphasis of the

---

[17] McNall, *The Mosaic of Atonement*, 38.

[18] A major book on the atonement has the simple title of *The Redemption*. See Gerald O'Collins, "Redemption: Some Crucial Issues," in *The Redemption*, ed. Stephen Davis, Daniel Kendall, and Gerald O'Collins (Oxford: Oxford University Press, 2004), 5. O'Collins speaks of redemption, atonement, and salvation as "equivalent terms" but acknowledges that "[u]sually 'atonement' is used more narrowly than 'redemption' or 'salvation,' and expresses the means of redemption or salvation" (5n4).

[19] Rutledge, *The Crucifixion*, 293. Emphasis in original.

[20] Leon Morris, *The Apostolic Preaching of the Cross* (Grand Rapids: Eerdmans, 1955), 58.

[21] William Arndt and F. Wilbur Gingrich, *A Greek-English Lexicon of the New Testament and Other Early Christian Literature*, 4th ed. (Chicago: University of Chicago Press, 1957), 72–73.

New Testament (1 Pet 1:18–19). Rutledge says ransom was by the payment of "an ultimate price. The cost of our redemption was the crucifixion of the Son of God. Otherwise we cannot find a place within our understanding for the sheer horror and godlessness of such a death."[22] What is not clear from the ransom motif alone is why the price was so costly, why it took the Son of God dying as our substitute to deliver us. We will find that the ransom motif needs supplementing from other ideas of the atonement to make that clear.

The idea of the atonement as victory is also explicitly endorsed in Scripture. In 1 Cor 15:54–56, Paul connects the theme of victory more to the resurrection than the cross, but Col 2:15 sees the triumph of Christ as accomplished by his death (Col 2:14). Michael Bird traces the theme of Christ's victory over all the powers of evil through the Gospels, the Pauline material, the Catholic epistles, and the Apocalypse to show the pervasiveness of the theme of Jesus's death as a victory throughout the New Testament.[23] John Stott likewise shows the pervasiveness of the theme of victory, but helpfully shows that it is not limited to the cross. Stott traces six stages of the victory of Christ in Scripture.[24] It is predicted perhaps as early as Gen 3:15 and certainly is present in messianic texts like Ps 2:8–9. We see the beginning of victory in the earthly ministry of Jesus as demons are cast out, the sick are healed, and the works of Satan begin to fall. But it is "the third and decisive stage" of the victory that is achieved at the cross,[25] and that is our concern here. These stages serve to remind us how the theme of victory informs the work of Christ from beginning to end.

Historical Development

The first major development of atonement as recapitulation came with the second-century patristic theologian Irenaeus. And if recapitulation is to involve reliving the entire human story, then it makes sense that his theory of the atonement begins with the incarnation. Irenaeus says of Christ: "when

---

[22] Rutledge, *The Crucifixion*, 302.
[23] Bird, *Evangelical Theology*, 393–95.
[24] Stott, *The Cross of Christ*, 231–36.
[25] Stott, 232.

He became incarnate, and was made man, He commenced afresh [Lat. *in seipso recapitulavit*] the long line of human beings, and furnished us, in a brief, comprehensive manner, with salvation, so that what we had lost in Adam . . . we might recover in Jesus."[26] But his interest is not merely in the incarnation; every stage of the earthly life is important to Irenaeus. He says of Jesus:

> He therefore passed through every age, becoming an infant for infants, thus sanctifying infants; a child for children, thus sanctifying those who are of this age. . . . So likewise he was an old man for old men, that he might be a perfect master for all. . . . Then, at last, he came even to death itself, that he might be "the first-born from the dead, that in all things he might have the pre-eminence" [Col 1:18], the prince of life, existing before all, and going before all.[27]

But while giving importance to the incarnation and life of Jesus, he does not deny the importance of the cross for atonement. He sees the obedience of Christ in hanging upon one tree, the cross, as undoing the old disobedience of Adam at the tree of the knowledge of good and evil.[28]

Recapitulation as an approach to the atonement does not loom large in the history of theology after Irenaeus. Even for Irenaeus, Oliver Crisp gives priority to the notion of "participation in the divine life through union with Christ" over that of recapitulation,[29] and Hans Boersma says Irenaeus is rightly associated with the Christus Victor theme of the atonement.[30] To be sure, Boersma also says that recapitulation is an "overarching concept" that allows Irenaeus to have "objective notions of sacrifice and propitiation," moral influence ideas, as well as Christus Victor elements in his thinking about the atonement: "recapitulation has a prophetic element (moral influence), a priestly element (representative punishment), and a royal element (Christus Victor)."[31] But most have not used recapitulation to arrive at or

---

[26] Irenaeus, "Against Heresies," *ANF* 1:446 (Book 3, chap. 18.1).
[27] Irenaeus, 390 (Book 2, chap. 22.2).
[28] Irenaeus, 547 (Book 5, chap. 19.1).
[29] Crisp, *Approaching the Atonement*, 36 (see chap. 12, n. 3).
[30] Boersma, *Violence, Hospitality, and the Cross*, 121.
[31] Boersma, 121–22.

develop these elements,[32] perhaps because, as Gordon Fee argues, in the NT the cross is central, not the incarnation and life of Christ.[33]

A second important early figure in these historical models is Athanasius. He too focuses more on the larger history of Christ rather than simply on his death. In particular, Athanasius sees the incarnation as crucial. This is seen in the title of his most famous work, "On the Incarnation of the Word." He sees Christ's death as that which "satisfied the debt" we owed. But in order to die he has first to become incarnate: "while it was impossible for the Word to suffer death, being immortal, and Son of the Father; to this end he takes a body capable of death, that it, by partaking of the Word who is above all, might be worthy to die in the stead of all."[34] He does occasionally use the language of satisfaction (Christ "satisfied the debt by His death"[35]) but he is better known as an advocate of *theosis*, or deification, as seen in his famous statement: "For He was made man that we might be made God."[36]

The ideas of ransom and victory developed together in church history because often, ransom was seen as the means of victory. Aulén argues, "The ransom is always regarded as paid to the powers of evil, to death, or to the devil; by its means they are overcome, and their power over men is brought to an end."[37] Aulén famously argued that this idea of victory via ransom was "the dominant idea of the Atonement" in the New Testament and "the ruling idea of the Atonement for the first thousand years of Christian history," and thus deserves to be called "the *classic Christian idea of the Atonement.*"[38]

---

[32] McNall, *The Mosaic of Atonement*, 44–46, argues that "the centuries since the Reformation have also witnessed a partial retrieval of Irenaeus's recapitulative logic," listing Calvin, John Owen, Karl Barth, Thomas Torrance, and Hans Boersma among those who have shown interest in recapitulation, but none make it as central a part of their atonement theology as does Irenaeus.

[33] Gordon Fee, "Paul and the Metaphors for Salvation: Some Reflections on Pauline Soteriology," in *The Redemption*, 50. Fee says, "Christ's *death* on the *cross* is the place where God effected his remedy for the human condition. From beginning to end, the focus is here" (emphasis in original).

[34] Athanasius, "On the Incarnation of the Word," *NPNF*² 4: 9, (40).

[35] Athanasius, 4:9, (41).

[36] Athanasius, 4:54, (65). For more on *theosis*, see the discussion in the previous chapter.

[37] Aulén, *Christus Victor*, 30.

[38] Aulén, 6–7. Emphasis in original.

But most today recognize that Aulén overstated his case. While ransom and Christ's victory are present in many patristic and medieval authors, to claim it as "the central view common to all, or almost all, theologians in the first thousand years of the church" is "not a sustainable position."[39] The importance of recapitulation and participation in the life of God (*theōsis*) as seen in Irenaeus and Athanasius as well as other themes in them and other patristic and medieval writers question the claim of this view to be the classic view.[40] Moreover, while they are often viewed as virtual synonyms in atonement literature, ransom and victory are distinct ideas,[41] and in recent times have developed independently. Thus, we will trace their development separately.

Development of the ransom idea began with consideration of the question, To whom was the ransom paid? Origen asked, "Could it not be the evil one? For he had us in his power, until the ransom for us should be given."[42] But the thinking also began that there was some divine deception involved in giving this ransom to Satan, that in taking it Satan was bringing about his own destruction. This was most famously expressed in the fishhook analogy of Gregory of Nyssa:

> [Christ's] Deity was hidden under the veil of our nature, that so, as with ravenous fish, the hook of the Deity might be gulped down along with the bait of flesh, and thus, life being introduced into the house of death, and light shining in darkness, that which is diametrically opposed to light and life might vanish.[43]

This same idea or some variation of it is found in a number of patristic authors: Irenaeus, Origen, Cyprian, Ambrose, John of Damascus, and later, even Martin Luther.[44] Augustine gives the picture of a mousetrap, but the

---

[39] Crisp, *Approaching the Atonement*, 48.

[40] Craig, *Atonement and the Death of Christ*, 111, argues that sacrifice combined with penal substitution was the dominant view by the fourth or fifth century, in West and East. But it should be recognized that this is a minority view.

[41] Crisp, *Approaching the Atonement*, 49.

[42] Origen, *Commentary on Matthew*, *ANF* 10:489.

[43] Gregory of Nyssa, *The Great Catechism*, *NPNF*[2], 5:493.

[44] See the citations in Crisp, *Approaching the Atonement*, 50, and McNall, *The Mosaic of Atonement*, 198.

idea of a ransom by which the devil "was not enriched but bound" is much the same.[45]

From the beginning, however, questions were raised about the idea that Satan should receive the ransom. The friend and colleague of Gregory of Nyssa, Gregory Nazianzus, almost immediately raised an objection. Satan, he said, had no right to a ransom, and the very idea that God would pay such a ransom to a robber, he saw as an "outrage."[46] Moreover, the idea that God would deceive the devil was seen as morally questionable, at best.[47] Fleming Rutledge summarizes, "The popularity of this notion [that the ransom was paid to the devil] persisted into the Middle Ages, but as consensus grew that Satan had no claim on or rights to anything, let alone the life of the Son of God, this semiliteral interpretation of the ransom motif fell permanently out of favor."[48] The prominence of ransom terminology in the New Testament and the wonderful meaning of deliverance signified by ransom assured that it would continue to be associated with the atonement and the victory won by Christ, but the question of who received the ransom would be answered differently in post-patristic church history, or not asked at all. Indeed, the church seems to have followed the lead of the New Testament, which as John Stott observes, "never presses the imagery to the point of indicating to whom the ransom was paid."[49]

The idea of the cross as a victory over the powers of darkness may not be as central in the New Testament or in church history as Aulén claimed, but it is undeniably present in most of the early church fathers. In Oliver Crisp's outline, the arguments of Irenaeus and Athanasius both contain points

---

[45] Augustine, *The Trinity*, trans. Stephen McKenna, in *The Fathers of the Church: A New Translation*, vol. 45 (Washington, DC: Catholic University of America Press, 1963), 13.15 (397–98). The mousetrap analogy itself is found in Augustine, "On the Ascension," in Augustine, *Sermons on the Liturgical Seasons*, trans. Mary Sarah Muldowney, Fathers of the Church Patristic Series (Washington, DC: Catholic University of America Press, 1984), Sermon 263.

[46] Gregory Naziansus, *Orations* 45.22 in *NPNF*[2], 7:427.

[47] McNall, *The Mosaic of Atonement*, 199–201, gives seven reasons why the idea of ransom as divine deception of the devil "all but disappeared from Christian history" (201). Stott, *The Cross of Christ*, 114, agrees that the devil has no rights and that "to attribute fraudulent action to God is unworthy of him."

[48] Rutledge, *The Crucifixion*, 285.

[49] Stott, *The Cross of Christ*, 179.

reflecting the belief that Christ's death gives believers victory over death, with Christ's resurrection as the confirmation.[50] Michael Bird says, "A search on the word 'cross' in the ante-Nicene fathers shows time and time again Jesus' death was part of a narrative of victory, triumph, and the defeat of sin and death."[51] How long Christus Victor remained the dominant theory is a matter of some discussion. Denny Weaver says the Christus Victor motif "faded away and lost favor after the sixth century,"[52] but Gregory Boyd said it remained dominant for the first millennium of church history.[53] Pretty much all agree that after AD 1000, discussion of Anselm's satisfaction theory took center stage. Among the Reformers, objective theories such as penal substitution became dominant, with the possible exception of Luther.[54] But Aulén's important work in 1931 did restore Christus Victor to a position of some prominence.

Today many argue for Christus Victor as the primary theme for the atonement, usually if not always without the idea of a ransom paid to the devil.[55] N. T. Wright recognizes that a variety of terms and motifs in the New Testament address the idea of atonement. In fact, he thinks all the major models—Christus Victor, substitution, and moral example—fit within the biblical story,[56] but he thinks the idea of victory deserves special prominence. He says,

> I suggest we give priority—a priority among equals, perhaps, but still a priority—to those Pauline expressions of the crucifixion of

---

[50] Crisp, *Approaching the Atonement*, 40, 44–45.

[51] Bird, *Evangelical Theology*, 396.

[52] Weaver, *The Nonviolent Atonement*, 15.

[53] Gregory Boyd, "Christus Victor View," in *The Nature of the Atonement: Four Views*, 46.

[54] Aulén, *Christus Victor*, 14, claims Luther as a proponent of what he calls the classic view against what he calls the Latin view. As Paul Althaus shows in *The Theology of Martin Luther*, Luther taught both penal substitution and Christus Victor equally.

[55] McNall, *The Mosaic of Atonement*, 202–6, sees something of the idea of a ransom paid to the devil in *The Lion, the Witch and the Wardrobe*, the first of C. S. Lewis's *Chronicles of Narnia*. It is more definitively found in Gregory Boyd, "Christus Victor View," 37, and in Darby Kathleen Ray's feminist approach, *Deceiving the Devil: Atonement, Abuse, and Ransom* (Cleveland: Pilgrim, 1998).

[56] Wright makes this point in N. T. Wright, Simon Gathercole, and Robert B. Stewart, *What Did the Cross Accomplish? A Conversation about the Atonement* (Louisville: Westminster John Knox, 2021), 26.

Jesus which describe it as the decisive victory over the 'principalities and powers.' Nothing in the many other expressions of the meaning of the cross is lost if we put this in the centre.[57]

Similarly, Hans Boersma, while recognizing the value of all three major approaches, affirms his belief that Christus Victor is "the most significant model of the atonement." He explains, "Moral influence and penal substitution are subordinate to Christus Victor as they are means toward an end."[58] Along the same lines, Michael Bird says, "I tentatively propose that the Christus Victor model is the crucial integrative hub of the atonement." He does so, not because he sees no value in the other models, but because Christus Victor "provides the canopy under which the other modes of atonement gain their currency."[59] These assessments seem to signal something of a shift in some sectors of evangelical theology—which historically has emphasized the objective theories of atonement, especially penal substitution—perhaps due to the criticism of the objective theories and especially penal substitution in recent years. Whether such a shift is merited is questioned by others, as will be considered below.

Theological Evaluation

Of these three historical models—recapitulation, ransom, and Christus Victor—by far the last has been the one most discussed in the history of theology. Recapitulation includes Christ's birth and life along with his death and resurrection in its model of atonement, but it is hard to miss the far greater centrality of Christ's death in New Testament teaching on atonement.[60] Boersma argues for an important place for recapitulation in seeing Christ's victory as the climax or result of the work of recapitulation,[61] but not many follow him. There is just not much on recapitulation in the Scriptures.

---

[57] N. T. Wright, *What St. Paul Really Said: Was Paul of Tarsus the Real Founder of Christianity?* (Grand Rapids: Eerdmans, 1997), 47.

[58] Boersma, *Violence, Hospitality, and the Cross*, 181–82.

[59] Bird, *Evangelical Theology*, 414.

[60] For example, the gospel summary in 1 Cor 15:3–4 is limited to death and resurrection, as is the preaching on the day of Pentecost in Acts 2 and throughout the book of Acts.

[61] Boersma, *Violence, Hospitality, and the Cross*, 181.

Ransom continues to have some currency, as it has a relative prominence in Scripture and resonates with many as descriptive of their experience of salvation. But here too, Crisp notes, "The ransom material has largely been eclipsed in some of this recent work by the Christus Victor theme."[62] So most of the attention given to the historical models has been focused on the Christus Victor model, and it is on Christus Victor that we will focus our theological evaluation.

Undoubtedly, victory deserves prominence in our thinking about atonement. We noted above the breadth of biblical teaching on the related ideas of ransom and redemption, and the idea of liberation from enemies and foes resonates with what many Christians have experienced. Indeed, almost every Easter hymn in traditional hymnals celebrates the victory of Christ over death. In many Majority World cultures the victory of Christ over all the powers of evil is an especially important part of gospel proclamation,[63] a part that Thomas Schreiner notes has "too often been ignored by Western evangelicals."[64] And as we noted above, a number of thoughtful students of atonement theology think victory deserves the central place in our thinking about atonement. However, one major theological critique questions whether the victory motif can stand in the center. That critique has been the lack of a mechanism of atonement in Christus Victor, or the lack of an answer to the questions of how and why.

Hans Boersma holds that Christus Victor is "the most significant model of the atonement," but acknowledges that it does not "explain *how* Christ gains the victory." He sees some of the other models, moral influence and "penal representation," as "the means toward an end," and thus the Christus Victor theme remains for him "the ultimate metaphor."[65] For Kathryn Tanner and Oliver Crisp, the lack of a mechanism disqualifies Christus Victor as a

---

[62] Oliver D. Crisp, ed., *Locating Atonement: Explorations in Constructive Dogmatics* (Grand Rapids: Zondervan, 2015), 53.

[63] Emily J. Choge Kerama, "Telling Our Stories: Salvation in the African Context," in *Majority World Theology*, 387, notes that the world of powers and principalities has been "predominant in the African worldview" and that there is a special need for the church in Africa "to proclaim the lordship of Jesus Christ over powers and principalities."

[64] Thomas Schreiner, "Penal Substitution Response," in *The Nature of the Atonement: Four Views*, 50.

[65] Boersma, *Violence, Hospitality, and the Cross*, 181–82.

genuine model of atonement.[66] In responding to Gregory Boyd's presentation of a Christus Victor view, Thomas Schreiner and Bruce Reichenbach both raise the same question: How does Jesus's death on the cross provide victory?[67] Or why was so costly a price necessary for our ransom? Some appeal to mystery or refuse to answer the "how" question on principle,[68] but several authors see a similar way to answer the "how" question: supplement Christus Victor with elements from other models of the atonement, especially elements from penal substitution. Oliver Crisp notes that this is what Irenaeus and Athanasius themselves did. Crisp says,

> In order to make the ransom/Christus Victor motifs more than mere metaphors, they need to have added to them something like the vicarious-substitutionary element found in Irenaeus and Athanasius, as well as making more prominent the way in which Christ's atonement has to do with the defeat of death as the penalty of human sin.[69]

Similarly, Hans Boersma sees the need to incorporate "[m]oral influence and penal representation" as the means by which Christ's death achieves victory.[70]

It is interesting that Crisp and Boersma both are uneasy with the category of penal substitution. Crisp uses the language of "vicarious substitution" and sees Christ taking upon himself "the penalty that is due for human sin, namely, death." But he insists that death in his thinking is not understood "as a punishment (as with classic penal substitution doctrines of atonement)."[71] Boersma refers to Christ's "representative punishment on the cross," and

---

[66] Kathryn Tanner, *Christ the Key* (Cambridge: Cambridge University Press, 2020), 252; Crisp, *Locating Atonement*, 56. Crisp sees not only Christus Victor but also the ransom motif as being subject to the same critique.

[67] See Boyd, "Christus Victor View"; Thomas Schreiner, "Penal Substitution Response"; and Bruce Reichenbach, "Healing Response"; all in *The Nature of the Atonement: Four Views*, 23–60.

[68] See the examples cited by Benjamin Myers, "The Patristic Atonement Model," in *Locating Atonement: Explorations in Constructive Dogmatics*, ed. Oliver Crisp and Fred Sanders (Grand Rapids: Zondervan, 2015), 71.

[69] Crisp, 59.

[70] Boersma, *Violence, Hospitality, and the Cross*, 182.

[71] Crisp, *Locating Atonement*, 58.

"penal representation,"[72] yet in his assessment, Jeremy Treat sees Boersma as agreeing that "penal substitution" is the 'how' of *Christus Victor*."[73] Crisp and Boersma are sensitive to the objections raised against penal substitution in recent years. It may be that penal substitution can be described and defined in such a way as to not be subject to such objections, but that is a topic for a later chapter. For now, we close this chapter with some applications.

Applications and Conclusion

The practical application that jumps out from the historical models is the incredible hope generated by the complete and certain victory Christ won at the cross. Christopher Wright expresses it well:

> *Ultimately, all that will be there in the new, redeemed creation will be there because of the cross. And conversely, all that will not be there (suffering, tears, sin, Satan, sickness, oppression, corruption, decay and death) will not be there because they will have been defeated and destroyed by the cross.* That is the length, breadth, height and depth of God's idea of redemption. It is exceedingly good news.[74]

At the same time, the claim that any of these historical models should be seen as *the* classical model, or *the* most significant, most central model of the atonement should be carefully qualified. They do have significant support in Scripture and strong support in history and among contemporary theologians. But these historical models do not do well standing alone as they fail to provide a mechanism for atonement or answer the questions of how the death of Christ provides atonement and as to why it should require the death of Christ to ransom us. They need to be supplemented by other atonement models, particularly elements from models such as penal substitution, to answer the how and why questions. In the next chapter, we turn to some of these other models.

---

[72] Boersma, *Violence, Hospitality, and the Cross*, 181–82.

[73] Jeremy Treat, *The Crucified King: Atonement and Kingdom in Biblical and Systematic Theology* (Grand Rapids: Zondervan, 2014), 222.

[74] Christopher Wright, *The Mission of God* (Downers Grove: IVP Academic, 2006), 315. Emphasis in original.

14

The Nature of the Atonement: Subjective Models

Introduction

In this chapter we turn to the second major approach to the nature of the atonement, subjective models. These models focus on the impact the work of the cross has on us. As we come to understand what Christ has done on the cross, it should elicit a response from us. Typically, two models are seen as taking this approach. In the moral influence model, we see the love of Christ displayed in the work of the cross, our resistance is melted away, and we gladly and unreservedly follow him. The moral example model sees Christ's death as an example of self-giving love that we are called to emulate.

Evangelicals have often associated these subjective models with liberal theology and thus viewed them with some suspicion. Bruce Demarest says proponents of these models "claim that Christ's death accomplished nothing objective; there were no obstacles in God that needed to be overcome in order for sinners to be restored to fellowship with their Creator. No satisfaction of justice and no placation of wrath was required on God's side."[1] This is no doubt true of many defenders of the subjective model, like the Reformation era heretic Faustus Socinus, and more recent liberals such as Hastings Rashdall, Horace Bushnell, and John Hick. But nothing in the subjective models requires denial of the validity of other models. As we will

---

[1] Bruce Demarest, *The Cross and Salvation* (Wheaton: Crossway, 1997), 153.

see in the historical development of these models, theologians in the past have often held to these and other models of the atonement, with no sense of conflict.

Thus evangelicals today should have no hesitancy about affirming the validity of some aspects of the subjective models. One of the strongest defenders of the objective penal substitutionary model of the atonement, J. I. Packer, says that his view "denies nothing asserted by the other two views [the classical or Christus Victor and subjective] save their assumption that they are complete," and that assumption need not be made. Packer adds, "It is a pity that books on the atonement so often take it for granted that accounts of the cross that have appeared as rivals in historical debate must be treated as intrinsically exclusive."[2] Oliver Crisp goes further and asserts that all accounts of the atonement incorporate some of the central ideas of the subjective models: "All Christian theologians think that Christ is a moral example to imitate and that his work on the cross is a supreme example of divine love that should elicit from us a loving response. That much is a kind of conceptual minimum for any account of atonement."[3]

The discussion of the subjective models here should be understood not as a denial of the validity of other views but as a possible supplement. As in the previous chapter, we will first consider the biblical support for these models, then the historical development, followed by a theological evaluation and practical applications.

Biblical Basis

We will begin by positing four claims associated with subjective models and then examine the biblical basis for each. The four claims are: 1) that Christ's death on the cross is an amazing manifestation of the love of God; 2) that this love should draw a response from humans; 3) that Christ's death is an example of how we should live; and 4) "[b]y imitating the example of Christ, human beings are saved."[4] This fourth claim should be carefully qualified. It

---

[2] J. I. Packer, "What Did the Cross Achieve?" in *In My Place Condemned He Stood*, ed. J. I. Packer and Mark Dever (Wheaton: Crossway, 2007), 72–73.

[3] Crisp, *Approaching the Atonement*, 90 (see chap. 12, n. 3).

[4] Crisp, 78.

is present only in some formulations of the moral example model and would be denied by many who see some validity in the first three claims.

As Alister McGrath puts it, the exemplarist believes that Christ is our example *"through whose imitation we are redeemed,"* while a moral influence model might say that Christ is our example *"because we are redeemed by him,"* and thus "we now wish to imitate him."[5] Similarly, Millard Erickson contrasts the emphasis of the example theory on Christ's death "as an example of the love we are to show for God," with the emphasis of the moral influence theory on Christ's death "as a demonstration of God's love."[6] Thus he sees the example theory emphasizing the third and fourth claims above, and moral influence focusing on the first. We will now consider the support Scripture gives to each of these four claims.

The first claim by far has the most emphatic biblical support. Perhaps the most well-known verse in the Bible is John 3:16. It sees the giving of the Son by the Father as showing the nature of the Father's love for us ("For God loved the world in this way"). Romans 5:8 is even more explicit: "But God proves his own love for us in that while we are still sinners, Christ died for us." The letter of 1 John couples the love of God with the giving of his Son to be "the atoning sacrifice" for our sins (1 John 4:10). The next verse makes the connection explicit: "God loved us in this way." It is striking that the Bible never tells Christians to look at their circumstances as proof of God's love; rather, it tells them to look to the cross; that is where we see the amazing love of God.

That this love should draw forth from us a response is also commonly taught in the New Testament. To continue in 1 John, John draws the obvious response to the manifestation of God's love: "Dear friends, if God loved us in this way, we must also love one another." Paul describes this divine love as compelling believers to respond, to "no longer live for themselves but for the one who died for them and was raised" (2 Cor 5:15). John says more simply, "We love because he first loved us" (1 John 4:19). Loving God presupposes the classic response to the gospel of repentance and faith, as in John 3:16 ("so that everyone who believes in him").

---

[5] Alister McGrath, "The Moral Theory of the Atonement: An Historical and Theological Critique," *Scottish Journal of Theology* 38, no. 2 (1985): 209. Emphasis in original.

[6] Erickson, *Christian Theology*, 717 (see chap. 13, n. 11).

The biblical support for these first two claims is so clear and has been so obvious that they are common themes in evangelical hymnody. Hymns are replete with affirmations of the amazing love of God shown in the cross, such as in Charles Wesley's hymn, "And Can It Be." The refrain exclaims, "Amazing love, how can it be / That Thou my God, shouldst die for me?" The response demanded by the love shown in the cross is given in the last line of "When I Survey the Wondrous Cross" by Isaac Watts: "Love so amazing, so divine / Demands my soul, my life, my all."

The third theme is not as celebrated or central in biblical teaching but has explicit support nonetheless. Perhaps most explicit is 1 Pet 2:21: "For you were called to this, because Christ also suffered for you, leaving you an example, that you should follow in his steps." Though not having the word "example," the idea is present in the words of Jesus: "Love one another as I have loved you. No one has greater love than this: to lay down his life for his friends" (John 15:12–13). The apostle John repeats the same idea in 1 John 3:16. After first reaffirming support for the first claim ("This is how we have come to know love: He laid down his life for us"), John calls on us to follow this example of love ("We should also lay down our lives for our brothers and sisters"). Finally, Eph 5:25 sees the self-giving love of Christ as an example for how husbands should love their wives: "Husbands, love your wives, just as Christ loved the church and gave himself for her."

It is the fourth claim that the Bible not only fails to support, but strongly opposes. Following the example of Christ is nowhere seen as the means by which humans are saved. Salvation in Scripture is everywhere dependent on what Christ has done for us; we receive salvation "by grace through faith" (Eph 2:8), and this is such classic and common evangelical teaching that we need not belabor that point.

Perhaps for this reason, few who champion subjective models make such bald statements as, "Humans are saved by following the example of Jesus." This fourth claim helps explain the hesitancy some evangelicals have shown to the subjective models. For example, of one version of moral exemplarism, Oliver Crisp says, "it eviscerates the Christian gospel of much of its distinctive doctrinal content."[7] A similar judgment is levied by Alister McGrath against others championing an exemplarist view: "It amounts to nothing

---

[7] Crisp, *Approaching the Atonement*, 85.

more than a doctrine of salvation by merit."[8] But when limited to the first three claims given above, subjective models are well supported by Scripture.

Historical Development

It has been common to begin discussion of the subjective models with the name of Peter Abelard as the pioneer and key advocate of such models, but there has been a movement in recent years to carefully qualify the degree to which such claims are true.[9] Even apart from that discussion, there is reason to think that some of the claims of the subjective models are so clearly supported in Scripture that they have been an assumed part of thinking about the atonement from the beginning and thus present long before Abelard.

For example, Hans Boersma claims that Irenaeus may be seen "as a significant protagonist of an exemplarist understanding of the atonement" because of the importance of example to his understanding of recapitulation. Boersma says, "Irenaeus did not just assert that Christ retraced all ages of all human beings, but he also insisted that Christ became an example for each of these age groups [from infants to old age]."[10] As our example and model, Christ calls on us to follow his example. Irenaeus is not teaching salvation by works, but following Christ's example is coupled with faith.[11] Joshua McNall points to Augustine as another possible early advocate of the subjective model in terms of seeing Christ as the manifestation of divine love. But the passages he cites from Augustine focus on the *incarnation* of Christ as the demonstration of God's love rather than the *crucifixion*.[12]

So while there may be some aspects of the subjective models that were assumed by virtually all theologians, and while there may be some

---

[8] McGrath, "The Moral Theory of the Atonement," 219.

[9] See McNall, *The Mosaic of Atonement*, 251–60 (see chap. 13, n. 11) for a survey of this movement and his evaluation of it.

[10] Boersma, *Violence, Hospitality, and the Cross*, 121, 126, citing Irenaeus, "Against Heresies," *ANF* 1, 391 (Book 2, chap. XXII, 4).

[11] Boersma, 130, says that Irenaeus does not "oppose faith to works," but "consistently keeps the two together."

[12] McNall, *The Mosaic of Atonement*, 260, cites Augustine's question, "What greater cause is there of the Lord's coming than to show God's love for us?" (Augustine, *On the Instruction of Beginners*, 4).

aspects of those models that have some part in the works of Irenaeus and
Augustine, there may still be reason to give some prominence of place to
Peter Abelard in the development of the subjective models, but with some
careful qualification.

The life of Peter Abelard (1079–1142) may be one of the most colorful
and controversial in all of church history. From his brilliance as a student who
challenged and defeated his own teachers in public debates, to his infamous
affair and subsequent love letters with Heloise, to his eventual excommuni-
cation on the grounds of teaching Pelagianism, he has left a large mark in
church history in the fields of ethics, philosophy, theology, with his mark in
theology specifically in the doctrine of the atonement.[13] In his own day, he
was charged by Bernard of Clairvaux and William of St. Thierry as teaching
that the atonement amounted "solely to a moral influence upon humanity."[14]
In the modern era, Hastings Rashdall claimed Abelard as his model in developing an exemplarist theory of the atonement,[15] and Steven Cartwright gives
a list of modern scholars who see Abelard as "an exemplarist par excellence."[16]

The basis for these charges concerning Abelard is a single passage from
his commentary on Romans. In discussing Rom 3:19–26, he reflects on how
we are reconciled to God through Christ's death. He rejected the popular
ransom theory of his day, which saw the ransom paid to Satan. He argued
that the fact that Satan had seduced humans gave him no rights over them.
He was also uneasy with the idea that the ransom was paid to God the
Father, though he did not explicitly reject the idea that some ransom had
been paid. Here then is the key passage. Abelard says that Christ reconciles
us to God by receiving our nature, "and in that nature, teaching us both by

---

[13] *The Cambridge Companion to Abelard*, ed. Jeffrey Brower and Kevin Guilfoy
(Cambridge: Cambridge University Press, 2004), provides a helpful biographical
sketch of Abelard's life, along with chapters examining his works in the fields of ethics, philosophy, and theology. For the famous love letters, see *The Letters of Abelard
and Heloise*, trans. Betty Radice (Hammondsworth, UK: Penguin, 1974).

[14] See McNall, *The Mosaic of Atonement*, 254. Emphasis in original.

[15] Hastings Rashdall, *The Idea of Atonement on Christian Theology* (London:
Macmillan, 1925), 360.

[16] Steven Cartwright, "Introduction," to Peter Abelard, *Commentary on
the Epistle to the Romans*, trans. Steven Cartwright, The Fathers of the Church,
Mediaeval Continuation, vol. 12 (Washington, DC: Catholic University of America
Press, 2011), 44–45.

word and example, preserved to the death and bound us to him even more through love, so that when we have been kindled by so great a benefit of divine grace, true charity might fear to endure nothing for his sake."[17]

This passage does seem to reflect the first three of the four claims we saw as important for subjective models. Both the incarnation and the crucifixion are seen as demonstrations of God's love (called "supreme love" later in this passage).[18] That love does call forth a response from us: "true charity might fear to endure nothing for his sake." The third claim, that Christ's death is an example of how we should live, is less clear. But he does quote John 15:13 in the context of this discussion: "No one has greater love than this: that he lays down his life for his friends."[19] And that verse is preceded in John 15 with the command to love one another in the same way that Christ has loved us, which seems to strongly imply that Christ's death is an example of how we should live. So the first three claims important to subjective models do seem to be present here in Abelard. But the absence of any affirmation of the fourth claim—that we are saved by obeying the example of Christ—is an important absence. It, along with a number of important pieces of evidence, has given rise to the reinterpretation of Abelard.

Joshua McNall allows that there may be some exemplarist ideas in Abelard but gives three reasons for denying that Abelard was exclusively exemplarist. He says, "Perhaps the most stunning evidence for Abelard's nonexemplarism comes in his explicit support for penal substitution."[20] In the same Romans commentary cited as evidence for his support for subjective theories, there are clear statements that support objective theories: "The Lord bore [and] endured the punishments of our sins. . . . We committed the sins for which he bore the punishment . . . by dying he might remove . . . the punishment of our sins."[21] McNall concludes, "Abelard's account of moral influence sits atop an objective foundation that includes even the idea of Christ bearing our penalty."[22]

---

[17] Abelard, *Commentary on Romans*, 167.

[18] Abelard, 168.

[19] Abelard.

[20] McNall, *The Mosaic of Atonement*, 255.

[21] Abelard, *Commentary on Romans*, 216. See also McNall, 256.

[22] McNall, 256. McNall points to Thomas Williams, "Sin, Grace, and Redemption," in *The Cambridge Companion to Abelard*, 258–78, for a more thorough

McNall also thinks that Abelard was wrongly charged and eventually excommunicated as a Pelagian, pointing to a second piece of evidence, Abelard's teaching on original sin. Because original sin has left us in "slavery to sin," we need more than an example to set us free.[23] And as his third piece of evidence, McNall argues that Abelard's teaching on God's love has been misunderstood or even mistranslated. It should not be seen as a love that calls us to follow its example, it is a love that redeems and binds us to God.[24] Concerning the love of God manifested in the cross, he quotes R. E. Weingart: "Its exemplary quality is secondary [and] consequent upon its redemptive character."[25]

Altogether these three pieces of evidence give ample reason to reject the idea that Abelard was an exclusive exemplarist. Alister McGrath goes even further. He says point blank that if by exemplarist we mean someone who teaches that we are saved by following Christ's example, "Abelard did not teach an exemplarist theory of the atonement," and sharply criticizes Hastings Rashdall for claiming to be following Abelard in developing his exemplarist views in the twentieth century.[26]

Abelard's case points to a need for precision in terminology in speaking of the subjective views. While both moral influence and example views can lay claim to being subjective views in focusing upon the effect of the cross subjectively on us, the two views have an important difference. Moral influence speaks of the response called forth in those who have been redeemed; example theories focus on what nonredeemed people must do to be redeemed. Moral influence theories can and in the minds and theologies of many, do coexist with other models of the atonement, models which make clear that our salvation does not come from following Christ's example but from accepting what Christ has done for us. When subjective views begin with a denial of the validity of other models, they tend to move toward exemplarism and often into heresy. We see that in the years following Abelard.

---

study.

[23] See Abelard, *Commentary on Romans*, 168; McNall, *The Mosaic of Atonement*, 256.

[24] McNall, 257.

[25] Richard E. Weingart, *The Logic of Divine Love: A Critical Analysis of the Soteriology of Peter Abailard* (Oxford: Clarendon, 1970), 78–96.

[26] McGrath, "The Moral Theory of the Atonement," 206.

In his study of the theology of Thomas Aquinas, Frederick Bauerschmidt says that medieval theology did not see the subjective view associated with Abelard as necessarily opposed to the objective, satisfaction view associated with Anselm. He says, "Thomas, like most medieval theologians, incorporated elements of both of these approaches, without seeing them as contradictory."[27] Though Bernard of Clairvaux was at times strongly critical of Abelard, Daniel Akin argues that, in the end, Bernard follows the pattern Bauerschmidt sees as typical of most medieval theologians: "In sum, Bernard affirmed the best elements in Abelard and Anselm."[28]

This changes with the sixteenth century work of Faustus Socinus, whose work on the atonement, *De Jesu Christo Servatore* (*On Jesus Christ the Savior*), is remembered chiefly "for its savage attack upon the whole idea of substitutionary atonement as understood by the Reformers."[29] Indeed, it is fair to question whether the Socinian view is an atonement view at all, for in his view, there was no need for atonement. God requires no payment for sin, and Jesus is merely a human and thus not able to make atonement for humanity, if it had been required. What Jesus did do is give us "an example of that total love for God that we must display if we are to experience salvation." He also gives us inspiration that displaying such love is not beyond us, reflecting his Pelagian view of the human condition "as spiritually and morally capable of fulfilling God's expectations."[30]

Socinus is a classical heretic on multiple counts. He denied the deity of Christ and thus the Trinity. He reduced human need from atonement and forgiveness to simply an inspiring example, provided by Jesus. He reduced salvation to a human accomplishment. Yet he became "the fount of much subsequent moral exemplarism in theology."[31] Enlightenment and post-Enlightenment thinkers and liberal theology in general moved to subjective models of the atonement in the eighteenth and nineteenth centuries, some

---

[27] Frederick Bauerschmidt, *The Essential* Summa Theologiae*: A Reader and Commentary*, 2nd ed. (Grand Rapids: Baker Academic, 2021), 327n27.

[28] Daniel Akin, "Bernard of Clairvaux and the Atonement," in *The Church at the Dawn of the 21st Century: Essays in Honor of W. A. Criswell*, ed. Paige Patterson, John Pretlove, and Luis Pantoja (Dallas: Criswell, 1989), 105.

[29] Crisp, *Approaching the Atonement*, 81.

[30] Erickson, *Christian Theology*, 716.

[31] Crisp, *Approaching the Atonement*, 80.

fully exemplarist but some still seeing the example of Christ as moving us to faith and not merely to imitation of his example.

One of the most widely known twentieth-century exemplarists is Hastings Rashdall. In his 1925 publication, *The Idea of Atonement in Christian Theology*, Rashdall credits Abelard with being the first since the days of the early fathers to state a view of the atonement "which thoroughly appeals to reason and conscience." He adds that it really was not original to Abelard, being fully present in the writings of Paul and John and the early fathers: "they all with one consent teach this—that it [the death of Christ] was a revelation of the love of God, intended to call forth answering love in man."[32]

But in the years since Rashdall, there have been few major presentations of subjective views. Albrecht Ritschl and R. S. Franks are mentioned as examples of some who preferred the subjective models,[33] but they are both roughly contemporaneous with Rashdall. Paul Fiddes and John Hick are suggested as more recent presentations, and Hick does seem to give an updated version of a moral exemplarism not far from Socinus, but neither has generated much of a following.[34] In fact, to find a subjective view contribution to their *Four Views* book, editors James Beilby and Paul Eddy enlisted the help of Bruce Reichenbach, whose healing view is quite different than most subjective views in history.[35] Traditionally, evangelicals have supported primarily objective views, and in recent years, when criticism has been raised against objective views, most have turned, not to subjective views, but to classical views, especially Christus Victor. Adam Kotsko says, "for much of the history of Christian thought, there was no particular need to bring forward exemplarism as a distinct theory because everyone

---

[32] Rashdall, *The Idea of Atonement on Christian Theology*, 360.

[33] See Albrecht Ritschl, *The Christian Doctrine of Justification and Reconciliation*, ed. H. R. Mackintosh and A. B. Macaulay (Edinburgh: Clark, 1900); R. S. Franks, *The Atonement* (London: Oxford University Press, 1934).

[34] For Fiddes, see Paul Fiddes, *Past Event and Present Salvation: The Christian Idea of Atonement* (Louisville: Westminster John Knox, 1989). See McNall, *The Mosaic of Atonement*, 260–65, for a fuller presentation and evaluation of Fiddes. For Hick, see John Hick, *The Metaphor of God Incarnate*, 2nd ed. (Louisville: Westminster John Knox, 2005). For an analysis of Hick, see Crisp, *Approaching the Atonement*, 83–84.

[35] See Bruce Reichenbach, "Healing View," in *The Nature of the Atonement: Four Views*, 117–42 (see chap. 13, n. 6).

assumed that Christ's work should have positive moral effects. It has only been in the modern period that exemplarism has become a 'stand-alone' theory, rather than a supplement to other theories."[36] The relative lack of historical development of subjective models may also be due to the fact that there are definite theological problems when subjective models are used in exclusion to other models.

Theological Evaluation

Despite the hesitations of some evangelicals toward the subjective models, we have already noted the assessment of others that there is an almost universal assumption among Christian theologians that Christ's death is an amazing manifestation of God's love, that it should melt our resistance and prompt loving responses from us, and that Christ's self-giving love is an example we should emulate. In an earlier section we gave the biblical support for these ideas. So at least the moral influence subjective model seems to merit a positive theological evaluation.[37]

However, as has long been noted, these subjective models leave some important questions unasked and often unrecognized. Most importantly, why is Christ's death a manifestation of God's love? As James Denney says in the classic illustration given more than a century ago, "If I were sitting at the end of a pier on a summer day, enjoying the sunshine and the air, and someone came along and jumped into the water and got drowned 'to prove his love for me,' I should find it quite unintelligible."[38] Only if we are in some sort of danger that Christ delivered us from at the cost of his life is his death a manifestation of God's love, and that danger is what the classical

---

[36] Adam Kotsko, "Exemplarism," in *T&T Clark Companion to Atonement*, 484–85.

[37] Such positive assessments are given in Packer, "What Did the Cross Achieve?", 72; Erickson, *Christian Theology*, 729; McNall, *The Mosaic of Atonement*, 259–60; Crisp, *Approaching the Atonement*, 94; Boersma, *Violence, Hospitality, and the Cross*, 132, and others.

[38] James Denney, *The Death of Christ*, ed. R. V. G. Tasker (London: Tyndale, 1951), 177. This is the same objection raised to the subjective view of Bruce Reichenbach in *The Nature of the Atonement: Four Views* by other contributors to that volume. See Thomas Schreiner, "Penal Substitution Response," 149, and Joel Green, "Kaleidoscopic Response," 154, in *The Nature of the Atonement: Four Views*.

and objective models supply. Thus any advocate of a subjective model that denies the validity of other models undermines the rationale of the subjective view itself, for Christ's death can only be seen as a manifestation of God's love that calls forth a grateful response from us if it delivers us from some danger. Oliver Crisp helpfully observes that subjective views may be "best understood . . . as ancillary to other, more developed ways of thinking about the reconciling work of Christ."[39]

A second question often unrecognized by advocates of the moral example version of the subjective view but recently raised by feminist critics is, Does seeing Christ as the example we are to emulate encourage women to passively accept abuse and unjust suffering? Darby Kathleen Ray articulates the objection arising from this question: "the salvific values of suffering, self-sacrifice, and obedience are too easily distorted into a theological tool of subjugation."[40] But this fails to notice that the call to follow Christ's self-sacrificing example is given not just or even especially to women.

In a radically countercultural move, Paul calls on husbands to follow Christ's example in how they love their wives (Eph 5:25) and Christ specifically calls those who would lead to follow his example (Mark 10:45). Sadly, many husbands and leaders have failed to follow Christ's example, but surely the failure is in the followers and not in the example they are called to follow. If we try to imagine a world in which there was no call to men to follow the example of Christ's self-giving love, it is unlikely that it would be a world in which there was less abuse than this present world, bad as it is.

Moreover, here is another place where subjective models may be helped by additional emphases in other models. For example, in the Christus Victor model there is the emphasis on Christ as the one who delivers us from all forms of enslavement, and we will see in a future chapter that objective models of the atonement can see the cross as God standing for justice, not endorsing injustice.

So we do not believe that these questions eliminate the theological value of at least some of the subjective models. To be sure, that is not true of all forms and uses of the subjective models. Those who take the exemplarist

---

[39] Crisp, *Approaching the Atonement*, 94.

[40] Darby Kathleen Ray, *Deceiving the Devil: Atonement, Abuse, and Ransom* (Cleveland: Pilgrim, 1998), 58.

view of the atonement to mean that it is by "imitating the example of Christ [that] human beings are saved" raise numerous troubling theological objections. Oliver Crisp calls such subjective models "no-atonement moral exemplarism," because in such a view "nothing about the life, work and death of Jesus brings about some kind of reconciliation with God." Indeed, there is no need for atonement, for God to be reconciled to humans; the only need is to elicit a change in humans, such that they follow Christ's example. Crisp says of such a view, "it eviscerates the Christian gospel of much of its distinctive doctrinal content" and seems "almost unrecognizable as a species of specifically *Christian* theology."[41]

Alister McGrath sees much the same problem in Hastings Rashdall's view. McGrath says that Rashdall, along with some earlier Enlightenment theologians, accepted the view that "man must find his way to salvation by his good works executed in the imitation of the example of Christ." In addition to missing the critique McGrath sees in Kant of the lack of human ability to successfully follow Christ's example, McGrath sees a further problem in Rashdall's view: "It amounts to nothing less than a doctrine of salvation by merit."[42]

Thus with subjective models as a whole, there are two theological objections. First, they lose their grounding and are vulnerable to objections if isolated from other, complementary models of the atonement. This can easily be rectified by using them along with other models. But, second, in some versions and uses of some subjective models, there are deeper problems, rooted in unorthodox understandings of the human problem and what is needed to provide salvation for humans. In these cases, some who use the subjective models do stray outside sound theological boundaries. Of such use, evangelicals should be wary. But this does not mean there is no positive value in any use of the subjective models. With one important specific application, we conclude this chapter.

Applications and Conclusion

With some forms of moral exemplarism leading to heterodox if not heretical ideas concerning salvation, and even the more biblical ideas of moral

---

[41] Crisp, *Approaching the Atonement*, 85–86. Crisp sees Socinus and Hick as the clearest examples of no-atonement moral exemplarism.
[42] McGrath, "The Moral Theory of the Atonement," 212, 219.

influence needing other models to be coherent, what value is there in subjective views of the work of Christ? Hans Boersma says, "Without the moral theory we lose sight of the freedom of the human response, of the significance of human action, and ultimately of the love of God itself."[43] The key contribution of the subjective views is that the cross is designed to move us to such response.

The Christus Victor view sees the cross as liberating us from our enemies; the objective models assure us that the barriers between us and God have been removed, such that God now welcomes all who come to him through Christ. But these aspects of the work of Christ can leave us still stubbornly resistant, turning away from all that has been done for us. The subjective views assure us that God does not leave us on our senseless, self-chosen path to destruction. The cross reveals the incredible lengths to which God will go to win our hearts. We see this amazing love, and to some, God issues an effectual call. It enables and provokes a response. We find that indeed, "the love of Christ compels us" (2 Cor 5:14). Yes, this is a human response, even a free human response. But it is a *response*; a response to what Christ has done. Like no other model of the atonement, the subjective models call forth our response. For that reason, at least some forms of these subjective models belong in a full-orbed view of the work of atonement.

---

[43] Boersma, *Violence, Hospitality, and the Cross*, 132.

15

The Nature of the Atonement: Objective Models

Introduction

We come now to the third family of atonement models, called objective models. By objective, we mean that in this family of models, the atonement is seen as accomplishing something outside the human subject. They do not see the atonement as in any way changing the character of God, but the atonement opens the way to a new type of relationship between God and humans. Some obstacle or barrier has been removed.

We agree with Michael Bird that three models belong in this family: satisfaction, governmental, and penal substitution.[1] In the first of these models it is "the gravity of sin and the majesty of God" that make satisfaction necessary. John Stott says, "God must not only respect us as the responsible beings we are, but he must also respect himself as the holy God he is. Before the holy God can forgive us, some kind of 'satisfaction' is necessary."[2] In the satisfaction model developed by Anselm, it is God's honor that is satisfied. Sin essentially is a dishonoring of God; it leaves humans in debt to God, owing him honor. But present obedience cannot repay the debt of past disobedience, so humans owe a debt they cannot pay. Christ lived a perfect life and so did not have to die. By nonetheless offering his life up on behalf of

---

[1] Bird, *Evangelical Theology*, 410 (see chap. 11, n. 6).
[2] Stott, *The Cross of Christ*, 110 (see chap. 13, n. 11).

humans he showed God ultimate honor and as God incarnate showed infinite honor, sufficient to pay the debt humans owed.[3]

In the second model in this family, it is not the honor of God that must be satisfied, but the demands of public justice. This view is identified with the name of Hugo Grotius, a seventeenth-century Dutch jurist and theologian. His major work, *A Defense of the Catholic Faith Concerning the Satisfaction of Christ, against Faustus Socinus*,[4] addressed two charges Socinus had made against traditional views of the atonement: that God could forgive without the need for any satisfaction, and that furthermore, it was impossible for one man to bear the punishment due to many others.[5] To the first objection, Grotius says that while God as sovereign could forgive without satisfaction, God as ruler (*rector*) has the duty to maintain justice and order in the government of the world. In biblical language, the Judge of all the earth must do what is right (Gen 18:25), and it is right that sin be punished. To the second objection, Grotius argued that Christ did not have to suffer the exact same punishment that sinners are due ("eternal death"), he only had to suffer something of the same worth.[6] Thus, Christ is not a substitute for humans, but an example of what would happen if God were to punish humans for their sins. This example is sufficient to justify God's moral government of the world but requires adapting the substitutionary language of Scripture to see it as fulfilled by Christ acting on our behalf if not in our place.[7]

---

[3] For Anselm's argument, see "Why God Became Man," in *A Scholastic Miscellany: Anselm to Ockham*, ed. Eugene Fairweather, Library of Christian Classics (Philadelphia: Westminster, 1956). For a critical evaluation of Anselm, see Rutledge, *The Crucifixion*, 146–66 (see chap. 13, n. 3).

[4] Hugo Grotius, *A Defence of the Catholic Faith Concerning the Satisfaction of Christ, against Faustus Socinus*, trans. Frank Hugh Foster (Andover, MA: Draper, 1889). The original, *Defenso fidei catholicae de satisfacione Christi adversus Faustum Socinum*, was written in 1617.

[5] These charges are found in Faustus Socinus, *De Jesu Christo Servatore* (*Concerning Jesus Christ the Savior*).

[6] See the description of this distinction in Gert van den Brink, "Hugo Grotius," in *T&T Clark Companion to Atonement*, 523–24. In Latin, the distinction is between the same (*idem*) and something of the same worth (*tantundem*).

[7] See the discussion in Crisp, *Approaching the Atonement*, 114–15 (see chap. 12, n. 3).

Of the three models in this family, by far the most influential, especially among evangelicals, has been the last, penal substitution. Joshua McNall compares penal substitution to a large hall with many smaller rooms or subdivisions, but he gives three elements that he sees all varieties of penal substitution sharing: substitution, penalty, and divine sanction.[8] All three are present in the thorough definition of penal substitution given by Thomas Schreiner:

> The Father, because of his love for human beings, sent his Son (who offered himself willingly and gladly) to satisfy God's justice, so that Christ took the place of sinners. The punishment and penalty we deserved was laid on Jesus Christ instead of us, so that in the cross both God's holiness and love are manifested.[9]

While this view sounds familiar to evangelical ears, it has also been the model most criticized, especially in the last twenty-five years, so much so that we devote the chapter following this one to the objections to the penal substitution model and responses to those objections. But we begin here with the biblical support for these three models.

Biblical Support

The biblical theme in support of all three of these models is the justice of God when confronted with human sin. In the words of Cornelius Plantinga, sin is "not the way it's supposed to be."[10] A similar sentiment is expressed by Fleming Rutledge in her assessment of human evil in the world: "Something is terribly wrong and needs to be set right."[11] Faced with an unjust world, the One who upholds justice must act.

Abraham realized this early on in the biblical narrative. As God prepares to judge Sodom and Gomorrah, Abraham asks, "Won't the Judge of the whole earth do what is just?" (Gen 18:25). The answer is yes, the Judge

---

[8] McNall, *The Mosaic of Atonement*, 101 (see chap. 13, n. 11).

[9] Schreiner, "Penal Substitution View," in *The Nature of the Atonement: Four Views*, 67. See the similar definition in Crisp, *Approaching the Atonement*, 97.

[10] See Cornelius Plantinga, Jr., *Not the Way It's Supposed to Be: A Breviary of Sin* (Grand Rapids: Eerdmans, 1995).

[11] Rutledge, *The Crucifixion*, 148.

of the whole earth will satisfy the demands of justice, because it is right for him to do so. From casting Adam and Eve out of the garden (Gen 3:23–24) to casting the wicked into the lake of fire after final judgment (Rev 20:15), sin moves God to act. But is it possible for justice to be satisfied without the penalty falling on the guilty humans? All three of these three models see the cross as the way God provides satisfaction. They see Scripture pointing to this in a variety of ways. The support for penal substitution is especially robust;[12] the satisfaction view shares some of the same support;[13] a lesser amount directly applies to the governmental theory,[14] but all three rest on the biblical theme of God acting to satisfy justice. The wonder of the New Testament is how love and justice meet at the cross.

The most pervasive means of making satisfaction for sin in the Old Testament is sacrifices. In the words of William Lane Craig, "No other atonement motif is so abundantly attested. This is convincing evidence that the motif of sacrifice anchors the doctrine of the atonement in the NT."[15] Joshua McNall concurs, saying "the theme of sacrifice is central for the New Testament writers. It was perhaps the first image by which the early Christians came to understand the atonement."[16]

This theme or motif of sacrifice seems to strongly support the penal substitution model. Bruce Demarest identifies the two key steps in the typical pattern of Old Testament sacrifices that reflect substitution and penalty: "The offerers placed their hands on the animal's head, denoting identification with the victim and the transfer of sin's penalty to the substitute"; second,

---

[12] Schreiner and Erickson both see the biblical support for penal substitution as so strong as to justify seeing it as "the anchor and foundation for all other dimensions of the atonement" (Schreiner, "The Penal Substitution View," 67) or as "the central theme of the atonement" (Erickson, *Christian Theology*, 732).

[13] Rutledge, *The Crucifixion*, 146, n. 1. She sees Anselm's insights as "anticipated" in texts like Isa 53:4–6; Rom 5:12–21; 8:3–4; 2 Cor 5:21; Gal 3:10–14; 1 Pet 2:24; 3:18 and others.

[14] The governmental theory emphasizes God's rectoral justice rather than his retributive justice but can still claim a biblical basis in texts such as Rom 3:24–26, which sees the cross as the way God deals righteously with sin as the moral governor of the world, and in all the texts dealing with Christ as our ransom paying the penalty due us (Crisp, *Approaching the Atonement*, 116–17).

[15] Craig, *Atonement and the Death of Christ*, 15 (see chap. 13, n. 13).

[16] McNall, *The Mosaic of Atonement*, 128–29.

"The animal was then slain, signifying death as the requisite punishment for sin."[17] Gordon Wenham says of these sacrifices, "They all presuppose that the animal victim is a substitute for the worshipper, makes atonement for him, and thereby restores him to favour with God."[18]

In addition to the sacrifices of animals, there is the haunting figure in Isaiah 53. The importance of this text for understanding the work of Christ is seen in the numerous allusions to it throughout the NT and in the words of Christ himself. Fleming Rutledge says of Isa 52:13–53:12, "The position taken here is that the passage serves as a guide or partial substructure for the New Testament as a whole."[19] This passage is further strong support for the penal substitution model, for these two elements (penal and substitution) seem to appear emphatically here. The Servant is "pierced because of our rebellion, crushed because of our iniquities; punishment for our peace was on him, and we are healed by his wounds" (Isa 53:5). Otfried Hofius calls penal substitution the "central and dominant theme" of the whole of Isaiah 53.[20]

Biblical support for the objective models is not limited to the Old Testament. The New Testament sees Jesus as the fulfillment of the sacrificial system, with John the Baptist calling Jesus "the Lamb of God who takes away the sin of the world" (John 1:29) and Peter comparing the blood of Jesus to that "of an unblemished and spotless lamb" (1 Pet 1:19) and thus qualified to be offered as a sacrifice. There are even a couple of verses that specifically associate the cross with giving honor to God, as Anselm's satisfaction theory claims (see John 17:1; Heb 2:9).

Jesus identifies himself with the Suffering Servant of Isaiah 53 in Mark 10:45, stating that he will give his life "as a ransom for many." Here,

---

[17] Demarest, *The Cross and Salvation*, 169 (see chap. 14, n. 1).

[18] Gordon Wenham, "The Theology of Old Testament Sacrifice," in *Sacrifice in the Bible*, ed. Roger Beckwith and Martin Selman (Grand Rapids: Baker, 1995), 84.

[19] Rutledge, *The Crucifixion*, 475. Craig, *Atonement and the Death of Christ*, 39, adds, "Ten of the twelve verses of the fifty-third chapter of Isaiah are quoted in the NT," including the words of Jesus in Mark 10:45.

[20] Otfried Hofius, "The Fourth Servant Song in the New Testament Letters," in *The Suffering Servant: Isaiah 53 in Jewish and Christian Sources*, ed. Bernd Jankowski and Peter Stuhlmacher (1996), trans. Daniel Bailey (Grand Rapids: Eerdmans, 2004), 164.

the support for the objective model is not found only in quoting from a text with clearly penal and substitutionary elements, but also in bringing in the whole idea of ransom or redemption. Intrinsic to the idea of a ransom is something very close to substitution. Fleming Rutledge calls one of the central ideas associated with redemption that of "equivalent exchange,"[21] or in Leon Morris's words, "a substitution."[22] The one being held captive or enslaved is freed in exchange for the ransom; the ransom is accepted as a substitute. Robert Peterson sees at least three texts where Christ's redemption is presented as substitutionary (Gal 3:13; 1 Tim 2:5–6; Titus 2:13–14), giving further support to objective models, especially penal substitution.[23] But Oliver Crisp also sees the ransom language as supportive of the governmental view. On that view, "Christ is a ransom. He does pay what would be the penalty due for human sin if it were visited upon us. For this reason he does release us from the requirements of the moral law by taking upon himself what would be the penal consequences of our sin as our penal example."[24]

In Gal 3:10–14, the nature of the penalty changes. Christ redeems us "by becoming a curse for us" (Gal 3:13). This passage supports objective models of the atonement in several ways. Fleming Rutledge calls it "perhaps the clearest statement of the substitution motif in Paul."[25] But alongside the substitutionary element there is the penal element. By becoming a curse for us, "He accepts as his own our legal status of condemned criminals and then endures our punishment to liberate us from such a state of condemnation."[26] The advocate of the governmental view could also see this as support for her view, seeing Christ becoming accursed for us as "our penal example—the one who takes on what would have been our punishment if God had meted out to us the penalty instead of making Christ the example."[27] Either way, the elements of penalty and substitution are present in this text.

---

[21] Rutledge, *The Crucifixion*, 294.
[22] Morris, *The Apostolic Preaching of the Cross*, 58 (see chap. 13, n. 20).
[23] Peterson, *Salvation Accomplished by the Son*, 357–58 (see chap. 11, n. 2).
[24] Crisp, *Approaching the Atonement*, 117.
[25] Rutledge, *The Crucifixion*, 472.
[26] Craig, *Atonement and the Death of Christ*, 76.
[27] Crisp, *Approaching the Atonement*, 117.

A final important biblical support for the objective models is found in Rom 3:21–26.[28] The mention of redemption in v. 24 brings in the substitutionary motif that has a part in all of the objective models. The phrase in v. 26 about God demonstrating his righteousness is claimed by advocates of the governmental view as support for their view.[29] But the single term that has generated the most discussion is found in v. 25, *hilastērion*.[30] The 1932 work of C. H. Dodd arguing that the meaning of *hilastērion* in Rom 3:25 "is that of expiation, not that of propitiation,"[31] eventually prompted responses by Leon Morris[32] and Roger Nicole,[33] who both concluded that Dodd went too far, especially in trying to remove any concept of the cross as satisfying the wrath of God. To explain simply the difference between the two terms, "expiation has to do with reparation for sin, propitiation connotes the idea of placating divine wrath."[34] And it is the idea of the cross satisfying the wrath of God that is at issue, even more than the proper translation of *hilastērion*.

Even after more than half a century of discussion, there is still no agreement, either on the meaning of *hilastērion* or even on who won the debate. Fleming Rutledge thinks that Morris acknowledges many of the points Dodd made against propitiation. She quotes Morris: "the God of the Bible is not a Being who can be propitiated after the fashion of a pagan deity," and concludes from that statement that "it should now be generally agreed that any concept of *hilastērion* in the sense of placating, appeasing, deflecting the

---

[28] Schreiner, "The Penal Substitution View," 87, calls it "a key text on penal substitution."

[29] Crisp, *Approaching the Atonement*, 117: "From the point of view of the defender of the governmental view, the passage indicates that God as a moral governor of the world must act righteously in dealing with sin, and that Christ is the means appointed to that end."

[30] There is even an entire dissertation devoted to this term. See Daniel Bailey, "Jesus as the Mercy Seat: The Semantics and Theology of Paul's Use of *Hilastērion* in Romans 3:25" (PhD diss., University of Cambridge, 1999).

[31] C. H. Dodd, *The Epistle of Paul to the Romans*, Moffatt New Testament Commentary (New York: Harper & Row, 1932), 360.

[32] Morris, *The Apostolic Preaching of the Cross*, 129.

[33] Roger Nicole, "C. H. Dodd and the Doctrine of propitiation," *WTJ* 17, no. 2 (1955): 117–57.

[34] Crisp, *Approaching the Atonement*, 98.

anger of, or satisfying the wrath of [God], is inadmissible."[35] But this is to misunderstand Morris and the position of many evangelicals and some non-evangelicals. In fact, D. A. Carson contends that it is widely recognized today that Dodd was wrong "in his central contentions,"[36] and support for the idea that the cross did involve the satisfaction of divine wrath is still widely held. What Morris and others would acknowledge is that the satisfaction of God's righteous and just wrath is far different than the placating of the capricious wrath of a pagan deity, and that the amazing love of God is seen in that God himself supplies the sacrifice that satisfies his divine wrath.

John Stott says quite categorically, "We strongly reject, therefore, every explanation of the death of Christ which does not have at its centre the principle of 'satisfaction through substitution,' indeed, divine self-satisfaction through divine self-substitution."[37] And what is satisfied is frankly stated as the righteous wrath of God. C. E. B. Cranfield, not seen as an evangelical scholar, nonetheless expresses agreement with much of Morris's critique of Dodd and concludes his exegesis of Rom 3:25–26 with these words:

> We take it that what Paul's statement that God purposed Christ as a propitiatory victim means is that God, because in His mercy he willed to forgive sinful men and, being truly merciful, willed to forgive them righteously, that is, without in any way condoning their sin, purposed to direct against His own very Self in the person of His Son the full weight of that righteous wrath which they deserved.[38]

Morris himself concludes his discussion of propitiation with the twin emphases that in the Bible "propitiation is thought of as springing from the love of God" and that with the heathen connotations stripped away, the central truth remaining is that "propitiation signifies the averting of wrath by the offering of a gift."[39] Thomas Schreiner says, "those who defend the notion

---

[35] Rutledge, *The Crucifixion*, 280, quoting Morris, *Apostolic Preaching*, 148.

[36] D. A. Carson, "Atonement in Romans 3:21–26," in *The Glory of the Atonement: Biblical, Historical, and Practical Perspectives*, ed. Charles Hill and Frank James III (Downers Grove: InterVarsity, 2002), 130.

[37] Stott, *The Cross of Christ*, 159.

[38] C. E. B. Cranfield, *A Critical and Exegetical Commentary on the Epistle to the Romans*, vol. 1, ICC (Edinburgh: T&T Clark, 1975), 217.

[39] Morris, *Apostolic Preaching*, 183.

of propitiation have the better argument, for the term [*hilastērion*] includes the sense of the averting of God's wrath—the appeasement or satisfaction of his righteousness." But he adds, "To be more precise, the term includes *both* notions, expiation *and* propitiation."[40]

In the last analysis, Oliver Crisp says it does not make much difference. He says, "an argument for penal substitution can be had irrespective of whether Christ is said to suffer a penalty for human sin in an act of expiation, or (in addition) is said to be punished in order to propitiate God's wrath." But the idea of the satisfaction of divine wrath is very important to this debate, and is related to a number of the objections to penal substitution, which we will mention below and address in more detail in the chapter to come.

Historical Development

The origin of the objective family of atonement theories is often thought to begin relatively late, with the satisfaction theory beginning with Anselm (c. 1033–1109), penal substitution with the Protestant Reformers, and the governmental theory with Hugo Grotius (1583–1645). But recent interpreters have seen much earlier roots for these theories.

Hans Boersma acknowledges that there are no "carefully articulated theories of the atonement among the early Fathers," but adds, "This is not to say there were no Anselmian themes in the early Church. They were present, and at times they were remarkably emphatic."[41] Boersma cites the second-century *Epistle to Diognetus*, Irenaeus, and Origen as among the earliest to sound such themes.[42] He sees not just broadly Anselmian themes but "penal substitutionary interpretations of the cross" as present "from the beginning of the tradition of the Church."[43]

---

[40] Schreiner, "The Penal Substitution View," 87. Emphasis in original. For further support for his conclusion, see Thomas Schreiner, *Romans*, BECNT (Grand Rapids: Baker, 1998), 176–99.

[41] Boersma, *Violence, Hospitality, and the Cross*, 159 (see chap. 13, n. 11).

[42] Boersma, 159–63. He cites the "principle of substitution" in the *Epistle to Diognetus*, the idea that Christ's death "is propitiatory in character and so is meant to deal with the wrath of God" in Irenaeus, and Origen as another early father who describes Christ's death as "propitiation."

[43] Boersma, *Violence, Hospitality, and the Cross*, 163.

Joshua McNall sees propitiation in Irenaeus but not "an explicit account of penal substitution."[44] He sees that not much later, in the work of Eusebius of Caesarea (c. 260–339). In his *Proof of the Gospel*, Eusebius writes that Christ "suffered a penalty He did not owe . . . He became the cause of the forgiveness of our sins, because He received death for us, and transferred to Himself the scourging, the insults, and the dishonor, which were due us, and drew down upon Himself the appointed curse, being made a curse for us."[45] McNall sees all three of the elements he identifies as "mere penal substitution" in these words: "substitution, penalty, and divine sanction."[46] He sees these same three elements present in the works of Athanasius.[47] He acknowledges that some have charged such a view as projecting Calvinist assumptions backwards onto Athanasius and other early Christian sources.[48] He agrees that penal substitution is not the center or dominant theme in Athanasius's thought on the atonement, but neither is penal substitution missing.[49]

J. N. D. Kelly sees Hilary of Poitiers (c. 315–367) as "one of the pioneers of the theology of satisfaction," and sees similar language in Hilary's contemporary, Victorinus, as well as in the works of the more well-known doctor of the Latin church, Ambrose (c. 339–97), who described Christ's death as "propitiatory."[50] Kelly says of Cyril of Alexandria, "his guiding idea is the familiar one of penal substitution,"[51] and McNall cites a section from Augustine's work *Against Faustus*,[52] about which he says, "It takes some

---

[44] McNall, *The Mosaic of Atonement*, 113.

[45] Eusebius of Caesarea, *Proof of the Gospel*, trans. and ed. W. J. Ferrar, vol. 2 (New York: Macmillan, 1920), 195.

[46] McNall, *The Mosaic of Atonement*, 114.

[47] McNall, 116, cites especially a famous passage from Athanasius, *On the Incarnation of the Word*, sect. 9, which contains the language of Christ "dying a sufficient exchange for all," and affirms that, in offering his body "as a substitute for the life of all, He fulfilled in death all that was required."

[48] This is the claim of Myers, "The Patristic Atonement Model," 84–86.

[49] McNall, *The Mosaic of Atonement*, 118–19. Rutledge, *The Crucifixion*, 477, concurs with McNall's judgment on this matter.

[50] J. N. D. Kelly, *Early Christian Doctrines*, rev. ed. (New York: Harper-SanFrancisco, 1960), 388–89. See Kelly for citations from the works of Hilary, Victorinus, and Ambrose.

[51] Kelly, 398.

[52] Augustine, *Against Faustus*, 14, 6–7 (*NPNF*[1], 4:209). The key phrase describes Christ "as our substitute, bearing our punishment."

fairly impressive interpretive maneuvers to read this as anything other than penal substitution."[53]

Others could be added to this list: Gregory Nazianzus, John Chrysostom, Gelasius, and Gregory the Great, just from the first six hundred years of church history. There may be some who have responded to the charge that the objective models are fairly recent with "overzealous attempts to find the model in every nook and cranny of the tradition,"[54] but when scholars as diverse as J. N. D. Kelly, Hans Boersma, Joshua McNall, and Fleming Rutledge all see support for the objective models in these early figures and can cite from their writings to do so, their conclusions seem hard to refute. Kelly, Boersma, and McNall specifically defend penal substitution as having been present from the earliest days of church history;[55] Rutledge's claim is more limited to the theme of substitution. She says, "The motif of substitution was present from the beginning."[56]

This is not to deny the importance of later figures, most of all the importance of Anselm[57] and his landmark book, *Cur Deus Homo* (*Why God Became Man*).[58] Oliver Crisp says of this book, "in terms of its influence on later theology, it may rank as the single most influential historic doctrine of atonement," since his position "was taken up and modified by later medieval theologians such as Thomas Aquinas and was a major influence on magisterial reformers such as Martin Luther and John Calvin, and subsequent post-Reformation theology."[59]

---

[53] McNall, *The Mosaic of Atonement*, 122.

[54] McNall, 108n37. He cites Steve Jeffery, Michael Ovey, and Andrew Sach, *Pierced for Our Transgressions: Rediscovering the Glory of Penal Substitution* (Wheaton: Crossway, 2007) as one possibly overzealous defense of penal substitution.

[55] Boersma, *Violence, Hospitality, and the Cross*, 163. From his examination of the writings of some of the figures we have mentioned, Boersma reaches this conclusion: "penal substitutionary interpretations of the cross had a place from the beginning of the tradition of the Church." McNall, *The Mosaic of Atonement*, 126, says: "The logic of penal substitution has been broadly present from almost the very beginning of church history."

[56] Rutledge, *The Crucifixion*, 480.

[57] For some of the literature on Anselm, see Katherine Sonderegger, "Anselmian Atonement," in *T&T Clark Companion to Atonement*, 175n1.

[58] For a recent translation, see *Cur Deus Homo* in Anselm, *Anselm, The Basic Works*, trans. Thomas Williams (Indianapolis: Hackett, 2007).

[59] Crisp, *Approaching the Atonement*, 63.

There are numerous objections to Anselm's satisfaction model, some of them shared by other models within this family, especially the penal substitution model, and we will deal with these objections in a separate chapter. But there is one objection unique to the satisfaction model that we will examine now, as it bears on one possible reason for modification of this theory by the reformers. This is the objection that Anselm's doctrine, with its reliance on concepts of honor and shame, is simply a product of the medieval feudal culture of his day. Those who make this objection say that the honor-shame code of conduct is no longer part of contemporary culture and thus Anselm's model no longer has purchase among people today. Moreover, the emphasis on sin as dishonoring God can create a confusing and difficult picture of God for modern minds. Is God like some "tin-pot dictator obsessed with his privileges?"[60]

There are three responses to this objection. One, mentioned by Oliver Crisp, is that this objection commits the "genetic fallacy."[61] This is the idea that the truth-value of a doctrine depends on its provenance. Anselm may be influenced in the concepts he used by his cultural context, but that does not mean that his doctrine is thereby true or false. For Christian theology, the truth-value of a doctrine is how well it explains and communicates the truths of Scripture. And as we saw above, the satisfaction theory of the atonement has substantial biblical support.

The second response is to deny that Anselm got his idea of satisfaction of God's honor from feudal culture at all. Eamon Duffy, in a review of a book by James Carroll, says Carroll and critics like him miss the context of Anselm's discussion of honor, which was a response to criticisms of Jewish intellectuals that Christianity's doctrine of incarnation dishonored God. Duffy says, "Anselm's insistence on 'honor' therefore, is not the product of fixation with feudal hierarchy, but an *argumentum ad hominem* addressed to intelligent Jews who felt that the Christian story debased God."[62] Oliver Crisp argues the same point from a different perspective. He says that it is not clear that Anselm is borrowing the notion of satisfaction from his

---

[60] Rutledge, *The Crucifixion*, 157.

[61] Crisp, *Approaching the Atonement*, 70.

[62] Eamon Duffy, "A Deadly Misunderstanding," *New York Review of Books*, July 5, 2001. The review is of James Carroll, *Constantine's Sword: The Church and the Jews* (New York: Houghton Mifflin, 2001).

medieval feudal perspective because the concept can be found in patristic theology. From a work by Tertullian, Crisp shows "that similar ways [to Anselm's] of thinking about satisfaction can be found in a theological work composed centuries before feudalism existed."[63]

A third response is to acknowledge that while Western culture may not operate largely on the basis of honor and shame, many cultures today still do, and Anselm's model seems to resonate well in those cultures. Some missionaries are finding those in such cultures understand the gospel better under the categories of honor and shame than by the categories more familiar in Western culture, like guilt and innocence.[64]

The second model in the objective family, penal substitution, is often seen as originating with the Reformers, and especially Calvin, whom Stephen Holmes credits with giving "the first fully worked out account of penal substitution."[65] Holmes acknowledges that some of the church fathers "said things that could be understood in penal substitutionary terms," but thinks most attempts to find penal substitution in them amount to "taking imagery that is more naturally read differently, and transposing it into penal substitutionary categories and imagery."[66]

Others see the evidence for penal substitution in the fathers in much more positive terms. As we mentioned above, Hans Boersma, Joshua McNall, J. N. D. Kelly, and others see clear support for penal substitution in the fathers. Even Holmes himself seems in an earlier writing to qualify his claim concerning Calvin. Perhaps Calvin was the first to give a "fully worked out account of penal substitution," but Holmes describes Gregory the Great as teaching penal substitution "clearly and unambiguously."[67] Contrary to

---

[63] Crisp, *Approaching the Atonement*, 71–72. The work of Tertullian to which he refers is Tertullian, "On Repentance," *ANF* 3:664 (chap. 9).

[64] See, for example, the work by Jackson Wu, *Saving God's Face: A Chinese Contextualization of Salvation Through Honor and Shame* (Pasadena, CA: William Carey International University Press, 2013).

[65] Stephen Holmes, "Penal Substitution," in *T&T Clark Companion to Atonement*, 307. But see the protest by Paul Dafydd Jones, "The Fury of Love: Calvin on the Atonement," in *T&T Clark Companion to Atonement*, 213–35, that Calvin's view "is rather more interesting" than just penal substitution (214).

[66] Holmes, "Penal Substitution," 306–7.

[67] Stephen Holmes, *The Wondrous Cross: Atonement and Penal Substitution in the Bible and History* (London: Paternoster, 2007), 51. Holmes does add that he thinks

the allegation that penal substitution is "primarily a modern innovation," McNall concludes, "The logic of penal substitution has been broadly present from almost the very beginning of church history. If there *is* a modern myth to be retired, it is the false notion that penal substitution first emerges with the Protestant Reformers."[68]

William Lane Craig gives this assessment of the relationship of the Reformers to earlier church history on this topic:

> The theological revolution wrought by the Protestant Reformers brought to full bloom the theory of the atonement that has come to be known as penal substitution. Though anticipated by the Church Fathers and approximated by Aquinas, the theory found its full expression and defense in the work of the Reformers and their scholastic progeny.[69]

Martin Luther is claimed by Gustav Aulén as the key figure in the recovery of the classical Christus Victor model,[70] and the note of victory is undeniably present in Luther.[71] But so are the key elements of penal substitution given by Joshua McNall (substitution, penalty, and divine sanction). Comparing penal substitution to a hall with many rooms, McNall says, "As is well known, John Calvin (1509–64) has a room off this hall, as do Martin Luther (1483–1546) and Charles Hodge (1797–1878)."[72]

Timothy George sees the idea of substitution in Luther's idea of "the joyous exchange," expressed perhaps most vividly in his comments on Gal 3:13. There Luther says that God the Father sends his Son into the world and says to him, "Be Peter the denier; Paul the persecutor, blasphemer, and

---

Gregory is the only early writer to do so.

[68] McNall, *The Mosaic of Atonement*, 126. Emphasis in original.

[69] William Lane Craig, *The Atonement and the Death of Christ: An Exegetical, Historical, and Philosophical Exploration* (Waco, TX: Baylor University Press, 2020), 125.

[70] Aulén, *Christus Victor*, 108 (see chap. 13, n. 5). He says that in Luther, "the patristic view has returned," only now "with greater depth and force than before."

[71] See the discussion and the numerous citations from Luther's works in Robert Kolb, "Martin Luther," in *T&T Clark Companion to Atonement*, 620, and the discussion in Timothy George, "The Atonement in Martin Luther's Theology," in *The Glory of the Atonement*, 275–76.

[72] McNall, *The Mosaic of Atonement*, 101.

assaulter; David the adulterer. . . . In short, be the person of all men, the one who has committed the sins of all men. And see to it that you pay and make satisfaction for them."[73] The way that Christ makes "satisfaction" is by paying our penalty.[74] And divine sanction is seen in the following striking statement from Luther: "God himself struck and punished Christ."[75]

Calvin is widely recognized as the key figure in the development of penal substitution, and rightly so. He states, "God's wrath and curse always lie upon sinners until they are absolved of guilt."[76] We are released from guilt through Christ taking our place: "This is our acquittal: the guilt that held us liable for punishment has been transferred to the head of the Son of God." He specifically calls this "substitution."[77] Fleming Rutledge wants to limit Calvin to advocacy of substitution and to see penal substitution as more a development after Calvin. But even she has to note Calvin's emphasis on the wrath of God and the language of "satisfaction" and "appease" and then try to explain it. She offers this opinion: "If Calvin were writing today, he would have to use different wording to make his points."[78] Most see penal substitution as clearly present in Calvin, though not at all a crude or coldly legal penal substitution,[79] and would not deny that other motifs are also present

---

[73] Martin Luther, *LW* 26: 280, as cited in George, "The Atonement in Martin Luther's Theology," 274–75.

[74] Wolfhart Pannenberg says, "Luther is probably the first since Paul and his school to have seen with full clarity that Jesus' death in its genuine sense is to be understood as vicarious penal suffering." Pannenberg, *Jesus—God and Man* (Philadelphia: Westminster, 1974), 279.

[75] Martin Luther, *WA* 40, part 3, 715. Translation given in Daniel Hill and Joseph Jedwab, "Atonement and the Concept of Punishment," in *Locating Atonement: Explorations in Constructive Dogmatics*, ed. Oliver Crisp and Fred Sanders (Grand Rapids: Zondervan, 2015), 151.

[76] Calvin, *Institutes*, 2.16.1 (1:504).

[77] Calvin, 2.16.5 (1:509–10).

[78] Rutledge, 486n50. See her wrestling uncomfortably with the emphasis on the wrath of God and satisfaction/appeasement language in Calvin (483–487).

[79] Robert Paul, *Atonement and the Sacraments* (New York: Abingdon, 1960), 105–8, sees Calvin as making three modifications of the penal substitution theory. But Henri Blocher, "The Atonement in John Calvin's Theology," in *The Glory of the Atonement*, 286, sees these modifications as applying only to caricatures of the theory. Paul Dafydd Jones, "The Fury of Love," in *T&T Clark Companion to Atonement*, 222, contrasts Calvin with those who treat the atonement as merely "a matter of legal

in Calvin's doctrine of the atonement.[80] Henri Blocher sees in Calvin's writings on the atonement a "constant reliance on the logic of penal-sacrificial substitution."[81] Others say more simply, "Calvin functions clearly with the concept of penal substitution."[82]

Holmes says, "After Calvin, penal substitution became so widespread as to be almost ubiquitous, at least among Protestant churches."[83] Yet that support began to wane rapidly in the nineteenth century, so much so that a history of the doctrine of the atonement published in 1920 could claim, "amongst reputable theologians the Penal theory is now extinct."[84] What could cause a theory that was unquestioned in 1700 to be declared extinct in 1900? There were no advances in the understanding of biblical teaching to account for this. Rather, as Stephen Holmes explains, there were cultural changes, especially in Europe, that rendered penal substitution less culturally plausible.[85] But the claim that the view was "extinct" among reputable theologians was probably untrue in 1920,[86] and was clearly untrue by the second half of the twentieth century with the revival of penal substitution initially through the works of Leon Morris, J. I. Packer, and John Stott,[87]

---

relation," but does not deny that all the elements of penal substitution are in Calvin (see 217–18 for substitution, sacrifice, propitiation of divine wrath).

[80] Robert Peterson, *Calvin and the Atonement*, rev. ed. (Fearn, Ross-shire: Mentor, 1999), chaps. 4–9. Peterson expounds Calvin's thought on the atonement with chapters on Christ as Second Adam, Victor, Legal Substitute, Sacrifice, Merit, and Example.

[81] Blocher, "The Atonement in John Calvin's Theology," 303.

[82] Roger Nicole, "John Calvin's View of the Extent of the Atonement," *WTJ* 47 (1985): 224.

[83] Holmes, "Penal Substitution," 307.

[84] L. W. Grensted, *A Short History of the Doctrine of the Atonement* (London: Longmans, Green & Co., 1920), 306.

[85] Holmes, "Penal Substitution," 308–09.

[86] The work of James Denney, *The Death of Christ* (London: Hodder & Stoughton, 1902) is a few years before 1920, but by 1934, a defense of penal substitution appears in the work of a reputable theologian, Emil Brunner, *The Mediator: A Study of the Central Doctrine of the Christian Faith*, trans. Olive Wyon (London: Lutterworth, 1934).

[87] It is hard to overstate the importance of Morris's first major work, *The Apostolic Preaching of the Cross*. It was initially published in 1955 but has gone through three editions and is still being reprinted today. The key book by J. I. Packer is *Knowing God*, in which penal substitution is defended in a chapter ("The Heart of the Gospel"). In

and today through the works of a wide array of evangelical theologians who claim that penal substitution is not the only biblical way to understand the atonement, but that it is undeniably one important way, and for many, the most important way.

The last model within the objective family, the governmental model, was the last to develop historically and has attracted the smallest following, with some questioning whether it should be seen as an objective or subjective model.[88] Moreover, in recent years some have given evidence that the figure most associated with the governmental model, Hugo Grotius, may not have fully affirmed all the ideas most associated with that model.[89] Nonetheless, at least some of the ideas which developed into the governmental theory do seem to come from Grotius, and so we will begin with his response to the criticism of penal substitution given by Faustus Socinus.

In his work *De Jesu Christo Servatore*, Socinus leveled numerous criticisms against the understanding of the atonement that had received such emphasis among the Reformers, penal substitution. Socinus argued that penal substitution was unnecessary, because God could remit sin without requiring some satisfaction, as in the parable of the king who forgives the

---

the first twenty years after its initial publication in 1973, it sold more than a million copies and was translated into more than a dozen languages, and sales are over 1.5 million copies today. The 1986 publication of John Stott, *The Cross of Christ*, marks his *magnum opus*, and added another very widely read and substantial support for penal substitution from one of the most well-known evangelical leaders. Its influence continues in a centennial edition of *The Cross of Christ*, published in 2021 to honor the centennial of Stott's birth.

[88] Erickson, *Christian Theology*, 722. While acknowledging that it has an "objective element," he says "in the main, the governmental theory is a subjective theory of the atonement—the chief impact was on human beings."

[89] This evidence is most fully presented in Garry J. Williams, "A Critical Exposition of Hugo Grotius's Doctrine of the Atonement in *De satisfactione Christi*" (PhD thesis, University of Oxford, 1999), and summarized in Garry J. Williams, "Punishment God Cannot Twice Inflict: The Double Payment Argument Redivivus," in *From Heaven He Came and Sought Her: Definite Atonement in Historical, Biblical, Theological, and Pastoral Perspective*, ed. David Gibson and Jonathan Gibson (Wheaton: Crossway, 2013), 490–93. Similarly, Craig, *Atonement and the Death of Christ*, 137, defends Grotius, claiming, "Grotius' theory is today widely misrepresented in the secondary literature. He is even accused of capitulating to Socinus and betraying the Reformers' theory of penal substitution."

debt of his servant in Matt 18:21–35. He argued further that penal substitution removes the idea of forgiveness. If someone pays the debt for another,
there is nothing left to forgive. Moreover, for him, penal substitution is inherently impossible. How could one person pay an eternal debt for a multitude
of people? And even if possible, the whole idea of penal substitution seemed
to him immoral. An innocent person cannot and should not be punished in
place of the guilty.[90]

Grotius drew upon his training in law and his experience in international relations[91] in responding to the objections of Socinus. First, he
acknowledged that as sovereign, God could indeed act as the king in the
parable in Matthew 18 and forgive freely, without requiring punishment.
He is subject to no one and no thing. However, as ruler or *rector*, God
"has the task of maintaining and establishing the order and the government of the world."[92] This contrast between rectoral justice, which "must
be satisfied," and retributive justice, which "may be 'relaxed' in order to save
fallen human beings,"[93] led to a further distinction. Rectoral justice does
not demand that Christ pay exactly what is due from sinners, but simply a
punishment of sufficient worth to uphold God's moral governance. Oliver
Crisp says it is as if God says, "if Christ performs this deterrent action by
becoming a penal example to you, then I do not need to punish you. My
moral government of the world will be upheld because Christ will have
shown you what would happen to human sin. His atoning work means
that I am able to relax the need to visit retribution upon you. Instead, I may
forgive you your sins."[94]

These distinctions answer the objections against penal substitution, in
part by distinguishing God's rectoral from his retributive justice and partly
by redefining the nature of Christ's death. In the governmental view, he is our

---

[90] For an exposition of Socinus, see Alan Gomes, "Socinus," in *T&T Clark
Companion to Atonement*, 753–56.

[91] R. G. Clouse, "Grotius, Hugo," in *Evangelical Dictionary of Theology*, 363:
"Grotius is remembered as 'father of international law' based on his work *De Jure
Belli et Pacis* (*Concerning the Law of War and Peace*), which appeared in 1625."

[92] Gert van den Brink, "Hugo Grotius," in *T&T Clark Companion to Atonement*,
523.

[93] Crisp, *Approaching the Atonement*, 118.

[94] Crisp, 118.

penal example, not our penal substitute.[95] Thus the objections of the impossibility of one paying the penalty of many, the impossibility of transferring guilt from one person to another, and the lack of need for retributive justice all fall.

But the governmental view also has some weaknesses. Rectoral justice carries with it a deterrence view of punishment. Under this view, Christ is not punished to satisfy the retributive justice demanded by the moral character of God but to deter others from prohibited actions and thus maintain order.[96] There is some truth to the idea of rectoral justice. God is the judge of all the earth and must maintain justice. But God's holiness and justice also are an essential part of his moral character, with retribution embedded in Scripture (Rom 12:19). Rectoral justice may be accepted alongside retributive justice but not to replace retributive justice.

Even more seriously, if Christ is punished, not to atone for our sins but only as a penal example of what our sins deserved, it raises the question as to "whether the governmental account of atonement is really a doctrine of atonement at all."[97] Making Christ merely a penal example and not a penal substitute is contrary to the biblical teaching we examined earlier in which substitution is seen as one of the central motifs, if not *the* central motif, of the atonement. This seems a serious shortcoming in governmental theories. While Grotius's view "had an enormous influence" in his day and well into the eighteenth century, it began to lose influence in the nineteenth century, with some German theologians seeing it as close to the views of Socinus himself and as a version of moral influence. That is an incorrect view of Grotius, but it began to influence the reception and perception of the governmental theory.[98] Today it is among the theories "not widely discussed in contemporary theological literature."[99]

---

[95] Crisp, 114, calls the governmental view "penal non-substitution."

[96] It is at this point that contemporary defenders of Grotius most strenuously object, arguing that Grotius maintained a proper emphasis on God's retributive justice. See Williams, "Punishment God Cannot Twice Inflict," 492: "There are writers who . . . deny God's inherent justice and retribution, . . . but Grotius is not of them." Likewise, Craig, *Atonement and the Death of Christ*, 138: "Grotius conceives of divine justice as retributive and of Christ's death as a punishment for our sins."

[97] Crisp, *Approaching the Atonement*, 122.

[98] Van den Brink, "Hugo Grotius," 524–25.

[99] Crisp, *Approaching the Atonement*, 114.

Theological Evaluation

We have mentioned several times the numerous objections to and criticisms of the models in the objective family, especially penal substitution. Responding to these objections would unduly lengthen this chapter and so we will defer such a response to the next chapter, but in this section of this chapter we will state what we see as the theological values of the objective theories, values that argue strongly for their inclusion in our theology of the atonement and thus argue for the need for cogent responses to the objections raised.

We begin our theological evaluation with the governmental model. We appreciate the need to respond to the type of criticism that Socinus posed to the penal substitution model, but we think the response given by the governmental model surrenders crucial and essential elements. Making Christ merely a penal example rather than our substitute is contrary to a wide swath of biblical teaching on the substitutionary nature of the atonement. From the implications of the sacrificial system, to the depiction of the suffering servant of Isaiah 53, to point blank statements of Jesus giving his life in exchange for man (Mark 10:45), to the nature of redemption and propitiation, substitution is an inescapable element of biblical teaching on the atonement. So while the governmental theory has an important place in the history of the doctrine of the atonement, and while some biblical teaching may be interpreted in governmental terms, the governmental model, as a whole, has more weaknesses than strengths. For that reason, its theological value is limited to giving one possible way to respond to some of the objections to satisfaction and penal substitution models through adding the category of rectoral justice.

As developed by Anselm, the satisfaction model draws deeply from the honor-shame motif common to Anselm's day. For that reason, some discount the value of the satisfaction model, as the honor-shame motif no longer resonates with Western culture. But we need to take off our ethnocentric lenses and realize that Western culture is far from the only culture in the world and that the honor-shame motif is still powerful in many parts of the world. Indeed the Bible itself was born in cultures that were predominantly honor and shame, more than guilt and innocence.[100] As mentioned earlier, mission-

---

[100] See Timothy Tennent, *Theology in the Context of World Christianity* (Grand Rapids: Zondervan, 2007), 83–91, for a short survey of honor and shame in the

aries are increasingly realizing the need to supplement the biblical teaching on the atonement in forensic and legal terms with equally biblical teaching on the atonement in honor and shame terms. As Timothy Tennent says, "This approach will also greatly help peoples in the Majority World to understand the significance and power of Christ's work, which has heretofore been told primarily from only one perspective."[101] We commend the satisfaction model as a valuable part of atonement theology for all Christians, as it has strong biblical support, but we especially commend its value in communicating the fullness of Christ's work in honor-shame cultures.

The penal substitution model has long been the favorite model among evangelical Christians. Indeed, some are tempted to see it as the only valid biblical model of the atonement, but that is not accurate. The preceding chapters have described the biblical bases for models in the historical and subjective families. The models in those families deserve a place in any understanding of the atonement that is fully biblical. But we believe a fair theological evaluation of the penal substitutionary model should conclude that it deserves a special, foundational place in any atonement theology for two reasons.

First, there is simply a stronger biblical basis for penal substitution than for any other theory. It is hard to overstate the importance of the sacrificial system in setting the context for atonement theology, for it was in and through those sacrifices that atonement was made in the Old Testament. It is equally hard to miss the centrality of penal and substitutionary elements in the sacrifices. The sacrifices were given as a substitute for the humans who symbolically transferred their sins to these animals; the penalty for sin was exacted on these animals—death. That sacrificial background is carried into the NT where Jesus is recognized as the Lamb of God, who takes away our sin by dying in our place. The earliest Christian definition of the gospel begins with the words, "Christ died for our sins" (1 Cor 15:3), with again the penal substitutionary overtones. The theme of redemption assumes that the ransom is accepted as the substitute for the one enslaved or kidnapped. And however translated, the *hilasmos/hilastērion* word group has ties to the temple, where atoning sacrifices were offered as substitutes for humans, taking the punishment due them. This is an undeniably strong biblical basis.

Old and New Testament.
[101] Tennent, 92.

Second, only the penal substitution answers some questions and gives some grounding for the other theories.[102] As Jeremy Treat puts it, "penal substitution has priority because of its explanatory power . . . it provides insight into many of the other aspects of the atonement."[103] This is most clearly seen in the moral influence theories. Why is Christ's death seen, not as a tragedy, but as a manifestation of amazing love? Only if Christ is seen as dying, not by accident or necessity, but deliberately in the place of sinners, bearing their sins. Only then do moral influence theories make sense.

Even the Christus Victor theory makes more sense when combined with penal substitution. Jeremy Treat has given careful attention to the relationship between the two. He asks, "How is Satan defeated? Christ defeats Satan (*Christus Victor*) by removing the ground of Satan's accusation, which Jesus does by paying the penalty for sin (penal substitution)." He adds, "*Christus Victor* apart from penal substitution, therefore, does not explain why Christ had to suffer to conquer Satan and actually undermines the victory."[104] Why does Christ achieve victory through the painful means of the cross? Why was it necessary for Christ to die? Why was that the Father's will? There may be many reasons, but part of it is God's desire to save us in a way that does not minimize the seriousness of sin. Sin cannot be simply decreed away; it must be atoned for. Death is the just penalty for sin; it cannot be abrogated; but when that penalty is paid, death no longer has a power over those united to Christ, and Christ's resurrection is the guarantee. God wins the victory over all our enemies, not just by might, but by right.

Applications and Conclusion

The objective family of atonement theories should bring unspeakable comfort to the Christian. What good would it be if our enemies were defeated and our hearts inflamed with love for Christ, if we then found the door to

---

[102] Craig, *Atonement and the Death of Christ*, 215–35, 259–63, shows the connection of penal substitution to both ransom/Christus Victor theories of the atonement and moral influence theories.

[103] Jeremy Treat, *The Crucified King*, 223–24 (see chap. 13, n. 73).

[104] Treat, 204–05. He sees "*Christus Victor* Through Penal Substitution" as the remedy for the human predicament and cites biblical texts like Heb 2:5–18; Col 2:13–15; Rev 12:9–11; and 1 John 3:4–9 as "strongly suggesting such a synthesis."

God's presence still locked? The objective theories say the door is open wide, the Father's arms are welcoming, all the barriers on God's side are down. Moreover, your sins have not been merely provisionally overlooked or temporarily forgotten; they have been atoned for, and the righteous wrath of God has been satisfied and will never fall upon us. Graham Cole even thinks we should ask, "Can there be Christian maturity without grasping penal substitution?" He explains, "To fail to incorporate the argument of Hebrews [especially Hebrews 6–10] concerning the nature of Christ's priesthood and substitutionary sacrifice into one's theology risks locking oneself into an arrested spiritual development."[105]

Yet some say the God of wrath who stands behind the penal substitutionary model is a God we need to be saved from. Others cannot understand why he would require death as the payment for sin. Still others shudder at the violence of the cross and turn away. These are among the objections that we must address in the next chapter.

---

[105] Graham A. Cole, *God the Peacemaker: How Atonement Brings Shalom*, ed. D. A. Carson, NSBT (Downers Grove: InterVarsity, 2009), 238.

16

Contemporary Objections to Penal Substitutionary Atonement

Introduction

We argued in the preceding chapter that the penal substitutionary theory of the atonement (PSA) is well supported biblically and historically, that it is of foundational importance in that it answers some theologically important questions and provides rationale for other major theories of the atonement, and that it is practically valuable in giving believers assurance of their complete acceptance by God. Following the classic exposition of this model of the atonement by Calvin, "penal substitution became so widespread as to be almost ubiquitous, at least among Protestant churches."[1] Despite some opposition over the years, most would grant that the PSA "remains standard in some conservative-evangelical circles,"[2] including the circle of the authors of this book.[3]

Yet within the past generation, this model has come under attack as never before, and not only by non-evangelicals but by some evangelicals as well.

---

[1] Stephen Holmes, "Penal Substitution," 307 (see chap. 15, n. 65).

[2] Rutledge, *The Crucifixion*, 488 (see chap. 13, n. 3).

[3] In the interests of full disclosure, the authors and editors of this book are Southern Baptists and the publishing house that is publishing this book is a Southern Baptist agency. The statement of faith of the Southern Baptist Convention specifically uses the adjective "substitutionary" to describe Jesus's death (*The Baptist Faith and Message 2000*, Article 2B. God the Son).

Garry Williams says, "It is no exaggeration to say that proponents of penal substitution are currently charged with advocating a biblically unfounded, systematically misleading, and pastorally lethal doctrine."[4] For example, one opponent of PSA has written of his conviction that this theory "has in some contexts muted the scandal of the cross, in other settings inappropriately scandalized people, and in still other circumstances made the saving significance of the cross and resurrection incomprehensible."[5]

This chapter will then, first, give a brief history of criticism of PSA. It will then give some consideration to the question of whether contemporary criticism is really of PSA itself or only of caricatures of it. Finally, it will then give what seem to be the most prevalent and significant objections to PSA and seek to give a cogent response to each.

A History of Criticism of PSA

The message of the cross has aroused opposition from the days of the apostles. Paul wrote, "The Jews ask for signs and the Greeks seek wisdom, but we preach Christ crucified, a stumbling block to the Jews and foolishness to the Gentiles" (1 Cor 1:22–23). While Paul steadfastly refused to remove the stumbling block of the cross, he did not totally ignore the objections. In the book of Acts, one can discern a different evangelistic strategy that Paul used with Jewish audiences compared to Gentile ones.[6] In doing so, he was not seeking to change the gospel message but he was contextualizing it to make it more readily comprehended. Contemporary defenders of PSA should respond in much the same way. We must refuse to compromise on the essence of the message, but let us all do all we can to make the message understandable and plausible. The objections raised by fellow evangelicals

---

[4] Garry Williams, "Penal Substitution: A Response to Recent Criticisms," *JETS* 50, no. 1 (March 2007): 86.

[5] Mark Baker, "Contextualizing the Scandal of the Cross," in *Proclaiming the Scandal of the Cross: Contemporary Images of the Atonement*, ed. Mark Baker (Grand Rapids: Baker Academic, 2006), 14.

[6] In Acts 13:16–41, Paul preaches in the synagogue a sermon tracing the history of Israel and citing texts from the Old Testament. In Acts 17:22–31 he preaches to a gathering of Gentiles a sermon from universal revelation and citing pagan poets.

deserve special consideration, as they do not see themselves as asking us in any way to compromise the message but to present it more correctly, more in keeping with biblical teaching. We want to give their critiques especially careful consideration.

With no fully orbed presentation of PSA in the patristic or medieval eras, there was of course no theory to critique, and after Constantine's 'conversion' in 312, there was little criticism of any Christian doctrine, including the doctrine of the atonement. But once a full presentation of PSA arrived, in the writings of John Calvin, objections were immediately raised, especially in the writings of Faustus Socinus.

Alan Gomes calls the work of Socinus, *De Jesu Christo Servatore* (*Concerning Jesus Christ the Savior*), "arguably the most trenchant critique" ever written of the doctrine of Christ's satisfaction of sin.[7] Oliver Crisp says "the work is remembered mainly for its savage attack upon the whole idea of substitutionary atonement as understood by the Reformers."[8] William Lane Craig adds that his "critique of penal substitution remains today unsurpassed in terms of its depth and breadth."[9] Some of his critiques are remarkably contemporary and will be among those we examine and respond to in some detail in a later section. For example, Socinus argues that there is nothing in God's nature that requires him to punish sin; that it would be immoral to punish an innocent person in the place of a guilty person; that satisfaction and remission are mutually contradictory.[10]

As discussed in the previous chapter, Hugo Grotius provided the first response to the objections of Socinus,[11] which eventually developed into the governmental theory of the atonement. Whether Grotius himself saw his work as developing a new theory of the atonement or merely shoring up the PSA view of the Reformers by supplementing it with new ways of thinking about how God's moral government of the world "could be brought to bear upon the atonement so as to meet the criticisms of Socinus"[12] is an

---

[7] Alan Gomes, "Socinus," in *T&T Clark Companion to Atonement*, 753.

[8] Crisp, *Approaching the Atonement*, 81 (see chap. 12, n. 3).

[9] Craig, *Atonement and the Death of Christ*, 128 (see chap. 13, n. 13).

[10] See Gomes, "Socinus," 755–56, for a full listing of Socinus's objections.

[11] See Hugo Grotius, *Defensio fidei catholicae de satisfactione Christi* (*A Defense of the Catholic Faith Concerning the Satisfaction of Christ*), published 1617.

[12] Crisp, *Approaching the Atonement*, 115.

open question.[13] But at any rate, Faustus was also anti-trinitarian and denied Christ's deity, justification by faith, and original sin, and some of his objections are linked to these denials. His patently heretical views, along with the response of Grotius, limited the serious consideration of his criticisms and so his work did not stop Calvin's formulation from becoming almost universally accepted among Protestants across Europe, a situation which lasted into the early decades of the nineteenth century, when the next wave of criticism began.

Stephen Holmes sees various changes in European culture in the late eighteenth and early nineteenth centuries rendering "penal substitution far less culturally plausible than it had been before."[14] Kevin Vanhoozer sees this as reflecting the "turn to the subject" in modernity: "The nineteenth century concern with human consciousness and experience, coupled with the tendency to reject divine retributive justice and affirm God's love, led to a second coming as it were of Abelard's moral influence theory."[15] Enlightenment thinking and liberal theology in general moved strongly toward subjective theories of the atonement and rejection of PSA throughout the nineteenth century and into the early twentieth century. To say, as L. W. Grensted did in 1920, that "among reputable theologians the Penal theory is now extinct"[16] is to considerably overstate the case, but from roughly 1800 to 1920, numerous theologians took issue with both the penal nature of the atonement and its substitutionary nature, but they were largely liberal or at least non-evangelical theologians.[17] On the other hand, evangelical defenders of

---

[13] Gert van den Brink, "Hugo Grotius," 524, sees several significant differences between the view of Grotius and the Reformers, particularly rectoral versus retributive justice, and sees Grotius's view as having "an enormous influence."

[14] Holmes, "Penal Substitution," 308.

[15] Kevin Vanhoozer, "Atonement," in *Mapping Modern Theology: A Thematic and Historical Introduction*, ed. Kelly Kapic and Bruce McCormack (Grand Rapids: Baker Academic, 2012), 178.

[16] Grensted, *A Short History of the Doctrine of the Atonement*, 308 (see chap. 15, n. 84).

[17] Vanhoozer, "Atonement," 178–183, cites Schleiermacher, Ritschl, and Harnack as representative of those who "took issue with the idea of satisfaction" (or the penal nature of satisfaction) and Edward Irving and J. McLeod Campbell as some who objected "to the idea of substitution" (180). He cites James Denney as one who in 1903 saw support for PSA as that which "divides interpreters of Christianity

PSA, some of them "reputable theologians," were numerous and influential: Charles Hodge, R. L. Dabney, and A. H. Strong in the United States; and Charles Spurgeon, R. W. Dale, and James Denney in England.

Speaking primarily of the situation in England, Holmes describes the situation as of 1920 in the following way: "Penal substitution remains an accepted doctrine for most evangelicals, but also a controversial one. Thoughtful evangelical theologians defend with energy the substitutionary character of the atonement and variously interpret that in penal or other categories."[18] Of those evangelicals who did reject PSA, Holmes says he sees "no new argument deployed by all these doubters that was not seen by the elders. I suspect, instead, that cultural change made previously assumed positions suddenly, if not untenable, at least much more difficult."

A final change in the pre-1920 debate over PSA was "a new theme within evangelical writings." Holmes adds, "For the first time, as far as I can see, we find writers insisting on penal substitution as the one and only correct way of talking about the atonement."[19] This last development may be seen as a natural response to attacks on an important doctrine, but unfortunately, insistence on PSA as the only correct way to speak about the atonement has provided opponents to PSA another objection to it, for careful study of the New Testament and the history of theology shows that there are multiple theories of the atonement with biblical grounding and theological validity. This is something many careful evangelical defenses of PSA have acknowledged and continue to do so today, as in this volume.[20]

Another new element entered the debate over PSA in the 1930s. This is an exegetical element denying the propriety of thinking of God as wrathful and of the cross as satisfying the wrath of God. In his 1932 commentary on Romans, C. H. Dodd argued that Paul uses the phrase "the wrath of God," not to mean "the attitude of God to man, but to describe an

---

into evangelical and non-evangelical." James Denney, *The Atonement and the Modern Mind* (New York: Eaton & Mains, 1903), 114.

[18] Stephen Holmes, "Ransomed, Healed, Restored, Forgiven: Evangelical Accounts of the Atonement," in *The Atonement Debate*, ed. Derek Tidball, David Hilborn, and Justin Thacker (Grand Rapids: Zondervan, 2008), 277.

[19] Holmes, 273, 276.

[20] As in Stott, *The Cross of Christ*, where three chapters (chaps. 7–9, pp. 167–251) give three major models of what the cross achieved.

inevitable process of cause and effect in a moral universe." He sees wrath as an attitude of God towards humans as inconsistent with the mercy of God, mercy as being something which "is inherent in the character of God." He concludes, "The idea of an angry God is a first attempt to rationalize the shuddering awe which men feel before the incalculable possibilities of appalling disaster inherent in life, but it is an attempt which breaks down as the rational element in religion advances."[21] With this understanding of the wrath of God, he interprets *hilastēron* in Romans 3:25, not as "propitiation," but as "a means by which guilt is annulled." He says, "The rendering **propitiation** is therefore misleading, for it suggests the placating of an angry God, and although this would be in accord with pagan usage, it is foreign to biblical usage."[22]

If correct, Dodd would be overturning a common idea in PSA. No defenders of PSA ever claimed that the penalty paid by Jesus was anything like a sacrifice to appease an angry pagan deity, but it was commonly seen that the penalty paid by Jesus satisfied the righteous wrath of God, which was seen as the right reaction of holiness toward sin. Dodd's position was challenged on exegetical grounds by Leon Morris in a 1955 book that has had an impact continuing today,[23] and by Roger Nicole in an article also from 1955.[24] We discussed this controversy in the previous chapter and found strong evidence that, while no one wants to compare God with a pagan deity, the concept of *hilastērion* includes both the annulling or erasing of guilt and the satisfaction of wrath. Yet one of the contemporary objections to PSA is that it "misunderstands the relationship between God's wrath and human sin."[25]

This brief history of the objections to PSA has led now to the present generation, where we have both growing opposition to PSA, even

---

[21] Dodd, *The Epistle of Paul to the Romans*, 23–24 (see chap. 15, n. 31).

[22] Dodd, 55.

[23] Morris, *The Apostolic Preaching of the Cross* (see chap. 13, n. 20).

[24] Roger Nicole, "C. H. Dodd and the Doctrine of Propitiation," 117–57.

[25] Jeffery, Ovey, and Sach, *Pierced for Our Transgressions*, 294–96 (see chap. 15, n. 54). The authors cite this objection as made by Mark D. Baker and Joel B. Green, *Recovering the Scandal of the Cross*; by Stephen Travis, *Christ and the Judgment of God: Divine Retribution in the New Testament* (Basingstroke: Marshall, Morgan & Scott, 1986); and to a lesser degree, by Paul Fiddes, *Past Event and Present Salvation: The Christian Idea of Atonement* (London: Darton, Longman & Todd, 1989).

among evangelicals, and also growing defense of it.[26] We will consider what we see as the most important and weighty contemporary objections below, but first, we turn to a preliminary question which merits at least brief consideration.

Are Contemporary Objections Really against PSA or Only a Caricature of It?

Joel Green and Mark Baker acknowledge that there are some presentations of the PSA model that are not subject to some of the objections that they raise, and that some have protested that, "rather than choosing the best example of penal substitution, we have chosen a caricature easy to critique." Green and Baker reply that they are not concerned with the carefully nuanced discussions in scholarly literature: "our concern is with popular understandings and articulations of the atonement."[27]

Joshua McNall points out a problem with such an approach. Almost every Christian doctrine has been poorly articulated in popular, nonacademic settings. The Trinity has especially been poorly articulated in popular settings, with common analogies implying tritheism, modalism, or other Trinitarian heresies. McNall states, "If the test of a doctrine's truth and usefulness is that it cannot possibly be misinterpreted or misapplied from the pulpit, then no Christian truth-claim would be left standing."[28] But McNall thinks that Green and Baker are not just objecting to "misconstruals" of PSA; "they are claiming that penal substitution is inherently problematic" but may be doing so based on less than the best representations of PSA.[29]

---

[26] Vanhoozer, "Atonement," 198: "That some evangelicals have joined the chorus of criticism against penal substitution has led others more vociferously to defend it." He cites three multiauthor volumes defending aspects of PSA appearing alongside the criticisms: David Peterson, ed., *Where Wrath and Mercy Meet: Proclaiming the Atonement Today; Papers from the Fourth Oak Hill College Annual School of Theology* (Carlisle, UK: Paternoster, 2001); Charles Hill and Frank James, eds., *The Glory of the Atonement* (see chap. 15, n. 36); and Jeffery, Ovey, and Sach, *Pierced for Our Transgressions.*

[27] Baker and Green, *Recovering the Scandal of the Cross*, 177.

[28] McNall, *The Mosaic of Atonement*, 163.

[29] McNall.

Garry Williams also considers the claim of some that the contemporary critics are attacking only a caricature of the doctrine. If so, then he says, "the way forward is simple: the critics need to say that they do believe in penal substitution itself and just not in warped forms of it." That the critics have not done so leads Williams to believe the attack is against penal substitution itself.[30] Fleming Rutledge says much the same. She is in sympathy with some of the objections, but says, "If the critiques were friendly, they would be accompanied by proposed reworkings of substitution. Instead, the critiques have generally—though not quite always—been accompanied by a wholesale rejection of the theme."[31] She herself believes the PSA model needs "a thorough overhaul" but does not at all want to eliminate "the substitution motif."[32]

To return to the question which we are addressing in this section, are the contemporary objections to PSA really objections to the doctrine itself or only caricatures of it, the answer seems to be something of both. In the list of twenty-six objections addressed by Jeffery, Ovey, and Sach,[33] there are some that are based on a caricature or frank misunderstanding of PSA, others that are debatable at best or matters of opinion, and some that are serious issues at the heart of PSA. Likewise, in the list of fourteen objections given by Fleming Rutledge, she herself acknowledges that some don't apply to all formulations of PSA and may be a matter of personal taste.[34] In what follows, we will follow the pattern of Oliver Crisp, who chooses to "focus in on a handful of really hard objections," and see what responses may be made.[35]

---

[30] Williams, "Penal Substitution," 86.

[31] Rutledge, *The Crucifixion*, 506. Something of an exception is seen in Baker and Green, *Recovering the Scandal of the Cross*, 184–90. They do not themselves propose a reworking of substitution, but they heartily commend that done by Kevin Vanhoozer, "The Atonement in Postmodernity: Guilt, Goats and Gifts," in *The Glory of the Atonement*, 367–404.

[32] Rutledge, *The Crucifixion*.

[33] Jeffery, Ovey and Sach, *Pierced for Our Transgressions*. See the lists of objections in the Table of Contents, 9–11.

[34] Rutledge, *The Crucifixion*. See 489–506 for her full list.

[35] Crisp, *Approaching the Atonement*, 100.

Major Objections to PSA and Attempted Responses

The Problem of Divine Violence

Some of the earliest and most vehement objections to PSA have come from feminist theologians. The objection is to divine violence in the atonement, especially what was provocatively called "'divine child abuse'—God the Father demanding and carrying out the suffering and death of his own son."[36] Within this problem are at least two questions that need individual consideration.

First, does PSA involve "divine child abuse"? There are numerous reasons why the answer is clearly no. The first and most important reason is the doctrine of the Trinity.[37] The Son who suffered on the cross is also the Eternal Son in the divine Trinity. And one belief that Christians have held about the Trinity for centuries is the doctrine of inseparable operations, expressed in the Latin phrase: *opera trinitatis ad extra sunt indivisa* ("the external works of the Trinity are undivided"). Adonis Vidu unpacks the implications of this doctrine, saying it affirms "that the Trinitarian persons act as a single agent in the economy, such that each trinitarian person is co-agent in each other's action tokens."[38] For the current question, this means that while it is the Son who became incarnate and suffered upon the cross, the work of redemption was the inseparable work of all three persons as one divine agent. It was the plan of the divine Trinity, and the second person was fully involved in the

---

[36] Joanne Carlson Brown and Rebecca Parker, "For God So Loved the World?" in *Christianity, Patriarchy, and Abuse: A Feminist Critique*, Joanne Carlson Brown and Carole Bohn, eds. (New York: Pilgrim, 1989), 26. The phrase "divine child abuse" was revised to "cosmic child abuse" by Steve Chalke and appears in Steve Chalke and Alan Mann, *The Lost Message of Jesus* (Grand Rapids: Zondervan, 2003), 182, and probably did as much as any single phrase to move ongoing discussions and criticisms of PSA to full out controversy, especially prompting response from those outraged to hear PSA compared to child abuse.

[37] Crisp, *Approaching the Atonement*, 103: "one would have to be willing to give up the Trinity for the objection to have any traction."

[38] Adonis Vidu, "Trinitarian Inseparable Operations and the Incarnation," *Journal of Analytic Theology* 4 (2016), 106. See the fuller defense and exposition of this doctrine in Adonis Vidu, *The Same God Who Works All Things: An Exposition and Defense of the Doctrine of Inseparable Operations* (Grand Rapids: Eerdmans, 2021).

making of that plan. As Crisp says, PSA "is not a doctrine that can entail 'divine child abuse' because only one divine entity is in view."[39]

Even apart from the Trinity, there are additional reasons for rejecting the idea of "divine child abuse." Jesus went to the cross voluntarily, knowing what it entailed. It is true that Jesus was deeply troubled at the prospect of drinking "the cup," an image of suffering the wrath of God, but he persevered in choosing to obey the Father's will (Matt 26:39).[40] His earlier comments in John 10 make it clear that this choice was in no way forced upon him: "This is why the Father loves me, because I lay down my life that I may take it up again. No one takes it from me, but I lay it down on my own" (John 10:17–18).

We have been chastened by recent events to never overlook any type of abuse, never to minimize the gravity of it,[41] and if PSA contributed to any acceptance of any type of abuse, that would be a very serious matter indeed. But it is difficult to see any intrinsic connection,[42] and Stephen Holmes says, "there is (as far as I am aware) not statistical evidence" of any correlation between belief in PSA and domestic abuse.[43] So we find no evidence to

---

[39] Crisp, *Approaching the Atonement*, 102.

[40] D. A. Carson, "Matthew," *EBC*, vol. 8 (Grand Rapids: Zondervan, 1984), 543: "The cup (*poterion*) refers not only to suffering and death but, as often in the OT . . . also to God's wrath."

[41] The revelations that have come out through the #MeToo movement have shocked and saddened many, and concerns over sexual abuse and cover-ups of those involved in it caused my own denomination, the Southern Baptist Convention, to commission an outside, independent agency to conduct a thorough investigation of how our leadership had handled sex abuse allegation over the twenty years 2001–2021. Their report, issued June 2022, documented a deeply disturbing pattern of denials, minimizing, cover-ups, and neglect of victims.

[42] Indeed, there may be a positive connection between PSA and properly dealing with sexual abuse. Rachel Denhollander gained worldwide attention as the first woman to publicly accuse Larry Nasser of abuse of female gymnasts. In a paper presented to the Evangelical Theological Society, she and her husband argue that "a proper account of penal substitution upholds a view of justice that is foundational for the treatment of both the victims and perpetrators of abuse." See Rachel and Jacob Denhollander, "Justice: The Foundation of a Christian Approach to Abuse," paper presentation, Evangelical Theological Society, Denver, Colorado, November 13, 2018; cited in McNall, *The Mosaic of Atonement*, 162–63n60.

[43] Holmes, "Penal Substitution," in *T&T Clark Companion to Atonement*, 302.

substantiate the idea that PSA encourages abuse; we deny that it affirms "divine child abuse," but acknowledge that there is at least one more question that goes beyond just the issue of divine child abuse.

Even if the cross and PSA do not imply divine child abuse, there is still the problem of divine violence. Why does the way of reconciliation of humans with God involve such violence? The traditional atonement models seem to entail "the valorization of violence," but these critics believe that "violent acts are morally objectionable" and that God would surely not act immorally in bringing about reconciliation. To state the objection bluntly, "Violence cannot bring about atonement."[44] Oliver Crisp believes that an adequate response to the problem of atoning violence must address two issues. The first is "the fact that the crucifixion of Christ is violent, and yet that atonement is about reconciliation." The second issue is the deeper one of "God's involvement in atoning violence."[45]

The response that Crisp himself offers and prefers is what he calls "the double effect response."[46] He compares the situation to that of a surgeon seeking to remove a cancerous mass from the womb of a pregnant woman. Such an operation is intended to heal and save and thus cannot be described as violence, because "violence requires an intention to harm." Yet the surgeon knows that the operation will have the unintended consequence of killing the fetus. "Thus her action in performing this surgical procedure has a double effect: one foreseen and intended, the other foreseen but not intended." In the same way, God acts to effect reconciliation; that is the reason for the crucifixion of Christ. Reconciliation is the positive and intended effect. God "ordains the circumstances in which Christ is crucified, including the violence of the Roman soldiers who whip and abuse him and eventually nail him to the cross. Yet, God does not *intend*

---

[44] This is the formulation of the problem of violence by Crisp, *Approaching the Atonement*, 131–32, but it is recognized as a problem by many and commented on extensively by Boersma, *Violence, Hospitality, and the Cross*, especially 38–51 (note the title of his book), and McNall, *The Mosaic of Atonement*, 159–64. Crisp himself devotes an entire chapter to "the problem of atoning violence" (131–45). See the attempt to omit violence from the atonement in Weaver, *The Nonviolent Atonement* (see chap. 13, n. 9).

[45] Crisp, *Approaching the Atonement*, 137.

[46] Crisp, 140–41.

the violence of the soldiers." Violence is a foreseen effect but not God's intended effect.[47]

Crisp does acknowledge a problem with the double effect response. Why is it that "God has to bring about human reconciliation by means of the violence of crucifixion?"[48] Indeed, Kevin Vanhoozer says "the acid test of any doctrine of atonement" is its ability to "explain the *necessity* of Jesus' sufferings on the cross."[49] Crisp acknowledges that in sketching out this response he has not included how it would argue for the necessity of the cross in the first place but suggests that defenders of this response could draw upon Anselm's idea, "that God must punish sin either in the person of the sinner in hell, or in the person of some suitable substitute able to offer satisfaction instead."[50] This is very close to a traditional formulation of PSA, but would bring with it numerous other standard objections to PSA we will examine shortly.

The second response to the problem of atoning violence is found in the work of Hans Boersma. In his book *Violence, Hospitality, and the Cross*, he examines atonement theology "as an expression of God's hospitality toward us," but a hospitality which "while necessarily involving violence, retains its integrity as hospitality." He asserts strongly, "Violence does not destroy hospitality"; rather, "we need to affirm the paradox of redemptive violence in order to retain the vision of unconditional hospitality."[51] He acknowledges that many "have instinctively negative reactions to the word 'violence,'" and that some, like Denny Weaver, call for a non-violent atonement.[52] But he is very hesitant to go in that direction for two reasons. First, he notes that all three of the main atonement models in the history of the church (Christus Victor, objective, and subjective) "associate God with violence." Thus, he concludes, "We can only shield God from the violence of the cross at the cost

---

[47] Though Crisp does not mention it, perhaps Acts 2:23 reflects something of the double effect idea in attributing the death of Jesus as happening in accordance with "God's determined plan and foreknowledge" but also as happening by the hands of "lawless people" who nailed him to the cross.

[48] Crisp, *Approaching the Atonement*, 143.

[49] Vanhoozer, "The Atonement in Postmodernity," 389.

[50] Crisp, *Approaching the Atonement*, 144.

[51] Boersma, *Violence, Hospitality, and the Cross*, 15–17.

[52] Boersma, 38, 40.

of parting ways with the Tradition of the Church."[53] Second, he thinks that the assumption that violence is always morally negative is open to question. He gives several reasons for questioning this assumption.

First is the fact that all three major approaches to the atonement involved God in violence and felt that it was not morally questionable to do so. Second is the just-war tradition, held by Augustine, Aquinas, Calvin and others, which assumes that "sometimes violence is not only unavoidable but also positively required."[54] Third, he suggests that we experience and may inflict on others various forms of discipline and coercion (which Boersma sees as violence)[55] without doing anything morally wrong. Finally, in contexts of sin and injustice, violence may be "morally required." Here Boersma transitions to a discussion of God's wrath and love, comparing them to violence and hospitality. "Just as divine hospitality requires at least some violence to make it flourish, so also God's love requires that he become angry when his love is violated. For God not to get angry when he is rejected by people made in his image (and redeemed in Christ) would demonstrate indifference, not love."[56] Thus, the violence of the cross is acceptable when it is seen that such violence is employed "in the interest of God's eschatological, undeconstructible justice."[57] Crisp says much the same thing when he says, "The language of 'wrath' and 'anger' may be understood as anthropomorphic ways of getting at the expression of his justice."[58] But the term "justice" leads to our next major objection to PSA.

---

[53] Boersma, 40, 43. Weaver, *Nonviolent Atonement*, 226, agrees with Boersma that a nonviolent atonement is "a new reading of the history of the doctrines of atonement and Christology."

[54] Boersma, 44.

[55] Boersma, 47: "Any use of force or coercion that involves some kind of hurt or injury—whether the coercion is physical or nonphysical—is a form of violence."

[56] Boersma, 49. For an argument that the wrath of God is an expression of the love of God, see Tony Lane, "The Wrath of God as an Aspect of the Love of God," in *Nothing Greater, Nothing Better: Theological Essays on the Love of God*, ed. Kevin Vanhoozer (Grand Rapids: Eerdmans, 2011), 138–67; see also Adam Johnson, "Violence," in *T&T Clark Companion to Atonement*, 794: "wrath is the entirely good and appropriate mode of God's love in relation to sin and the sinner."

[57] Boersma, 51.

[58] Crisp, *Approaching the Atonement*, 104.

The Problem of Retributive Justice

The idea of *penalty* in penal substitution rests on an assumption of retributive justice.[59] We are justly deserving of punishment because of our sins. Only if someone were to take the penalty for sin in our place could we be justly released from our punishment. God can be just (or righteous) and declare those who were manifestly sinners to be justified (righteous) only because of what Christ has done (Rom 3:25–26). This idea of justice in society and government, which seems to have clear biblical testimony,[60] was once widely held in the West and still is held today almost everywhere outside the secularized West. Eric Johnson recognizes the contemporary objections to retributive justice but says, "the principles of retributive justice and reciprocal exchange might be easier to appreciate if one recognizes their universality. . . . They did not originate in the Mosaic covenant but are found across cultures and across time." He adds, retributive justice is practiced, "*basically, wherever wrongdoing is punished.*"[61] Yet, retributive justice is widely denied today and has been seen as a major objection to penal understandings of the atonement.

There are two main reasons for the rejection of retributive justice. The first is found in the work of the philosopher Eleonore Stump. She sees many problems with what she calls Anselmian theories of the atonement (with PSA seen as one variant of Anselmian theories), but chief of them is that such theories are contrary to the love of God. Under the logic of retributive justice, she says, "absent satisfaction, God would not love the wrongdoer. But, as the biblical text 1 John 4:8 claims, God is love. To suppose, then, that God would not forgive or accept reconciliation unless satisfaction had been made to God is to suppose that, without satisfaction, God is not God."[62] The insistence on the necessity of satisfying the wrath of God distorts God's character

---

[59] Grensted, *A Short History of the Doctrine of the Atonement*, 313: "The assertion that retribution is the primary function of justice is ardently combated, and is ardently defended. And by the result of the debate the Penal theory must stand or fall."

[60] See Rom 12:19: "'Vengeance belongs to me; I will repay,' says the Lord"; Rev 22:12: "Look, I am coming soon, and my reward is with me to repay each person according to his work."

[61] Eric Johnson, *God & Soul Care: The Therapeutic Resources of the Christian Faith* (Downers Grove: IVP Academic, 2017), 363. Emphasis in original.

[62] Eleonore Stump, *Atonement* (Oxford: Oxford University Press, 2018), 111.

as free to show mercy. In the words of Paul Fiddes, "Penal substitution fails to unify the love of God with his wrath."[63]

Fellow philosopher William Lane Craig examines Stump's argument and finds numerous problems with it. One is the connection between love and forgiveness. He asks, "How is the universality of God's love and forgiveness incompatible with there being preconditions of forgiveness, like the satisfaction of God's justice?"[64] As to the idea that PSA exaggerates the wrath of God in a way inconsistent with God's love, the nature of God's love as holy love requires a proper recognition of the wrath of God as a necessary concomitant of the love of God.[65] Indeed, Scripture sees God's love as present before the satisfaction of his wrath and as the motivation for providing for the satisfaction of that wrath: "Love consists in this: not that we loved God, but that he loved us and sent his Son to be the atoning sacrifice for our sins" (1 John 4:10). When the condition for forgiveness is met by the one requiring it, and met by dying in their place, there would seem to be no room for complaint that this particular exercise of retributive justice is contrary to love. The NT seems to see this provision for the demands of retributive justice as the proof of divine love (John 3:16; Rom 5:8; 1 John 3:16).

The more often mentioned reason for the objection to retributive justice is changes in Western culture. Kevin Vanhoozer notes how "the nineteenth century concern with human consciousness and experience" became linked to a "tendency to reject retributive justice and affirm God's love."[66] Stephen Holmes tracks the changes in European thinking on punishment in general, from seeing punishment as serving retributive justice to punishment serving the purposes of deterrence or reform of the offender.[67] Opposition to retributive justice is also strong in postmodern thought: "Postmoderns criticize any theory that tries to make sense of the cross in terms that might legitimate

---

[63] Fiddes, *Past Event and Present Salvation*, 103.

[64] Craig, *The Atonement and the Death of Christ*, 165n40 (see chap. 13, n. 13).

[65] As argued by Lane, "The Wrath of God as an Aspect of the Love of God," in *Nothing Greater, Nothing Better: Theological Essays on the Love of God*, 138–67.

[66] Vanhoozer, "Atonement," 178.

[67] Holmes, "Penal Substitution," 309. These two theories of punishment are called retributive and consequentialist. The latter claims punishment is moral if good consequences flow from it; the former says punishment is moral if deserved.

violence, or in terms of retribution, or in terms of economic exchange."[68] Joel Green and Mark Baker go further, arguing that retributive justice is not only opposed by modern and postmodern culture, it is contrary to the concept of justice in Scripture. Speaking specifically of the formulation of PSA by J. I. Packer, they say his "concepts of moral law, guilt, and retributive justice . . . are more at home in his time and place than in the biblical materials."[69] The Biblical materials call for a framework of justice that is "covenantal and relational," not legal and retributive.[70]

What response can we offer to this second objection to retributive justice? It might be helpful, first, to guard against the intrusion of caricatures. Retributive justice does affirm the idea of the cross as the satisfying of God's just and righteous wrath. But that should not be confused with the idea that "the God of the Bible can be propitiated after the fashion of a pagan deity."[71] Thus, terms such as "vindictive," "placate," or "appease," which can be associated with a pagan deity, should be distinguished from the rightful satisfaction of just wrath.[72] Vanhoozer specifically decries caricatures of God's wrath that pictures him as "emotion-laden" and "ever on the verge of striking out."[73] The question, "Does God need to be placated before he can love and forgive?"[74] is one that may properly be attributed to a caricature of PSA, but not to any fully biblical formulation of PSA (see 1 John 4:10).

---

[68] Vanhoozer, "The Atonement in Postmodernity," 371.

[69] Baker and Green, *Recovering the Scandal of the Cross*, 180.

[70] Baker and Green.

[71] Morris, *The Apostolic Preaching of the Cross*, 148.

[72] This is the mistake of Fleming Rutledge in her very fine work, *The Crucifixion*, 280. She quotes with approval the words of Morris saying we should not see God "after the fashion of a pagan deity," and says that "it should now be generally agreed that any concept of *hilastērion* in the sense of placating, appeasing, deflecting the anger of, or satisfying the wrath of, is inadmissible." Morris would want to distance himself from terms like "placate," "appease" and perhaps "deflect the anger of." But he, and numerous other defenders of PSA, would affirm that the propitiatory work of the cross does satisfy the wrath of God.

[73] Vanhoozer, "The Atonement in Postmodernity," 376, citing this caricature from Baker and Green, *Recovering the Scandal of the Cross*, 53.

[74] Vanhoozer, 372. This is one of the questions Vanhoozer sees postmodern critics asking those who affirm retributive justice. It may reflect an inaccurate understanding of what retributive justice involves for those affirming PSA.

A second preliminary point may be to ask how much changes in culture should prompt changes in theology. Fleming Rutledge acknowledges that many say "penal substitution cannot be viable today because it is based in nineteenth-century concepts of justice." She further acknowledges, "There is certainly some merit in understanding context," but asks, "how much should we allow it [context] to guide our assessment of a theological text or doctrine?"[75] How important is "cultural plausibility?" Stephen Holmes affirms that it is not more important than Scripture: "If we take it [PSA] as something found in the Scriptures, then we are not at liberty to set it aside." We affirm such a doctrine whether it is "culturally comprehensible" or "prophetic and challenging."[76] Indeed, from the beginning, many elements of the gospel message were "stumbling blocks" to first-century culture,[77] but were nonetheless proclaimed. PSA may be such an element today.

A third preliminary point also deserves mention. Is the loss of cultural plausibility, which Holmes sees as the key reason for the controversy over penal substitution,[78] really universal, or are we guilty of Western ethnocentrism? Eric Johnson says, "Outside the secularized West, few reject the notions of retributive justice and reciprocal exchange." Rather than being the product of earlier Western culture, such notions "are found across cultures and across time." Johnson speculates that "they are likely embedded in the human genome."[79] Even in the West, there has been a recent renaissance of defenses of retributive justice.[80] Similarly, Fleming Rutledge questions the

---

[75] Rutledge, *The Crucifixion*, 491.

[76] Holmes, "Ransomed, Healed, Restored, Forgiven," 284.

[77] McNall, *The Mosaic of Atonement*, 166: "it seems odd and even somewhat unchristian, to sideline a particular doctrine because it presents a 'stumbling block' to a given group." He cites Justin Martyr, who says the cross was so nonsensical in his day that to believe in it was a sign of "madness." See Justin Martyr, *First Apology* 13 (*ANF* 1:166–67).

[78] Holmes, "Ransomed, Healed, Restored, Forgiven," 284. Speaking of the loss of cultural plausibility, he says, "Everything else, I think, depends on this."

[79] Johnson, *God and Soul Care*, 364, 363.

[80] See Mark White, *Retributivism: Essays on Theory and Policy* (Oxford: Oxford University Press, 2011); Michael Tonry, ed., *Retributivism Has a Past: Has It a Future?* Studies in Penal Theory and Philosophy (Oxford: Oxford University Press, 2011). I am indebted to Craig, *Atonement and the Death of Christ*, 175–76n2 for calling my attention to this development.

argument against substitution on the grounds that "people in other cultures do not see themselves in the categories we have been discussing" (categories like guilty and in need of forgiveness). On the contrary, she says, "the more one hears, the more the categories seem to pop up."[81]

Still, we shouldn't dismiss this objection too cavalierly. While we cannot let cultural plausibility determine our theology, neither can we disregard it. It is helpful if our atonement theology "has sufficient cultural purchase to be useful in the proclamation of the gospel."[82] Here Kevin Vanhoozer has responded to the objection that retributive justice is to be rejected as contrary to modern and postmodern culture by offering "a constructive proposal" that takes seriously the postmodern objection and still manages to retain a place for retributive justice and PSA as a whole.

Vanhoozer recognizes that the postmodern critique of retributive justice is linked to its dislike of "a divine 'economy' in which God distributes a particular resource (forgiveness) only after the appropriate payment (Jesus' death)." In place of this idea of economic exchange, he argues for an economy of excess: "God pours himself out for us, not in an economic exchange, but in an excess of justice and love,"[83] justifying this motif of excess by the prominence of the Greek preposition *hyper*. He says, "The death of Jesus exceeds our attempts to explain it. Postmodern treatments of the cross are thus '*hyper*-economic.'" Yet Vanhoozer draws from *hyper* the motif of substitution too: "Substitution is the principle that best corresponds to the preposition (*hyper*)," and affirms substitution as "a necessary, if not sufficient, condition for understanding the saving significance of the cross."[84]

Many of the objections to retributive justice he overcomes by affirming both/and for a number of possible dichotomies. Thus, the penalty is not just for breaking a law, as in Western legal systems, but also for covenant disobedience. The penalty itself is exile, which is both penal (legal) and relational. He makes room for a justice that is both retributive and restorative, that sees Christ's death as making things right, both objectively and subjectively, a

---

[81] Rutledge, *The Crucifixion*, 491.
[82] Holmes, "Penal Substitution," 313.
[83] Vanhoozer, "The Atonement in Postmodernity," 403.
[84] Vanhoozer, 403n114.

rightness that is both legal and interpersonal.[85] Even Green and Baker, who oppose most formulations of PSA, affirm Vanhoozer for taking the context for justice, not from a Western courtroom, but from a context where "justice is defined by faithfulness to commitments and covenants, and the role of the judge is to rectify and reconcile. If this judge demands payment or punishment, the purpose is restorative."[86] Yet retributive justice is not so much denied as reconfigured into an economy of excess.

For those in the West, who see the retributive justice embedded in penal substitution as making the saving significance of the cross incomprehensible, Vanhoozer has done us a service by reframing it in a way that addresses the concerns of such critics without abandoning the substance of PSA. But there is a further problem linked to retributive justice.

The Problem of Justice in Punishing an Innocent

Retributive justice says that those who do wrong should be punished because they deserve it; justice demands that they be punished. This is seen in the Bible's commands to judges to acquit the innocent and condemn the guilty to the punishment they deserve (Deut 25:1–2). But under PSA, it is the innocent one, Jesus, who suffers the punishment that guilty humans deserve. Eleonore Stump asks, "How is justice or goodness served by punishing a completely innocent person or exacting from him what he does not owe?"[87] William Lane Craig sees this objection as originating with Socinus and calls it "by far and away the most prevalent and powerful objection" to PSA.[88]

It is linked to a second, related objection. If it is claimed that the first problem, that of punishing an innocent person instead of the guilty ones, is resolved by claiming the sin and guilt of the guilty ones is transferred to the innocent one, the problem now is the non-transferability of sin and guilt. Oliver Crisp considers various possible parallels in criminal justice but finds none that match the problem here. One person may pay a parking fine for

---

[85] Vanhoozer, 398, 381.

[86] Baker and Green, *Recovering the Scandal of the Cross*, 189.

[87] Stump, *Atonement*, 24.

[88] Craig, *Atonement and the Death of Christ*, 130, 173.

another, but human sin seems to be much more serious, something more comparable to a felony, and "the guilt for this crime is bound up with the one who committed it. It 'attaches' to that person; it cannot be transferred to another."[89] He believes that having a substitute suffer the punishment due a felon, and ascribing the sin and guilt of that felon to the substitute, "would be a miscarriage of justice." He asks, "What about the theological application of penal substitution means an exception can be made in the case of Christ, which is not a traducing of justice?"[90]

Joshua McNall takes seriously this problem of penal transference, but thinks it is possible to question the assumption that the innocent one, Jesus, and the guilty ones, humans, are disconnected. He claims, "we are truly bound together with all humanity in a way that counters the currents of modern individualism." One way Christian theology has affirmed this connectedness of all humanity is in federal theology, in which "God has sovereignly covenanted that human destiny would hinge upon the faithfulness of just one man acting on behalf of the many." But McNall combines this federalism with an appeal to Irenaeus: "For Irenaeus, Christ acts as the true head of all humanity because he is both the creator and the archetype after which the human creature was formed in the beginning. . . . Christ's life and ours share a mysterious but real connection."[91] This explains why Jesus can be the recapitulation of life for all humans. McNall thinks this helps deal with the problem of penal transference:

> If all humanity is somehow bound up *in* and *with* the Son, then the cross presents us not with one innocent and disconnected individual bearing the punishment for other guilty ones. Instead, the cross involves the judgment of the sin of the entire human race in the body of the one person who really does (somehow) contain us all.[92]

He concludes, "In short, Christ may bear the judgment for our sin because he does, in some sense, *bear us*."[93]

---

[89] Crisp, *Approaching the Atonement*, 109.
[90] Crisp, 111.
[91] McNall, *The Mosaic of Atonement*, 81.
[92] McNall, 82; emphasis in original.
[93] McNall, 83; emphasis in original.

McNall's account helps us make sense of biblical language that does seem to say that sin and guilt are in some way transferable. What else is meant by the symbolism of the sacrificial system of the OT, when the one offering the sacrifice lays his hand on the animal and the animal is offered up on his behalf? What else is meant by the word spoken of the suffering servant in Isaiah 53:6, "the LORD has punished him for the iniquity of us all"?[94] How else can Jesus, the righteous one, suffer for the sins of the unrighteous (1 Pet 3:18)? The reality of transference seems assumed in Scripture. Luther saw this reality of transference illustrated in marriage, in which each spouse takes on the debts and credits of the other: "sins, death and damnation will be Christ's, while life, grace, and salvation will be the soul's; for if Christ is a bridegroom, he must take upon himself the things which are his bride's and bestow upon her the things which are his."[95]

But some may say that even so, does this idea of our connectedness in Christ really make penal transference just? A second part of a possible response is to ask, "Who or what determines what is just or unjust?" William Lane Craig raises metaethical considerations to argue that there is no external law of justice to which God must conform. He must act in a manner consistent with his nature, but "if He wills to take on human nature in the form of Jesus of Nazareth and give His own life as a sacrificial offering for sin, who is to forbid Him?" It seems eminently consistent with his justice and mercy.[96]

Finally, it may be worthwhile to consider the alternative. If Christ cannot take the punishment due sinners, how can we possibly escape the punishment due our sins? Thankfully, the Bible seems to clearly say that Christ did pay our debt, he did suffer the punishment due us. The possibility that

---

[94] Rutledge, *The Crucifixion*, 493, suggests that perhaps we are being too rationalistic here: "Christ does not take our guilt upon himself in any way that can be described in ordinary human terms; it is not logical in that sense, and analogies are doomed to inadequacy. Like so much of Scripture, the idea in Isaiah 53 that 'the Lord has laid on him the iniquity of us all' is *poetic* truth, to be received in faith; it is not a statement that we can rationally explain."

[95] Martin Luther, "The Freedom of a Christian," in *Martin Luther's Basic Theological Writings*, ed. Timothy Lull, 2nd ed. (Minneapolis: Fortress, 2005), 397, uses the analogy of husband and wife.

[96] Craig, *Atonement and the Death of Christ*, 177. See 177n5 for proponents of such a metaethical theory.

this would be unjust is answered in Rom 3:25–26. The cross demonstrates God's justice in accepting us because of what Christ has done.

Conclusion

We have not nearly exhausted all the contemporary objections to PSA, but we think we have given honest consideration to those we consider the most serious and pressing. Though less crucial, perhaps it would be good to respond briefly to the objection that PSA defenders claim the penal substitution is the only biblical model of the atonement[97] by simply stating that no major contemporary advocate denies that there is value in the other major theories of the atonement. That objection applies at best to a caricature of PSA. The admission of value in other theories means that objections that PSA is too little concerned with the human response to the cross,[98] or has too little emphasis on the resurrection,[99] do not really count against PSA, for defenders of PSA look to subjective theories to discuss the human response, and see the importance of the resurrection in Christus Victor theories. We do not think PSA says all there is to say about the atonement.

Other objections about the biblical and historical support for PSA we think we answered sufficiently in the previous chapter. There are also a number of minor objections, such as that if satisfaction for sins is made, there is nothing left to forgive, or that Christ did not suffer eternal condemnation and so did not fully pay for our sins,[100] but these can be answered briefly by recognizing that satisfaction does not replace forgiveness but makes forgiveness just and that allowing the debt to be paid by a substitute is part of God's forgiveness and that the infinite nature of Christ as God makes the penalty suffered by him likewise infinite.[101]

---

[97] Baker and Green, *Recovering the Scandal of the Cross*, 50. PSA "at the very least, constrains overmuch the richness of biblical thinking concerning the death of Jesus."

[98] Fiddes, *Past Event and Present Salvation*, 99. PSA "does not integrate the human response to God, and the healing of the human personality here and now, into the act of atonement."

[99] Baker and Green, *Recovering the Scandal of the Cross*, 180.

[100] These are among the objections made by Socinus (Gomes, "Socinus," 756) and Stump (*Atonement*, 24–25).

[101] See Craig, *Atonement and the Death of Christ*, 207–11.

In short, we see none of the objections raised by contemporary critics as sufficient to justify an abandonment of PSA or a diminishing of the claims of its centrality. Perhaps incorporating some of the elements of Vanhoozer's proposal (seeing the context as legal and covenantal, seeing God's justice as retributive and restorative, seeing both reciprocal exchange and excess as involved in God's response) would be wise.[102] Perhaps we should take care to describe the satisfaction of God's wrath as motivated by the already existing love of God (1 John 4:10) and clearly differentiate this righteous and just wrath from that of pagan deities. But it is hard to avoid the likelihood that much of the contemporary opposition to PSA stems from the thought of many modern people, that, while they may not be perfect and sinless, surely their sin is not so heinous that someone would need to die to make them acceptable before God. The response to such thinking is surely the fundamental biblical teaching that "the wages of sin is death" (Rom 6:23).[103] To those who question whether the wages of sin should be so costly, we suggest that since sin is against God (Ps 51:4), only God has the right to set its cost, and such a question is, at any rate, far above the "pay grade" of any human.

---

[102] Vanhoozer, "The Atonement in Postmodernity," 367–404.

[103] Rutledge, *The Crucifixion*, 506: "a good deal of the opposition to the substitution motif is rooted in an aversion to its fundamental recognition of the rule of Sin and God's judgment upon it."

17

The Extent of the Atonement[1]

Introduction

In this chapter, we turn from the somewhat extensive consideration we gave to the nature of the atonement to a briefer consideration of an important but secondary issue: the extent of the atonement. While most theologians use the word *extent* in referring to this issue, Louis Berkhof clarifies that the key issue is the *design* or *intent* of God in the death of Christ: "Did the Father in sending Christ, and did Christ in coming into the world, to make atonement for sin, *do this with the design or for the purpose of saving only the elect or all men?*"[2] In other words, what was God's intention (or intentions) in the atonement made by Christ?

The first position is perhaps best known as limited atonement, but was called by some early Baptists particular redemption (Christ died not for all but for the elect in particular).[3] Today most of its advocates prefer definite atonement as a more accurate title. They say that Christ did not die to make

---

[1] This chapter is adapted from the larger work by this author on the same topic, John Hammett, "Multiple-Intentions View of the Atonement," in *Perspectives on the Extent of the Atonement: Three Views*, ed. Andrew Naselli and Mark Snoeberger (Nashville: B&H Academic, 2015), 143–94. Used with permission.

[2] Louis Berkhof, *Systematic Theology*, 4th ed. (Grand Rapids: Eerdmans, 1949), 394. Emphasis in original.

[3] For the origin of the Particular Baptists, see David Bebbington, *Baptists Through the Centuries: A History of a Global People* (Waco, TX: Baylor University Press, 2010), 46–48; for a classical statement of their belief about the atonement, see the London Confession of 1644, art. XVII.

salvation possible for all, but to make it definite for the elect, and so definite atonement is the way we will most often refer to this view in this chapter.[4] The opposing position is sometimes called general or more often universal atonement, but this view should be distinguished from universalism, the idea that all will be saved. For this reason, some prefer to call this view unlimited atonement.[5] Universal or unlimited atonement affirms that Christ died with the intention of making salvation possible for all, but that only those who respond to the gospel message with repentance and faith will be saved.

There have been numerous attempts to combine something of these two views, to see the death of Christ as in some sense universal or unlimited and in some sense limited or definite. The most famous is the formulation of the twelfth-century theologian Peter Lombard. Of Christ's death, he said that Christ died "for all with regard to the sufficiency of the price, but only for the elect with regard to its efficacy."[6] This sufficiency/efficiency distinction was developed by some British theologians in the seventeenth and eighteenth centuries into a position called hypothetical universalism; a similar position developed by the French theologian Moise Amyraut is called Amyraldianism.[7] In the first, Christ died conditionally for all but effectually only for the elect.[8] In Amyraut's version, "Christ procured atonement for all.

---

[4] This is the preferred term in David Gibson and Jonathan Gibson, eds., *From Heaven He Came and Sought Her: Definite Atonement in Historical, Biblical, Theological, and Practical Perspective* (Wheaton: Crossway, 2013); Shawn Wright, *40 Questions About Calvinism* (Grand Rapids: Kregel Academic, 2019), 181–201; and Carl Trueman, "Definite Atonement View," in *Perspectives on the Extent of the Atonement: Three Views*, 19–61.

[5] David Allen, *The Extent of the Atonement: A Historical and Critical Review* (Nashville: B & H Academic, 2016), xxii: Allen says, "Throughout this volume, I will regularly use 'unlimited atonement' as a synonym for 'universal atonement' to avoid confusion."

[6] Peter Lombard, *The Sentences: Book 3; On the Incarnation of the Word*, trans. G. Silano, Medieval Sources in Translation 45 (Toronto: Pontifical Institute of Medieval Studies, 2008), 86.

[7] For more on various issues and versions of Amyraldism, see Michael Bird and Scott Harrower, ed., *Unlimited Atonement: Amyraldism and Reformed Theology* (Grand Rapids: Kregel Academic, 2023).

[8] For a discussion of British hypothetical universalism, see Leo Gattis, "The Synod of Dort and Definite Atonement," in *From Heaven He Came and Sought Her*, 143–63.

But it is hypothetical, for salvation is effectual only when and if the condition of faith is realized."[9]

Another way to see both universal and definite elements in the atonement is to go beyond the sufficient/efficient distinction to affirm multiple intentions in the atonement. While David Allen sees a "dualistic" view of God's intentions in the atonement as characteristic of those he calls "moderate Calvinists,"[10] this view has been more explicitly developed in recent years by a number of authors,[11] including the author of this chapter.[12] This view will be given consideration in this chapter, along with definite and unlimited views.

One possible view included in a recent book on this topic that will not be included here is Christian universalism. It is defined as "the hope that, because of the sovereign loving of God, the extent of the atonement will be universal not only in potentiality but in its actuality"; that is, "the reception of salvation is not conditional upon either a profession of faith or the eternal decision of God to elect or reject the individual: God has elected all in God's love, and it is for these all that God atones in the person of Christ."[13] Though universalism can claim some adherents in Christian history, from

---

[9] See the thorough presentation of Amyraut's position in Amar Djaballah, "Controversy on Universal Grace: A Historical Survey of Moise Amyraut's *Brief Traitté de la Predestination*," in *From Heaven He Came and Sought Her*, 165–99; quotation from 191. Djaballah, 166n5, comments on the key difference between British hypothetical universalism and Amyraldianism: "the difference between the two positions centers mainly on the order of decrees," with Amyraut seeing the decree of election as coming after the decree of redemption while the British hypothetical universalists do not necessarily follow that pattern.

[10] Allen, *The Extent of the Atonement*, xix.

[11] See Bruce Demarest, *The Cross and Salvation: The Doctrine of Salvation* (Wheaton: Crossway, 1997), 189–93; and Gary Shultz, Jr., "A Biblical and Theological Defense of a Multi-Intentioned View of the Atonement" (PhD diss., The Southern Baptist Theological Seminary, 2008). Shultz wrote his dissertation under the supervision of Bruce Ware, who advocates for this view but has only written on it in unpublished documents (Bruce Ware, "Extent of the Atonement: Outline of the Issue, Positions, Key Texts, and Key Theological Arguments").

[12] Hammett, "Multiple-Intentions View of the Atonement," 143–94.

[13] Tom Greggs, "Christian Universalist View," in *Five Views on the Atonement*, ed. Adam Johnson (Grand Rapids: Zondervan, 2019), 197–217; quotations from 217 and 198.

Origen to Karl Barth—and though Christian universalism is receiving some attention among evangelicals today[14]—the biblical and theological evidence against it is overwhelming, and so it will not be included among the options considered here.[15]

The Case for an Unlimited Atonement

While it is possible to list numerous arguments in support of this view, most fit within two broad categories.[16] One argument not included below that some advocates of unlimited atonement include in their defense of their position is the historical support that universal atonement enjoys.[17] While it is indisputably the majority position in the history of the church, to what degree there was some support for definite atonement, especially before the Reformation, is a matter of some dispute.[18] Today there is significant support for both positions, and so the choice here is to focus on two major arguments.

Biblical Texts

The case for a universal (or unlimited) view of the atonement consists largely of various groups of biblical texts. David Allen says boldly, "That Christ died for the sins of all people is clearly taught in Scripture in numerous places,"

---

[14] See Thomas Talbott, "A Case for Christian Universalism," in *Universal Salvation? The Current Debate*, ed. Robin Parry and Christopher Partridge (Grand Rapids: Eerdmans, 2003).

[15] For an evangelical critique of universalism, see Christopher Morgan and Robert Peterson, eds., *Hell Under Fire* (Grand Rapids: Zondervan, 2004).

[16] Walter Elwell, "Atonement, Extent of," in *Evangelical Dictionary of Theology*, 100–101, lists eight arguments in support of "general redemption."

[17] Allen's work, *The Extent of the Atonement*, is perhaps the most complete presentation of the historical support for unlimited atonement, with more than 650 pages of his volume devoted to historical matters.

[18] Allen, *The Extent of the Atonement*, xvi–xvii, claims that definite atonement was a "novelty" before the late sixteenth century. Raymond Blacketer, "Definite Atonement in Historical Perspective," in *The Glory of the Atonement*, 313 (see chap. 15, n. 36), offers a slightly different perspective: "There is a trajectory of thought in the Christian tradition running from the patristic era through the Middle Ages that stresses a specific, particular and defined purpose of God in salvation; but it is a minority position and is frequently ambiguous."

and lists thirteen texts, with an additional fifteen that "implicitly affirm unlimited atonement."[19] Grant Osborne sees this as the major argument for universal atonement and lists eighteen texts.[20] Gary Shultz gives attention to fifteen specific texts;[21] a similar list is found in the work of Norman Douty,[22] and could be duplicated in most significant presentations of the universal view. Due to space limitations, we will consider only two of these texts.

One of the strongest and most often cited of these texts is 1 John 2:2: "He himself [Jesus] is the atoning sacrifice for our sins, and not only for ours, but also for those of the whole world." The key phrase is the last one, "the whole world." The word "world" is an important one for John,[23] but it is used in a number of different senses,[24] with the meaning in any individual verse determined by context. Advocates of definite atonement concede that in John, "*kosmos* is frequently used to emphasize the scope of God's redemptive work," but they claim that the scope is "all people without distinction" (Jew and Gentile), not all people without exception.[25]

This differentiation of "all without distinction" versus "all without exception" is a major part of the response of advocates of definite atonement to the whole group of universal texts, for most of these texts contain words like "world" or "all." But is it exegetically defensible to give such universal words a limited meaning? Certainly in some cases it seems to be a very sound approach. When Jesus says, "If I am lifted up, I will draw all people to myself" (John 12:32), "all without distinction" (Jew and Gentile) makes good sense for two reasons. First, the "all without exception" meaning would lead to universal salvation, which is contrary to the overwhelming overall teaching

---

[19] Allen, *The Extent of the Atonement*, 156.

[20] Osborne, "General Atonement View," 107–20.

[21] Shultz, "Multi-Intentioned View," 100.

[22] Norman Douty, *The Death of Christ: Did Christ Die Only for the Elect?* (Irving, TX: William & Watrous, 1978), 68–127.

[23] Of the 186 occurrences of *kosmos* in the NT, 105 are in the Johannine corpus of writings.

[24] The standard Greek lexicon (Arndt and Gingrich, *A Greek-English Lexicon of the New Testament and Other Early Christian Literature*, 446–48) gives eight major categories for the meanings for *kosmos*, with additional sub-meanings in several of the major categories.

[25] Matthew Harmon, "For the Glory of the Father and the Salvation of His People," in *From Heaven He Came and Sought Her*, 282.

of the New Testament. Second, the presence of Greeks seeking Jesus is in the near context (John 12:20–22) and may have prompted the "all people" language. The "all people" that Jesus will draw to himself in this text seems likely to mean "Jew and Greek" or "all without distinction."

But does "all without distinction" make sense in all uses of "all" or "the world"? Specifically, what meaning should we assign to "world" in 1 John 2:2? David Allen notes the presence of the adjective "whole" preceding "world" in 1 John 2:2, a phrase only found in one other place in John's writings. In 1 John 5:19, "the whole world," under the sway of the evil one, is contrasted with believers. In that verse, seeing the "whole world" as "all without distinction" does not seem to fit. This would seem to argue for seeing the "whole world" in 1 John 2:2 in a similar way, as meaning all people without exception.[26] Another factor that tips the scales toward the "all without exception" meaning would be the fact that the NT has numerous ways to express "all without distinction." Paul specifically says "Jew and Gentile" repeatedly (Rom 1:16; 2:9–10; 3:22) and can use fuller formulae to make "all without distinction" even clearer, such as "neither Jew nor Gentile, neither slave nor free, nor is there male and female" (Gal 3:28). John can affirm that Jesus will die not only for the "Jewish nation" but also "the scattered children of God" (John 11:51–52). There are many biblical phrases that can be used to mean "all without distinction." But what phrase would a biblical writer use to mean "all without exception"? The "whole world" would seem a likely choice.

A second strong universal text is 1 Tim 4:10, especially the last phrase, referring to God as "the Savior of all people, and especially of those who believe." The difficulty for definite atonement with this text is that the extent of God's saving work here seems to extend beyond just the elect ("those who believe") to "all people." Here again "all without distinction" is a problem for definite atonement. As long as God is described as Savior of some in addition to "those who believe," the atonement can no longer be restricted to the elect, for those who believe and the elect are the same group.

Thomas Schreiner engages this and other "problematic texts for definite atonement" and rejects some of the ways other definite atonement defenders have attempted to resolve this problem. He rejects the notion that *malista* should be translated as "namely" rather than "especially." Schreiner rejects

---

[26] Allen, *The Extent of the Atonement*, 158–59.

this translation and gives the strong evidence for *malista* as "especially."[27] He likewise considers and rejects the idea that the salvation in view in calling God "Savior" is not salvation from sin, but what is called God's common grace. Schreiner rejects this interpretation as "quite unlikely."[28] How does he resolve the problem for definite atonement? He argues that 1 Tim 4:10 teaches two truths: that God is "the *available* Savior for all kinds of people . . . while at the same time being the *actual* Savior for only those who believe."[29] But there is nothing in the text or context that justifies applying Savior in one sense to "all people," and in another sense to "those who believe." This is justifiably recognized as one of the strongest texts for universal atonement.

In addition to texts teaching the universal salvific will of God and texts that seem to teach that Christ died for all without exception, there is a group of texts that seem to show that some of those for whom Christ died are, in the end, lost.[30] Under definite atonement, this would not be possible; the salvation of all those for whom Christ died is definite. Within this group of texts, 2 Pet 2:1 is one of the most prominently recognized as "problematic" for the definite atonement view.[31] The last part of the verse describes false teachers as those who deny "the Master who bought them" and as a consequence, bring "swift destruction on themselves." The difficulty lies in the fact that the language of buying people in every other instance in the New Testament refers to redemption or atonement.[32] But under definite atonement, the only ones bought by Christ are the elect. They would not fit the description of being "false teachers" or "bringing swift destruction upon themselves." If the atonement includes even those such as these false teachers, it is clearly not limited to the elect, and universal atonement seems the interpretation that best fits this verse.

---

[27] Thomas Schreiner, "'Problematic Texts' for Definite Atonement in the Pastoral and General Epistles," in *From Heaven He Came and Sought Her*, 380–82.

[28] Schreiner, 383–84.

[29] Schreiner, 386. Emphasis in original.

[30] Osborne, "General Atonement View," 117–18, lists Rom 14:15; 1 Cor 8:11; Heb 10:20; and 2 Pet 2:1 in this group of texts.

[31] Schreiner, "'Problematic Texts,'" 387–92. In his chapter on problematic texts for definite atonement, Schreiner devotes six pages to 2 Pet 2:1.

[32] Schreiner, 387–88: "We have no instance in the NT where the *agorazō* word group, when it is associated with the death of Christ, has a nonsoteriological meaning."

Speaking of this verse, Matthew Pinson observes, "It is hard to avoid the force of this description."[33] How do defenders of definite atonement respond? Schreiner offers this interpretation: "Peter's language is phenomenological. In other words, it *appeared as if* the Lord had purchased the false teachers with his blood (v. 1), though they did not truly belong to the Lord."[34] Schreiner acknowledges that the Arminian (or unlimited atonement) interpretation of the text is "straightforward and clear" and that some may charge him with "an artificial interpretation introduced to support a theological bias." But he links 2 Pet 2:1 with 2 Pet 2:20 and the further description of these false teachers as having "the knowledge of the Lord and Savior Jesus Christ." Schreiner argues that unless we see the language of both 2 Pet 2:1 and 2:20 as phenomenological, we "compromise the doctrine of the perseverance of the saints."[35] But this is not the only option. There are interpretations of 2 Peter 2 that do not see the false teachers as ever being believers and thus the doctrine of the perseverance of the saints does not come into play.[36] What is not only compromised but contradicted is definite atonement. Second Peter 2:1 is a strong text for the unlimited atonement view.

Preaching the Gospel

A final argument advocates of unlimited atonement offer in support of their view is the claim that only their view is consistent with the preaching of the gospel to all. They ask, How can we offer the gospel to all if God has not made provision for all?[37] Gary Shultz makes the further point that Paul begins his definition of the gospel with the words: "Christ died for our sins"

---

[33] J. Matthew Pinson, *40 Questions About Arminianism* (Grand Rapids: Kregel Academic, 2022), 125.

[34] Schreiner, "'Problematic Texts,'" 390. Emphasis in original.

[35] Schreiner, 391–92.

[36] See, for example, Edwin Blum, "2 Peter," in *EBC*, vol. 12 (Grand Rapids: Zondervan, 1981), 276–77, 282; Robert Lightner, *The Death Christ Died: A Biblical Case for Unlimited Atonement*, 2nd ed. (Grand Rapids: Kregel, 1998), 74–76.

[37] David Allen, *The Extent of the Atonement*, 786–87, is particularly emphatic about this. See also Berkhof, *Systematic Theology*, 462. Though a strong defender of definite atonement, he said of this charge, "It need not be denied that there is a real difficulty at this point."

(1 Cor 15:3). But how could Paul have preached that in Corinth? He didn't know who the elect were, and according to definite atonement, it is not true to preach to the non-elect that Christ died for their sins. Definite atonement makes preaching the gospel, as Paul defined it in 1 Cor 15:3, very difficult.[38]

Wayne Grudem feels this difficulty. He objects to some who insist on being such purists in their language that they object to an evangelist telling a crowd of nonbelievers, "Christ died for your sins." While that statement is technically contrary to definite atonement, Grudem thinks advocates of definite atonement (Grudem is one) should have no problem with such a statement "if it is made clear in the context that is necessary to trust in Christ before one can receive the benefits of the gospel offer." He thinks we can understand "Christ died for your sins" to mean "Christ died to offer you forgiveness for your sins," or "Christ died to make available forgiveness for your sins."[39] It is undeniable that many advocates of definite atonement, past and present, have been zealous evangelists.[40] But the very fact that Grudem feels it necessary to modify a strict construction of the definite atonement view shows a possible weakness in that view in terms of its impact upon the preaching of the gospel to all.

Definite Atonement View

The case for definite atonement "does not depend on the understanding of any single text, nor does any single text explicitly teach it."[41] But this does not mean it is derived purely as a logical implication or only as part of a larger system. Rather, it "emerges from holding together various soteriological texts while at the same time synthesizing internally related doctrines," and thus it may be called "a biblico-systematic doctrine."[42] Jonathan Gibson shows that there are

---

[38] Shultz, "Multi-Intentioned View," 168.

[39] Grudem, *Systematic Theology*, 601–3 (see chap. 11, n. 16).

[40] Perhaps the most famous example would be Charles Spurgeon, who was a passionate evangelist and an advocate of definite atonement. It is fair to note, however, that Spurgeon did at times seem to preach in a way not fully consistent with that belief. See Allen, *Extent of the Atonement*, 503–6.

[41] Carl Trueman, "Definite Atonement View," in *Perspectives on the Extent of the Atonement*, 23.

[42] Jonathan Gibson, "The Glorious, Indivisible, Trinitarian Work of God in Christ," *in From Heaven He Came and Sought Her*, 332.

both particularistic and universalistic texts in Paul and thus thinks that these individual texts "neither prove nor disprove the doctrine of definite atonement . . . a larger soteriological framework must be respected."[43] In a similar way, Robert Letham thinks we should consider this issue within "the wider biblical framework," and sees multiple biblical doctrines that point to definite atonement.[44] Here are two major arguments that emerge from such a framework.

Christ's Effective Atonement

The first argument that emerges from this synthesis of biblical texts and related doctrines is the idea *"that Christ's death actually saves"*;[45] others use the phrase, "the objective efficacy of Christ's work."[46] Or as Shawn Wright puts it, "The New Testament does not speak of a potential salvation procured by our Savior if we just add our part. Rather, Christ accomplished his work."[47] Robert Letham argues that the most accurate term for definite atonement is "effective." By contrast, universal atonement is "limited in efficacy."[48] To put it more bluntly, this view believes that seeing Jesus as Savior as opposed to Possibility-Maker argues for definite atonement.

The doctrine of penal substitution, which we argued for in an earlier chapter, is seen as also supporting this argument: "because Christ does not win a hypothetical salvation for hypothetical believers, but rather a real salvation for his people, the effectiveness of the atonement flows from its penal, substitutionary nature."[49] Indeed, penal substitution is seen by Shawn

---

[43] Gibson, "The Glorious, Indivisible, Trinitarian work of God in Christ," 332. His examination of the particularistic and universalistic texts in Paul is in an earlier chapter in the same book, "For Whom Did Christ Die? Particularism and Universalism in the Pauline Epistles," 289–330. Still earlier chapters in the same book (*From Heaven He Came and Sought Her*) examine important texts in the Pentateuch, Isaiah, and the Synoptics and Johannine Literature, but they do not seek to make the case for definite atonement from any specific texts.

[44] Letham, *The Work of Christ*, 233 (see chap. 11, n. 1).

[45] Michael Horton, "Traditional Reformed View," in *Five Views on the Extent of the Atonement*, 126. Emphasis in original.

[46] Trueman, "Definite Atonement View," 23.

[47] Wright, *40 Questions About Calvinism*, 187.

[48] Letham, *The Work of Christ*, 229, 233.

[49] David Gibson and Jonathan Gibson, "Sacred Theology and the Reading of the Divine Word," in *From Heaven He Came and Sought Her*, 48.

Wright as a major argument for definite atonement in and of itself: "the Bible teaches that Jesus substituted himself for particular persons and bore their penalty completely."[50] Garry Williams agrees: "Penal substitutionary atonement rightly understood entails definite atonement."[51] Robert Letham is emphatic: "only effective atonement does justice to the biblical insistence that the cross was a work of penal substitution."[52]

John Owen explains that with penal substitution, the options are universal salvation or definite atonement in his famous "double jeopardy" argument. In his classic work, *The Death of Death in the Death of Christ*, he gives these as the options: "God imposed his wrath due unto, and Christ underwent the pains of hell for, either all the sins of all men, or all the sins of some men, or some sins of all men."[53] If only some sins of all men are atoned for, then none would be saved and thus the third option (Christ died for some sins of all men) is untenable. Of the first option, that Christ died for all the sins of all men, he says this would lead to universal salvation. If Christ died for all the sins of all people, how could God justly judge and send any to hell? Their sins were paid for by Christ's death; to judge the sinner now for his sins would be double jeopardy. The only possible option is the second, that Christ died for all the sins of some men.[54]

Trinitarian Unity

The second major argument for definite atonement has to do with what Wright calls "Trinitarian Unity in Salvation."[55] Michael Horton explains more fully, "*this view displays the cooperation of the Trinity in the one work*

---

[50] Wright, *40 Questions About Calvinism*, 195. He devotes all of question 26 to "Does Substitutionary Atonement Imply Particular Redemption?" 195–201.

[51] Garry Williams, "The Definite Intent of Penal Substitutionary Atonement," in *From Heaven He Came and Sought Her*, 461.

[52] Letham, *The Work of Christ*, 233.

[53] John Owen, *The Death of Death in the Death of Christ*, in *The Works of John Owen*, ed. William H. Goold (Edinburgh: Banner of Truth, 1967), 10:173–74.

[54] J. I. Packer makes almost the same argument in "What Did the Cross Achieve? The Logic of Penal Substitution," in *In My Place Condemned He Stood: Celebrating the Glory of the Atonement*, ed. J. Packer and Mark Dever (Wheaton: Crossway, 2007), 90.

[55] Wright, *40 Questions About Calvinism*, 190.

of redemption, united in purpose and accomplishment."[56] David Gibson and brother Jonathan give the specifics: "the Father elects and sends, the Son becomes incarnate and dies, the Spirit draws and vivifies."[57] Why does this require definite atonement? If Christ dies for all but the Father only elects some and the Spirit only draws some, "a fatal disjunction is introduced . . . the divine persons are cleaved from each other in their saving intentions."[58]

They see this idea of Trinitarian unity in the work of salvation not as a logical deduction but as biblical teaching. Shawn Wright states, "Scripture is replete with the notion that the persons of the Trinity are united in their intention on the cross," citing John 6:37–44 as evidence.[59] From his study of the Pauline epistles, Jonathan Gibson argues that the saving work of God in Christ is both Trinitarian and "indivisible." The different moments of salvation (redemption predestined, redemption accomplished, redemption applied) may be distinct, but they are "integrally connected."[60] Thus to suggest that the moment of redemption predestined includes only some, but the moment of redemption accomplished includes all and the moment of redemption applied includes only some is contrary to how Paul sees the work of God in salvation. Paul allows for distinctions in the moments of salvation, but not "disjunctions" because "the saving work of God is indivisible."[61]

These are the two major arguments for definite atonement: (1) the objective efficacy of Christ's penal substitutionary work on the Christ (he doesn't just make salvation possible; he saves); and (2) the unity of the Trinity in the work of salvation, such that all those elected by the Father are the ones for whom Christ dies, and the ones to whom the Spirit applies the saving benefits of Christ's works.

---

[56] Horton, "Traditional Reformed View," 127. Emphasis in original.

[57] David Gibson and Jonathan Gibson, "Sacred Theology and the Reading of the Divine Word," 49.

[58] Gibson and Gibson.

[59] Wright, *40 Questions About Calvinism*, 181.

[60] Gibson, "The Glorious, Indivisible, Trinitarian Work of God," 334–38. He works initially through Eph 1:3–14, then expands into numerous other Pauline texts to make his case.

[61] Gibson, 345.

Other arguments are cited by some.[62] Most arguments for definite atonement include some mention of the verses that speak of Christ coming to save "his people" (Matt 1:21); laying down his life for his "sheep" (John 10:11) or his "church" (Eph 5:25–27).[63] But Jonathan Gibson wisely acknowledges the limitation of these texts: they "do not *in themselves* rule out Christ making atonement for the non-elect," because "Scripture nowhere states that Christ died for the elect *alone* or for them *only*."[64] So this is not a major argument for definite atonement.

Carl Trueman makes much of the high-priestly role of Christ as grounding the objective efficacy of the cross and making "intentional particularism" the outcome of substitutionary atonement. As high priest, Christ is mediator of a definite group; he intercedes for them and died for them.[65] But Christ as high priest does not exhaust the biblical teaching on the atonement. We can grant that the mediatorial role of Christ as high priest supports a particular intention in the atonement, but we cited ample biblical evidence for a universal intention earlier in this chapter. Thus, like Bruce Demarest, we may see the high-priestly work of Christ as supporting the limited application of the atonement, without seeing it as overturning the biblical teaching on the universal provision.[66]

---

[62] Elwell, "Atonement, Extent of," 100–01, lists eight arguments for what he calls "particular redemption," but most fit under one of the two major arguments in the text.

[63] Trueman, "Definite Atonement View," 24–27; Grudem, *Systematic Theology*, 595; Letham, *The Work of Christ*, 244; and many other older standard Reformed works (such as Berkhof, *Systematic Theology*, 395).

[64] Jonathan Gibson, "For Whom Did Christ Die," in *From Heaven He Came and Sought Her*, 292. Emphasis in original.

[65] See Trueman's discussion of the high-priestly role of Christ and the importance of the Old Testament background for properly understanding the work of Christ in Trueman, "Definite Atonement View," 41–50. He also criticizes other views for their lack of attention to Christ's high-priestly mediatorial role and the need to set it within the OT context. He says this failure is "the major weakness" in the case made by Hammett for the multiple-intentions view and the case made by Grant Osborne for the universal atonement view (Trueman, "Response by Carl R. Trueman" in *Perspectives on the Extent of the Atonement*, 208). Letham, *The Work of Christ*, 236–37, sees the "unity of Christ's high priestly work" as "compatible" with definite atonement but does not claim it requires definite atonement.

[66] Demarest, *The Cross and Salvation*, 192–93.

This then is the case for definite atonement. We believe that these two arguments give strong support to the idea that there is a definite or particular or limited intention in the atonement. We do not think these arguments preclude there also being a universal or unlimited intention in the atonement. The atonement may be understood as involving both provision and application. Is there any reason why the provision could not be universal or unlimited and the application definite? Further, if the plan devised by the Trinity includes both a universal and a definite intention, there can be no breakdown of the unity of the Trinity in accomplishing both intentions, only a fulfilling of the Trinitarian plan.

The Case for a Multiple-Intentions View of the Atonement

The multiple-intentions view agrees with advocates of unlimited atonement that Christ died for all and not just hypothetically for all (as advocates of hypothetical universalism or Amyraldianism affirm).[67] They disagree with the assertion that Christ's death only makes salvation possible for all; it makes salvation definite for some. The multiple-intentions view of the atonement agrees with advocates of definite atonement that Jesus actually saves some; they disagree that this precludes a universal intention to make provision for all. This view believes it can combine the best points of both the unlimited view and the definite view in a non-contradictory way.

The Universal Intention

To begin with the universal intention, the multiple-intentions view thinks there is impressive exegetical support for the idea that Christ died in some sense for "all," or for "the world," and that in the sense of "all without exception." The Johannine verses with "world" as the object of Jesus's atonement (such as 1 John 2:2), Pauline verses stating that Christ died for all (1 Tim 2:6 and 4:10 especially), and the Petrine statement that Christ "bought" some

---

[67] Demarest, 193. The adjective "hypothetical" does not fit the multiple-intention view. God intended to make a universal provision and did so; God intended to make a definite application and did so.

who appear to be outside the elect (2 Pet 2:1) are all difficult for definite atonement advocates to interpret without resorting to "a strained exegesis."[68]

But how can one affirm that Christ died for all without that affirmation leading to universalism, the idea that all are saved? John Owen reasons that if God's intention in sending Christ was to provide a ransom for all people, then either God failed to accomplish his intention, which is to Owen "blasphemous," or all are saved.[69] But this is to ignore the two aspects of the atonement: the provision and the application. This distinction of provision and application is crucial to this view. Provision alone does not save anyone. Calvin himself says the objective accomplishment of atonement on the cross does not save anyone apart from subjective appropriation: "As long as Christ remains outside of us, and we are separated from him, all that he has suffered and done for the salvation of the human race remains useless and of no value to us."[70] Thus, the atonement can make a universal provision without leading to universal salvation. God's honor and righteous wrath can be satisfied; the debt of sin and its penalty can be fully paid, but if sinful hearts still run from Christ and hide in the dark (Rom 3:11; John 3:19), none will be saved.

If one asks, why Christ would make provision for all, knowing that not all will make subjective appropriation, one might make a comparison with universal revelation. God's "eternal power and divine nature" (Rom 1:20) are revealed to all, even though many "by their unrighteousness suppress the truth" (Rom 1:18). Nevertheless, universal revelation is important in that it creates universal accountability: all are "without excuse" (Rom 1:20). In the same way, universal atonement is important, even though not all take advantage of it. Gary Shultz sees the universal intention important in grounding a universal gospel call, in providing a basis for the gift of common grace, in giving the supreme revelation of God's character, and even in creating an additional basis of condemnation.[71] But most of all, and first of all, affirming

---

[68] This is the phrase of Timothy George, himself a defender of definite atonement, in reference to attempts to interpret "all" as "all without distinction." See Timothy George, *Amazing Grace: God's Pursuit, Our Response*, 2nd ed. (Wheaton: Crossway, 2011), 94.

[69] Owen, *Death of Death*, 159.

[70] John Calvin, *Institutes*, 20:537 (3.1.1).

[71] Shultz, "Multi-Intentioned View," 161–203. Shultz calls these "general intentions of the atonement" (161), but it seems to this author they are more results that

God's intention to provide a universal provision for all to be forgiven is important because it seems to be the inescapable teaching of Scripture.

The Particular Intention

We mentioned earlier that most definite atonement advocates don't appeal as much to specific texts as they do to "a larger soteriological framework."[72] They sometimes mention the verses that speak of Christ's dying for a specific group: his "people" (Matt 1:21), his "sheep" (John 10:11) or his "church" (Eph 5:25–27). They acknowledge that these verses don't say Christ died for this specific group alone,[73] so these verses have limited importance for them. However, for advocates of multiple intentions, these verses don't have to say that Christ died for a specific group *alone*; but they may indicate that Christ died for a specific group with a particular or definite intention.[74] Indeed, some of the verses cited seem to go beyond merely a universal provision. In Matt 1:21, Jesus will not just make salvation possible for all, he "will save his people from their sins." Romans 5:9 says "we have now been justified by his blood." Most inclusive is Eph 5:26–27. Jesus did not die merely to make universal provision; he died to make his church "holy" and "to present the church to himself in splendor." This seems to go beyond universal provision, and within a multiple intentions perspective, these verses can have more force. However, the strongest support for a particular intention continues to be the reality of salvation. Jesus doesn't just make our salvation possible; he is called Savior more than twenty times. But as we said above, the universal provision made by the cross in itself does not save anyone. How then does Christ's atonement have a particular or definite application?

Most discussions of application focus on the work of the Spirit in bringing persons to repentance and faith. Thomas McCall says, "whatever

---

flow from the single universal intention to make universal provision. The last of Shultz's "general intentions" ("cosmic triumph over all sin," 203–22) is omitted here, as it is seen by this author as another separate intention.

[72] Gibson, "The Glorious, Indivisible, Trinitarian Work of God in Christ," 332.

[73] Gibson, "For Whom Did Christ Die?," 292.

[74] Demarest, *The Cross and Salvation*, 192 (see chap. 14, n. 1), sees these verses as supporting the limited or particular intention of the atonement, that of limited application.

'objective' and 'efficacious' mean, theologically they do not mean that the process of salvation is complete before a sinner comes to faith or that application by the spirit is 'actual' apart from the work of the Spirit in the life of the believer." On this, he says, "proponents of both definite and general atonement can—and should—agree."[75] On this, proponents of definite atonement do agree. Jonathan Gibson says, "Our salvation is not a 'done deal' at the 'when' of the cross." The moment of "redemption accomplished" is distinct from the moment of "redemption applied," but defenders of definite atonement insist that these different moments are "integrally connected."[76]

But if it is the Spirit who brings about the application of redemption, how is it truly part of the atonement? As the Spirit is the agent in application, some separate application from atonement *per se*.[77] However, most connect the Spirit to the work of the cross. This connection is hinted at in John 7:39, where we are told "the Spirit had not yet been given because Jesus had not yet been glorified." The hour of glorification draws near in John 17:1, as Jesus makes his way toward the cross. In his discussion of the atonement, Kevin Vanhoozer offers this thesis: "The saving significance of Christ's death consists in making possible God's gift of the Holy Spirit."[78] Gary Shultz more categorically states, "Christ secured the salvation of the elect in the atonement by dying for their sin in order then to send the Holy Spirit to apply salvation to the elect."[79] Thus, the particular or definite intention of the cross is accomplished by the work of the Spirit, who only applies salvation to the elect.

But perhaps it is possible to tie the application of the atonement even more tightly to the cross. Earlier chapters examined various models of the nature of the atonement. We saw the models in the objective family as seeing

---

[75] Thomas McCall, "Response by Thomas H. McCall and Grant R. Osborne," in *Perspectives on the Extent of the Atonement*, 69.

[76] Gibson, "The Glorious, Indivisible, Trinitarian Work of God in Christ," 337–38.

[77] A. H. Strong, *Systematic Theology* (Valley Forge, PA: Judson, 1907), 773: "Christ is specially the Savior of those who believe, in that he exerts a special power of his Spirit to procure their acceptance of his salvation. This is not, however, a part of his work of atonement; it is the application of the atonement."

[78] Kevin Vanhoozer, "The Atonement in Postmodernity," in *The Glory of the Atonement*, 398–99.

[79] Shultz, "A Multi-Intentioned View," 226.

atonement as satisfying God's honor or paying the penalty required by righteous wrath or vindicating God's moral governance of the world. All these
objective models seem to correlate with the objective accomplishment of
the cross and the universal intention, to make universal provision. On God's
side, redemption was accomplished. We also looked at a family of models we
called subjective, as they see the atonement as designed to impact us subjectively. One such model is called moral influence. It claims that the cross has
the power to move us. We see the love of Christ displayed in the cross and
we find this love of Christ "compels us" (2 Cor 5:14). Some find they can no
longer live for themselves but "for the one who died for them and was raised"
(v. 15). More succinctly, 1 John 4:19 says, "We love because he first loved us,"
and John sees that love supremely displayed in the cross (1 John 4:10). As the
objective models correlate with the universal intention of the cross, subjective models correlate with the definite intention. The cross makes provision
for all; it draws some (a definite group) to application.

The Cosmic Intention

Some believe that the atonement must include a third, cosmic intention. If
the atonement "is designed to resolve the macroscopic problem of sin and
evil,"[80] a problem clearly cosmic in scope, then the solution must also be "cosmic in scope."[81] In a relatively short but provocative chapter, Adam Johnson
considers the atonement and its relationship to God himself, to the good
angels, to animals, to creation, even to the demons, along with its relationship to humankind.[82] Such an atonement could be fairly described as cosmic.

Something of a cosmic intention seems indicated by the fact that
several New Testament texts point to God's future plans for this cosmos.
Romans 8:19–23 speak of the future redemption or liberation of the created
order. In 2 Cor 5:19, the object of God's reconciling work is "the world."
Admittedly, this could very well mean the world of humans, since humans

---

[80] Scot McKnight, *A Community Called Atonement* (Nashville: Abingdon, 2007), 61.

[81] Adam Johnson, *Atonement: A Guide for the Perplexed* (London: T&T Clark,
2015), 143.

[82] Johnson, 143–73. While including all of humankind as receiving some of "the
benefits of the atonement" (155), Johnson never directly relates his chapter to our
question of the extent of the atonement.

are the ones in need of having God not count their trespasses against them. But Philip Edgcumbe Hughes sees an implication here of cosmic reconciliation: "it is applied in the first place to mankind; but since man, as the crown of God's creation, in his fall brought a curse upon the subordinate realm also, so in man's restoration the whole created order (*cosmos*) will also be restored."[83] This seems confirmed by Paul's statement on reconciliation in Col 1:20. Through Christ, God has reconciled to himself not just people, but "everything . . . whether things on earth or things in heaven." Even the new heavens and new earth of 2 Pet 3:13 are seen by many to be not a new cosmos created *ex nihilo*, but a refinement and renewal of this cosmos.[84] And if the new creation is this creation renewed and restored, then the grandest cosmic intention of all is seen and fulfilled in Rev 21:5: "I am making everything new."

If God has cosmic intentions for this creation which involve the lifting of the curse placed on this creation in Genesis 3 (see Rev 22:3) and the removal of all the marks of sin, are those intentions linked to the cross and resurrection? The association of this intention with reconciliation in 2 Cor 5:19 and Col 1:20 and with redemption in Rom 8:23 suggest that they are. Here we find an appealing symmetry.

We found in the objective models of the atonement a correlation with the universal intention of the atonement. On God's side, all the barriers are down. Universal satisfaction has been made. In the subjective models of the atonement, we have found correlation with the particular intention of the atonement. The cross moves some to a responding love; it draws them to faith and repentance. In addition to the objective and subjective families of models of the atonement, in earlier chapters we considered a family we called the historical models, which have to do with victory over all our foes and enemies (this family often is designated as Christus Victor).[85] Could the cosmic intention of God be correlated with the Christus Victor model of atonement?

---

[83] Philip Edgcumbe Hughes, *Paul's Second Epistle to the Corinthians*, NICNT (Grand Rapids: Eerdmans, 1962), 209.

[84] See Hoekema, *The Bible and the Future*, 280–81 (see chap. 12, n. 40) for arguments for seeing the new creation as this creation renewed.

[85] See the classic book on this model, Gustaf Aulén, *Christus Victor: An Historical Study of the Three Main Types of the Idea of Atonement*.

Some advocates of definite atonement mention this cosmic intention briefly and believe it is included within their view but do not see it as an issue in the debate between universal and definite atonement and thus do not give it any detailed consideration.[86] Gary Shultz sees "the cosmic triumph over all sin" as one of five general (or universal) intentions he sees in the cross. He argues, "The reconciliation of all things to God through Christ's atonement is only possible if Christ's atonement was for all sin, and not just for the sin of the elect."[87] But even Shultz in the end brings in the Christus Victor model as part of his explanation of how the cosmic triumph over sin is made possible.[88]

Since the cosmic intention goes beyond the issue of atonement for elect or for all, it seems better to designate it under neither the universal intention nor under the definite intention, but as a third intention. Within a multiple-intention model there is no need to limit one's thinking to one or even two intentions if Scripture seems to indicate a third. And as there are three main families of models of the nature of the atonement, there seems to be a fitting correlation of models of the nature of the atonement with intentions on the scope of the atonement: the objective models ground the universal intention, the subjective models show how the definite intention is accomplished, and the Christus Victor models fit the cosmic intention.

This is especially fitting in that the Christus Victor model strongly connects the cross and resurrection,[89] and the resurrection seems especially important for the cosmic intention of the atonement. N. T. Wright links the resurrection of creation itself to the resurrection of Christ. He calls the act of

---

[86] Berkhof, *Systematic Theology*, 398–99, sees it as an ancillary element under "the wider bearing of the atonement"; Roger Nicole, *Our Sovereign Saviour* (Ross-shire, UK: Christian Focus, 2002), 58–59, sees it as a benefit of the cross that flows to all and thus not one of the issues in dispute; R. B. Kuiper, *For Whom Did Christ Die?* (Grand Rapids: Eerdmans, 1959), 98, sees this as part of the "cosmic significance" of the cross and part of the "divine design" of the atonement that advocates of definite atonement may affirm but does not explain why. Robert Letham, 233, mentions that Christ's death has "objective cosmic dimensions" but develops this idea more fully in connection with Christ's mediatorial kingship than in connection with the extent of the atonement.

[87] Shultz, "A Multi-Intentioned View," 205.

[88] Shultz, 206.

[89] For more on the resurrection in relation to the atoning work of Christ, see chapter 8 of this book.

new creation, which applies to "the entire cosmos," as "parallel to and derived from the act of new creation when God raised Jesus from the dead."[90]

The details of what it will look like for all things to be reconciled to God are left largely undefined by Scripture, and there are some difficult questions. Does the reconciliation of all things to God include the lost and the fallen angels? With the fate of the lost and the fallen angels described as eternal punishment (see Matt 25:41, 46), their reconciliation does not mean that they are eventually accepted by God; rather, perhaps its meaning is that there is now peace between them and God because they are fully vanquished and no longer able to war against God.[91] There is need for modesty here, but Christopher Wright gives a stirring statement of what the Christus Victor model could mean for the cosmic intention of the atonement. Though we have already cited his statement in an earlier chapter, it bears repeating here. Wright says:

> *Ultimately all that will be there in the new, redeemed creation will be there because of the cross. And conversely, all that will not be there (suffering, tears, sin, sickness, oppression, corruption, decay and death) will not be there because they will have been defeated and destroyed by the cross.* That is the length, breadth, height and depth of God's idea of redemption. It is exceedingly good news. It is the font of all our mission.[92]

Conclusion

While still a minority position, there are three reasons why we support the multiple-intentions view. First and most important, it best incorporates all the biblical data. It allows for a straightforward reading of the universalistic texts, gives full value to the definite atonement texts, and does not overlook the texts indicating a cosmic intention in the atonement.

---

[90] N. T. Wright, *Surprised by Hope: Rethinking Heaven, the Resurrection, and the Mission of the Church* (New York: HarperOne, 2008), 99.

[91] See the provocative but not fully persuasive discussion in Johnson, *Atonement: A Guide for the Perplexed*, 155–58, 166–71.

[92] Christopher Wright, *The Mission of God: Unlocking the Bible's Grand Narrative* (Downers Grove: IVP Academic, 2006), 315. Emphasis in original.

Second, it is more theologically comprehensive than either of the two traditional positions because it includes the best points of both. It can affirm the universal love of God and joyfully proclaim that the debt and penalty of sin has been fully paid because of the universal provision of Christ's atoning cross. It does not lead to universal salvation because the universal intention is limited to provision. But it also can affirm the reality and certainty of the salvation of the elect, because God's Spirit works subjectively in the hearts of some, accomplishing the particular intention of saving a definite number, drawing them to respond to the work done for them by Christ. Furthermore, in adding a cosmic intention, it broadens the scope of salvation beyond that of humanity, looking to the future completion of salvation.

Finally, the multiple-intentions view addresses the objections the two major camps have with each other. Universal atonement advocates think definite atonement contradicts the universal love of God and makes a genuine offer of the gospel to all problematic. But including a universal intention removes those concerns. Definite atonement advocates are concerned that universal atonement makes the salvation won by Christ merely possible or leads to universal salvation. But including a particular intention makes the salvation of the elect certain and because it is particular, universal salvation is not entailed.

Thus, we commend the multiple-intention view with respect to the question of the extent of the atonement.

18

From Resurrection to Return

Introduction

The cross is the focal point of the work of Christ. For that reason, we have devoted several chapters to the important questions of the nature and extent of the atonement. But the cross does not exhaust or conclude the work of Christ. Thus, in previous chapters we have included consideration of Christ's work as the Eternal Word, through whom the world was made; his work as the preincarnate One who was even before his birth with his people in various manifestations; his work in the very act of incarnation; and his work during his earthly ministry. Now we turn to the work of Christ from the time after his death to the time of the end, "when he hands over the kingdom to God the Father, when he abolishes all rule and all authority and all power" (1 Cor 15:24). In the title to this chapter, we mention the resurrection and return of Christ as two major chronological mileposts on the way to the end, but we will begin this chapter with one possible element of Christ's work in the time between his death and resurrection and will conclude with another possible element of Christ's work after his return, depending on one's interpretation of the millennium.

The Work of Christ on Holy Saturday

Where was the soul or spirit of Jesus on Holy Saturday, that day between the crucifixion event of Good Friday and the resurrection event of Easter

Sunday, and did he accomplish any work during that time?[1] His body was in the tomb, but Jesus had said to the thief on the cross, "today you will be with me in paradise" (Luke 23:43), so it would seem that Jesus's soul was in paradise on Holy Saturday. But the Apostles' Creed places the phrase "he descended into hell" between the phrases affirming his death and his resurrection.[2] How could he descend into hell if he was in paradise? Some see this difficulty and frankly advocate removing the descent phrase from the Creed.[3] But in a recent book-length treatment of this issue, Matt Emerson argues strongly that doctrine of the descent was "virtually universally believed" from the second century through the medieval period, that there is substantial biblical support for the descent doctrine, and that evangelicals should be slow to reject the "derivative authority" of the Creed as a statement that has been seen by many generations of believers as "an accurate summary of biblical content."[4]

Part of the problem comes from a simple translation error. The Latin phrase in the Creed, *ad inferos*, means "to the grave, the place of the dead," or *hades*. To get the translation "descended into hell," the Latin would require the words *ad inferno*, "the place of punishment after death" (*Gehenna*), instead of *ad inferos*.[5] A "descent to the place of the dead" seems much less problematic than "a descent into hell." The former seems to fit Acts 2:31; Christ was not abandoned to *hades*. Moreover, if Emerson is right in asking us to see "the place of the dead" as one place consisting of three levels, there is no conflict between Jesus being in "paradise" and in "the place of the dead."[6] Emerson thus gives this interpretation of Christ's descent to the dead. It means Christ

---

[1] While the words "soul" and "spirit" can have differing meanings, both are used in Scripture for the nonmaterial aspect of humans that can survive the death of the body (see Heb 12:23 and Rev 6:9).

[2] Christ "was crucified, dead and buried; he descended into hell; the third day he rose from the dead."

[3] Wayne Grudem, "He Did Not Descend into Hell: A Plea for Following Scripture instead of the Apostles' Creed," *JETS* 34 (1991): 107–12.

[4] Matthew Emerson, *"He Descended to the Dead": An Evangelical Theology of Holy Saturday* (Downers Grove: IVP Academic, 2019), 82, 33–65, 11.

[5] For this translation error, see Bird, *Evangelical Theology*, 433 (see chap. 11, n. 6).

[6] See Emerson, *"He Descended to the Dead,"* 33 (Fig. 2.2). Emerson sees "the place of the dead" as composed of "the place of the righteous dead (paradise or Abraham's

experienced death as all humans do: his body remained in the grave, and his soul remained in the place of the righteous dead. He did not suffer there, but, remaining the incarnate Son, proclaimed the victory procured by his penal substitutionary death to all those in the place of the dead—fallen angels, the unrighteous dead, and the OT saints.[7]

The first part of this explanation, that Christ "experienced death as all humans do," seems well warranted and might even have been envisioned by Christ as part of what it would mean for him to "empty himself" (Phil 2:7) and fully identify with humanity. If so, then even choosing to experience death as all humans do fits under the work of incarnation. But is there some work of Christ unique to Holy Saturday? Emerson's claim that on Holy Saturday, Christ proclaimed his victory to fallen angels and others, seems less well-founded. If so, it would fit better with the work of resurrection, which is the more obvious visual proclamation of victory (1 Cor 15:54: "Death has been swallowed up in victory"). But in fact, the two texts that could be associated with a proclamation of victory—Eph 4:8 and 1 Pet 3:18–19—are better associated with the incarnation (Eph 4:8–9) and the post-resurrection time (1 Pet 3:18–19) than with Holy Saturday.[8]

Thus, the work of Christ on Holy Saturday seems quite limited. In keeping with his commitment to fully identify with humans, he went down to the place of the dead, as all humans do. Unlike them, though, he conquered death, as we see in the work of resurrection. The proclamation of his victory to those in the place of the dead seems less likely to have taken place on Holy Saturday.

---

bosom), "the place of the unrighteous dead (*hades, sheol, gehenna*)," and "the prison for fallen angels (*Tartarus*)."

[7] Emerson, 103.

[8] For Eph 4:8, see Markus Barth, *Ephesians*, AB, vol. 34A (Garden City, NY: Doubleday. 1974), 433–34. He gives six reasons why Eph 4:8–9 should not be seen as supporting the descent to the place of the dead, but rather referring to the incarnation and crucifixion. For 1 Pet 3:18–19, see R. T. France, "Exegesis in Practice: Two Examples," in *New Testament Interpretation: Essays on Principles and Methods*, ed. I. Howard Marshall (Grand Rapids: Eerdmans, 1977), 252–81. France makes a strong case that the time when Jesus went and made proclamation to fallen angels was post-Resurrection and not Holy Saturday.

The Work of Christ in the Resurrection

There is a preliminary question that needs at least a brief consideration before we explore the significance of the work of resurrection. Since "the habitual New Testament form of expression is that the Father raised the Son,"[9] should we even see the resurrection as part of the work of Christ? Is it not more properly the work of the Father? There are three reasons for resisting this conclusion.

The first is the doctrine of inseparable operations, the idea that "the trinitarian persons act as a single agent in the economy, such that each trinitarian person is co-agent in each other's actions."[10] Adonis Vidu thinks the cross, along with incarnation, resurrection, and Pentecost all need "to be integrated into a broader unified (and single) action of the Trinitarian God."[11] Even if the particular work of resurrection is more particularly "appropriated" to one member of the Trinity than the others, it is not the work of that one member exclusively.[12]

Second, even if the resurrection is not seen as fitting under the doctrine of inseparable operations, there is "a strand of New Testament teaching"[13] that sees Jesus's active participation in his resurrection. There is the explicit statement of Jesus in John 10:18, seeing both his death and resurrection as volitional acts of Jesus. Of his life, he says, "I have the right to lay it down, and I have the right to take it up again." Also suggestive are the verses that have Jesus as the subject of the verb "rose" (Acts 10:41; 17:3; 1 Thess 4:14; also John 2:19: "I will raise").

Third, the cross and resurrection are inseparable. They appear together in all three passion predictions in the Synoptic Gospels (Matt 16:21; 17:23;

---

[9] Morris, *The Gospel According to John*, (see chap. 6, n. 17).

[10] Adonis Vidu, "Trinitarian Inseparable Operations and the Incarnation," *Journal of Analytic Theology* 4 (May 2016): 106.

[11] Adonis Vidu, "The Place of the Cross Among the Inseparable Operations of the Trinity," in *Locating Atonement: Explorations in Constructive Dogmatics*, ed. Oliver Crisp and Fred Sanders (Grand Rapids: Zondervan, 2015), 39.

[12] Gregg Allison and Andreas Köstenberger, *The Holy Spirit*, Theology for the People of God, ed. David Dockery, Nathan Finn, and Christopher Morgan (Nashville: B&H Academic, 2020), 283. Allison gives the incarnation as an example: "while having specific reference to the Son, the incarnation is not exclusively his work."

[13] Morris, *Gospel of John*, 513n49.

20:19; parallels in Mark and Luke), both are found in Peter's sermon on the day of Pentecost (Acts 2:23–24), and Paul includes both in his summary of the gospel (1 Cor 15:3–4). Calvin argues that even when only one is explicitly mentioned, both are to be understood as included:

> Whenever mention is made of his death alone, we are to understand at the same time what belongs to his resurrection. Also, the same synecdoche applies to the word "resurrection": whenever it is mentioned separately from death, we are to understand it as including what has to do especially with his death.[14]

Thus the resurrection is as much an integral part of the work of Christ as the cross. The specific significance of that part of his work is our next topic.

There has been surprisingly little scholarly attention given to the theological significance of the resurrection for the work of Christ.[15] What attention has been given to the resurrection has been primarily in arguing for its historical reality as crucial for apologetics.[16] While the present author has found the strong evidence for the historical reality of the resurrection important in grounding his own faith, our concern here is limited to the

---

[14] Calvin, *Institutes*, 1:521 (2.16.13).

[15] Erickson, *Christian Theology*, 709–10, devotes only one page to resurrection in his section on the work of Christ. Grudem, *Systematic Theology*, 614–15, has a chapter on the resurrection following his chapter on the work of Christ, but only two pages are devoted to the doctrinal significance of the resurrection. Bird, *Evangelical Theology*, 435–48, has the most substantive section on the theological significance of the resurrection of any systematic theology text examined. Of books on the work of Christ, Letham, *The Work of Christ*, 220–23, has only three pages, while Peterson, *Salvation Accomplished by the Son*, 117–50 (see chap. 11, n. 2), has by far the fullest treatment. N. T. Wright's 700+ page work, *The Resurrection of the Son of God* (Minneapolis: Fortress, 2003), focuses on the historical reality and biblical teaching on the resurrection, with little consideration of the theological significance of it in relation to the work of Christ. Only W. Ross Hastings, *The Resurrection of Jesus Christ: Exploring Its Theological Significance and Ongoing Relevance* (Grand Rapids: Baker Academic, 2022), addresses the theological significance of the resurrection in a book-length treatment, but this author found a number of his interpretations questionable.

[16] This is the focus of the massive work of N. T. Wright, *The Resurrection of the Son of God*, and that of numerous works by Gary Habermas and Michael Licona, including their joint work, *The Case for the Resurrection of Jesus* (Grand Rapids: Kregel, 2004).

resurrection's importance for the work of Christ. We will consider that importance under five headings.

1. The resurrection vindicates Jesus's identity and is God's seal of approval on the work of the cross. Ross Hastings notes that in the first post-resurrection sermon in Acts 2, "the three declarations that God raised Jesus are in fact all meant as a vindication of the *identity* of Jesus as the One he claimed to be: conqueror of death, Lord of life, Lord and Christ."[17] The fact that he is described as raised by the Father shows the Father's approval and acceptance of his work. All that Jesus had claimed to be and claimed to be able to do has been proven to be true. God had vindicated his claims, because only God's power could effect a resurrection.

2. The resurrection completes the work of salvation. Evangelicals typically focus on the cross and the cross alone, as the place where salvation is accomplished. But Paul pairs being "delivered up for our trespasses," referring to the cross, with "being raised for our justification," referring to the empty tomb (Rom 4:25). Michael Bird sees the resurrection as "the objective grounds of salvation";[18] Robert Peterson says more bluntly, "Christ's resurrection saves."[19] Anthony Thiselton boldly declares, "Without the resurrection of Christ, Christ's death alone has no atoning, redemptive, or liberating effect in relation to human sin."[20]

But how is this so? If the full payment for sin was paid on the cross, what can the resurrection add? Calvin reminds us that all that Christ has done for us brings no benefit to us apart from union with him.[21] Ross Hastings states what is obvious but important: "We can be brought into union only with someone who is alive."[22] No resurrection; no union with Christ. No union with Christ; no salvation. The resurrection of Jesus is essential for salvation.

---

[17] Hastings, *The Resurrection*, 26. Emphasis in original.

[18] Bird, *Evangelical Theology*, 443.

[19] Peterson, *Salvation Accomplished by the Son*, 139.

[20] Anthony Thiselton, *The First Epistle to the Corinthians*, NIGNTC (Grand Rapids: Eerdmans, 2000), 1220.

[21] Calvin, *Institutes*, 1:537 (3.1.1).

[22] Hastings, *The Resurrection of Jesus Christ*, 31.

Another element of salvation is adoption. Paul associates adoption with the redemption of our bodies (Rom 8:23). But the redemption of our bodies is dependent on the resurrection of Jesus's body (1 Cor 15:49; Phil 3:21). The cross alone does not guarantee the redemption of our bodies. That is added by the resurrection of Jesus.

3. Resurrection inaugurates new creation. Death is characteristic of this fallen creation. Creation today is described by Paul as "subjected to futility," in "bondage to decay" and "groaning" (Rom 8:20–22). It awaits liberation and even transformation into a new creation (2 Pet 3:13; Rev 21:1) where God will make all things new. We argued in the previous chapter that the atonement has a cosmic intention, with Paul's statement that God has reconciled "everything to himself . . . by making peace through his blood, shed on the cross" (Col 1:20) as one of the clearest indications. But there is also a cosmic intention in the resurrection. It is found in the language of "firstfruits."

In 1 Cor 15:24, Paul looks forward to a time when every power in the cosmos is under Jesus's authority. N. T. Wright says that in this passage, "Paul is clearly articulating a theology of *new creation*," a new creation that is "parallel to and derived from the act of new creation when God raised Jesus from the dead."[23] This is based on Jesus being the firstfruits, not just of other believers but of all creation. Oliver O'Donovan sees this cosmic renewal as part of the gospel proclaimed by the apostles: "in proclaiming the resurrection of mankind, they proclaimed the renewal of all creation with him."[24] At the same time, we shouldn't jump too quickly over the first application Paul makes of Christ as firstfruits: "Christ, the firstfruits; afterward, at his coming, those who belong to Christ" (1 Cor 15:23). Christ's resurrection guarantees the resurrection of believers, even though it is delayed until Christ's return, when the cosmic renewal then begins to take effect.[25]

Ross Hastings says this connection of resurrection to new creation means that the resurrection, bodily as it was, involves a reaffirmation of

---

[23] Wright, *Surprised by Hope*, 99 (see chap. 17, n. 90).

[24] Oliver O'Donovan, *Resurrection and Moral Order: An Outline for Evangelical Ethics* (Leicester, UK: Inter-Varsity, 1986), 31.

[25] Bird, *Evangelical Theology*, 442. The "trajectory" of God's creative power is Christ first, then church, then creation.

creation, with numerous implications for how we think about science, the arts, embodiment, even the cultural mandate.[26] This leads to a fourth point of significance.

4. Resurrection empowers Christian living and shapes the mission of the church. Michael Bird coins a new word, "anastasity" (from the Greek term for resurrection, *anastasis*), to refer to "experiencing the power of Christ's resurrection flowing into our lives.[27] He sees this "anastasity" as having four implications for Christian living. First, resurrection power is the power of the Christian life. Paul says our union with Christ in his death, symbolized by baptism, is matched by union with Christ in new life, resurrection life: "just as Christ was raised from the dead by the glory of the Father, so we too may walk in newness of life" (Rom 6:4). Our new life is possible only because of the resurrection. Second, the resurrection is our hope in the face of death (2 Cor 4:14). Third, because we are raised with Christ, we are to have a new focus and kingdom perspective (Col 3:1–2). Fourth, the resurrection is the goal that sustains us in losing all things for the sake of Christ and pressing on to know him, even when it means sharing in his sufferings. The goal is to "know the power of his resurrection," and somehow to "reach the resurrection from among the dead" (Phil 3:10–11).[28] The same idea is seen in 1 Corinthians 15. After his longest discussion of the resurrection, Paul draws the conclusion: "Therefore . . . be steadfast, immovable, always excelling in the Lord's work"; the resurrection means we know that our "labor in the Lord is not in vain" (1 Cor 15:58).

What about the claim that the resurrection shapes the mission of the church? Many today see that the mission of the church must be rooted in the mission of God (*missio Dei*).[29] In the words of Christopher Wright, "the

---

[26] Hastings, *The Resurrection of Jesus Christ*, 133–48, 57–58.

[27] Bird, *Evangelical Theology*, 445.

[28] Bird, 445–46.

[29] Craig Ott, "Preface," to *The Mission of the Church: Five Views in Conversation*, ed. Craig Ott (Grand Rapids: Baker Academic, 2016), vii: "Consensus among nearly all branches of Christianity has gradually emerged regarding the missionary nature of the church, which has its source in the very character and acts of the Triune God, in the *missio Dei* (mission of God)." This may be a slight overstatement, as there are

mission of the church flows from the mission of God," which is "the redemption of humanity and the creation of the new heavens and new earth," or "the redemption of the whole creation."[30] But the resurrection of Jesus is the firstfruits of the redemption of the whole creation, as the inauguration of the new creation. N. T. Wright draws this conclusion: "The church is called to a mission of implementing Jesus's resurrection and thereby anticipating the final new creation."[31] Michael Bird makes a similar connection: "The resurrection means that God's new world has broken into our own world." Therefore, the mission of the church is "the task of proclaiming and embodying before the world exactly what this new creation is and what it looks like."[32] Drawing out the specifics of that mission differs from author to author and would take us beyond our specific concerns in this chapter[33] but the mission of the church must be shaped by the revelation of God's mission as seen in the resurrection of Jesus.

5. The resurrection marks the transition from Christ's humiliation to his exaltation. Paul traces something of this transition, marking the low point of his humiliation in Phil 2:8: "death on a cross." The next phrase in Phil 2:9 is "For this reason God highly exalted him," but other texts make clear that the first step in God's exaltation of Christ is the resurrection (Eph 1:20). The exaltation will also include his ascension and entry into his ministry as our great high priest, interceding for us.

---

still some differing views of the mission of the church in evangelicalism. See the differing views of Kevin DeYoung and Greg Gilbert, *What Is the Mission of the Church?* (Wheaton: Crossway, 2011) versus Christopher Wright, *The Mission of God's People: A Biblical Theology of the Church's Mission* (Grand Rapids: Zondervan, 2010).

[30] Christopher Wright, *The Mission of God: Unlocking the Bible's Grand Narrative* (Downers Grove: IVP Academic, 2006), 67.

[31] Wright, *Surprised by Hope*, 212.

[32] Bird, *Evangelical Theology*, 447.

[33] For example, N. T. Wright sees justice, beauty, and evangelism as major categories for the church's mission (*Surprised by Hope*, 213–30); Christopher Wright sees "cultivating the church through evangelism and teaching . . . engaging society through compassion and justice [and] caring for creation" as the three major "domains" of the church's mission. Wright, "Participatory Mission: The Mission of God's People Revealed in the Whole Bible Story," in *Four Views on the Church's Mission*, ed. Jason Sexton (Grand Rapids: Zondervan, 2017), 81.

But the resurrection is not just a marker, it is the necessary prerequisite for the ascension and session. In one sense, this is obvious. He had to be alive to ascend and take his place at the Father's right hand. There are several qualifications for his exaltation as our great high priest that are linked to his resurrection. Hebrews 1:3 teaches that it was only after "making purification for sins [that] he sat down at the right hand of the Majesty on high," and as we have said above, atoning for sins involved both crucifixion and resurrection. Further, it is only "by the power of an indestructible life" (Heb 7:16) that Jesus qualifies for priesthood in the order of Melchizedek, and that life is his resurrected life. Moreover, his ability to remain in office and save "completely" those for whom he intercedes (Heb 7:24–25) is grounded in the fact that he lives forever, as a consequence of resurrection.

These five statements are far from an exhaustive presentation of the significance of the resurrection for the work of Christ, but perhaps they can at least partially fill the gap in theological studies of this topic. We turn now to the next aspect of the work of Christ, the ascension.

The Work of Christ in the Ascension

Though the title of this section includes only the word "ascension," we are using it inclusively to refer to both the event of the ascension itself and all that Christ does as the ascended one.[34] We saw above that the theological significance of the resurrection has been "relatively neglected in evangelical theology"; the neglect of the ascension has been "even more."[35] Patrick Schreiner offers five reasons for this customary neglect, but also gives five additional reasons why it should not be neglected, the two weightiest being that there is far more biblical teaching on the ascension than is commonly realized, and the second being its special importance to our topic, as the

---

[34] Patrick Schreiner, *The Ascension of Christ: Recovering a Neglected Doctrine* (Bellingham, WA: Lexham, 2020), xv: "When I refer to the ascension, I imply the session. When I refer to the session, I imply the ascension." Peterson, *Salvation Accomplished by the Son*, 151–250, prefers to separate the two and has separate chapters on Ascension and Session and additional chapters on Pentecost and Intercession.

[35] Bird, *Evangelical Theology*, 449.

ascension is the "vital hinge on which the work of Christ turns."[36] We will follow the pattern of others in examining the work of Christ in the ascension under the rubric of his threefold office, as prophet, priest, and king.[37]

The Ascension and Christ's Prophetic Work

The primary way that Christ continues his prophetic work as the ascended one is through sending the Holy Spirit upon his church. It is the Gospel of John that first makes clear this connection between the ascension and the sending of the Spirit. In some verses, the Spirit is spoken of as the gift of the Father (John 14:16–17), but more often, the Son is specified as the one actually giving this gift, with John 14:26 saying the Father will send the Spirit in Jesus's name, and John 15:26 saying that the Spirit is sent by Jesus from the Father. John 16:7 gives the necessity of the ascension as prerequisite to the giving of the Spirit: "if I don't go away the Counselor will not come to you. If I go, I will send him to you."[38]

Curiously, the text does not say specifically why it was necessary for Christ to ascend ("go away") for the Spirit to be sent. D. A. Carson says we should not seek for some "unarticulated metaphysical reason"; there is nothing that prevents the Son and Spirit from operating on earth at the same time. Rather, he says, "The thought is eschatological . . . this saving

---

[36] Schreiner, *The Ascension of Christ*, 17. For the five reasons for neglecting and not neglecting the ascension, see 2–17. For the biblical material on the ascension, Schreiner cites 37 verses from seven different New Testament books in which terms like "go up," "go away," "go through," "go into," "to sit," "to be taken up," or "to be exalted" are used in reference to Jesus's ascension. Moreover, there are numerous references to what Jesus does as the ascended one. Peterson, *Salvation Accomplished by the Son*, 183–202, 228–47, cites 16 texts relating to Christ's session, and more than a dozen referring to the intercessory work of Christ.

[37] This is the pattern of Schreiner (see chapters 2, 3, and 4 of his book, on "Ascension of the Prophet . . . Priest . . . [and] King); Peterson, *Salvation Accomplished by the Son*, 203; and Gerrit Dawson, *Jesus Ascended: The Meaning of Christ's Continuing Incarnation* (Phillipsburg, NJ: P & R, 2004), 8.

[38] John 7:39 says the Spirit had not been given, "because Jesus had not been glorified." Peterson, *Salvation Accomplished by the Son*, 158: "Christ's glorification in this verse does not indicate his ascension specifically but speaks of the events surrounding the crucifixion as a whole, including the ascension." For further connection of ascension and glorification, see John 17:5; Acts 3:13.

reign of God cannot be fully inaugurated until Jesus has died, risen from the dead, and been exalted to this Father's right hand."[39] In similar words, G. R. Beasley-Murray says the exaltation of Jesus to the throne of God "brings about the turn of the ages that ushers in the saving sovereignty of God in fullness."[40] At any rate, it is from the Father that Jesus receives the Spirit (Acts 2:33) and then pours it out upon the church on the day of Pentecost. How is this a demonstration of the work of Christ as prophet?

During his earthly ministry, Christ taught the people directly; now, as the ascended Lord, he will continue to teach his people, through the Spirit. Jesus promises that the Spirit "will teach you all things and remind you of everything I have told you" (John 14:26). Indeed, the Spirit "will guide you into all the truth" (John 16:13). These promises would seem to apply in the most direct sense to the apostles,[41] as they would be the ones responsible for teaching the church (Acts 2:42). Through the Scriptures, written by the apostles but inspired by the Spirit, the prophetic work of Jesus is not just continued, but also amplified and multiplied.[42]

The prophetic work of Jesus is also carried out through the Spirit in all God's people. Joel 2:28 says that one of the results of the outpouring of the Spirit would be "Your sons and daughters will prophesy." Not only will they prophesy, they will witness in the power of the Spirit (Acts 1:8). Thus, the prophetic ministry of Jesus continues through the Spirit in his people: "The followers of Jesus become the hands and feet of Jesus as they go out and speak about the Lord Jesus and performs signs and wonders, thus building and growing his church."[43]

In all this, it should be noted that the Spirit is not acting independently; it truly is Jesus, working through the Spirit. He promised in John 14:18 that

---

[39] D. A. Carson, *The Gospel According to John*, PNTC (Grand Rapids: Eerdmans and Leicester, UK: Apollos, 1991), 329, says much the same thing. The Spirit could not be given until the Son had completed his work.

[40] G. R. Beasley-Murray, *John*, WBC, 2nd ed. (Nashville: Thomas Nelson, 1999), 36:280.

[41] Carson, *The Gospel According to John*, 505: "the promise of v. 26 has in view the Spirit's role in the first generation of disciples, not to all subsequent Christians."

[42] Schreiner, *The Ascension of Christ*, 30, 35: "The word becomes Christ's scepter through which his prophetic office continues."

[43] Schreiner, 37. See also Bird, *Evangelical Theology*, 451.

he would not leave his followers as orphans, but would come to them, in the person of the Spirit. The Spirit is sent in Jesus's name (John 14:26); in teaching them all things, the Spirit will remind them of what Jesus had said (John 14:26);[44] in guiding his followers into all truth, Jesus says of the Spirit, "he will not speak on his own," but "will take from what is mine and declare it to you" (John 16:13–14). It is through pouring out the Spirit that Jesus continues his prophetic work.

The Ascension and Christ's Priestly Work

Hebrews 2:17 gives making atonement for his people as one of the duties of a high priest. Evangelical theology typically emphasizes the once-for-all sacrifice of Christ as the all-sufficient atonement for sin, and it is true that no further sacrifice is necessary. But there is another sense in which the cross did not completely accomplish all that is necessary for salvation. I. Howard Marshall says, "The work of atonement was not completed until something had been done in heaven that ratified what had been done on the cross."[45] That "something more" that needed to be done in heaven was the presentation of the sacrifice before the Father.[46]

We want to be careful here. There is no suggestion that the sacrifice of Christ needs to be repeated or supplemented. Even the idea that the ascended Christ presents his blood to the Father to complete the work of atonement has been objected to by some.[47] But Hebrews 9:12 does say that Christ "entered the most holy place once for all time, not by the blood of goats and calves, but by his own blood, having obtained eternal redemption."

---

[44] Morris, *The Gospel According to John*, 657: "the Spirit will not dispense with the teaching of Jesus. The teaching to be recalled is his."

[45] I. Howard Marshall, "Soteriology in Hebrews," in *The Epistle to the Hebrews and Christian Theology*, ed. Richard Bauckham, et al. (Grand Rapids: Eerdmans, 2009), 271.

[46] Peterson, *Salvation Accomplished by the Son*, 176n22; Schreiner, *The Ascension of Christ*, 63.

[47] F. F. Bruce, *The Epistle to the Hebrews*, NICNT (Grand Rapids: Eerdmans, 1964), 201, acknowledges that in the Old Testament it was necessary first for sacrificial blood to be shed in the court and then brought into the Holy of Holies, but he believes that under the New Covenant, "no such division of our Lord's sacrifice into two phases is envisaged."

Robert Peterson is careful to say that this does not mean "that we must envision Christ literally taking his blood before the Father," but it does mean that "the death of Christ on the cross is the means by which he enters the heavenly tabernacle to perform his high priestly work,"[48] which includes the presentation of the sacrifice before the Father.[49] This in no way denigrates the work of the cross, for when Christ presented that sacrifice, he, unlike the priests of the Old Testament, "sat down at the right hand of God" (Heb 10:12). No more offering for sin is needed; Christ's priestly work was "complete, perfect, and utterly effective."[50] But this priestly work could only be completed by the ascended Christ; only he could enter the true tabernacle; only he could then sit down at the right hand of God.

A second crucial aspect of Christ's priestly work as the ascended one is his work of intercession.[51] The verb "intercede" is found twice in the New Testament, Rom 8:34 and Heb 7:25. In Rom 8:34, Paul lists Christ's death, resurrection, ascension and intercession all as grounds for assurance that we will not suffer condemnation. Hebrews 7:25 goes even further, saying that Jesus is able to save us "completely," because "he always lives to intercede for them." Here the completeness of salvation, understood either temporally or qualitatively,[52] is linked not only to Jesus's resurrection and unending life, but also to his intercession. This is far from a casual prayer; it is intimately linked to salvation. What form might this intercession take?

Both F. F. Bruce and Robert Peterson look to Luke 22:31–32 and Jesus's earlier prayer for Peter to answer this question. Bruce says, "If it be asked what form His heavenly intercession takes, what better answer can be given

---

[48] Peterson, *Salvation Accomplished by the Son*, 244.

[49] Both Schreiner (*The Ascension of Christ*, 63–64) and Peterson (243) speak of the presentation of the sacrifice before the Father as part of Christ's priestly work.

[50] Peterson, 204.

[51] Schreiner, 65, sees intercession as the second priestly action of the ascended Christ; Peterson (245) sees the presentation of the sacrifice as the first part of the intercession. In the end, it makes little difference, for what Peterson treats as the second part of intercession is the same topic that Schreiner treats as the intercession itself.

[52] Peterson, *Salvation Accomplished by the Son*, 243n22. The Greek phrase in Heb 7:25, *eis to panteles*, "has been interpreted in two ways: in a temporal sense, 'forever,' and in a qualitative sense, 'completely.'" Peterson opts for the translation "absolutely," which includes both senses.

than that He still does for His People at the right hand of God what He did for Peter on earth?"[53] Peterson goes further to connect Christ's prayers of intercession to assurance of the believer's final perseverance: "In the way that Christ effectively prays for Peter's perseverance because of Satan's attack, he prays continually and effectively for all believers to continue in the faith and arrive at final salvation."[54]

With only two texts explicitly referring to Christ's intercession, it may not be wise to be dogmatic on this point, but the idea that Christ's intercession is his effectual prayers for the final perseverance of his people fits very well with the assurance of freedom from condemnation in Rom 8:34 and the completeness of salvation promised in Heb 7:25, both grounded upon Christ's priestly work of intercession. Again, we are reminded by Heb 7:25 that this priestly work is continual and ongoing; he "always lives" to make such intercession, showing that while seated, this high priest is also active in his ministry (see Heb 8:1–2).

The Ascension and Christ's Kingly Work

Though we come to Christ's kingly work in the ascension last in our discussion here, it is seen by many to be first in importance. Robert Peterson says that while Christ's session pertains to all three of his messianic offices, "it especially pertains to his royal office."[55] Patrick Schreiner is even more emphatic: of the three offices, "kingship is the root metaphor and provides the most momentous implications for Christ's ascension."[56] From his birth to his death, Jesus was proclaimed to be the king of the Jews.[57] In his person and actions the kingdom of God had dawned (Matt 12:28). His miracles showed his kingly power over nature, disease, demons, even death. So what is new or distinctive about Jesus's kingly work as the ascended one?

Schreiner describes it well: "Jesus had to be *installed* as king; he had to be enthroned; he had to be recognized as king; he had to ascend to the

---

[53] Bruce, *Hebrews*, 154–55.
[54] Peterson, *Salvation Accomplished by the Son*, 233.
[55] Peterson, 203.
[56] Schreiner, *The Ascension of Christ*, 76.
[57] See Matt 2:2 and Luke 1:32–33; John 19:19.

right hand of the Father, sit on the throne, and receive from him all dominion and authority."[58] Christ's ascension fulfills all the Old Testament expectation of the true king, a son of David, who would ascend to the throne
(2 Sam 7:16). Christ's ascension is the completion of his exaltation by the
Father (Phil 2:9–11; Eph 1:20–23). His disciples had called Jesus "Lord"
and "Christ" (John 6:68; Matt 16:16), but now by resurrection and ascension, God "has made" Jesus "Lord and Christ" (Acts 2:32–36). The term
"made" does not denote some change in Jesus's nature, such that he is now
something he was not before; rather, "it is God's open avowal that the messianic work has been accomplished and that Jesus now has the full right to
assume the messianic title; that the exaltation of Jesus is the proclamation of
his lordship."[59] Without this "open avowal" and recognition, "Christ's kingly
work is unfinished."[60]

The New Testament makes clear that the rule of Jesus as King is universal. Seated at God's right hand, Jesus is exalted "far above every ruler
and authority, power and dominion, and every title that is given, not only
in this age but in the one to come" (Eph 1:21). It is true that in Col 2:15,
Jesus is spoken of as triumphing over the evil powers by the cross, but in
Eph 1:20 and 1 Pet 3:21–22, the importance of resurrection and ascension
are included. The great New Testament textual critic Bruce Metzger com-
mends the celebration of Ascension Day in the Christian calendar, remind-
ing us that "Christ's ascension is the guarantee that he has triumphed over
the principalities and powers."[61] Without the ascension, a throne in heaven
is unoccupied; the victory is not yet certain. Now that throne is occupied; he
is installed as Lord of all.

Christ's kingly rule over all opposing powers is matched by his rule of
his church. As the one seated at God's right hand, God has appointed Christ
as "head over everything for the church" (Eph 1:22). Jesus had promised that

---

[58] Schreiner, 75. Emphasis in original.

[59] Richard Longenecker, "The Acts of the Apostles," in *EBC*, vol. 9 (Grand
Rapids: Zondervan, 1981), 281.

[60] Schreiner, *The Ascension of Christ*, 90.

[61] Bruce Metzger, "The Meaning of Christ's Ascension," in *Search the Scriptures:
New Testament Studies in Honor of Raymond T. Stamm*, ed. J. M. Myers, O. Reimherr,
and H. N. Bream (Leiden: Brill, 1969), 128. I thank Michael Bird (*Evangelical
Theology*, 459) for alerting me to this reference.

he would build his church (Matt 16:18). That work he began in his earthly ministry; now, as the ascended King, he continues it. It is as the ascended "ruler and Savior" that Jesus grants "repentance . . . and forgiveness of sins" (Acts 5:31) so that lost people may become part of his church. It is as the ascended one (Eph 4:10) that he builds the church by giving them leaders (Eph 4:11–12). It is from the exalted Head that the whole body "grows with growth from God" (Col 2:19).

The Ongoing Work of the Ascended One

Christ continues his threefold work as the Ascended One throughout the entire interadvent era. He continues his prophetic work of speaking to the church by his Spirit through his Word. He continues his priestly work, always living to make intercession for his people. And he continues his kingly work, ruling over all things as Lord of all. But we do not yet see every knee bowing, or every tongue confessing him as Lord (Phil 2:10–11). We do not yet see "those of every people, nation, and language" serving him (Dan 7:14). He has not yet abolished "all rule and all authority and power" with "all his enemies under his feet" (1 Cor 15:24–25). This reality raises the question, to what degree should we expect to see Christ's kingly rule implemented in this age, or is that part of the work of Christ at his return?

There is one school of thought that is very optimistic about the possibility of seeing Christ's kingly rule largely implemented during this age. Kenneth Gentry Jr. gives the following definition for the basic idea of postmillennialism:

> Postmillennialism expects the proclaiming of the Spirit-blessed gospel to win the vast majority of human beings to salvation in the present age. Increasing gospel success will gradually produce a time in history prior to Christ's return in which faith, righteousness, peace, and prosperity will prevail in the affairs of people and of nations.[62]

---

[62] Kenneth Gentry Jr., "Postmillennialism," in *Three Views on the Millennium and Beyond*, ed. Darrell Bock (Grand Rapids: Zondervan, 1999), 13–14. See also Keith Mathison, *Postmillennialism: An Eschatology of Hope* (Phillipsburg, NJ: P & R, 1999).

But representatives of the other major eschatological options (amillennialism and premillennialism) see serious problems with the postmillennialist view. Amillennialist Robert Strimple says that while Christ "gave himself for our sins to rescue us from this evil age" (Gal 1:4), "yet it remains true that the church continues to live in this age, this *present* age, this *evil* age, and will continue to do so until Christ comes again." As a further problem with the postmillennial view, he adds the fact that "Our Lord knows only of two ages, the present age and the age to come," and that suffering is the "characteristic mark" of this age.[63] Premillennialist Craig Blaising critiques Gentry's treatment of key texts. Gentry fails to notice in Matt 13:40 that the wheat and tares are both still present at the end of the age, he fails to deal adequately with the whole biblical theme of the day of the Lord, and has a very poor treatment of Revelation 20. Blaising also adds an observation from the last two thousand years of history. If the kingdom is gradually advancing, "After almost two thousand years, should we not be able to see this progress?"[64]

Postmillennialism is the definite minority view in terms of how much progress we may expect in seeing Christ's universal rule manifested in human history, and in view of the problems pointed out by amillennialists and premillennialists, it deserves to be the minority view. Christ is still active in his prophetic, priestly, and kingly offices from the ascension to the second coming, but there is much that is deferred until the second coming. We now turn to that stage of Christ's work.

Christ's Work in the Second Coming

The second coming of Christ looms prominently throughout the New Testament. Jesus himself repeatedly tells his disciples of his coming again (Matt 25:31; John 14:3); his return is promised from immediately after his ascension (Acts 1:11) to the close of the New Testament (Rev 22:20); it is what believers are to long for (1 Cor 16:22) as their "blessed hope"

---

[63] Robert Strimple, "An Amillennialist Response," in *Three Views on the Millennium and Beyond*, 63–64.

[64] Craig Blaising, "A Premillennial Response," in *Three Views on the Millennium and Beyond*, 75–79.

(Tit 2:13); it is the most often prophesied future event (with scores of references, including some in almost every New Testament book).[65] The obvious question raised by such emphasis on a future event is, why will Jesus return? What more work does he have to do?

One phrase that encompasses much of the work of Christ in his return is the **completion of our salvation**.[66] While it is entirely biblical to speak of salvation in the past tense as an accomplished reality (Eph 2:5, 8: we "have been saved), it is also a present experience (1 Cor 1:18: we are "being saved"); and a future expectation (Rom 5:9, 10: we "will we be saved").[67] This future aspect of salvation is specifically connected to Christ's second coming in Heb 9:28: "Christ . . . will appear a second time, not to bear sin, but to bring salvation to those who are waiting for him."

This completion of our salvation will especially involve our bodies, which will be resurrected, transformed, and glorified (1 Cor 15:51–53). This is specifically described as the work of Christ (Phil 3:21: "he will transform" our bodies "into the likeness of his glorious body, by the power that enables him to subject everything to himself"). But his transforming work will involve more than just our bodies. The transformation of our characters into Christlikeness, which begins with our conversion and progresses as part of our sanctification will be completed when Christ returns and we see him: "when he appears, we shall be like him" (1 John 3:2). We are not told exactly how this change happens. Robert Yarbrough suggests,

---

[65] Some see some of these verses as referring not to the second coming, but to the rapture, which they see as an event preceding the second coming. For more on this debate within eschatology, see Alan Hultberg, ed., *Three Views on the Rapture: Pretribulation, Prewrath, or Posttribulation*, 2nd ed. (Grand Rapids: Zondervan, 2010).

[66] Peterson, *Salvation Accomplished by the Son*, 266–69, lists "seven particular ways in which Christ's second coming saves." The list given in the text differs in some ways from his but was aided by his reflections.

[67] The ESV translates *este sesōsmenoi* in Eph 2:5, 8 as "are saved," but the perfect participle is rendered by most translations as "have been saved" (NIV, ESV, NRSV) to convey the sense of a "completed deed of God." Barth, *Ephesians*, AB, 34:221 (see chap. 13, n. 16). Barth, n. 66, adds, "The perfect tense of 'save' in Eph 2:5, 8 replaces the present, future, or aorist tenses found elsewhere in Pauline literature," citing numerous texts with each tense, but noting, "The future [tense] is preferred by Paul."

"A coming glimpse of Jesus will complete the redemptive work that the incarnation inaugurated."[68]

Some of the most exalted descriptions of what the completion of salvation will involve in all of Scripture are in Rev 7:9–17, 21:3–5, and 22:3–4. It is true that these texts are not directly connected to the return of Christ,[69] but one of the purposes of Christ's return is to take us to be with him (John 14:2–3; 1 Thess 4:17). Without the return of Christ, we could not experience this completion of salvation and no account of the completion of our salvation would be complete without these amazing accounts of what Christ will do for us. For the returned Christ now becomes our shelter and Shepherd (7:15, 17); he dries all our tears and removes all that could cause tears (7:16–17; 21:4); he provides for ultimate healing and the beatific vision (*visio dei*), seen by many as the highest goal of heaven (22:3–4).[70] This is complete salvation.

A second major theme of Christ's work at his return is **the conquest of all his enemies**. This is stated in broad outline in 1 Cor 15:24: "Then comes the end, when he hands over the kingdom to God the Father, when he abolishes all rule and authority and power." More specifically, the conquest is of a figure called "the man of lawlessness" (2 Thess 2:3), or "the beast" (Rev 13:1) or a second beast allied with the first beast and called "the false prophet" (Rev 19:20). Sometimes these figures are referred to as the Antichrist, but that term is used by John for people present in his day, and in a general way for anyone who denies that Jesus is the Christ (1 John 2:18, 22). Whatever term is used, the real power behind all of these figures is the power of the evil one himself, the one called "your adversary" (1 Pet 5:8).

At any rate, when Christ returns, all these figures and forces are vanquished. Speaking of the man of lawlessness, Paul says, "The Lord Jesus will

---

[68] Robert Yarbrough, *1–3 John*, BECNT (Grand Rapids: Baker Academic, 2008), 179. I thank Peterson, *Salvation Accomplished by the Son*, 264, for calling my attention to Yarbrough's statement.

[69] Indeed, on the interpretation of the book of Revelation given by premillennial eschatology, the events of Revelation 21 and 22 are separated from Christ's return by his millennial reign.

[70] See the helpful discussion of the beatific vision in G. C. Berkouwer, *The Return of Christ* (Grand Rapids: Eerdmans, 1972), 359–86, and Michael Allen, *Grounded in Heaven: Recentering Christian Hope and Life on God* (Grand Rapids: Eerdmans, 2018), 59–86.

destroy him with the breath of his mouth and will bring him to nothing at the appearance of his coming" (2 Thess 2:8). Revelation 19 depicts the return of Christ as a rider on a white horse. The beast and the false prophet are captured and thrown into the lake of fire that burns with sulfur; those that followed them "were killed with the sword that came from the mouth of the rider on the horse" (Rev 19:21). Depending on one's eschatology, the devil joins the beast and false prophet in the lake of fire and sulfur, either immediately upon Christ's return or after the millennial kingdom.[71]

One final conquest is of those who are persecuting Christians. Paul promises the Thessalonian Christians that justice will be served: God will repay the ones afflicting them with affliction and give them relief. He says, "This will take place at the revelation of the Lord Jesus from heaven" (2 Thess 1:7). He will take vengeance on them, inflicting upon them "the penalty of eternal destruction" (2 Thess 1:9).

Christ reigns, but there is one last enemy to be destroyed, death. It had been defeated in the resurrection, but now it is to be "abolished" (1 Cor 15:26). This leads to a third theme in the work of Christ at his second coming: **the transformation of all things**. The return of Christ will mean completion and transformation not just for believers, but for the whole cosmos. We are promised a new creation, one in which that final enemy, death, will be abolished. Along with the end of death, in this new creation, there will be no more grief, crying, or pain (Rev 21:4). The scope of this transformation is made clear in Rev 21:5: "Then the one seated on the throne said, 'Look, I am making everything new.'"

The reference to "the one seated on the throne" may cause us to wonder if this new creation is the work of God the Father, or the work of Christ.[72]

---

[71] Premillennialists see an earthly millennial reign intervening between the return of Christ and the casting of the devil into the lake of fire and sulfur; amillennialists and postmillennialists see no such intervening period. See Richard Clouse, ed., *The Meaning of the Millennium: Four Views* (Downers Grove: InterVarsity, 1977) or Darrell Bock, ed., *Three Views on the Millennium and Beyond* (Grand Rapids: Zondervan, 1999) for more on the issue of the millennium.

[72] According to the doctrine of inseparable operations, creation is among the works to be attributed to all three members of the Trinity; new creation would presumably be the same. But as the original creation was the Father creating through the Son and by the Spirit, we are considering now if that may also be true of the new creation.

As Mounce says, "Elsewhere in Revelation the One seated upon the throne is the Father."[73] But the original work of creation was by the Father but "through the Son" (see John 1:3; 1 Cor 8:6; Col 1:16; Heb 1:2); will the new creation be the same? Some think this is implied in the statement of Acts 3:21: "Heaven must receive him [Jesus] until the time of the restoration of all things." F. F. Bruce says the "final inauguration of the new age" is in view here.[74] Anthony Hoekema sees 2 Pet 3:10–13 as teaching "with unmistakable clarity that the Second Coming will be followed at once by the dissolution of the old earth and the creation of the new earth."[75] Premillennialists would disagree with the phrase "at once" in Hoekema's interpretation of 2 Pet 3:10–13, but premillennialist Eckhard Schnabel still sees reason to see the new creation as the work of Christ in his return. He says, "Jesus' return brings about the new heavens and new earth."[76]

This serves as a fitting conclusion to our study of the work of Christ. The One who was the Father's agent in creation in the beginning manifested his concern for his people even before his incarnation, as the "angel of the Lord," the fourth man in the fiery furnace (Dan 3:25), and even the rock from which Moses and the people drank in the wilderness (1 Cor 10:4). His love was most evidently shown in the works of incarnation and crucifixion, and thus we devoted multiple chapters to these focal points of the work of Christ. But his death was not the end of Christ, or of his work for us. In this last chapter, we have traced his work in his resurrection, ascension, and return. We have come full circle. The One through whom all things were made in the beginning is the One through whom we have been healed and through whom all things have been made new. As we gaze upon this awesome work, the only fitting response is for every knee to bow and every tongue confess that Jesus Christ is Lord, to the glory of God the Father!

---

[73] Robert Mounce, *The Book of Revelation*, NICNT (Grand Rapids: Eerdmans, 1977), 364. Mounce cites Rev 4:2, 9; 5:1, 7, 13; 6:16; 7:10, 15; and 19:4 as supporting his claim.

[74] Bruce, *Acts*, 91n36.

[75] Hoekema, *The Bible and the Future*, 185–86 (see chap. 12, n. 40).

[76] Eckhard Schnabel, *40 Questions About the End Times* (Grand Rapids: Kregel Academic, 2011), 250.

CONCLUSION

T hus far, our focus has been on the work of Christ—from Genesis to Revelation, and from Creation to New Creation. In this conclusion, we want to briefly note some of the responses the work of Christ calls for from us.

First, Christ's role as the one through whom God the Father made all things (John 1:3) and the one through whom God will make all things new (Rev 21:5) calls for a comprehensive creation-wide response from God's people. Such a response should take two forms. One would begin by recognizing that if Christ is Creator of all, he must be Lord of all: Lord over every human culture, all human vocations, over "the whole fabric of human existence."[1] As Abraham Kuyper famously said, "There is not a square inch in the whole domain of our human existence over which Christ, who is Sovereign over all, does not cry, 'Mine!'"[2] Thus, the Christian's response must be to proclaim and live out Christ's lordship in every area of life. The second form of response would begin with recognizing that Christ's lordship specifically includes the natural creation, leading to the response of creation care. Sadly, in our day creation care has become a political issue, but in Scripture it is part of the mandate given to humans from the beginning (Gen 1:28; 2:15) and one especially appropriate for Christians in recognition of Christ as Creator.[3]

---

[1] Bruce Ashford, *Every Square Inch: An Introduction to Cultural Engagement for Christians* (Bellingham, WA: Lexham, 2015), 6.

[2] Abraham Kuyper, "Sphere Sovereignty," in *Abraham Kuyper: A Centennial Reader*, ed. James Bratt (Grand Rapids: Eerdmans, 1998), 488.

[3] Christopher Wright, *The Mission of God*, 412–20, especially connects creation care with the mission of the church, and there are an increasing number of books devoted to this topic by Christian theologians. For one recent example, see Douglas

Second, the Nicene Creed describes the work of Christ as "for us and for our salvation." This multifaceted work includes ministering to his people even before his incarnation, as the rock that followed Israel in the wilderness (1 Cor 10:4), identifying with us in his incarnation, life and death, bearing our sin in his crucifixion and conquering our enemies in his resurrection. This multifaceted work has always called forth a multifaceted response, instinctively and irrepressibly from Christian hearts. Exclamations of gratitude burst forth from Paul: "Thanks be to God for his indescribable gift!" (2 Cor 9:15); Peter speaks of rejoicing with an "inexpressible and glorious joy" (1 Pet 1:8); John finds himself moved to love: "We love because he first loved us" (1 John 4:19). Paul says the response called for by "the mercies of God" is the presentation of our entire lives as living sacrifices (Rom 12:1).

The various aspects of Jesus's atoning death inspire a series of different responses. Because Jesus's death atoned for our sin, believers at last find peace with God. We who vainly struggled to satisfy God by our own attempts at goodness renounce that false hope and exclaim, "Nothing in my hand I bring, Simply to thy cross I cling."[4] Sinners wracked with guilt over the gravity and immensity of our sin find relief for our tormented consciences. The gripping conviction that "he laid down his life for us" (1 John 3:16) serves to "reassure our hearts before him whenever our hearts condemn us" (1 John 3:19–20). The full forgiveness provided through the cross alleviates our fear of the wrath of God that we justly deserve. We treasure our new standing before the holy Judge as those who are "holy, faultless, and blameless before him" (Col 1:22) through Jesus's death.

Because Jesus's death was the sacrifice that enacts the new covenant, we can be assured that believers are not only forgiven, but also transformed. As the new covenant promised, God has inscribed his law on our hearts and minds (Jer 31:33; 2 Cor 3:3; Heb 8:10) to compel us from within to do what is pleasing to him (Rom 2:14–15). God has imparted his Spirit to us to cause us to follow his statutes and carefully observe his ordinances (Ezek 36:27). The transformed heart and indwelling Spirit give us new power for holy

---

Moo and Jonathan Moo, *Creation Care: A Biblical Theology of the Natural World* (Grand Rapids: Zondervan, 2018).

[4] Augustus M. Toplady, "Rock of Ages, Cleft for Me."

living. As Augustus Toplady so beautifully penned, the blood which flowed from Jesus's wounded side was "of sin the double cure" since it both saves from wrath and makes us pure.[5]

And because of our union with Christ in his death, we can celebrate a new identity. The old person that we used to be was "crucified with Christ" (Gal 2:20). As a result, we "are no longer enslaved to sin" (Rom 6:6), and sin will no longer rule over us (Rom 6:14). We are no longer the helpless slaves of our old sinful habits since we "have been set free from sin and become enslaved to God" (Rom 6:22). By our participation in Christ's death, we died to the tyranny of sin, the authority of the old covenant, and the influences of a corrupt world (Rom 7:1–6; Gal 6:14). The death of Christ shatters the chains that kept us enslaved to old sinful habits and liberates us to obey "from the heart the pattern of teaching to which you were handed over" (Rom 6:17) and to offer ourselves "as slaves of righteousness, which results in sanctification" (Rom 6:19).

Ambrose of Milan repeated the fable of a young man who abandoned his home because of his love for a prostitute. He eventually repented and returned home. When he later encountered his old lover, he saw her but ignored her. Shocked by his rebuff, she assumed that he did not recognize her. At their next random encounter, the woman identified herself and shouted, "It is I." Yet the repentant man replied, "But I am not the old I."[6] Our co-crucifixion changes our character and our behavior. Through our union with Jesus in his death, we have "put off the old self with its practices" and have "put on the new self" which is being renewed according to the image of our Creator (Col 3:9–10).

Because the death of Christ defeated Satan (John 12:31–32), believers are no longer helpless victims of the tempter (Eph 2:2; Col 2:15). Neither are they defenseless defendants against the accuser (Rev 12:10–11). They do not tremble or cower in the face of death because God, through Jesus's death, destroyed the devil who held the power of death (Heb 2:14–15).

---

[5] Toplady, "Rock of Ages, Cleft for Me." The original lyric was, "Be of sin the double cure, Save me from its guilt and power," which was later adapted to, "Be of sin the double cure, Save from wrath and make me pure."

[6] Ambrose, *Paen.* 2.10 §96.

These responses to the work of Christ in Scripture have been seen also in the similar responses from God's people down through the centuries. Hymnwriters pondering the cross give praise for "amazing grace" and "amazing love," love that "demands my soul, my life, my all."[7] Artists and sculptors have been drawn to it time and again, attempting to depict it visually. John Stott is especially helpful in describing the proper response to the cross as "living under the cross," and fleshes that out by describing cross-shaped relationships "to God, to ourselves, to other people both inside and outside the Christian fellowship, and to the grave problems of violence and suffering."[8] His four chapters are filled with many specific responses; here we will only sketch the major elements.

We respond to the cross by joining in "the community of celebration," by following Jesus's example of self-denial, self-affirmation, and self-sacrificial love, by standing for justice and overcoming evil with good, and by accepting that suffering may be "God's appointed path to sanctification . . . multiplication . . . and glorification," for us as it was for Jesus.[9] Stott boldly says, "I could never myself believe in God, if it were not for the cross." He explains, "He laid aside his immunity to pain. He entered our world of flesh and blood, tears and death. He suffered for us. Our sufferings become more manageable in the light of his."[10] The cross calls forth a response of devotion.

As the completion of Christ's work for our salvation, the resurrection of Christ has also called forth responses. Again, the biblical writers are drawn to worship.[11] According to Michael Bird, that is our proper response, too: "if the resurrection drives us to do anything, surely it must be to worship."[12] It is a worship characterized by boldness and confidence, as these are proper responses to the victory of the resurrection.[13] As with the cross, hymnwriters

---

[7] The phrases cited are from John Newton, "Amazing Grace"; Charles Wesley, "And Can It Be"; and Isaac Watts, "When I Survey the Wondrous Cross."

[8] Stott, *The Cross of Christ*, 255–56 (see chap. 13, n. 11).

[9] These responses are developed more fully in Stott, 255–337.

[10] Stott, 335–36.

[11] See the response of Thomas in John 20:28; that of all the eleven disciples in Matt 28:17.

[12] Bird, *Evangelical Theology*, 447 (see chap. 11, n. 6).

[13] For boldness, see Heb 10:19; for confidence, see Rom 8:37–39.

down through the centuries have responded to the resurrection with songs, but for the resurrection, the songs are those filled with the themes of exultation and victory.[14]

The resurrection also begins the final phase of Christ's work, for it leads to exaltation, ascension, and intercession and makes possible the work associated with his return. What type of response does this part of the work of Christ call for on the part of his people? There is a twofold response. The first depends upon recognizing the resurrection as the sign that "God's new world has broken into our own world." Once we recognize that, we see our response: "we have the task of proclaiming and embodying before the world exactly what this new creation is and what it looks like." We show how it "impacts people when it is worked out in daily life, family life, and community life."[15]

This is true not just of individuals but of the church as a whole. N. T. Wright says, "The church is called to a mission of implementing Jesus's resurrection and thereby anticipating the final new creation."[16] But sometimes that final new creation seems far, far away. That makes even more important the last response engendered by the resurrection and the last phase of Christ's work, the response of an unflagging, energizing hope. Peter calls the hope given to us in the resurrection a "living hope" (1 Pet 1:3), and Paul calls the hope of his return "the blessed hope" (Titus 2:13). The energizing effect of this hope is seen in these words of Paul, which indicates that our response to the work of Christ is one that never ends: "Therefore, my dear brothers and sisters, be steadfast, immovable, always excelling in the Lord's work, because you know that your labor in the Lord is not in vain" (1 Cor 15:58).

---

[14] Almost all the hymns on the resurrection focus on its victory, such as Charles Wesley, "Christ the Lord Is Risen Today," or Gloria and William Gaither, "Because He Lives."

[15] Bird, *Evangelical Theology*, 447.

[16] Wright, *Surprised by Hope*, 212 (see chap. 17, n. 90).

BIBLIOGRAPHY

Abelard, Peter. *Commentary on the Epistle to the Romans.* Translated by Steven R. Cartwright. Fathers of the Church, Mediaeval Continuation 12. Washington, DC: Catholic University of America Press, 2011.

Abelard, Peter and Heloise. *The Letters of Abelard and Heloise.* Translated by Betty Radice. Hammondsworth: Penguin, 1974.

Abernethy, Andrew T., and Gregory Goswell. *God's Messiah in the Old Testament: Expectations of a Coming King.* Grand Rapids: Baker, 2020.

Akin, Daniel L. *1,2,3 John.* New American Commentary. Nashville: B&H, 2001.

———. "Bernard of Clairvaux and the Atonement." Pages 103–28 in *The Church at the Dawn of the 21st Century: Essays in Honor of W. A. Criswell.* Edited by Paige Patterson, John Pretlove, and Luis Pantoja. Dallas: Criswell, 1989.

———. "The Person of Christ." Pages 391–438 in *A Theology for the Church.* Edited by Daniel L. Akin. Revised. Nashville: B&H, 2014.

Alcorn, Randy. *Heaven.* Carol Stream, IL: Tyndale House, 2004.

Alexander, Ralph H. "Ezekiel." Pages 735–996 in *Isaiah, Jeremiah, Lamentations, Ezekiel.* Vol. 6 of *Expositor's Bible Commentary.* Grand Rapids: Zondervan, 1986.

Alexander, T. Desmond. "Further Observations on the Term Seed in Genesis." *TynBul* 48 (1997): 363–67.

———. *The Servant King: The Bible's Portrait of the Messiah.* Vancouver: Regent College, 2003.

Allan, John A. "The 'in Christ' Formula in Ephesians." *NTS* 5 (1958): 54–62.

Allen, David L. *The Atonement: A Biblical, Theological and Historical Study of the Cross of Christ.* Nashville: B&H Academic, 2019.

———. *The Extent of the Atonement: A Historical and Critical Review.* Nashville: B&H, 2016.

Allen, Michael. *Grounded in Heaven: Recentering Christian Hope and Life on God.* Grand Rapids: Eerdmans, 2018.

Allison, Dale. *The New Moses: A Matthean Typology.* Minneapolis: Fortress, 1993.

Allison, Gregg R., and Andreas J. Köstenberger. *The Holy Spirit.* Theology for the People of God. Nashville: B&H, 2020.

Anderson, A. A. *2 Samuel.* Word Biblical Commentary. Nashville: Nelson, 2000.

Anselm. *Anselm: Basic Writings.* Translated by Thomas Williams. Indianapolis: Hackett, 2007.

Archer, Gleason L., trans. *Jerome's Commentary on Daniel.* Grand Rapids: Baker, 1958.

Arndt, William, and F. Wilbur Gingrich. *A Greek-English Lexicon of the New Testament and Other Early Christian Literature.* 4th ed. Chicago: University of Chicago Press, 1957.

A Select Library of Nicene and Post-Nicene Fathers of the Christian Church, Series 2. Edited by Philip Schaff and Henry Wace. 28 vols. Grand Rapids: Eerdmans, 1890–1900.

Augustine. *Sermons on the Liturgical Seasons.* Fathers of the Church 38. Washington, DC: Catholic University of America Press, 1984.

———. *The Trinity.* Translated by Stephen McKenna. Fathers of the Church 45. Washington, DC: Catholic University of America Press, 1963.

Aulén, Gustaf. *Christus Victor: An Historical Study of the Three Main Types of the Idea of the Atonement.* Translated by A. G. Hebert. London: SPCK, 1931.

Bailey, Daniel P. "Jesus as the Mercy Seat: The Semantics and Theology of Paul's Use of Hilasterion in Romans 3:25." PhD diss., University of Cambridge, 1999.

———. "Jesus as the Mercy Seat: The Semantics and Theology of Paul's Use of Hilasterion in Romans 3:25." *TynBul* 51 (2000): 155–58.

Baker, Mark D. "Contextualizing the Scandal of the Cross." Pages 13–36 in *Proclaiming the Scandal of the Cross: Contemporary Images of the Atonement.* Edited by Mark D. Baker. Grand Rapids: Baker, 2006.

Baldwin, Joyce G. *1 and 2 Samuel: An Introduction and Commentary.* Tyndale Old Testament Commentaries. Downers Grove: InterVarsity, 1988.

Bandstra, Andrew. "Interpretation in 1 Cor. 10:1–11." *CTJ* 6 (1971): 5–21.

Barnett, Paul. *The Second Epistle to the Corinthians.* New International Commentary on the New Testament. Grand Rapids: Eerdmans, 1997.

Barrett, C. K. *Acts.* International Critical Commentary. Edinburgh: T&T Clark, 1994.

Barth, Karl. *Church Dogmatics, 1/2.* Edited by G. W. Bromiley and Thomas F. Torrance. Translated by G. T. Thompson and Harold Knight. Edinburgh: T&T Clark, 1956.

Barth, Markus. *Ephesians 1–3.* Anchor Bible. Garden City, NY: Doubleday, 1974.

Bauckham, Richard. *Jude, 2 Peter.* Word Biblical Commentary. Dallas: Word, 1983.

Bauerschmidt, Frederick Christian. *The Essential Summa Theologiae: A Reader and Commentary.* 2nd ed. Grand Rapids: Baker, 2021.

Beale, G. K. *1–2 Thessalonians.* IVP New Testament Commentary. Downers Grove: InterVarsity, 2003.

———. *The Book of Revelation.* New International Commentary Greek Testament Commentary. Grand Rapids: Eerdmans, 1998.

———. *Colossians and Philemon.* Baker Exegetical Commentary on the New Testament. Grand Rapids: Baker, 2019.

————. "The Use of Hosea 11:1 in Matthew 2:15: One More Time." *JETS* 55 (2012): 697–715.

Beasley-Murray, George R. *John*. Word Biblical Commentary. Dallas: Word, 1999.

Bebbington, David W. *Baptists Through the Centuries: A History of a Global People*. Waco, TX: Baylor University Press, 2010.

Belcher, Jr. Richard P. *The Messiah and the Psalms: Preaching Christ from All the Psalms*. Fearn, Scotland: Mentor, 2006.

Belleville, Linda L. *2 Corinthians*. IVP New Testament Commentary. Downers Grove: InterVarsity, 1996.

Bercot, David W., ed. *A Dictionary of Early Christian Beliefs*. Peabody, MA: Hendrickson, 2002.

Bergen, Robert D. *1, 2 Samuel*. New American Commentary. Nashville: B&H, 1996.

Berkhof, Louis. *Systematic Theology*. 4th ed. Grand Rapids: Eerdmans, 1949.

Berkouwer, G. C. *The Return of Christ*. Edited by Martin J. van Elderen. Translated by James van Oosterom. Grand Rapids: Eerdmans, 1972.

————. *The Work of Christ*. Translated by Cornelius Lambregtse. Grand Rapids: Eerdmans, 1965.

Bird, Michael F. *Evangelical Theology: A Biblical and Systematic Introduction*. Grand Rapids: Zondervan, 2020.

Blacketer, Raymond A. "Definite Atonement in Historical Perspective." Pages 304–23 in *The Glory of the Atonement: Biblical, Historical & Practical Perspectives: Essays in Honor of Roger Nicole*. Edited by Charles E. Hill and Frank A. James. Downers Grove: InterVarsity, 2002.

Blaising, Craig A. "A Premillennial Response." Pages 72–80 in *Three Views on the Millennium and Beyond*. Edited by Darrell L. Bock. Grand Rapids: Zondervan, 1999.

Blocher, Henri. "Biblical Metaphors and the Doctrine of the Atonement." *JETS* 47 (2004): 629–45.

Block, Daniel I. *The Book of Ezekiel: Chapters 25–48.* New International Commentary on the Old Testament. Grand Rapids: Eerdmans, 1998.

———. "My Servant David: Ancient Israel's Vision of the Messiah." Pages 17–56 in *Israel's Messiah in the Bible and the Dead Sea Scrolls.* Edited by Richard S. Hess, Carroll R., and M. Daniel. Downers Grove: Baker, 2003.

Bock, Darrell L. *Luke 1:1–9:50.* Baker Exegetical Commentary on the New Testament. Grand Rapids: Baker, 1994.

———. *Luke 9:51–24:53.* Baker Exegetical Commentary on the New Testament. Grand Rapids: Baker, 1996.

———, ed. *Three Views on the Millennium and Beyond.* Grand Rapids: Zondervan, 1999.

Boersma, Hans. *Violence, Hospitality, and the Cross: Reappropriating the Atonement Tradition.* Grand Rapids: Baker, 2004.

Borchert, Gerald L. *John 1–11.* New American Commentary. Nashville: B&H, 1996.

———. *John 12–21.* New American Commentary. Nashville: B&H, 2002.

Boyd, Gregory A., and James K. Beilby, eds. *The Nature of the Atonement: Four Views.* Downers Grove: InterVarsity, 2006.

Bray, Gerald. "The Church Fathers and Their Use of Scripture." Pages 157–74 in *The Trustworthiness of God: Perspectives on the Nature of Scripture.* Edited by Paul Helm and Carl R. Trueman. Grand Rapids: Eerdmans, 2002.

Briggs, Charles A. *Messianic Prophecy: The Prediction of the Fulfillment of Redemption Through the Messiah: A Critical Study of the Messianic Passages of the Old Testament in the Order of Their Development.* New York: Scribner, 1886.

Brink, Gert van den. "Hugo Grotius." Pages 525–26 in *T&T Clark Companion to Atonement.* Edited by Adam J. Johnson. New York: Bloomsbury, 2015.

Brookins, Timothy A., and Bruce W. Longenecker. *1 Corinthians 10–16: A Handbook on the Greek Text.* Baylor Handbook on the Greek New Testament. Waco, TX: Baylor University Press, 2016.

Brower, Jeffrey E., and Kevin Guilfoy, eds. *The Cambridge Companion to Abelard*. Cambridge: Cambridge University Press, 2004.

Brown, Joanne Carlson, and Rebecca Parker. "For God So Loved the World?" Pages 1–30 in *Christianity, Patriarchy, and Abuse: A Feminist Critique*. Edited by Joanne Carlson Brown and Carole R. Bohn. New York: Pilgrim, 1989.

Brown, Raymond E. *The Gospel According to John I–XII*. Vol. 1 of *Anchor Bible*. Garden City, NY: Doubleday, 1966.

Bruce, F. F. *The Book of Acts*. New International Commentary on the New Testament. Grand Rapids: Eerdmans, 1988.

———. *The Epistle to the Hebrews*. New International Commentary on the New Testament. Grand Rapids: Eerdmans, 1964.

———. *Philippians*. San Francisco: Harper & Row, 1983.

Brunner, Emil, and Olive Wyon. *The Mediator: A Study of the Central Doctrine of the Christian Faith*. London: Lutterworth, 1934.

Calvin, John. *Calvin: Institutes of the Christian Religion*. Edited by John T. McNeill. Translated by Ford Lewis Battles. 2 vols. Library of Christian Classics. Philadelphia: Westminster, 1960.

———. *The Gospel According to St. John, Part 1:1–10*. Translated by T. H. L. Parker. Calvin's New Testament Commentaries 4. Grand Rapids: Eerdmans, 1961.

———. *The Gospel According to St. John, Part 2:11–21, and the First Epistle of John*. Translated by T. H. L Parker. Calvin's New Testament Commentaries 5. Grand Rapids: Eerdmans, 1959.

Carpenter, Eugene E. *Ezekiel, Daniel*. Edited by Philip W. Comfort. Cornerstone Biblical Commentary. Carol Stream, IL: Tyndale, 2010.

Carroll, James. *Constantine's Sword: The Church and the Jews: A History*. New York: Houghton Mifflin, 2001.

Carson, D. A. "Atonement in Romans 3:21–26." Pages 119–39 in *The Glory of the Atonement: Biblical, Historical & Practical Perspectives: Essays in*

Honor of Roger Nicole. Edited by Charles E. Hill and Frank A. James. Downers Grove: InterVarsity, 2002.

———. *The Gospel According to John*. Pillar New Testament Commentary. Grand Rapids: Eerdmans, 1991.

———. "Matthew." Pages 1–599 in *Matthew, Mark, Luke*. Vol. 8 of *The Expositor's Bible Commentary*. Grand Rapids: Zondervan, 1984.

Chafer, Lewis Sperry. *Systematic Theology*. Dallas: Dallas Theological Seminary, 1948.

Chalke, Steve. *The Lost Message of Jesus*. Grand Rapids: Zondervan, 2003.

Childs, Brevard S. *Introduction to the Old Testament as Scripture*. Philadelphia: Fortress, 1979.

Christensen, Michael J., and Jeffery A. Wittung, eds. *Partakers of the Divine Nature: The History and Development of Deification in the Christian Traditions*. Grand Rapids: Baker, 2007.

Clements, R. E. "The Messianic Hope in the Old Testament." *JSOT* 43 (1989): 3–19.

Clendenen, E. Ray. *Haggai, Malachi*. New American Commentary. Nashville: B&H, 2004.

———. "Malachi 3:1; 4:1–5: The Messiah as the Messenger of the Lord." Pages 1327–38 in *The Moody Handbook of Messianic Prophecy: Studies and Expositions of the Messiah in the Old Testament*. Edited by Michael Rydelnik and Edwin Blum. Chicago: Moody, 2019.

Clendenin, Daniel B. *Eastern Orthodox Christianity: A Western Perspective*. Grand Rapids: Baker, 2003.

———. "Partakers of Divinity: The Orthodox Doctrine of *Theosis*." *JETS* 37 (1994): 365–79.

Clouse, Robert G. "Grotius, Hugo." Page 675 in *Evangelical Dictionary of Theology*. Edited by Daniel J. Treier and Walter A. Elwell. 3rd ed. Grand Rapids: Baker, 2017.

————, ed. *The Meaning of the Millennium: Four Views*. Downers Grove: InterVarsity, 1977.

Cockerill, Gareth Lee. *The Epistle to the Hebrews*. New International Commentary on the New Testament. Grand Rapids: Eerdmans, 2012.

Cole, Graham A. *Against the Darkness: The Doctrine of Angels, Satan, and Demons*. Foundations of Evangelical Theology. Wheaton: Crossway, 2019.

————. *God the Peacemaker: How Atonement Brings Shalom*. NSBT. Downers Grove: InterVarsity, 2009.

————. *God Who Became Human: A Biblical Theology of Incarnation*. New Studies in Biblical Theology. Downers Grove: InterVarsity, 2013.

Collins, C. J. "A Syntactical Note (Genesis 3:15): Is the Woman's Seed Singular or Plural?" *TynBul* 48 (1997): 139–48.

Cook, John Granger. *Crucifixion in the Mediterranean World*. Wissenschaftliche Untersuchungen Zum Neuen Testament. Tübingen: Mohr Siebeck, 2014.

Cortez, Marc. *Resourcing Theological Anthropology: A Constructive Account of Humanity in the Light of Christ*. Grand Rapids: Zondervan, 2017.

Coxe, A. Cleveland, ed. *St. Augustin: Expositions on the Book of Psalms*. Vol. 8 of *The Nicene and Post-Nicene Fathers* 1. New York: Christian Literature Company, 1888.

Craig, William Lane. *Atonement and the Death of Christ an Exegetical, Historical, and Philosophical Exploration*. Waco, TX: Baylor University Press, 2020.

Cranfield, C. E. B. *A Critical and Exegetical Commentary on the Epistle to the Romans*. Vol. 1 of *International Critical Commentary*. Edinburgh: T&T Clark, 1975.

Crisp, Oliver. *Approaching the Atonement: The Reconciling Work of Christ*. Downers Grove: InterVarsity, 2020.

————. "Did Christ Have a Fallen Human Nature?" *International Journal of Systematic Theology* 6 (2004): 270–88.

————. *Divinity and Humanity: The Incarnation Reconsidered.* Current Issues in Theology. Cambridge: Cambridge University Press, 2007.

————. "Methodological Issues in Approaching the Atonement." Pages 315–34 in *T&T Clark Companion to Atonement.* Edited by Adam J. Johnson. New York: Bloomsbury, 2015.

————. "T. F. Torrance on *Theosis* and Universal Salvation." *SJT* 74 (2021): 12–25.

Davids, Peter H. *A Theology of James, Peter, and Jude: Living in the Light of the Coming King.* Biblical Theology of the New Testament. Grand Rapids: Zondervan, 2014.

Davidson, Ivor J. "Atonement and Incarnation." Pages 35–56 in *T&T Clark Companion to Atonement.* Edited by Adam J. Johnson. New York: Bloomsbury, 2015.

Davis, Stephen T. *Christian Philosophical Theology.* New York: Oxford University Press, 2006.

Dawson, Gerrit S. *Jesus Ascended: The Meaning of Christ's Continuing Incarnation.* Phillipsburg, NJ: P&R, 2004.

Delitzsch, Franz. *Biblical Commentary on the Prophecies of Isaiah.* Translated by James Kennedy. Clark's Foreign Theological Library. Edinburgh: T&T Clark, 1890.

Demarest, Bruce A. *The Cross and Salvation: The Doctrine of God.* Wheaton: Crossway, 1997.

Denhollander, Rachel, and Jacob Denhollander. "Justice: The Foundation of a Christian Approach to Abuse." Paper presented at Evangelical Theological Society. Denver. November 13, 2018. Quoted in Joshua M. McNall. *The Mosaic of Atonement: An Integrated Approach to Christ's Work.* Grand Rapids: Zondervan, 2019.

Denney, James. *The Atonement and the Modern Mind.* New York: Eaton & Mains, 1903.

————. *The Death of Christ.* Edited by R. V. G. Tasker. London: Tyndale, 1951.

DeSilva, David A. *The Letter to the Galatians.* New International Commentary on the Old Testament. Grand Rapids: Eerdmans, 2018.

DeWeese, Garrett. "One Person, Two Natures: Two Metaphysical Models of the Incarnation." Pages 114–53 in *Jesus in Trinitarian Perspective: An Intermediate Christology.* Edited by Fred Sanders and Klaus Issler. Nashville: B&H, 2007.

DeYoung, Kevin, and Greg Gilbert. *What Is the Mission of the Church?: Making Sense of Social Justice, Shalom, and the Great Commission.* Wheaton: Crossway, 2011.

Djaballah, Amar. "Controversy on Universal Grace: A Historical Survey of Moise Amyraut's Brief Traitté de La Predestination." Pages 165–99 in *From Heaven He Came and Sought Her: Definite Atonement in Historical, Biblical, Theological, and Pastoral Perspective.* Edited by David Gibson and Jonathan Gibson. Wheaton: Crossway, 2013.

Dodd, C. H. *According to the Scriptures: The Sub-Structure of New Testament Theology.* New York: Scribner, 1953.

———. *The Epistle of Paul to the Romans.* Moffatt New Testament Commentary. New York: Harper & Row, 1932.

Douty, Norman F. *The Death of Christ: A Treatise Which Considers the Question: "Did Christ Die Only for the Elect?"* Irving, TX: Williams & Watrous, 1978.

Dyrness, William A., and Veli-Matti Kärkkäinen, eds. *Global Dictionary of Theology: A Resource for the Worldwide Church.* Downers Grove: InterVarsity, 2008.

Edwards, James R. *The Gospel According to Mark.* Pillar New Testament Commentary. Grand Rapids: Eerdmans, 2002.

Elliott, John H. *1 Peter.* Anchor Bible 37B. New York: Doubleday, 2000.

Elwell, Walter A. "Atonement, Extent Of." Pages 201–2 in *Evangelical Dictionary of Theology.* Edited by Daniel J. Treier and Walter A. Elwell. 3rd ed. Grand Rapids: Baker, 2017.

Emerson, Matthew Y. *"He Descended to the Dead": An Evangelical Theology of Holy Saturday*. Downers Grove: InterVarsity, 2019.

Erickson, Millard J. *Christian Theology*. 3rd ed. Grand Rapids: Baker, 2013.

Eusebius. *The Proof of the Gospel*. Edited and translated by W. J. Ferrar. Vol. 2. New York: Macmillan, 1920.

Evans, C. Stephen. *Exploring Kenotic Christology: The Self-Emptying of God*. New York: Oxford University Press, 2006.

Evans, Craig. "The Old Testament in the New." Pages 130–45 in *The Face of New Testament Studies: A Survey of Recent Research*. Edited by Scot McKnight and Grant R. Osborne. Grand Rapids: Baker, 2004.

Evans, Mary J. *1 and 2 Samuel*. New International Biblical Commentary on the Old Testament. Peabody, MA: Hendrickson, 2000.

Ezigbo, Victor. "Jesus as God's Communicative and Hermeneutical Act: African Christians on the Person and Significance of Jesus Christ." Pages 133–47 in *Majority World Theology: Christian Doctrine in Global Context*. Edited by Gene L. Green, Stephen T. Pardue, and K. K. Yeo. Downers Grove: InterVarsity, 2020.

Fairweather, Eugene Rathbone. *A Scholastic Miscellany: Anselm to Ockham*. Library of Christian Classics. Philadelphia: Westminster John Knox, 1956.

Fee, Gordon D. *The First Epistle to the Corinthians*. New International Commentary on the New Testament. Grand Rapids: Eerdmans, 1987.

———. *The First Epistle to the Corinthians*. Revised. New International Commentary on the New Testament. Grand Rapids: Eerdmans, 2014.

———. "Paul and the Metaphors for Salvation: Some Reflections on Pauline Soteriology." Pages 43–68 in *The Redemption: An Interdisciplinary Symposium on Christ as Redeemer*. Edited by Stephen T. Davis, Daniel Kendall, and Gerald O'Collins. Oxford: Oxford University Press, 2004.

Fiddes, Paul S. *Past Event and Present Salvation: The Christian Idea of Atonement*. Louisville: Westminster John Knox, 1989.

Fiorenza, Elisabeth Schüssler. *Jesus: Miriam's Child, Sophia's Prophet: Critical Issues in Feminist Christology.* 2nd ed. New York: Bloomsbury, 2015.

France, R. T. "Exegesis in Practice: Two Examples." Pages 252–81 in *New Testament Interpretation: Essays on Principles and Methods.* Edited by I. Howard Marshall. Grand Rapids: Eerdmans, 1977.

———. *The Gospel of Matthew.* New International Commentary on the New Testament. Grand Rapids: Eerdmans, 2007.

———. "The Servant of the Lord in the Teaching of Jesus." *TynBul* 19 (1968): 26–52.

Franke, Chris. *Isaiah 46, 47, and 48: A New Literary-Critical Reading.* Winona Lake, IN: Eisenbrauns, 1994.

Franks, R. S. *The Atonement.* London: Oxford University Press, 1934.

Fryer, N. S. L. "The Meaning and Translation of Ἱλαστήριον in Romans 3:25." *EvQ* 59 (1987): 99–116.

Garland, David E. *1 Corinthians.* Baker Exegetical Commentary on the New Testament. Grand Rapids: Baker, 2003.

———. *2 Corinthians.* New American Commentary. Nashville: B&H, 1999.

Garrett Jr., James Leo. *Systematic Theology: Biblical, Historical, and Evangelical.* Grand Rapids: Eerdmans, 1990.

Gathercole, Simon. *Defending Substitution: An Essay on Atonement in Paul.* Grand Rapids: Baker, 2015.

Gentry Jr., Kenneth L. "Postmillennialism." Pages 11–57 in *Three Views on the Millennium and Beyond.* Edited by Darrell L. Bock. Grand Rapids: Zondervan, 1999.

Gentry, Peter J. "Daniel's Seventy Weeks and the New Exodus." *SBJT* 14 (2010): 26–44.

Gentry, Peter J., and Stephen J. Wellum. *Kingdom Through Covenant: A Biblical-Theological Understanding of the Covenants.* 2nd ed. Wheaton: Crossway, 2018.

George, Timothy. *Galatians*. New American Commentary. Nashville: B&H, 1994.

Gibson, David, and Jonathan Gibson. "Sacred Theology and the Reading of the Divine Word." Pages 33–56 in *From Heaven He Came and Sought Her: Definite Atonement in Historical, Biblical, Theological, and Pastoral Perspective*. Edited by David Gibson and Jonathan Gibson. Wheaton: Crossway, 2013.

Gill, John. *An Exposition of the New Testament from Galatians 2:1 to Revelation 21:21*. Vol. 3 of *Expositions of the New Testament*. London: Mathews and Leigh, 1809.

Goldingay, John, ed. "Old Testament Sacrifice and the Death of Christ." Pages 3–20 in *Atonement Today: A Symposium at St John's College, Nottingham*. London: SPCK, 1995.

Gomes, Alan W. "Socinus." Pages 753–58 in *T&T Clark Companion to Atonement*. Edited by Adam J. Johnson. New York: Bloomsbury, 2015.

Gordon, Robert P. *1 & 2 Samuel*. Exeter: Paternoster, 1986.

Gore, Charles. *The Incarnation of the Son of God*. Bampton Lectures. London: John Murray, 1898.

Gorman, Michael J. *The Death of the Messiah and the Birth of the New Covenant: A (Not So) New Model of the Atonement*. Eugene, OR: Cascade, 2014.

Green, Gene L. *The Letters to the Thessalonians*. Pillar New Testament Commentary. Grand Rapids: Eerdmans, 2002.

Green, Gene L., Stephen T. Pardue, and K. K. Yeo, eds. *Majority World Theology: Christian Doctrine in Global Context*. Downers Grove: InterVarsity, 2020.

Green, Joel B., and Mark D. Baker. *Recovering the Scandal of the Cross: Atonement in New Testament and Contemporary Contexts*. 2nd ed. Carlisle: Paternoster, 2003.

Greggs, Tom. "Christian Universalist View." Pages 197–217 in *Five Views on the Extent of the Atonement*. Edited by Adam J. Johnson. Grand Rapids: Zondervan, 2019.

Grensted, L. W. *A Short History of the Doctrine of the Atonement*. London: Longmans, Green, 1920.

Grotius, Hugo. *A Defence of the Catholic Faith Concerning the Satisfaction of Christ, against Faustus Socinus*. Translated by Frank Hugh Foster. Andover, MA: Draper, 1889.

Grudem, Wayne. "He Did Not Descend into Hell: A Plea for Following Scripture Instead of the Apostles' Creed." *JETS* 34 (1991): 103–13.

———. *Systematic Theology: An Introduction to Biblical Doctrine*. Grand Rapids: Zondervan, 1994.

Guelich, Robert A. *Mark 1–8:26*. Word Biblical Commentary. Dallas: Word, 1989.

Gurtner, Daniel M., John Nolland, and James M. Hamilton Jr., eds. "'The Virgin Will Conceive': Typological Fulfillment in Matthew 1:18–23." *Built Upon the Rock: Studies in the Gospel of Matthew*. Grand Rapids: Eerdmans, 2008.

Guthrie, George H. *2 Corinthians*. Baker Exegetical Commentary on the New Testament. Grand Rapids: Baker, 2015.

Habermas, Gary R., and Michael R. Licona. *The Case for the Resurrection of Jesus*. Grand Rapids: Kregel, 2004.

Hallonsten, Gösta. "*Theosis* in Recent Research: A Renewal of Interest and a Need for Clarity." Pages 281–93 in *Partakers of the Divine Nature: The History and Development of Deification in the Christian Traditions*. Edited by Michael J. Christensen and Jeffery A. Wittung. Grand Rapids: Baker, 2007.

Hamilton, James. "The Skull Crushing Seed of the Woman: Inner-Biblical Interpretation of Genesis 3:15." *SBJT* 10 (2006): 30–54.

Hammett, John S. "Multiple-Intentions View of the Atonement." Pages 143–94 in *Perspectives on the Extent of the Atonement: Three Views*. Edited by Andrew David Naselli and Mark A. Snoeberger. Nashville: B&H, 2015.

Hansen, G. Walter. *The Letter to the Philippians*. Pillar New Testament Commentary. Grand Rapids: Eerdmans, 2009.

Harris, Murray J. *Prepositions and Theology in the Greek New Testament*. Grand Rapids: Zondervan, 2012.

———. *The Second Epistle to the Corinthians*. New International Greek Testament Commentary. Grand Rapids: Eerdmans, 2005.

Hastings, W. Ross. *The Resurrection of Jesus Christ: Exploring Its Theological Significance and Ongoing Relevance*. Grand Rapids: Baker, 2022.

Hick, John. *The Metaphor of God Incarnate: Christology in a Pluralistic Age*. 2nd ed. Louisville: Westminster John Knox, 2005.

Hiestand, Gerald. "Put Pain Like That Beyond My Power." *Beauty, Order, and Mystery: A Christian Vision of Human Sexuality*. Edited by Gerald Hiestand and Todd Wilson. Downers Grove: InterVarsity, 2017.

Hill, Andrew E. *Haggai, Zechariah and Malachi: An Introduction and Commentary*. Tyndale Old Testament Commentaries. Downers Grove: InterVarsity, 2012.

Hill, Benjamin, and Joseph Jedwab. "Atonement and the Concept of Punishment." Pages 139–53 in *Locating Atonement: Explorations in Constructive Dogmatics*. Edited by Oliver Crisp and Fred Sanders. Grand Rapids: Zondervan, 2015.

Hill, Charles E., and Frank A. James, eds. *The Glory of the Atonement: Biblical, Historical & Practical Perspectives: Essays in Honor of Roger Nicole*. Downers Grove: InterVarsity, 2002.

Hill, Robert C. *Didymus the Blind: Commentary on Zechariah*. Fathers of the Church 111. Washington, DC: Catholic University of America Press, 2006.

Hoehner, Harold W. *Ephesians: An Exegetical Commentary*. Grand Rapids: Baker, 2002.

Hoekema, Anthony. *The Bible and the Future*. Grand Rapids: Eerdmans, 1979.

Hofius, Otfried. "The Fourth Servant Song in the New Testament Letters." Pages 163–88 in *The Suffering Servant: Isaiah 53 in Jewish and Christian Sources*. Edited by Bernd Jankowski and Peter Stuhlmacher, Translated by Daniel Bailey. Grand Rapids: Eerdmans, 2004.

Holmes, Stephen R. "Ransomed, Healed, Restored, Forgiven: Evangelical Accounts of the Atonement." Pages 267–92 in *The Atonement Debate: Papers from the London Symposium on the Theology of Atonement*. Edited by Derek Tidball, David Hilborn, and Justin Thacker. Grand Rapids: Zondervan, 2008.

———. *The Wondrous Cross: Atonement and Penal Substitution in the Bible and History*. London: Paternoster, 2007.

Horton, Michael. *Introducing Covenant Theology*. Grand Rapids: Baker, 2009.

House, Paul R. *Daniel: An Introduction and Commentary*. Tyndale Old Testament Commentaries. Downers Grove: InterVarsity, 2018.

———. *Isaiah: A Mentor Commentary*. 2 vols. Fearn, Tain, Ross-Shire, UK: Mentor, 2019.

———. *The Unity of the Twelve*. Journal for the Study of the Old Testament Supplement Series 97. Sheffield: Almond, 1990.

Huey, Jr., F. B. *Jeremiah, Lamentations*. New American Commentary. Nashville: B&H, 1993.

Hugenberger, G. P. "The Servant of the Lord in the 'Servant Songs' of Isaiah: A Second Moses Figure." Pages 105–40 in *The Lord's Anointed: Interpretation of Old Testament Messianic Texts*. Edited by Philip Satterthwaite, Richard Hess, and Gordon Wenham. Carlisle: Paternoster, 1995.

Hughes, Philip Edgcumbe. *Paul's Second Epistle to the Corinthians*. New International Commentary on the New Testament. Grand Rapids: Eerdmans, 1962.

Issler, Klaus. "Jesus' Example: Prototype of the Dependent, Spirit-Filled Life." Pages 189–225 in *Jesus in Trinitarian Perspective: An Intermediate Christology*. Edited by Fred Sanders and Klaus Issler. Nashville: B&H, 2007.

Jeffery, Steve, Michael Ovey, and Andrew Sach. *Pierced for Our Transgressions: Rediscovering the Glory of Penal Substitution*. Wheaton: Crossway, 2007.

Johnson, Adam J. *Atonement: A Guide for the Perplexed*. London: Bloomsbury, 2015.

Johnson, Alan. "Revelation." Pages 397–603 in *Hebrews through Revelation*. Vol. 12 of *Expositor's Bible Commentary*. Grand Rapids: Zondervan, 1981.

Johnson, Eric L. *God & Soul Care: The Therapeutic Resources of the Christian Faith*. Downers Grove: InterVarsity, 2017.

Jones, Paul Dafydd. "The Fury of Love: Calvin on the Atonement." Pages 213–36 in *T&T Clark Companion to Atonement*. Edited by Adam J. Johnson. New York: Bloomsbury, 2015.

Kaiser, Walter C. "Exodus." Pages 285–497 in *Genesis, Exodus, Leviticus, Numbers*. Vol. 1 of *Expositor's Bible Commentary*. Grand Rapids: Zondervan, 1990.

———. *The Messiah in the Old Testament*. Grand Rapids: Zondervan, 1995.

Kaiser, Walter C. et al. *Hard Sayings of the Bible*. Downers Grove: InterVarsity, 1996.

Kapic, Kelly M. "The Son's Assumption of a Human Nature: A Call for Clarity." *International Journal of Systematic Theology* 3 (2006): 154–66.

Keener, Craig S. *The Gospel of John: A Commentary*. Vol. 2. Peabody, MA: Hendrickson, 2003.

Keil, Carl Friedrich, and Franz Delitzsch. *Biblical Commentary on the Old Testament*. Translated by James Martin et al. 25 vols. Edinburgh, 1857–1878. Repr., 10 vols., Peabody, MA: Hendrickson, 1996.

Keller, Timothy. *Center Church: Doing Balanced, Gospel-Centered Ministry in Your City*. Grand Rapids: Zondervan, 2012.

Kellum, L. Scott. *Acts*. Exegetical Guide to the Greek New Testament. Nashville: B&H, 2020.

Kelly, J. N. D. *Early Christian Doctrines*. Revised. New York: HarperSanFrancisco, 1960.

Kerama, Emily J. Choge. *Telling Our Stories: Salvation in the African Context*. Edited by Gene L. Green, Stephen T. Pardue, and K. K. Yeo. Downers Grove: InterVarsity, 2020.

Klein, George L. *Zechariah*. New American Commentary. Nashville: B&H, 2008.

Knight, George W. *The Pastoral Epistles*. New International Greek Testament Commentary. Grand Rapids: Eerdmans, 1992.

Koehler, Ludwig, Walter Baumgartner, and Johann J. Stamm. *The Hebrew and Aramaic Lexicon of the Old Testament*. Translated and edited under the supervision of Mervyn E. J. Richardson. 2 vols. Leiden: Brill, 2001.

Kolb, Robert. "Martin Luther." Pages 613–22 in *T&T Clark Companion to Atonement*. Edited by Adam J. Johnson. New York: Bloomsbury, 2015.

Köstenberger, Andreas J. *A Theology of John's Gospel and Letters*. Biblical Theology of the New Testament. Grand Rapids: Zondervan, 2009.

Köstenberger, Andreas J., L. Scott Kellum, and Charles L. Quarles. *The Cradle, the Cross, and the Crown: An Introduction to the New Testament*. 2nd ed. Nashville: B&H, 2016.

Kotsko, Adam. "Exemplarism." Pages 485–88 in *T&T Clark Companion to Atonement*. Edited by Adam J. Johnson. New York: Bloomsbury, 2015.

Kruse, Colin G. *John: An Introduction and Commentary*. 2nd ed. Tyndale Old Testament Commentaries. Downers Grove: InterVarsity, 2017.

———. *The Letters of John*. Pillar New Testament Commentary. Grand Rapids: Eerdmans, 2020.

Kuiper, R. B. *From Whom Did Christ Die?* Grand Rapids: Eerdmans, 1959.

Ladd, G. E. *Jesus and the Kingdom: The Eschatology of Biblical Realism*. New York: Harper & Row, 1964.

———. *The Presence of the Future: The Eschatology of Biblical Realism*. Grand Rapids: Eerdmans, 1974.

Lalleman, Hetty. *Jeremiah and Lamentations: An Introduction and Commentary*. Tyndale Old Testament Commentaries. Downers Grove: InterVarsity, 2013.

Landgraf, Paul. "The Structure of Hebrews: A Word of Exhortation in Light of the Day of Atonement." Pages 19–27 in *A Cloud of Witnesses: The Theology of Hebrews in Its Ancient Contexts*. Edited by Richard Bauckham et al. The Library of New Testament Studies 387. London: T&T Clark, 2008.

Lane, Tony. "The Wrath of God as an Aspect of the Love of God." Pages 138–67 in *Nothing Greater, Nothing Better: Theological Essays on the Love of God*. Edited by Kevin J. Vanhoozer. Grand Rapids: Eerdmans, 2001.

Lane, William L. *The Gospel According to Mark*. New International Commentary on the New Testament. Grand Rapids: Eerdmans, 1974.

Lanier, Gregory R. "The Curious Case of צמח and ἀνατολή: An Inquiry into Septuagint Translation Patterns." *JBL* 134 (2015): 505–27.

Letham, Robert. *The Work of Christ*. Contours of Christian Theology. Downers Grove: InterVarsity, 1993.

Lincoln, Andrew T. *Ephesians*. Word Biblical Commentary. Dallas: Word, 1980.

Lindars, Barnabas. *The Theology of the Letter to the Hebrews*. Cambridge: Cambridge University Press, 1991.

Longenecker, Richard N. *Galatians*. Word Biblical Commentary. Dallas: Word, 1990.

———. "The Acts of the Apostles." *John and Acts*. Vol. 9 of *Expositor's Bible Commentary*. Grand Rapids: Zondervan, 1981.

Longman III, Tremper. *Daniel*. NIV Application Commentary. Grand Rapids: Zondervan, 1999.

Lucas, Ernest C. *Daniel*. Apollos Old Testament Commentary. Downers Grove: InterVarsity, 2002.

Luther, Martin. *Luther's Works: Lectures on Galatians Chapters 1–4*. Edited by Jaroslav Jan Pelikan. Vol. 26. St. Louis: Concordia, 1963. Quoted in George, Timothy. "The Atonement in Martin Luther's Theology." Pages 263–78 in *The Glory of the Atonement: Biblical, Historical & Practical Perspectives: Essays in Honor of Roger Nicole*. Edited by Charles E. Hill and Frank A. James. Downers Grove: InterVarsity, 2002.

———. *Martin Luther's Basic Theological Writings*. Edited by Timothy F. Lull. Minneapolis: Fortress, 2005.

Lyonnet, Stanislas, and Léopold Sabourin. *Sin, Redemption, and Sacrifice: A Biblical and Patristic Study*. Analecta Biblica. Roma: Pontificio Istituto Biblico, 1971.

Macleod, Donald. *The Person of Christ*. Contours of Christian Theology. Downers Grove: InterVarsity, 1998.

Marshall, I. Howard. "Soteriology in Hebrews." Pages 253–79 in *The Epistle to the Hebrews and Christian Theology*. Edited by Richard Bauckham et al. Grand Rapids: Eerdmans, 2009.

———. *The Epistles of John*. New International Commentary on the New Testament. Grand Rapids: Eerdmans, 1978.

Martin, R. A. "The Earliest Messianic Interpretation of Genesis 3:15." *JBL* 84 (1965): 425–27.

Martin, Ralph P. *2 Corinthians*. 2nd ed. Word Biblical Commentary. Grand Rapids: Zondervan, 2014.

———. *Carmen Christi: Philippians 2:5–11 in Recent Interpretation and in the Setting of Early Christian Worship*. Cambridge: Cambridge University Press, 1967.

Martin, Ralph P., and Gerald F. Hawthorne. *Philippians*. Revised. Word Biblical Commentary. Nashville: Nelson, 2004.

Mathison, Keith A. *Postmillennialism: An Eschatology of Hope*. Phillipsburg, NJ: P&R, 1999.

McCall, Thomas H. *Against God and Nature: The Doctrine of Sin*. Foundations of Evangelical Theology. Wheaton: Crossway, 2019.

McComiskey, Thomas. "Angel of the Lord." Page 54 in *Evangelical Dictionary of Theology*. Edited by Daniel J. Treier and Walter A. Elwell. 3rd ed. Grand Rapids: Baker, 2017.

McConville, J. Gordon. "Messianic Interpretation of the Old Testament in Modern Context." *The Lord's Anointed: Interpretation of Old Testament Messianic Texts*. Edited by Philip Satterthwaite, Richard Hess, and Gordon Wenham. Eugene, OR: Wipf and Stock, 2012.

McDonald, H. D. *The Atonement of the Death of Christ: In Faith, Revelation, and History*. Grand Rapids: Baker, 1985.

McDonough, Sean M. *Christ as Creator Origins of a New Testament Doctrine*. Oxford: Oxford University Press, 2009.

McGrath, Alister E. "The Moral Theory of the Atonement: An Historical and Theological Critique." *SJT* 38 (1985): 205–20.

McIntyre, John. *The Shape of Soteriology*. Edinburgh: T&T Clark, 1992.

McKinley, John E. *Tempted for Us: Theological Models and the Practical Relevance of Christ's Impeccability and Temptation*. Eugene, OR: Wipf & Stock, 2009.

McKnight, Scot. *A Community Called Atonement: Living Theology*. Nashville: Abingdon, 2007.

———. *The Letter to the Colossians*. New International Commentary on the New Testament. Grand Rapids: Eerdmans, 2018.

McNall, Joshua M. *The Mosaic of Atonement: An Integrated Approach to Christ's Work*. Grand Rapids: Zondervan, 2019.

Melick, Richard R. *Philippians, Colossians, Philemon*. New American Commentary. Nashville: B&H, 1991.

Menken, Maarten J. J. "The Textual Form and the Meaning of the Quotation from Zechariah 12:10 in John 19:37." *CBQ* 55 (1993): 494–511.

Merrill, Eugene H. *Deuteronomy*. New American Commentary. Nashville: B&H, 1994.

Metzger, Bruce M. "The Meaning of Christ's Ascension." Pages 118–28 in *Search the Scriptures: New Testament Studies in Honor of Raymond T. Stamm*. Edited by J. M. Myers, O. Reimherr, and H. N. Bream. Leiden: Brill, 1969.

Milgrom, Jacob. *Leviticus 1–16*. Anchor Bible. New York: Doubleday, 1991.

Miller, Stephen R. *Daniel*. New American Commentary. Nashville: B&H, 1994.

Moo, Douglas J. *The Epistle to the Romans*. The New International Commentary on the New Testament. Grand Rapids: Eerdmans, 1996.

———. *Galatians*. Baker Exegetical Commentary on the New Testament. Grand Rapids: Baker, 2013.

———. *The Letters to the Colossians and to Philemon*. Pillar New Testament Commentary. Grand Rapids: Eerdmans, 2008.

———. *The Letter to the Romans*. 2nd ed. New International Commentary on the New Testament. Grand Rapids: Eerdmans, 2018.

———. *A Theology of Paul and His Letters*. Biblical Theology of the New Testament. Grand Rapids: Zondervan, 2021.

Moreland, J. P., and William Lane Craig. *Philosophical Foundations for a Christian Worldview*. Downers Grove: InterVarsity, 2003.

Morgan, Christopher W. *Christian Theology: The Biblical Story and Our Faith*. Nashville: B&H, 2020.

Morris, Leon. *The Apostolic Preaching of the Cross*. Grand Rapids: Eerdmans, 1955.

———. *The Atonement: Its Meaning and Significance*. Downers Grove: InterVarsity, 1983.

———. *The Gospel According to John*. New International Commentary on the New Testament. Grand Rapids: Eerdmans, 1995.

Moulder, W. J. "The Old Testament Background and the Interpretation of Mark x. 45." *NTS* 24 (1977): 120–27.

Mounce, Robert H. *The Book of Revelation*. New International Commentary on the New Testament. Grand Rapids: Eerdmans, 1977.

Mounce, William D. *Pastoral Epistles*. Word Biblical Commentary. Nashville: Nelson, 2000.

Mouw, Richard J. *He Shines in All That's Fair: Culture and Common Grace*. Grand Rapids: Eerdmans, 2001.

Murray, David. *Jesus on Every Page: 10 Simple Ways to Seek and Find Christ in the Old Testament*. Nashville: Nelson, 2020.

Myers, Benjamin. "The Patristic Atonement Model." Pages 71–88 in *Locating Atonement: Explorations in Constructive Dogmatics*. Edited by Oliver Crisp and Fred Sanders. Grand Rapids: Zondervan, 2015.

Neyrey, Jerome H. *2 Peter, Jude*. Anchor Bible 37C. New York: Doubleday, 1993.

Nicole, Roger R. "C. H. Dodd and the Doctrine of Propitiation." *WTJ* 17 (1955): 117–57.

———. "John Calvin's View of the Extent of the Atonement." *WTJ* 47 (1985): 197–225.

———. *Our Sovereign Saviour*. Ross-shire, UK: Christian Focus, 2002.

Nolland, John. *Luke 18:35–24:53*. Word Biblical Commentary. Dallas: Word, 1993.

North, Christopher R. *The Suffering Servant in Deutero-Isaiah: An Historical and Critical Study*. London: Cumberlege, 1956.

O'Brien, Peter. "Colossians." Pages 1260–76 in *New Bible Commentary*. Edited by Gordon J. Wenham, J. A. Motyer, D. A. Carson, and R. T. France. 4th ed. Downers Grove: InterVarsity, 1994.

O'Collins, Gerald. "Redemption: Some Crucial Issues." Pages 1–24 in *The Redemption: An Interdisciplinary Symposium on Christ as Redeemer*. Edited by Stephen T. Davis, Daniel Kendall, and Gerald O'Collins. Oxford: Oxford University Press, 2004.

O'Donovan, Oliver. *Resurrection and Moral Order: An Outline of Evangelical Ethics.* Leicester: InterVarsity, 2018.

Osborne, Grant R. "2 Peter." Pages 273–354 in *James-Revelation.* Cornerstone Biblical Commentary. Carol Stream, IL: Tyndale House, 2011.

———. "General Atonement View." Pages 81–142 in *Perspectives on the Extent of the Atonement: Three Views.* Edited by Andrew David Naselli and Mark A. Snoeberger. Nashville: B&H, 2015.

———. *Revelation.* Baker Exegetical Commentary on the New Testament. Grand Rapids: Baker, 2002.

———. *Romans.* IVP New Testament Commentary. Downers Grove: InterVarsity, 2004.

———. *The Gospel of John.* Cornerstone Biblical Commentary. Carol Stream, IL: Tyndale House, 2007.

Osterhaven, M. E. "Covenant Theology." Pages 215–16 in *Evangelical Dictionary of Theology.* Edited by Daniel J. Treier and Walter A. Elwell. 3rd ed. Grand Rapids: Baker, 2017.

Oswalt, J. N. "New International Dictionary of Old Testament Theology & Exegesis." משח 2:1123–27.

Oswalt, John N. *The Book of Isaiah: Chapters 1–39.* New International Commentary on the Old Testament. Grand Rapids: Eerdmans, 1986.

———. *The Book of Isaiah: Chapters 40–66.* New International Commentary on the Old Testament. Grand Rapids: Eerdmans, 1998.

Ott, Craig, ed. *The Mission of the Church: Five Views in Conversation.* Grand Rapids: Baker, 2016.

Owen, John. *Hebrews.* Crossway Classic Commentaries. Wheaton: Crossway, 1998.

———. *The Death of Death in the Death of Christ.* London: Banner of Truth, 1959.

————. *The Works of John Owen*. Edited by William Gould. Avon, Great Britain: Johnstone & Hunter, 1850–53. 10 vols. Repr., Carlisle, PA: Banner of Truth Trust, 1967.

Packer, J. I. *Knowing God*. Downers Grove: InterVarsity, 1993.

————. "What Did the Cross Achieve? The Logic of Penal Substitution." Pages 53–100 in *In My Place Condemned He Stood: Celebrating the Glory of the Atonement*. Edited by J. I. Packer and Mark E. Dever. Wheaton: Crossway, 2007.

Pannenberg, Wolfhart. *Jesus—God and Man*. Philadelphia: Westminster, 1974.

Paul, Ian. *Revelation: An Introduction and Commentary*. Tyndale Old Testament Commentaries. Downers Grove: InterVarsity, 2018.

Paul, Robert S. *The Atonement and the Sacraments: The Relation of the Atonement to the Sacraments of Baptism and the Lord's Supper*. New York: Abingdon, 1960.

Payne, J. Barton. *The Theology of the Older Testament*. Grand Rapids: Zondervan, 1962.

Peter Lombard. *The Sentences: Book 3: On the Incarnation of the Word*. Translated by Giulio Silano. Medieval Sources in Translation 45. Toronto: Pontifical Institute of Mediaeval Studies, 2008.

Peterson, Anthony. "A New Form-Critical Approach to Zechariah's Crowning of the High Priest Joshua and the Identity of 'Shoot' (Zechariah 6:9–15)." *The Book of the Twelve and the New Form Criticism*. Edited by Mark J. Boda, Michael H. Floyd, and Colin M. Toffelmire. SBL Ancient Near East Monographs 10. Atlanta: SBL, 2015.

Peterson, David. *The Acts of the Apostles*. Pillar New Testament Commentary. Grand Rapids: Eerdmans, 2009.

————. *Where Wrath and Mercy Meet: Proclaiming the Atonement Today: Papers from the Fourth Oak Hill College Annual School of Theology*. Carlisle: Paternoster, 2001.

Peterson, Robert A. *Calvin and the Atonement*. Revised. Fearn, Ross-shire: Mentor, 1999.

———. *Salvation Accomplished by the Son: The Work of Christ*. Wheaton: Crossway, 2012.

Pinson, J. Matthew. *40 Questions About Arminianism*. Grand Rapids: Kregel, 2022.

Piotrowski, Nicholas G. "'I Will Save My People from Their Sins': The Influence of Ezekiel 36:28b-29a; 37:23b on Matthew 1:21." *TynBul* 64 (2013): 33–54.

Piper, John. *Does God Desire All to Be Saved?* Wheaton: Crossway, 2013.

Plantinga Jr., Cornelius. *Not the Way It's Supposed to Be: A Breviary of Sin*. Grand Rapids: Eerdmans, 1995.

Postell, Seth D. "Messianism in the Psalms." Pages 457–76 in *The Moody Handbook of Messianic Prophecy: Studies and Expositions of the Messiah in the Old Testament*. Edited by Michael Rydelnik and Edwin Blum. Chicago: Moody, 2019.

Quarles, Charles L. *A Theology of Matthew: Jesus Revealed as Deliverer, King, and Incarnate Creator*. Phillipsburg, NJ: P&R, 2013.

———. "Lord or Legend: Jesus as the Messianic Son of Man." *JETS* 62 (2019): 103–24.

———. *Matthew*. The Exegetical Guide to the Greek New Testament. Nashville: B&H, 2017.

———. "Matthew 27:52–53: Meaning, Genre, Intertextuality, Theology, and Reception History." *JETS* 59 (2016): 271–86.

———. *Matthew: Evangelical Biblical Theology Commentary*. Evangelical Biblical Theology Commentary. Bellingham, WA: Lexham, 2022.

———. "New Creation: Spirituality According to Jesus." Pages 79–106 in *Biblical Spirituality: God's Holiness and Our Spirituality*. Edited by Christopher W. Morgan. Wheaton: Crossway, 2019.

————. "'Out of Egypt I Called My Son': Intertextuality and Metalepsis in Matthew 2:15." *STR* 8 (2017): 3–19.

————. *Sermon on the Mount: Restoring Christ's Message to the Modern Church.* NAC Studies in Bible & Theology. Nashville: B&H, 2011.

Rad, Gerhard von. *Old Testament Theology.* Translated by D. M. G. Stalker. 2 vols. New York: Harper & Row, 1962.

————. *The Message of the Prophets.* Translated by D. G. M. Stalker. New York: Harper & Row, 1965.

Rashdall, Hastings. *The Idea of Atonement in Christian Theology.* London: Macmillan, 1925.

Ray, Darby Kathleen. *Deceiving the Devil: Atonement, Abuse, and Ransom.* Cleveland: Pilgrim, 1998.

Rendtorff, Rolf. *The Canonical Hebrew Bible: A Theology of the Old Testament.* Translated by David Orton. Tools for Biblical Study Series 7. Leiden: Deo, 2011.

Richards, E. Randolph, and Brandon J. O'Brien. *Misreading Scripture with Western Eyes: Removing Cultural Blinders to Better Understand the Bible.* Downers Grove: InterVarsity, 2012.

Rico, Christophe, and Peter J. Gentry. *The Mother of the Infant King, Isaiah 7:14: 'almâ and Parthenos in the World of the Bible, a Linguistic Perspective.* Eugene, OR: Wipf & Stock, 2020.

Ritschl, Albrecht. *The Christian Doctrine of Justification and Reconciliation: The Positive Development of the Doctrine.* Edited by H. R. Mackintosh and A. B. Macaulay. Edinburgh: Clark, 1990.

Rooker, Mark F. *Leviticus.* New American Commentary. Nashville: B&H, 2000.

Rosenberg, A. J., trans. *Mikraoth Gedoloth: The Twelve Prophets.* New York: Judaica, 1996.

Rosner, Brian S., and Roy E. Ciampa. *First Letter to the Corinthians.* Pillar New Testament Commentary. Grand Rapids: Eerdmans, 2010.

Ruether, Rosemary Radford. *Sexism and God-Talk: Toward a Feminist Theology.* Boston: Beacon, 1983.

Rutledge, Fleming. *The Crucifixion: Understanding the Death of Jesus Christ.* Grand Rapids: Eerdmans, 2015.

Rydelnik, Michael. *The Messianic Hope: Is the Hebrew Bible Really Messianic?* NAC Studies in Bible & Theology. Nashville: B&H, 2010.

Rydelnik, Michael, and Edwin Blum, eds. *The Moody Handbook of Messianic Prophecy: Studies and Expositions of the Messiah in the Old Testament.* Chicago: Moody, 2019.

Ryrie, Charles. *Dispensationalism Today.* Chicago: Moody, 1965.

Sailhamer, John H. *The Meaning of the Pentateuch: Revelation, Composition and Interpretation.* Downers Grove: InterVarsity, 2009.

———. *The Pentateuch as Narrative: A Biblical-Theological Commentary.* Grand Rapids: Zondervan, 1992.

Sanderegger, Katherine. "Anselmian Atonement." Pages 175–94 in *T&T Clark Companion to Atonement.* Edited by Adam J. Johnson. New York: Bloomsbury, 2015.

Schemm, Jr., Peter. "The Agents of God: Angels." Pages 249–82 in *A Theology for the Church.* Edited by Daniel L. Akin. Revised. Nashville: B&H, 2014.

Scherman, *Isaiah: The Later Prophets with a Commentary Anthologized from the Rabbinic Writings.* Milstein Edition. New York: Mesorah, 2013. Quoted in J. Randall Price, "Isaiah 2:2–4/Micah 4:1–5: The Restoration of Israel in the Messianic Age." Pages 785–802 in *The Moody Handbook of Messianic Prophecy: Studies and Expositions of the Messiah in the Old Testament.* Edited by Michael Rydelnik and Edwin Blum. Chicago: Moody, 2019.

Schmiechen, Peter. *Saving Power: Theories of Atonement and Forms of the Church.* Grand Rapids: Eerdmans, 2005.

Schnabel, Eckhard J. *40 Questions About the End Times.* Grand Rapids: Kregel, 2011.

Schnackenburg, Rudolf. *The Gospel According to St. John.* Edited by J. Massingberd Ford and Kevin Smyth. Translated by Kevin Smyth. Vol. 1. New York: Herder and Herder, 1968.

Schreiner, Patrick. *Ascension of Christ: Recovering a Neglected Doctrine.* Bellingham, WA: Lexham, 2020.

Schreiner, Thomas R. *1, 2 Peter, Jude.* New American Commentary. Nashville: B&H, 2003.

———. *Hebrews.* Evangelical Biblical Theology Commentary. Bellingham, WA: Lexham, 2020.

———. *1 Corinthians: An Introduction and Commentary.* Tyndale Old Testament Commentaries. Downers Grove: InterVarsity, 2018.

———. *Paul, Apostle of God's Glory in Christ: A Pauline Theology.* 2nd ed. Downers Grove: InterVarsity, 2020.

———. *Romans.* Baker Exegetical Commentary on the New Testament. Grand Rapids: Baker, 1998.

———. *Romans.* 2nd ed. Baker Exegetical Commentary on the New Testament. Grand Rapids: Baker, 2018.

Scobie, Charles H. H. *The Ways of Our God: An Approach to Biblical Theology.* Grand Rapids: Eerdmans, 2003.

Seifrid, Mark A. *The Second Letter to the Corinthians.* Pillar New Testament Commentary. Grand Rapids: Eerdmans, 2014.

Selman, Martin J. "Messianic Mysteries." Pages 281–301 in *The Lord's Anointed: Interpretation of Old Testament Messianic Texts.* Edited by Philip Satterthwaite, Richard Hess, and Gordon Wenham. Carlisle: Paternoster, 1995.

Shepherd, Michael B. *A Commentary on the Book of the Twelve: The Minor Prophets.* Kregel Exegetical Library. Grand Rapids: Kregel, 2018.

———. *Daniel in the Context of the Hebrew Bible.* Studies in Biblical Literature 123. New York: Peter Lang, 2009.

Shultz, Jr., Gary L. "A Biblical and Theological Defense of a Multi-Intentioned View of the Extent of the Atonement." PhD diss., The Southern Baptist Theological Seminary, 2008.

Smith, Gary V. *Isaiah 1–39*. New American Commentary. Nashville: B&H, 2007.

———. *Isaiah 40–66*. New American Commentary. Nashville: B&H, 2009.

Smothers, Thomas G. *Jeremiah 26–52*. Word Biblical Commentary. Dallas: Word, 1995.

Sprinkle, Preston M. *Embodied Transgender Identities, the Church, and What the Bible Has to Say*. Colorado Springs: David C. Cook, 2021.

Stein, Robert H. *Jesus the Messiah: A Survey of the Life of Christ*. Downers Grove: InterVarsity, 1996.

———. *Luke*. New American Commentary. Nashville: B&H, 1992.

———. *Mark*. Baker Exegetical Commentary on the New Testament. Grand Rapids: Baker, 2008.

———. *The Method and the Message of Jesus' Teachings*. Philadelphia: Westminster, 1978.

Steinmann, Andrew E. *Daniel*. Concordia Commentary. St. Louis: Concordia, 2008.

———. *Genesis: An Introduction and Commentary*. Tyndale Old Testament Commentaries. Downers Grove: InterVarsity, 2019.

Stott, John. *The Cross of Christ*. Downers Grove: InterVarsity, 1986.

Strimple, Robert B. "An Amillennialist Response." Pages 58–71 in *Three Views on the Millennium and Beyond*. Edited by Darrell L. Bock. Grand Rapids: Zondervan, 1999.

Strong, A. H. *Systematic Theology*. Valley Forge, PA: Judson, 1907.

Stump, Eleonore. *Atonement*. Oxford: Oxford University Press, 2018.

Suggit, John N., trans. *Oecumenius: Commentary on the Apocalypse.* Fathers of the Church 112. Washington, DC: Catholic University of America Press, 2006.

Talbott, Thomas. "A Case for Christian Universalism." Pages 3–54 in *Universal Salvation?: The Current Debate.* Edited by Robin A. Parry and Christopher H. Partridge. Grand Rapids: Eerdmans, 2003.

Tanner, Kathryn. *Christ the Key.* Cambridge: Cambridge University Press, 2010.

Tasker, R. V. G. *The Second Epistle of Paul to the Corinthians: An Introduction and Commentary.* Tyndale Old Testament Commentaries. Grand Rapids: Eerdmans, 1958.

Tennent, Timothy C. *For the Body: Recovering a Theology of Gender, Sexuality, and the Human Body.* Grand Rapids: Zondervan, 2020.

———. *Theology in the Context of World Christianity: How the Global Church Is Influencing the Way We Think about and Discuss Theology.* Grand Rapids: Zondervan, 2007.

The Ante-Nicene Fathers. Edited by Alexander Roberts and James Donaldson. 1885–1887. 10 vols. Repr., Peabody, MA: Hendrickson, 1994.

The Nicene and Post-Nicene Fathers, Series 1. Edited by Philip Schaff. 1886–1889. 14 vols. Repr., Peabody, MA: Hendrickson, 1994.

Thiselton, Anthony C. *The First Epistle to the Corinthians.* New International Greek Testament Commentary. Grand Rapids: Eerdmans, 2000.

Thompson, J. A. *The Book of Jeremiah.* New International Commentary on the Old Testament. Grand Rapids: Eerdmans, 1980.

Thompson, John. *Deuteronomy.* Tyndale Old Testament Commentaries. Downers Grove: InterVarsity, 1974.

Thomson, C. J. "The 'Seven Eyes' of Zech 3:9 and the Meaning of the Dual Form." *VT* 62 (2012): 115–28.

Tonry, Michael, ed. *Retributivism Has a Past: Has It a Future?* Studies in Penal Theory and Philosophy. Oxford: Oxford University Press, 2011.

Torrance, Thomas F. *Atonement: The Person and Work of Christ.* Edited by Robert T. Walker. Downers Grove: InterVarsity, 2009.

———. *Incarnation: The Person and Life of Christ.* Edited by Robert T. Walker. Milton Keynes, UK: Paternoster, 2008.

———. "Justification: Its Radical Nature and Place in Reformed Doctrine and Life." *SJT* 13 (1960): 225–46.

———. *The Trinitarian Faith: The Evangelical Theology of the Ancient Catholic Church.* Edinburgh: T&T Clark, 1988.

Towner, Philip H. *The Letters to Timothy and Titus.* New International Commentary on the New Testament. Grand Rapids: Eerdmans, 2006.

Travis Stephen H. *Christ and the Judgement of God: Divine Retribution in the New Testament.* Basingstoke: Marshall, Morgan & Scott, 1986.

Treat, Jeremy R. *The Crucified King: Atonement and Kingdom in Biblical and Systematic Theology.* Grand Rapids: Zondervan, 2014.

VanderKam, James, and Peter Flint. *The Meaning of the Dead Sea Scrolls: Their Significance for Understanding the Bible, Judaism, Jesus, and Christianity.* San Francisco: Harper, 2002.

Vanhoozer, Kevin J. "Atonement." Pages 175–202 in *Mapping Modern Theology: A Thematic and Historical Introduction.* Edited by Kelly M. Kapic and Bruce L. McCormack. Grand Rapids: Baker, 2012.

———. "The Atonement in Postmodernity: Guilt, Goats and Gifts." Pages 367–404 in *The Glory of the Atonement: Biblical, Historical & Practical Perspectives: Essays in Honor of Roger Nicole.* Edited by Charles E. Hill and Frank A. James. Downers Grove: InterVarsity, 2002.

Vidu, Adonis. "The Place of the Cross Among the Inseparable Operations of the Trinity." Pages 21–42 in *Locating Atonement: Explorations in Constructive Dogmatics.* Edited by Oliver Crisp and Fred Sanders. Grand Rapids: Zondervan, 2015.

———. *The Same God Who Works All Things: Inseparable Operations in Trinitarian Theology.* Grand Rapids: Eerdmans, 2020.

———. "Trinitarian Inseparable Operations and the Incarnation." *Journal of Analytic Theology* 4 (2016): 106–27.

Wallace, Ronald S. *The Message of Daniel: The Lord Is King*. Bible Speaks Today. Downers Grove: InterVarsity, 1979.

Ware, Bruce A. *The Man Christ Jesus: Theological Reflections on the Humanity of Christ*. Wheaton: Crossway, 2013.

Watts, John D. W. *Isaiah 1–33*. Waco, TX: Word Books, 1985.

Weaver, J. Denny. *The Nonviolent Atonement*. Grand Rapids: Eerdmans, 2001.

Wegner, Paul. "A Reexamination of Isaiah IX 1–6." *VT* 42 (1992): 103–12.

Weima, Jeffrey A. D. *1–2 Thessalonians*. Baker Exegetical Commentary on the New Testament. Grand Rapids: Baker, 2014.

Weingart, Richard E. *The Logic of Divine Love: A Critical Analysis of the Soteriology of Peter Abailard*. Oxford: Clarendon, 1970.

Wells, David F. *The Person of Christ: A Biblical and Historical Analysis of the Incarnation*. Westchester, IL: Crossway, 1984.

Wellum, Stephen J. *God the Son Incarnate: The Doctrine of Christ*. Foundations of Evangelical Theology. Wheaton: Crossway, 2016.

Wenham, Gordon J. *Numbers*. Tyndale Old Testament Commentaries. Downers Grove: InterVarsity, 1981.

———. "The Theology of Old Testament Sacrifice." Pages 75–87 in *Sacrifice in the Bible*. Edited by Roger Beckwith and Martin Selman. Grand Rapids: Baker, 1995.

Westcott, B. F. *The Epistle to the Hebrews: The Greek Text with Notes and Essays*. 3rd ed. London: Macmillan, 1903.

White, Mark D. *Retributivism: Essays on Theory and Policy*. Oxford: Oxford University Press, 2011.

Williams, Garry J. "A Critical Exposition of Hugo Grotius's Doctrine of the Atonement in De Satisfactione Christi." PhD diss., University of Oxford, 1999.

———. "Penal Substitution: A Response to Recent Criticisms." *JETS* 50 (2007): 71–86.

———. "Punishment God Cannot Twice Inflict: The Double Payment Argument Redivivus." Pages 483–516 in *From Heaven He Came and Sought Her: Definite Atonement in Historical, Biblical, Theological, and Pastoral Perspective*. Edited by David Gibson and Jonathan Gibson. Wheaton: Crossway, 2013.

Wilson, Gerald H. *The Editing of the Hebrew Psalter*. Society of Biblical Literature Dissertation Series. Chico, CA: Scholars, 1985.

Witherington III, Ben. *Conflict and Community in Corinth: A Socio-Rhetorical Commentary on 1 and 2 Corinthians*. Grand Rapids: Eerdmans; Carlisle, U.K: Paternoster, 1995.

Wright, Christopher J. H. "Participatory Mission: The Mission of God's People Revealed in the Whole Bible Story." Pages 63–91 in *The Mission of the Church: Five Views in Conversation*. Edited by Jason Sexton. Grand Rapids: Zondervan, 2017.

———. *The Mission of God: Unlocking the Bible's Grand Narrative*. Downers Grove: InterVarsity, 2006.

———. *The Mission of God's People: A Biblical Theology of the Church's Mission*. Grand Rapids: Zondervan, 2010.

Wright, N. T. *Surprised by Hope: Rethinking Heaven, the Resurrection, and the Mission of the Church*. New York: HarperOne, 2008.

———. *The Climax of the Covenant: Christ and the Law in Pauline Theology*. Minneapolis: Fortress, 1992.

———. *The Resurrection of the Son of God*. Minneapolis: Fortress, 2003.

———. *What Saint Paul Really Said: Was Paul of Tarsus the Real Founder of Christianity?* Grand Rapids: Eerdmans, 1997.

Wright, N. T., Simon Gathercole, and Robert B. Stewart. *What Did the Cross Accomplish?: A Conversation About the Atonement*. Louisville: Westminster John Knox, 2021.

Wright, Shawn D. *40 Questions About Calvinism*. Grand Rapids: Kregel, 2019.

Wu, Jackson. *Saving God's Face: A Chinese Contextualization of Salvation Through Honor and Shame*. Pasadena, CA: William Carey International University Press, 2013.

Yarbrough, Robert W. *1–3 John*. Baker Exegetical Commentary on the New Testament. Grand Rapids: Baker, 2008.

Young, E. J. *Studies in Isaiah*. Grand Rapids: Eerdmans, 1955.

NAME INDEX

Harris, Murray, 114–15
Hastings, W. Ross, 309–11
Hawthorne, Gerald, 185
Hick, John, 221, 233
Hilary of Poitiers, 244
Hill, Andrew, 61
Hiyya bar Abba, 13
Hodge, Charles, 248, 263
Hoekema, Anthony, 301, 326
Hofius, Otfried, 239
Holmes, Stephen, 247, 250, 262–63,
    268, 273, 275
Horton, Michael, 293
Huey, F. B., 46
Hughes, Paul Edgcumbe, 301

I

Irenaeus, 182, 207, 210–14, 218, 225–26,
    243, 278
Irving, Edward, 262
Issler, Klaus, 185

J

Jeffery, Steve, 266
Jerome, 51
John of Damascus, 213
Johnson, Adam, 271, 300
Johnson, Eric, 272, 275
Jones, Paul Dafydd, 249
Julius Africanus, 50
Justin Martyr, 177, 275

K

Kaiser, Walter, 26, 144, 176–77
Keener, Craig, 85
Kelly, J. N. D., 244–45, 247
Keown, Gerald, 47
Kerama, Emily J. Choge, 217
Kimchi, David, 60
Klein, George, 57
Köstenberger, Andreas, 95
Kotsko, Adam, 230
Kreider, Glenn, 10
Kruse, Colin, 86, 90, 120

Kuiper, R. B., 302
Kuyper, Abraham, 327

L

Ladd, G. E., 191
Lalleman, Hetty, 47
Landgraf, Paul, 140
Lanier, Gregory R., 35
Letham, Robert, 1, 173, 190–91, 194–
    95, 197, 202, 292–93, 295, 302,
    309
Lincoln, Andrew, 125
Lindars, Barnabas, 140–41
Lombard, Peter, 284
Longenecker, Richard, 105–6
Longman, Tremper III, 3, 178
Lopéz, Réne, 177
Luther, Martin, 213, 215, 245, 248–49,
    279

M

Macleod, Donald, 184
Marshall, I. Howard, 86, 317
Martin, R. A., 16
Martin, Ralph, 114
McCall, Thomas, 298
McConville, J. Gordon, 9
McDonough, Sean, 174–75
McGrath, Alister, 223–24, 228, 233
McIntyre, John, 206
McKnight, Scot, 130, 177
McNall, Joshua, 207–8, 212, 214–15,
    225, 227–28, 237–38, 244–45,
    247–48, 265, 275, 278–79
Merrill, Eugene, 20
Metzger, Bruce, 320
Moo, Douglas, 104, 127, 130
Moreland, J. P., 185
Morgan, Christopher, 206
Morris, Leon, 89–90, 209, 240–42, 250,
    264, 274, 317
Motyer, J. Alec, 43
Mounce, Robert, 326
Murray, David, 10, 12

SUBJECT INDEX

SCRIPTURE INDEX